Subjects, Citizens and Others

Studies in British and Imperial History
Published for the German Historical Institute, London
Editor: Andreas Gestrich, Director of the German Historical Institute, London

Volume 1
The Rise of Market Society in England, 1066–1800
Christiane Eisenberg
Translated by Deborah Cohen

Volume 2
Sacral Kingship between Disenchantment and Re-enchantment
The French and English Monarchies, 1587–1688
Ronald G. Asch

Volume 3
The Forgotten Majority
German Merchants in London, Naturalization and Global Trade, 1660–1815
Margit Schulte-Beerbühl
Translated by Cynthia Klohr

Volume 4
Crown, Church and Constitution
Popular Conservatism in England, 1815–1867
Jörg Neuheiser
Translated by Jennifer Walcoff Neuheiser

Volume 5
Between Empire and Continent
British Foreign Policy before the First World War
Andreas Rose
Translated by Rona Johnston

Volume 6
Unearthing the Past to Forge the Future
Colin Mackenzie, the Early Colonial State and the Comprehensive Survey of India
Tobias Wolffhardt
Translated by Jane Rafferty

Volume 7
Subjects, Citizens and Others
Administering Ethnic Heterogeneity in the British and Habsburg Empires, 1867–1918
Benno Gammerl
Translated by Jennifer Walcoff Neuheiser

SUBJECTS, CITIZENS AND OTHERS

Administering Ethnic Heterogeneity in the British
and Habsburg Empires, 1867–1918

Benno Gammerl
Translated by Jennifer Walcoff Neuheiser

berghahn
NEW YORK · OXFORD
www.berghahnbooks.com

Published in 2018 by
Berghahn Books
www.berghahnbooks.com

English-language edition © 2018 Benno Gammerl

German-language edition © 2010 Vandenhoeck & Ruprecht GmbH & Co. KG

Originally published in 2010 as *Untertanen, Staatsbürger und Andere: Der Umgang mit ethnischer Heterogenität im britischen Weltreich und im Habsburgerreich 1867–1918* by Vandenhoeck & Ruprecht GmbH & Co. KG, Göttingen

The translation of this work was funded by Geisteswissenschaften International – Translation Funding for Humanities and Social Sciences from Germany, a joint initiative of the Fritz Thyssen Foundation, the German Federal Foreign Office, the collecting society VG WORT and the Börsenverein des Deutschen Buchhandels (German Publishers and Booksellers Association).

Library of Congress Cataloging-in-Publication Data
A C.I.P. cataloging record is available from the Library of Congress

British Library Cataloguing in Publication Data
A catalogue record for this book is available from the British Library

ISBN 978-1-78533-709-3 hardback
ISBN 978-1-78533-710-9 ebook

CONTENTS

ILLUSTRATIONS

Maps, Tables and Figures

Maps

Tables

Figures

ACKNOWLEDGEMENTS

The making of this book was rendered possible when the German Historical Institute in London awarded me the Wolfgang J. Mommsen Prize for my Ph.D. thesis on the administration of ethnic heterogeneity in the British and Habsburg empires. This prize covered the cost of translating my work into English, and thus granted me the fantastic opportunity to thoroughly revise my German monograph (published in 2010), and to share this research with a much broader audience. I am extraordinarily grateful to the institute's director Andreas Gestrich, to the deputy director Michael Schaich and to his predecessor Benedikt Stuchtey for granting me this opportunity and for their support in realizing this project. It is certainly no easy tas4$k to convert academic German into elegant English, but I could fortunately rely on Jennifer Neuheiser in this respect. Her ability to recreate, time and again, the original version in a smart and skilful idiom amazed me.

I started working on this project in 2004 when I joined the Berlin School for Comparative European History. Its managing director Arnd Bauerkämper, Bernhard Struck and many others deserve the gratitude of numerous Ph.D. students who profited from the school's stimulating atmosphere. There can hardly be a better place for pursuing one's research. Colleagues from various East and West European countries benefited from each other's criticism and encouragement. My Ph.D. research was financially most generously supported by the Gerda Henkel Foundation, the German Academic Exchange Service and the Austrian Exchange Service. In terms of being provided with materials and information I could thankfully rely on the very helpful staff of the Public Records Office and the British Library in London, as well as the Österreichisches Staatsarchiv and the Österreichische Nationalbibliothek in Vienna. Last, but certainly not least, I profited intellectually from the cues and the advice so generously provided by my supervisors Dieter Gosewinkel and Jürgen Kocka. Looking back, I more and more appreciate their supportive mentoring that enabled and inspired me to start my career as a historian.

This career has meanwhile taken me to the Center for the History of Emotions within the Max Planck Institute for Human Development, whose director, Ute Frevert, also facilitated my work on this book. Along the way I have engaged in fruitful exchanges with many inspiring colleagues and friends who allowed me to benefit from their expertise and knowledge. For thought-provoking discussions I want to thank in particular Hannelore Burger, Daniela Caglioti,

Johannes Feichtinger, Christa Hämmerle, Pieter Judson, Jacqueline Krikorian, Jörn Leonhard, Marcel Martel, Maren Möhring, Georg Neuhaus, Margrit Pernau, Helmut Reifeld, Sven Rücker, Karen Schönwälder, Adrian Schubert and Heidemarie Uhl.

I furthermore want to express my gratitude to Berghahn Books and to Chris Chappell, Amanda Horn and Caroline Kuhtz in particular, who diligently guided the manuscript towards publication. My thanks also go to Karola Rockmann, who allowed me to rely on her impressive accuracy in revising the bibliography. For permissions to use images I am very grateful to the British Library, the City of Vancouver Archives, the Österreichisches Staatsarchiv, the Österreichische Nationalbibliothek, the Public Records Office and the Sudetendeutscher Rat. And finally, I am very thankful for Frank Kurt Schulz's help who skilfully edited the images and charts for this book.

ABBREVIATIONS

ABGB   Allgemeines Bürgerliches Gesetzbuch [General Civil Code]
k.k.   kaiserlich-königlich [imperial-royal] (Austrian or Cisleithanian)
k.u.   königlich-ungarisch [royal-hungarian] (Hungarian or Transleithanian)
k.u.k.   kaiserlich und königlich [imperial and royal] (Austro-Hungarian)

INTRODUCTION

In spring 2014 the campaigns for the European Elections in May entered a critical stage. While Andreas Mölzer, the front runner of the right-wing Freedom Party of Austria (FPÖ), had to step down after referring to the European Union (EU) as a 'conglomerate of niggers',[1] the leader of Britain's UK Independence Party (UKIP), Nigel Farage, continued to lament 'uncontrolled immigration' and 'the downgrading of Christianity in our national life'.[2] Simultaneously, Cypriots nourished hopes that the long-standing conflict between the Greek- and Turkish-speaking populations would be resolved as nationalist politicians in Hungary intensified their antiziganistic rhetoric and stirred up conflicts surrounding the so-called Szekler minority in Romania.

These four examples from different parts of the former British and Habsburg empires aptly demonstrate that dealing with ethnic heterogeneity in a peaceful and agreeable manner is still quite a challenge. In some places around the world, attempts are still being made to evade this seemingly insurmountable task by opting for outright discrimination and exclusion on the basis of ethnicity instead. Given the pressing nature of problems associated with European integration and global migration, however, these questions of how polities with ethnically diverse populations could and should deal with heterogeneity are of paramount importance. Although this book does not intend to offer ready-made political advice, it investigates the ways in which ethnic diversity has been handled in the past, and thereby hopes to contribute to a thorough re-evaluation of this issue in contemporary politics.

Rather than focusing on the supposedly more modern and democratic context of the nation-state, it looks at two empires over the course of the last third of the long nineteenth century. While attempts to create or maintain an ethnically

Notes for this chapter begin on page 15.

homogeneous nation or people within the framework of the nation-state have received quite a lot of scholarly attention over the last decades, imperial states such as Britain and Austria have largely, yet undeservedly, fallen under the radar. Nonetheless, these empires are a promising empirical prism for analysing the legal and administrative handling of ethnic heterogeneity, especially because of the characteristic entanglement of ethnic difference and asymmetrical power relations inherent within their structures. That said, however, such constellations are not merely a feature of the imperialist past as they still apply to the contemporary world. Consequently, this comparison between the British and the Habsburg empires in the late nineteenth and early twentieth centuries traces the imperial roots of present-day issues by outlining the strategies with which legislatures, governments and administrations addressed similar problems, thereby offering a new dual perspective that speaks to historical as well as contemporary circumstances.

Nationality and Citizenship as Concepts

In order to maintain a manageable scope, this book focuses on questions of nationality and citizenship in relation to the handling of ethnic heterogeneity. Nationality laws determine who belongs to a polity and who is excluded. Within this national polity, citizenship laws define the rights and duties of members – by regulating suffrage, for example. If the two legal concepts of nationality and citizenship are examined together, which historians have seldom done, not only external boundaries become apparent, but also grades of differentiation within a polity itself. Moreover, nationality and citizenship laws reflect the degree to which ethnic identities and differences have played a role in external as well as internal processes of inclusion and exclusion. These two concepts thus offer an ideal perspective for analysing the political, legal and administrative handling of ethnic heterogeneity.

This study of the lines of differentiation present within imperial constellations in the late nineteenth and early twentieth centuries therefore promises to enrich our general understanding of the role of ethnicity in imperial contexts. To start with, empires are by definition ethnically and politically heterogeneous.[3] They rule over diverse populations, and they employ different regimes of control and governance that are often marked by highly asymmetrical constellations of power. It is particularly challenging, yet equally rewarding, to trace the ways in which ethnic diversity was woven into and simultaneously formed by this complex web of power relations. This is especially true for the period around 1900, when the rise of nationalism and demands for democratic participation signalled and propelled significant changes and shifts within imperial formations. As different as these two empires may seem at first glance, both were faced with the question of how they could and should mediate between their imperial structures and rising demands for national homogeneity and democratic equality at the turn of the twentieth century.[4] Furthermore, this comparison makes it possible to critically reassess what has almost become an unquestioned dichotomy within scholarship between allegedly 'modern' liberal solutions for dealing with this issue in the western half of Europe and the supposed 'backward' approaches shaping policies in the eastern half of the continent.[5]

Within this framework, examining the significance of ethnic difference in terms of nationality and citizenship certainly promises to enrich existing scholarly perspectives. Who was a national? Everyone who was born within the borders of the empire or all those whose parents were nationals of the empire? Was it the place of birth (*ius soli*) – or rather descent (*ius sanguinis*) – that mattered? To what extent did these regulations affect processes of inclusion and exclusion? What happened to the legal status of nationals who married foreigners, or foreigners who married nationals? What role did ethnic identities and differences play in terms of immigration laws and naturalization practices? How was the right of suffrage regulated? Who profited from social welfare provisions such as health insurance and pension schemes, but also who was denied access to these systems? Were there different types of citizenship that conferred more rights and duties than others? Alongside these rather legal questions, this study also looks at the cultural underpinnings behind the different approaches to dealing with ethnic heterogeneity. What bases of knowledge and concepts did these approaches rest upon, and how were they justified?

This analysis focuses primarily on the political and administrative elite, and seeks to outline the perspectives and principles that guided these actors in dealing with ethnic diversity. As a result, it leans heavily towards a macrohistory perspective 'from above', only touching on microhistoric questions related to subaltern actors in passing. This, of course, also correlates with the source base for this study. The primary sources consulted consist mostly of laws and regulations, parliamentary debates and administrative records produced by state institutions. For the British case, the Home Office, the Colonial Office, the Foreign Office and the India Office were the key organs of state; the major players in the Habsburg Empire were the Cisleithanian Interior Ministry and the Austro-Hungarian Foreign Ministry. In addition, contemporary publications, especially those of a legal nature, were consulted. The insights gleaned from these sources only minimally reflect perspectives 'from below'. Yet, the sometimes wilful strategies that individual actors employed in conflicts with the law and government administration, as well as dealings with ethnic diversity in everyday life, do come to light within certain empirical examples. Thus, on multiple levels, this study improves our historical understanding of the ways in which both of these empires dealt with ethnic heterogeneity.

Nation-State, Statist and Imperialist Approaches?

Using three idealized interpretative models, this book traces a cohesive analytical thread through the sometimes overwhelming abundance of sources and scholarship on ethnic heterogeneity in these empires. The well-researched ways in which nation-states dealt with this issue serve as a springboard for further investigation within an imperial context. The nation-state approach combines internal homogenization in terms of citizenship with a sharpening of external borders on the basis of nationality.[6] Within its boundaries, the extension of political and social rights as well as the enforcement of duties, mostly military in nature, ensured legal equality.[7] Simultaneously, the determination of who belonged to this community of equals became all the more precise over time. These inclusive and exclusive mechanisms affected migrants in general, but especially those seeking naturalization, as well as individuals who were married to foreigners. Often, the ethnic identity of those in question determined whether they would be excluded or admitted.[8] Within this national community, ethnic differences were either eliminated through homogenizing assimilation processes or – in the case of multi-ethnic states – patched together into a heterogeneous national entity. In sum, the nation-state approach sought to achieve the integration of the members of the nation.

In contrast to the emphasis on individuals within the nation-state framework, the statist approach followed a territorial principle that stressed the need for congruency between the resident population and the citizens of the state.[9] This was supposed to make it easier for the state administration to manage and exert control over its nationals. The core of this statist logic was the enlightened-absolutist notion that all those residing in the country should be equal in the eyes of the state. Correspondingly, this resulted in a tendency towards processes of legal equalization. However, the end goal was not necessarily to integrate the entire community, but rather to enable the state to pursue its political, military and economic interests without hindrance. In this respect, ethnic differences were characteristically irrelevant within the statist framework; laws related to nationality as well as citizenship therefore strove for ethnic neutrality. However, if ethnic identities proved to be a source of potential conflict that threatened to disrupt domestic peace, the statist government could take on the role of a supra-ethnic referee. As such, it then sought to ensure a peaceful and equal coexistence of different groups through the recognition of difference.[10]

The imperialist approach, in contrast, rested on a discriminatory process of differentiation according to ethnic criteria within the community of nationals. It privileged one group at the expense of others. The imperialist model became highly significant in colonial contexts,[11] as it brought the question of who was to enjoy privileges and who was to be excluded from them to centre stage. Issues of nationality tended to recede into the background because the question was not necessarily who belonged to the already heterogeneous community of nationals but rather where the line of discrimination was to be drawn internally between those entitled to the privileges of citizenship and those denied them. Whereas the imperialist model rested on a hierarchy established on the basis of ethnic criteria, the statist approach promoted the egalitarian coexistence of individuals or ethnic groups, and the nation-state model sought to integrate all those who belonged to the national community.

Correspondingly, these three different approaches were tightly linked to three methods of dealing with ethnic heterogeneity. First of all, the law and administrative praxis could be ethnically neutral, meaning that all individuals regardless of their ethnicity were to be treated equally. Or, secondly, they could differentiate between different ethnic groups and acknowledge them in order to endow them, as collective entities, with equal rights.[12] Within this model of recognition, so-called positive discrimination measures represent a special case because they aim to better the status of less privileged groups.[13] Such policies of neutrality or recognition were typical of the statist model. The imperialist approach, in contrast, was defined by a kind of negative discrimination in which certain ethnic groups within the community of nationals enjoyed fewer privileges. The nation-state model, on the other hand, chiefly discriminated against those who were not considered to be part of the nation. These individuals were either supposed to be integrated into the national community through cultural assimilation processes, or excluded from the community of nationals as foreigners.[14]

It is important to note that these three models corresponded, generally speaking, with three forms of political organization – the nation-state, the state and the empire – but they were by no means always inherently congruent. This is most clearly the case with the imperialist model. Although it mostly appeared within imperial contexts, the reverse was not true as not every imperial formation was marked by imperialist mechanisms of discrimination. As this book will show, statist and nation-state approaches were also effective within imperial frameworks. Which of these three models shaped how ethnic heterogeneity would be dealt with in certain parts of each empire depended on whether a territory was directly or indirectly subject to imperial control, and whether it was located at the centre, on the periphery, or somewhere in between. Accordingly, this analysis looks at the specific combinations of nation-state, statist and imperialist approaches, and the conflicts between advocates of different policies, to help to explain shifts in ways of dealing with ethnic heterogeneity.

The Contours of Ethnicity Defined

A comparison between the British and Habsburg empires necessitates the use of a broad definition of ethnicity that can encompass different forms of ethnic identification and differentiation in both imperial contexts.[15] For this reason, it is important to clarify how the terms 'ethnic' and 'ethnicity' are to be defined for the purposes of this book with respect to the extensive scholarly debates on these notions.[16] Neither term should be misunderstood as describing a primordial or essentialist category, or as defining fixed and unchangeable lines of demarcation between different groups of people. Assuming that ethnic identities are inherent and static would harbour the danger that racist patterns of thought could reappear, merely cloaked in a different 'language' of terminology.[17]

In order to avoid an essentialist understanding of ethnicity, this analysis emphasizes that the building of ethnic groups does not necessarily depend on objective criteria; rather, what is important is whether or not individual actors consider themselves as belonging to a specific ethnic community.[18] According to widely accepted sociological and anthropological theories, the foundation for such a sense of ethnic unity lies in cultural, religious and linguistic commonalities that are channelled into an ethnic identity through the construction of a shared history and ancestry. Ethnicity, therefore, is less culturally determined than it is socially constructed. The so-called instrumentalist approach therefore focuses on the processes of interaction that lead to the formation of ethnic groups and the social groups that foster them (i.e. ethnicization through elites 'from above' or as a social movement 'from below'), as well as their economic and political interests. However, some scholars have emphasized that the construction of ethnic identities on the basis of shared interests by no means occurs in a vacuum, because pre-existing cultural traditions and institutions are also key to these processes.[19]

A focus on the boundaries between groups serves as another safeguard against the assumption of ethnicity as a primal and unchangeable phenomenon.[20] According to this concept, an ethnic group is not comprised through identity and homogeneity within, but rather through the creation of differences and alterity with respect to other groups along its boundaries. In this respect, ethnological approaches emphasize the symbolic communication processes and the dynamic nature of patterns of ethnic identification and differentiation that have to be continually adapted and incorporated by those involved. One advantage of these theories is that they can account for heterogeneity within ethnic groups. At the same time, however, these approaches are problematic because – taken to the extreme – they reject the existence of any criteria for determining ethnicity, turning the concept into a general and vague description of differences between 'us' and 'them'.

A third way to argue against an essentialist definition of ethnicity is to work from the assumption that ethnic differences cannot be clearly delineated and fixed. Post-structuralist and post-colonial theorists point out that the imperial differentiation between colonial rulers and colonial subjects was ambiguous in nature, often producing hybrid subjects.[21] This questioning of ethnic difference goes further than the concept of multiple identities in other theories of ethnicity that postulate, for example, the simultaneous and compatible nature of a Styrian, Austrian and European sense of belonging. The post-colonial approach with its theories of difference, on the other hand, pleads for the possibility that seemingly contradictory identities can coexist within a single subject.

When woven together, these three strains of critique against the objective truth, invariability and clarity of ethnic identities make for an approach that understands ethnic differences as constructed, dynamic and unstable.[22] Accordingly, this book refers to ethnic differences and ethnic identities primarily when lawmakers and government offices attributed certain groups with a shared identity that went beyond religious or linguistic commonalities. The assumption of a shared ancestry or feelings of belonging often played a significant role in this respect, but it must be said that most historical actors perceived of these identities as pre-existing and unquestionable matters of fact.

Owing to the fact that this book focuses on legislation and administrative praxis, its working definition of 'ethnic' and 'ethnicity' is mainly associated with the production of ethnicity 'from above'. Accordingly, the emergence or reproduction of ethnic identities vis-à-vis individual actors only comes into view peripherally or as part of individual examples. In contrast, the degree to which state involvement and government activities shaped the establishment of patterns of ethnic difference will be closely examined. Interestingly, some of the questions that are still relevant for scholarly debate today were already being hotly discussed in government offices over a hundred years ago. In Austria, for example, statisticians and politicians were debating whether the determination of ethnicity should be based on a subjective sense of belonging or rather on objective criteria.

The working definition of ethnicity used here therefore emphasizes that the specific points of reference for the formation of ethnic differences varied case by case. In this respect, the discrepancy between ethnocultural and 'race-based' differences came into play. The latter relied on the assumption of biological differences that were usually considered to be phenotypically apparent or discernible.[23] Whereas an ethnocultural identity could be considered as learned or acquired and therefore malleable, 'race' was seen as hereditary and therefore static. Distinctions made according to 'race'-based criteria were often linked with colonial hierarchies and pejorative categorizations that refused to acknowledge equality for the 'other race'.[24] Such 'race'-based differentiation tended towards racism, discriminating against the group perceived to be the 'other'. This biological understanding of 'race' corresponds to that of most of the contemporary actors in question. This analysis, however, works from the contradictory premise that 'racial' differences are just as constructed, malleable and unstable as ethnic identities.[25] Consequently, it sees 'racial' difference as a specific manifestation of 'ethnic' difference.[26]

Lastly, a distinction must be made between nationality and ethnicity.[27] The major difference between the two is that the concept of nationality is more closely linked to the political sphere and the state.[28] In some cases, nations may be congruent with an ethnic group, but in others supra-ethnic national integration occurs;[29] however, it would be entirely misleading to define ethnic groups as deficient nations. Such an understanding emerges if one accepts that a dichotomy exists between the 'backward' nationalism without a state, typical of Central Europe, and the 'modern', state-based nationalism characteristic of the west of the continent. The qualitative difference between ethnicity and national-ity is not one of superiority or inferiority. There is no necessary or irreversible path leading from an ethnic to a national identity-building process. Rather, what is more interesting in this respect is the question of when, under what cir-cumstances and on which levels nationalization processes took place. When did opposing tendencies appear that depoliticized ethnic identities? And when were transitional forms of ethnonational identification established? Especially within the context of empires, the relationship between ethnicity and nationality often proved to be far more complex than is suggested by linear narratives that trace a line of development from the building of ethnic identities to demands for politi-cal autonomy that ultimately led to national emancipation.[30]

Empires and Nations

When viewed from such teleological perspectives, the achievement of national self-determination was judged to be a decisive step on the path to a better future, for example in the American War of Independence or the decolonialization processes of the twentieth century. Accordingly, the nation-state was seen as a guarantor of modernity, in contrast to the empire as a rather antiquated form of political organization.[31] Given the predominance of this perspective, historical research on nationality and citizenship has largely focused on nation-states. Only in recent years have transnational and global history perspectives gained ground. These studies have brought the stateless people who fall outside the system of national belonging, and whose number increased dramatically in the twenti-eth century as a result of wars and catastrophic displacement policies, into the picture.[32] These changing perspectives have also prompted a growing scholarly interest in nationality and citizenship in imperial formations.[33]

Analyses that move beyond the fixation with the nation-state have shown that the nation was by no means the only relevant point of reference for historic development in the nineteenth and twentieth centuries. Even today, imperial forms of governance continue to shape political, social and cultural develop-ments throughout the world. The ubiquity of empires becomes entirely clear if one considers the fact that Switzerland is the only European nation-state that has neither been a metropolitan nor a peripheral part of an imperial structure over the last two hundred years. Broader transnational perspectives, moreover, have not only pointed out how firmly national units were embedded within alternative structures of power and communication, but have simultaneously exposed the fictional character of the mostly implicit and unquestioned assumption of the ethnic homogeneity and unity of nation-states. If the imperial complexity of the interactions between metropolis and the periphery is taken into account, it quickly becomes apparent that a strict distinction between the homogeneity of the nation-state and the heterogeneity of the empire cannot hold. Nation and empire may sometimes have collided as opposites, but they could also be symbiotic and inseparably entangled.

Studies of imperial forms of state that often swing between two extremes in their appraisals present dangers quite similar to those of analyses of the nation-state. On the one hand, some scholars paint the nation-state as the glory and culmination of historical development, as well as the political form most compatible with a cosmopolitan spirit (*Weltgeist*). On the other hand, the majority of historians now launch harsh critiques, depicting the nation-state as the origin of all evils, ranging from war to the exploitation of the working classes to the exclusion of minorities. Empires face similar accusations regarding the devastation left in their wake. From this perspective, empires rest on problematic asymmetrical power relations, making it justifiable to hold them accountable for wars, exploitation and discrimination.

Given this negative balance sheet, it seems all the more surprising that an increasing number of positive interpretations of empires have appeared in recent years, although it must be said that they differ quite markedly in their approaches. Some emphasize the modernizing and ordering power of imperial structures in keeping with 'traditional' discourses. They celebrate the successes of imperial endeavours and recommend the empire as a model for contemporary neo-conservative world politics.[34] This book clearly distances itself from any such blatantly affirmative arguments. Others draw on post-colonial theories and employ analytic approaches that welcome the hybridity produced by imperial formations. Some studies on British nationality interpret the existence of ambiguous legal statuses as an advantage because they supposedly allowed for multiple forms of belonging and were therefore inclusive.[35] This book does not deny the fact that subaltern actors benefited from the spaces of negotiation provided by such productive ambiguities,[36] but their problematic dimensions must not be forgotten. For example, in most cases, they strengthened hegemonic hierarchies in which those with a hybrid status were denied any kind of protection and were often subject to extralegal mechanisms of discrimination.

When analysing empires – just like nation-states – a balanced perspective is needed that takes into account positive as well as negative dimensions. Which features of a specific imperial order unfurled within processes of discrimination, equalization or recognition? As exaggerated praise and demonization undoubtedly detract from the usefulness of a historical analysis, this study not only considers the seemingly unavoidable collapse and decline of the two empires, but also their chances of survival and their potential for integration. In doing so, it provides a basis for dealing with imperial legacies fairly, neither celebrating nor condemning them altogether, and it paves the way for a cogent assessment of present-day imperial tendencies.

Likewise, the use of the broader concept of 'imperial formations' as opposed to the narrower notion of 'empire',[37] and the consistent distinction between the imperial and imperialist exercise of power also serve this purpose. Not all dimensions of imperial rule rested in equal measure on hierarchies and asymmetrical constellations. Such differentiations make it possible to compare the British Empire as a prototypical western European colonial empire with the Habsburg Empire as a typical continental central European imperial example. However, this book quite consciously seeks to undermine a number of East–West dichotomies.

The Pitfalls of an East–West Dichotomy

The distinction between maritime colonial empires (e.g. the British, French, Dutch or Portuguese) and contiguous continental empires (e.g. the Habsburg, Russian or Ottoman) is part of the standard repertoire of scholarship on empires.[38] Akin to the differentiation between liberal and authoritarian forms of rule, or between politically inclusive or ethnically exclusive nationalism, this scholarly field tends to align itself with the historic schema that divides the European continent into a 'progressive' western half and a 'backward' eastern half. The perhaps unusual comparative constellation of this book seeks to question these dichotomies without denying the fact that there were indeed significant differences between the two empires in question. Through a mindful examination of the similarities and differences, as well as the use of refined analytical categories, it pulls at the anchors of this East–West dichotomy to offer a fresh perspective that moves beyond existing scholarly assumptions.

Without a doubt, there were indeed major differences between the British and Habsburg empires in terms of geographic scope and the rate of expansion in the nineteenth century. Moreover, as this study will show, the mechanisms involved in the establishment of ethnic differences and identities also varied, thanks in part to these factors. Likewise, there were lines of contrast between the two empires in terms of economics and politics. These differences resulted in divergent self-images that were at least partly constructed explicitly in opposition to the respective other. At the same time, both empires competed in the same international or inter-imperial arena to preserve their prestige as global powers. Domestically, both faced similar demands coming from national movements, such as those of Irish, Indian, Czech and South Slavic origin. As a result, the significance of ethnonational differences and the degree of political heterogeneity grew in both cases. In 1867, which marks the beginning of the period in question here, both the British and Habsburg empires underwent a reorganization of their political structures with the British North America Act and the Austro-Hungarian Compromise, respectively. With the advent of the First World War, the endpoint of this book's analysis, disintegration processes were set into motion that led to the catastrophic collapse of the Habsburg Empire and the slow decline of the British Empire, which began with the partition of Ireland and dragged on well into the second half of the twentieth century.

Given these commonalities, the two empires should not be cursorily categorized as mutually exclusive types of imperial rule. Rather, shared phenomena and developments that resulted from transfers and reciprocal dynamics must also be taken into account. Nuanced analytical categories that make it possible to tease out the gradual differences related to particularities and individual territories of both empires are necessary for such an undertaking. If one considers 'the extent of inequality between center and periphery',[39] for example, it becomes apparent that Bosnia's underprivileged position in the Habsburg context was not that dissimilar from the situation of some British colonies than it may seem at first glance.[40] Additionally, a look at the relationship between 'incorporation and differentiation'[41] or the 'degrees of tolerance, of difference, of domination, and of rights'[42] exposes parallels and gradients where otherwise only categorical differences could be detected. Such similarities in terms of the ways in which both empires dealt with demands for autonomy, or shifted between discrimination and recognition, will reappear throughout this book.

Yet another element of the East–West dichotomy has been the distinction often made between authoritarian, police-state modes of exercising power in the Habsburg 'prison of nations', and liberal, democratic forms of rule in the British 'empire of rights'.[43] It is quite apparent that this opposition rests on a number of oversimplifications. On the one hand, it glosses over the colonial-imperialist dimensions of the British Empire; on the other hand, it blocks out the constitutional character of Habsburg rule. Furthermore, this simplified dichotomy between the authoritarian East and the liberal West ignores the complex differences that emerged out of the varying traditions of codified Roman law and precedence-based common law.

The goal of this analysis goes beyond the mere inversion of the conventional schema by pointing out the illiberal aspects of the British Empire and the quasi anti-authoritarian character of the Austro-Hungarian Empire, as it criticizes the liberal–authoritarian dichotomy itself.[44] In doing so, it draws on theories that contrast older forms of sovereign power over life and death with more recent structures of biopower and governmentality that aim to preserve and foster life.[45] Whereas sovereign power subjugates the individual person as a legal entity, biopower sees the population as a biological species and a public entity that can be assessed and managed through demographic and prognostic methods such as birth counts, migration statistics and opinion polls.[46] Unlike sovereign rule, which imposes its will on the unformed nature of its subjects, the biopolitical or governmental exercise of power rests on population dynamics, perceived as natural or spontaneous, that it strives to use or channel to its own ends. This understanding of biopower clearly differs from other prominent theories.[47] Instead of emphasizing the exploitation and the suffering experienced in concentration and other camps as the 'biopolitical paradigm of the modern', it highlights the decisively less abysmal and unsettling role that systems of health insurance and old-age provision played within the framework of governmentality.

The rather abstract distinction between sovereign power and biopower is useful in terms of an analysis of the ways in which heterogeneity was dealt with as it can describe concrete power techniques that either regulate, discipline and rule in a sovereign fashion or govern by encouragement and incentives in a biopolitical laissez-faire manner.[48] Following this line of thought, this book will differentiate between prohibitive and promotive mechanisms of power. In contrast to the authoritarian–liberal dichotomy, which traces a progressive development with increasing degrees of freedom, the distinction between prohibition and promotion suggests that 'liberal' forms of government did not necessarily reduce the quantitative extent of the exercise of power, but rather they changed its qualitative modus.[49] From this perspective, the implementation of liberal demands did not lead to more freedom, but rather to the establishment of new, promotive techniques of government. These appeared alongside the older prohibitive mechanisms, which led to the conflict-ridden coexistence of both in Habsburg as well as British migration policies, for example. Ultimately, an analysis of these dynamics is decidedly more productive than insisting upon a general dichotomy between the liberal West and the authoritarian East.

The alleged contrast between the backward, ethnically exclusive nationalism characteristic of Eastern Europe and the progressive, politically inclusive notions of the nation in Western Europe is closely connected to this assumption. This has been a critical distinction for research on nationality and citizenship. Older, mostly legal history approaches were predominantly interested in the relationship between the state and its constitutive people in modern Europe and the transition from territorial understandings of the state to notions that rested on the idea of a community of people.[50] Building on this foundation, more recent studies have looked at how states have gathered information about and controlled their subjects with the help of documents and registration apparatuses.[51] At the same time, sociohistorical scholars have also shifted their gaze to look at ways of dealing with ethnic differences. As part of this endeavour, Franco-German comparisons of nationality in particular have emphasized the contrast between the legal principles of *ius sanguinis* (i.e. the descent-based model predominant in modern Germany) and *ius soli* (i.e. the territorial-based model generally followed in France); in theory at least, a German national was an individual born to a German national, while a French national was an individual born in France. Whereas the German principle of descent corresponded with an ethnically exclusive understanding of the nation, as the argument is usually put forth, the French principle of birthplace reflected a politically inclusive concept of the nation.[52] This rather cursory dichotomy has not gone unchallenged. On the one hand, critics have suggested that the German *ius sanguinis* was initially a component of statist strategies that primarily served the interests of the state for purposes of clarity and control, and that only took on ethnically exclusive dimensions in the early twentieth century.[53] On the other hand, they emphasize the fact that French laws based on *ius soli* could and did have ethnically exclusive ramifications.[54]

Merely looking at the formal legal distinctions between nationals and non-nationals, however, does not suffice as it is important to question who enjoyed the rights of citizenship and who was excluded from its privileges in part or whole. Whereas liberal-leaning historical narratives of citizenship operate from the premise that an increasing portion of the population came to enjoy civic, political and social rights through processes of integration in the nation-state,[55] critical studies point to the dialectic of inclusion and exclusion, as well as the fact that the integration of marginalized groups often went hand in hand with the marginalization of other groups defined on the basis of gender, social status or ethnicity.[56] This study takes up with such critical perspectives to the extent that it emphasizes the concurrence of legal equality with the establishment of administrative mechanisms of discrimination as well as the paradoxical logic of inclusive exclusion. The comparison between the British and Habsburg empires also contributes to a revision of the schematic juxtaposition of the principle of descent as ethnically exclusive and the principle of birthplace as politically inclusive. In the British case, if one takes into account the entire imperial context, including its colonial dimensions,[57] even a cursory look reveals that the *ius soli* proved to be compatible with the discrimination against and exclusion of certain ethnic groups; however, the Habsburg *ius sanguinis* by no means ruled out the possibility of inclusive policies resting on the recognition of differences.[58] Accordingly, this book offers a critical re-examination of the dichotomy between 'modern', politically inclusive nation-states in Western Europe and 'backward', ethnically exclusive nations in Eastern Europe.

Comparing Empires

Without a doubt, comparisons between countries have indeed contributed to the establishment of such dichotomies. They have often reinforced the assumption of timeless differences, but, unfortunately, this has not discouraged historians from constructing pithy contrasts in order to put forth more trenchant theses. This means that historians constantly face the historiographical task of unmasking such exaggerated contrasts in order to challenge the arguments that emerge from them. Comparisons can, however, also be used as a tool for dismantling such assertions when they consciously seek to tease out differences as well as similarities, without losing sight of the dynamic interplay between national contexts and cross-border processes in turn.[59] Just like everything that has a history, even firmly established contrasts can change or even evaporate. For this reason, this book does not intend to confirm the common assumptions of either British modernity or Habsburg backwardness, nor does it simply want to overturn this dichotomy by painting the Austro-Hungarian Empire as the 'true' modern imperial formation. Rather, its goal is to analyse the different forms of imperial modernity found within both empires, shedding light on beneficial as well as detrimental aspects. British law resulted in discriminating as well as empowering effects that made it possible for marginalized groups to make their voices heard. Conversely, policies of recognition in the Habsburg case coexisted with strongly exclusive mechanisms. Without denying the existence of differences, this book by no means intends to establish new dichotomies or reinforce old ones.

Accordingly, this study is not structured around contrasts. Indeed, despite the seemingly apparent differences between land-based and maritime empires, more recent scholarship has exposed a myriad of commonalities between these two types of imperial formations.[60] These similarities are the subject of the first three chapters, which examine the ways in which ethnic heterogeneity was dealt with in specific parts of both empires on a theoretical as well as practical level. The territories selected for this analysis not only reflect the political heterogeneity of both imperial formations, but also they each depict one of the three approaches to dealing with ethnic differences. Chapter 1, for example, outlines the nation-state approach that prevailed in the largely self-governing dominion of Canada and in the so-called Transleithanian or Hungarian portion of the Habsburg Empire, whose government enjoyed a great deal of autonomy in terms of its domestic affairs. In conclusion, this chapter illuminates the complex relationship between nation and empire in imperial formations. Chapter 2 directs its gaze to the Austrian half of the empire located on the other side of the Leitha River, and compares the statist approach of its mostly autonomous government with the approaches that emerged in the colonial context of India the larger part of which was directly subject to British rule. The last section of this chapter discusses the extent to which censuses and other forms of the imperial production of knowledge contributed to the creation and determination of ethnic identities and differences. Chapter 3 investigates the imperialist policies effective within the British protectorate of East Africa, whose legal and administrative status differed little from that of a 'true' colony, and the (quasi-)colonial territory of Bosnia-

Herzegovina, which was occupied by the Austro-Hungarian Empire in 1878 and annexed in 1908. It concludes with some thoughts on the relationship between imperial policies and different forms of racism.

This focus on individual territories within these empires makes it possible to trace local elements of large-scale developments as well as to investigate mutual interdependencies, not only between the metropolises and peripheries but also between different peripheral spaces. Likewise, this approach overcomes the typical focus on the metropolises or the metropolitan effects of peripheral developments characteristic of much new scholarship on the history of empires by suggesting a multipolar perspective.[61] Chapter 4 builds upon this line of thought by emphasizing the particularities of the United Kingdom that do not seem to fit clearly into any one of the three models, and concludes with a look at the interplay between ethnic and religious as well as social and gender differences. Chapter 5 then analyses both imperial formations at large, and questions how the ways of dealing with ethnic heterogeneity were moulded and changed at the level of the joint government of Austria–Hungary and the entire British Empire. It ends with a discussion of the relationship between biopower and ethnicization. The conclusion offers a summary of the answers to the questions posited at the outset of the book, as well as a brief overview of further developments in the twentieth century.

Notes

1. D. Griesser, 'Schwarze haben kaum Vertrauen in heimische Behörden', *derStandard.at* (16 April 2014). Retrieved 2 May 2014 from http://derstandard.at/1397520714967/Schwarze-haben-kaum-Vertrauen-in-Behoerden.

2. N. Farage, 'Flip-flopping Cameron is beginning to sound like my little echo', *The Daily Express* (25 April 2014). Retrieved 2 May 2014 from http://www.express.co.uk/news/uk/472409/Flip-flopping-Cameron-is-beginning-to-sound-like-my-little-echo-says-Nigel-Farage.

3. C. McGranahan and A.L. Stoler, 'Introduction: Refiguring Imperial Terrains', in A.L. Stoler, C. McGranahan and P.C. Perdue (eds), *Imperial Formations* (Santa Fe, NM: School for Advanced Research Press, 2007), 8–11; H. Münkler, *Reich, Nation, Europa: Modelle politischer Ordnung* (Weinheim: Beltz, Athenäum, 1996); C. Pierson, *The Modern State* (London: Routledge, 1996); S.N. Eisenstadt, *The Political Systems of Empire* (New York: Free Press, 1969); U. v. Hirschhausen and J. Leonhard, 'Beyond Rise, Decline and Fall: Comparing Multi-ethnic Empires in the Long Nineteenth Century', in J. Leonhard and U. v. Hirschhausen (eds), *Comparing Empires: Encounters and Transfers in the Long Nineteenth Century* (Göttingen: Vandenhoeck & Ruprecht, 2011), 12. On the British Empire, see J. Darwin, 'Britain's Empires', in S. Stockwell (ed.), *The British Empire: Themes and Perspectives* (Malden, MA: Blackwell, 2008), 1–20. On the Habsburg Empire, see H.-C. Maner (ed.), *Grenzregionen der Habsburgermonarchie im 18. und 19. Jahrhundert: Ihre Bedeutung und Funktion aus der Perspektive Wiens* (Münster: Lit, 2005).

4. D. Lieven, 'Dilemmas of Empire 1850–1918: Power, Territory, Identity', *Journal of Contemporary History* 34(2) (1999), 165; K. Barkey and M. v. Hagen, 'Conclusion', in K. Barkey and M. v. Hagen (eds), *After Empire: Multiethnic Societies and Nation-Building* (Boulder, CO: Westview Press, 1997), 182; McGranahan and Stoler, 'Introduction', 7.

5. D. Gosewinkel, *Schutz und Freiheit? Staatsbürgerschaft in Europa im 20. und 21. Jahrhundert* (Berlin: Suhrkamp, 2016), 24.

6. E. Nathans, *The Politics of Citizenship in Germany: Ethnicity, Utility and Nationalism* (Oxford: Berg, 2004). D. Gosewinkel, 'Citizenship, Subjecthood, Nationality: Concepts of Belonging in the Age of Modern Nation States', in K. Eder and B. Giesen (eds), *European Citizenship between National Legacies and Postnational Projects* (Oxford: Oxford University Press, 2001), 17–35; T.H. Marshall and T. Bottomore, *Citizenship and Social Class* (London: Pluto Press, 1992); P. Weil, *Qu'est-ce qu'un Français? Histoire de la nationalité française depuis la Révolution* (Paris: Grasset, 2002); D. Gosewinkel, *Einbürgern und Ausschließen: Die Nationalisierung der Staatsangehörigkeit vom Deutschen Bund bis zur Bundesrepublik Deutschland* (Göttingen: Vandenhoek & Ruprecht, 2001); R. Brubaker, *Citizenship and Nationhood in France and Germany* (Cambridge, MA: Harvard University Press, 1992).

7. T. Hippler, *Citizens, Soldiers and National Armies: Military Service in France and Germany, 1789–1830* (London: Routledge, 2008); G.Q. Flynn, *Conscription and Democracy: The Draft in France, Great Britain, and the United States* (Westport, CT: Greenwood Press, 2002); G. Finlayson, *Citizen, State, and Social Welfare in Britain, 1830–1990* (Oxford: Clarendon Press, 1994); C. Conrad and J. Kocka, 'Einführung', in C. Conrad and J. Kocka (eds), *Staatsbürgerschaft in Europa: Historische Erfahrungen und aktuelle Debatten* (Hamburg: Ed. Körber-Stiftung, 2001), 9–28.

8. Gosewinkel, *Einbürgern und Ausschließen*, 178–90, 278–302. On British nationality from a legal perspective, see L. Fransman, *Fransman's British Nationality Law*, 3rd edn (London: Bloomsbury Professional, 2011). On British law between liberal inclusiveness and ethnic exclusiveness, see K. Schönwälder and I. Sturm-Martin (eds), *Die britische Gesellschaft zwischen Offenheit und Abgrenzung: Einwanderung und Integration vom 18. bis zum 20. Jahrhundert* (Berlin: Philo, 2001); A. Fahrmeir, *Citizens and Aliens: Foreigners and the Law in Britain and the German States, 1789–1870* (New York: Berghahn Books, 2000). M.P. Baldwin, 'Making British Subjects: The Development of British Nationality Law, 1870–1939'. (Ph.D. dissertation, University of London, 2003); D. Cesarani, 'The Changing Character of Citizenship and Nationality in Britain', in D. Cesarani and M. Fulbrook (eds), *Citizenship, Nationality and Migration in Europe* (London: Routledge, 1996), 57–73; A. Dummett, *Citizenship and Nationality* (London: Battley, 1976). On exclusion in the Canadian context, see P.E. Roy, *A White Man's Province: British Columbia Politicians and Chinese and Japanese Immigrants, 1858–1914* (Vancouver: University of British Columbia Press, 1989). On the Habsburg context, see H. Burger, *Heimatrecht und Staatsbürgerschaft österreichischer Juden: Vom Ende des 18. Jahrhunderts bis in die Gegenwart* (Vienna: Böhlau, 2014); U. v. Hirschhausen, 'Von imperialer Inklusion zur nationalen Exklusion: Staatsbürgerschaft in Österreich-Ungarn 1867–1923', WZB Discussion Papers (Berlin: Social Science Research Center Berlin, SP IV 2007–403), retrieved 22 February 2017 from http://hdl.handle.net/10419/49610. On other case studies, see O. Trevisiol, *Die Einbürgerungspraxis im Deutschen Reich 1871–1945* (Göttingen: V&R unipress, 2006); D. Müller, *Staatsbürger*

auf Widerruf: Juden und Muslime als Alteritätspartner im rumänischen und serbischen Nationscode. Ethnonationale Staatsbürgerschaftskonzepte 1878–1941 (Wiesbaden: Harrassowitz, 2005).

9. A. Fahrmeir, 'Nineteenth-Century German Citizenships: A Reconsideration', *Historical Journal* 40(3) (1997), 27f., 67f. On the conflict between statist and nation-state modi in the German case, see Gosewinkel, *Einbürgern und Ausschließen*.

10. On dimensions of recognition in Austrian citizenship laws, see G. Stourzh, 'The Multinational Empire Revisited: Reflections on Late Imperial Austria', *Austrian History Yearbook* 23 (January 1992), 1–22; idem, *Die Gleichberechtigung der Nationalitäten in der Verfassung und Verwaltung Österreichs 1848–1918* (Vienna: Verlag der Österreichischen Akademie der Wissenschaften, 1985); D. Baier, *Sprache und Recht im alten Österreich: Art. 19 des Staatsgrundsetzes vom 21. Dezember 1867, seine Stellung im System der Grundrechte und seine Ausgestaltung durch die oberstgerichtliche Rechtsprechung* (Munich: Oldenbourg, 1983); A. Wandruszka and P. Urbanitsch (eds), *Die Habsburgermonarchie 1848–1918*, vol. 2, *Verwaltung und Rechtswesen* (Vienna: Verlag der Österreichischen Akademie der Wissenschaften, 1975). For critical perspectives on the highly stylized multicultural portrayal of Habsburg politics, see A. Komlosy, 'Habsburgermonarchie, Osmanisches Reich und Britisches Empire: Erweiterung, Zusammenhalt und Zerfall im Vergleich', *Zeitschrift für Weltgeschichte* 9(2) (2008), 20. See also J. Kusber, 'Grenzregionen, Randprovinzen, Vielfalt der Peripherie im Habsburgerreich: Zusammenfassende Anmerkungen und Ausblick', in H.-C. Maner (ed.), *Grenzregionen der Habsburgermonarchie im 18. und 19. Jahrhundert: Ihre Bedeutung und Funktion aus der Perspektive Wiens* (Münster: Lit, 2005), 235–43. On the 'principled tolerance of religious, cultural, and linguistic variations', see also McGranahan and Stoler, 'Introduction', 22.

11. T.K. Oommen (ed.), *Citizenship and National Identity: From Colonialism to Globalism* (New Delhi: Sage, 1997); Gosewinkel, *Einbürgern und Ausschließen*, 303f.; L. Wildenthal, 'Race, Gender, and Citizenship in the German Colonial Empire', in F. Cooper and A.L. Stoler (eds), *Tensions of the Empire: Colonial Cultures in a Bourgeois World* (Berkeley, CA: University of California Press, 1997), 263–83; E. Saada, *Les Enfants de la colonie: Les métis de l'Empire français entre sujétion et citoyenneté* (Paris: La Découverte, 2007). On discrimination according to 'racial' criteria in the Indian context (with a focus after 1945), see A.N. Sinha, *Law of Citizenship and Aliens in India* (London: Asia Publishing House, 1962).

12. C. Taylor, 'The Politics of Recognition', in idem, *Multiculturalism and 'the Politics of Recognition': An Essay*, edited by Amy Gutman (Princeton, NJ: Princeton University Press, 1992), 25–74; G. Alderman (ed.), *Governments, Ethnic Groups and Political Representation* (Aldershot: Dartmouth, 1993); Conrad and Kocka, 'Einführung'; G. Britz, *Kulturelle Rechte und Verfassung: Über den rechtlichen Umgang mit kultureller Differenz* (Tübingen: Mohr Siebeck, 2000); R. Bauböck, A. Heller and A.R. Zolberg (eds), *The Challenge of Diversity: Integration and Pluralism in Societies of Immigration* (Aldershot: Avebury, 1996); F. Cooper, *Citizenship between Empire and Nation: Remaking France and French Africa, 1945–1960* (Princeton, NJ: Princeton University Press, 2014), 11, 24. For a critical perspective on recognition, see R.J.F. Day, *Multiculturalism and the History of Canadian Diversity* (Toronto: University of Toronto Press, 2000), 216–22.

13. M. Galanter, *Competing Equalities: Law and the Backward Classes in India* (Berkeley, CA: University of California Press, 1984).

14. Such dynamics of assimilation could also play a role in imperial contexts; see S. Belmessous, *Assimilation and Empire: Uniformity in French and British Colonies, 1541–1954* (Oxford: Oxford University Press, 2013), 2.

15. Carsten Wieland justifies using a broad definition of ethnicity because it allows for his comparison between Bosnia and South Asia; see C. Wieland, *Nationalstaat wider Willen: Politisierung von Ethnien und Ethnisierung der Politik: Bosnien, Indien, Pakistan* (Frankfurt am Main: Campus, 2000), 35.

16. On the debate over ethnicity, see for example R. Jenkins, *Rethinking Ethnicity: Arguments and Explorations* (London: Sage, 1997); M. Guibernau and J. Rex (eds), *The Ethnicity Reader: Nationalism, Multiculturalism and Migration* (Cambridge: Polity Press, 1997); J. Hutchinson and A.D. Smith (eds), *Ethnicity* (Oxford: Oxford University Press, 1996); T.H. Erikson, *Ethnicity and Nationalism: Anthropological Perspectives* (London: Pluto Press, 1993); H. Esser, 'Ethnische Differenzierung und moderne Gesellschaft', *Zeitschrift für Soziologie* 17(4) (1988), 235–48. According to Robert Young, the term 'ethnicity' was first used in English in 1941; see R.J.C. Young, *The Idea of English Ethnicity* (Malden, MA: Blackwell, 2008), X.

17. C. Giordano, 'Ethnizität und das Motiv des mono-ethnischen Raumes in Zentral- und Osteuropa', in U. Altermatt (ed.), *Nation, Ethnizität und Staat in Mitteleuropa* (Vienna: Böhlau, 1996), 25.

18. M. Weber, 'Wirtschaft und Gesellschaft: Die Wirtschaft und die gesellschaftlichen Ordnungen und Mächte', in H.G. Kippenberg, P. Schilm and J. Niemeier (eds), *Nachlaß* (Tübingen: Mohr, 2001), vol. 2, *Religiöse Gemeinschaften*, 172f.

19. A.D. Smith, *The Ethnic Origins of Nations* (Oxford: Blackwell, 1986).

20. A.P. Cohen (ed.), *Signifying Identities: Anthropological Perspectives on Boundaries and Contested Values* (London: Routledge, 2000); F. Barth (ed.), *Ethnic Groups and Boundaries: The Social Organization of Culture Difference* (Boston, MA: Little, Brown & Company, 1969).

21. M. Wieviorka, *Kulturelle Differenz und kollektive Identitäten*, trans. R. Voullié (Hamburg: Hamburger Edition, 2003); H.K. Bhaba, *The Location of Culture*, reprint (London: Routledge, 1994). With respect to nationality law, see S. Conrad, 'Doppelte Marginalisierung: Plädoyer für eine transnationale Perspektive auf die deutsche Geschichte', *Geschichte und Gesellschaft* 28 (2002), 167f. On the question of to what extent post-colonial approaches can be applied to Austria-Hungary, see J. Feichtinger, U. Prutsch and M. Csáky (eds), *Habsburg postcolonial: Machtstrukturen und kollektives Gedächtnis* (Innsbruck: Studien-Verlag, 2003).

22. In response to such definitions of ethnicity and other identities, see the critique in R. Brubaker and F. Cooper, 'Beyond "Identity"', *Theory and Society* 29(1) (2000), 1–47, which argues that the 'soft' lines of ethnicity may blur the 'hard' effects of ethnic attribution, and proposes the alternative terms 'identification' and 'groupness'.

23. M. Banton, *Racial Theories*, 2nd edn (Cambridge: Cambridge University Press, 1998); W. Conze, 'Rasse', in O. Brunner, W. Conze and R. Koselleck (eds), *Geschichtliche Grundbegriffe*, reprint, vol. 5, *Pro–Soz* (Stuttgart: Klett-Cotta, 1994) 135–78.

24. However, ethnocultural patterns of difference could also be marked by privileges and hierarchies. For this kind of argument in relation to the Habsburg context, see D. Hoerder, 'Revising the Monocultural Nation-State Paradigm: An Introduction to Transcultural Perspectives', in D. Hoerder, C. Harzig and A. Shubert (eds), *The Historical Practice of Diversity: Transcultural Interactions from the Early Modern*

Mediterranean to the Postcolonial World (New York: Berghahn Books, 2003), 3; Kusber, 'Grenzregionen', 240.

25. Even 'physical features' can be seen as cultural constructs. M. Nash, *The Cauldron of Ethnicity in the Modern World* (Chicago, IL: University of Chicago Press, 1989), 10f. See also Day, *Multiculturalism*, 5; M.M. Smith, *How Race Is Made: Slavery, Segregation, and the Senses* (Chapel Hill, NC: University of North Carolina Press, 2006). On the debate over racism, see also C. Geulen, *Wahlverwandte: Rassendiskurs und Nationalismus im späten 19. Jahrhundert* (Hamburg: Hamburger Edition, 2004), 15–19, 42–47. Owing to the desire to maintain an analytical distance from biologist concepts, the terms 'race' and 'racial' are placed in quotes throughout this book, as are other problematic terms such as 'native' and 'European', which were often used by contemporaries in a racist sense.

26. On the distinction between 'race' and 'ethnicity', see also Young, *English Ethnicity*, Xf., 42.

27. On the debate over the concepts of nation and nationalism, see, among others, M. Hroch, *European Nations: Explaining their Formation*, trans. by K. Graham (London: Verso, 2015); H. Kriesi and K. Armingeon (eds), *Nation and National Identity: The European Experience in Perspective* (Chur: Rüegger, 1999); R. Koselleck, 'Volk, Nation, Nationalismus, Masse', in O. Brunner, W. Conze and R. Koselleck (eds), *Geschichtliche Grundbegriffe: Historisches Lexikon zur politisch-sozialen Sprache in Deutschland*, vol. 7, *Verw–Z* (Stuttgart: Klett-Cotta, 1992), 141–431; E.J. Hobsbawm, *Nations and Nationalism since 1780: Programme, Myth, Reality* (Cambridge: Cambridge University Press, 1991).

28. Erikson, *Ethnicity*, 6, 99.

29. On interesting examples of multi-ethnic nation-states, see R. Argast, *Staatsbürgerschaft und Nation: Ausschließung und Integration in der Schweiz 1848–1933* (Göttingen: Vandenhoeck & Ruprecht, 2007), on Switzerland; as well as Day, *Multiculturalism*, and E. Winter, 'Neither "America" nor "Québec": Constructing the Canadian Multicultural Nation', *Nations and Nationalism* 13(3) (2007), 481–503, on Canada.

30. R. Emerson, *From Empire to Nation: The Rise to Self-Assertion of Asian and African People* (Cambridge, MA: Harvard University Press, 1967); R.L. Rudolph, 'Nationalism and Empire in Historical Perspective', in R.L. Rudolph and D.F. Good (eds), *Nationalism and Empire: The Habsburg Empire and the Soviet Union* (New York: St. Martin's Press, 1992), 3–12; R.R. Pierson and N. Chaudhuri (eds), *Nation, Empire, Colony: Historicizing Gender and Race* (Bloomington, IN: Indiana University Press, 1998).

31. For an unfavourable comparison between imperial asymmetries and equality in nation-states, see T.H. Parsons, *The Rule of Empires: Those Who Built Them, Those Who Endured Them, and Why They Always Fall* (Oxford: Oxford University Press, 2010), 3, 15. For a critique of this over-simplified contrast, see Cooper, *Citizenship*; S. Berger and A. Miller, 'Nation-Building and Regional Integration, c. 1800–1914: The Role of Empires', *European Review of History* 15(3) (2008), 317–30; Hirschhausen and Leonhard, 'Beyond Rise', 9. On the growing interests in empires, see H.-H. Nolte (ed.), *Imperien: Eine vergleichende Studie* (Schwalbach: Wochenschau-Verlag, 2008); C. Layne and B.A. Thayer, *American Empire: A Debate* (New York: Routledge, 2007); H. Münkler, *Imperien: Die Logik der Weltherrschaft: Vom Alten Rom bis zu den Vereinigten Staaten*, 2nd edn (Berlin: Rowohlt, 2005); G. Steinmetz, 'Return to Empire: The New U.S. Imperialism in Comparative Historical Perspective', *Sociological Theory* 23(4) (2005), 339–67; J. Osterhammel, 'Imperien im 20. Jahrhundert: Eine Einführung', *Zeithistorische*

Forschungen 3(1) (2006), 4–13, retrieved 23 February 2017 from http://www.zeithisto-rische-forschungen.de/1-2006/id=4627.

32. M. Rürup, 'Lives in Limbo: Statelessness after Two World Wars', *Bulletin of the German Historical Institute* 49 (Fall 2011), 113–34; M. Stiller, *Eine Völkerrechtsgeschichte der Staatenlosigkeit: Dargestellt anhand ausgewählter Beispiele aus Europa, Russland und den USA* (Vienna: Springer, 2011).

33. F. Cooper, 'From Imperial Inclusion to Republican Exclusion? France's Ambiguous Postwar Trajectory', in C. Tshimanga, D. Gondola and P.J. Bloom (eds), *Frenchness and the African Diaspora: Identity and Uprising in Contemporary France* (Bloomington, IN: Indiana University Press, 2009), 91–119; J. Burbank, 'An Imperial Rights Regime: Law and Citizenship in the Russian Empire', *Kritika* 7(3) (2006), 397–431; Weil, *Qu'est-ce qu'un Français?*; Saada, *Les enfants de la colonie*; Wildenthal, 'Race, Gender, and Citizenship'.

34. N. Ferguson, *Empire: The Rise and Demise of the British World Order and the Lessons for Global Power* (New York: Basic Books, 2002). For a critique of Ferguson's argument, see Parsons, *Empires*, 3; J. Leonhard and U. v. Hirschhausen, '"New Imperialism" oder "Liberal Empire"? Niall Fergusons Empire-Apologetik im Zeichen der "Anglobalization"', *Zeithistorische Forschungen* 3(1) (2006), 121–28, retrieved 9 December 2015 from http://www.zeithistorische-forschungen.de/1-2006/id=4525.

35. R. Karatani, *Defining British Citizenship: Empire, Commonwealth, and Modern Britain* (London: Frank Cass, 2003); cf. D. Gorman, *Imperial Citizenship: Empire and the Question of Belonging* (Manchester: Manchester University Press, 2006); K. Grant, P. Levine and F. Trentmann (eds), *Beyond Sovereignty: Britain, Empire and Transnationalism, c.1880–1950* (Basingstoke: Palgrave Macmillan, 2007); Cooper, *Citizenship*.

36. L. Benton, *A Search for Sovereignty: Law and Geography in European Empires, 1400–1900* (Cambridge: Cambridge University Press, 2010); S.B. Kirmse, 'Law and Empire in Late Tsarist Russia: Muslim Tatars Go to Court', *Slavic Review* 72(4) (2013), 778–801 (doi: 10.5612/slavicreview.72.4.0778).

37. C. McGranahan, A.L. Stoler and P.C. Perdue (eds), *Imperial Formations* (Santa Fe, NM: School for Advanced Research Press, 2007).

38. On this distinction, see E.J. Hobsbawm, 'The End of Empires', in K. Barkey and M. v. Hagen (eds), *After Empire: Multiethnic Societies and Nation-Building* (Boulder, CO: Westview Press, 1997), 12–16; Lieven, 'Dilemmas of Empire', 164. On the critique of such contrasts, see A. Miller, 'The Value and the Limits of a Comparative Approach to the History of Contiguous Empires on the European Periphery', in K. Matsuzato (ed.), *Imperiology: From Empirical Knowledge to Discussing the Russian Empire* (Sapporo: Slavic Research Center, Hokkaido University, 1997), 20.

39. C. Tilly, 'How Empires End', in K. Barkey and M. v. Hagen (eds), *After Empire: Multiethnic Societies and Nation-Building* (Boulder, CO: Westview Press, 1997), 3; cf. Komlosy, 'Habsburgermonarchie', 57.

40. M. Koller, 'Bosnien und die Herzegowina im Spannungsfeld von "Europa" und "Außereuropa": Der Aufstand in der Herzegowina, Südbosnien und Süddalmatien (1881–1882)', in H.-C. Maner (ed.), *Grenzregionen der Habsburgermonarchie im 18. und 19. Jahrhundert: Ihre Bedeutung und Funktion aus der Perspektive Wiens* (Münster: Lit, 2005), 200; Komlosy, 'Habsburgermonarchie', 10, 28f.; K. Kaps and J. Surman, 'Postcolonial or Post-colonial? Post(-)colonial Perspectives on Habsburg Galicia', *Historyka: Studia Metodologiczne* 42 (2012), 20.

41. F. Cooper, 'Empire Multiplied: A Review Essay', *Comparative Studies in Society and History* 46(2) (2004), 269.

42. C. McGranahan and A.L. Stoler, 'Preface', in A.L. Stoler, C. McGranahan and P.C. Perdue (eds), *Imperial Formations* (Santa Fe, NM: School for Advanced Research Press, 2007), XI.

43. L. Péter, *Hungary's Long Nineteenth Century: Constitutional and Democratic Traditions in European Perspective.* Collected Studies, edited by M. Lojkó (Leiden: Brill, 2012), 281–304; F. Lindström, *Empire and Identity: Biographies of the Austrian State Problem in the Late Habsburg Empire* (West Lafayette, IN: Purdue University Press, 2008).

44. Burbank, 'Imperial Rights', 399; Geulen, *Wahlverwandte*, 37f.

45. M. Foucault, *Histoire de la sexualité*, vol. 1, *La volonté de savoir* (Paris: Gallimard, 1976); idem, *Security, Territory, Population: Lectures at the Collège de France, 1978–79*, ed. M. Senellart, trans. G. Burchell (Basingstoke: Palgrave Macmillan, 2007); T. Lemke, 'Eine Analytik der Biopolitik: Überlegungen zu Geschichte und Gegenwart eines umstrittenen Begriffs', *Behemoth – A Journal on Civilisation* 1(1) (2008), 80. The relevance of this approach for the analysis of developments in nationality and citizenship is stressed in Argast, *Staatsbürgerschaft*, 16, 46–60.

46. Foucault, *Security, Territory, Population*; idem, *The Birth of Biopolitics: Lectures at the Collège de France, 1978–79*, ed. M. Senellart, trans. G. Burchell (Basingstoke: Palgrave Macmillan, 2008). This emphasis on the population in the context of biopower corresponds with the fundamental transition from an understanding of the state focusing on territory to a form of statehood focusing on population and membership. See R. Grawert, *Staat und Staatsangehörigkeit: Verfassungsgeschichtliche Untersuchung zur Entstehung der Staatsangehörigkeit* (Berlin: Duncker & Humblot, 1973). See also D. Schmidt, *Statistik und Staatlichkeit* (Wiesbaden: Verlag für Sozialwissenschaften, 2005).

47. Lemke, 'Analytik der Biopolitik', 73; J. Gledhill, 'The Power of Ethnic Nationalism: Foucault's Bio-power and the Development of Ethnic Nationalism in Eastern Europe', *National Identities* 7(4) (2005), 347–68; Geulen, *Wahlverwandte*, 374.

48. Lemke, 'Analytik der Biopolitik', 80. On this distinction, see also Argast, *Staatsbürgerschaft*, 20, 324f., 332.

49. 'So, comparing the quantity of freedom between one system and another does not in fact [make] much sense. And we do not see what type of demonstration, what type of gauge or measure we could apply' (Foucault, *Birth of Biopolitics*, 62f).

50. Grawert, *Staat und Staatsangehörigkeit.*

51. J. Caplan and J. Torpey (eds), *Documenting Individual Identity: The Development of State Practices in the Modern World* (Princeton, NJ: Princeton University Press, 2001); J. Torpey, *The Invention of the Passport: Surveillance, Citizenship and the State* (Cambridge: Cambridge University Press, 2000).

52. Brubaker, *Citizenship and Nationhood.* Uri Ra'anan draws the border between the 'national' West and the 'ethnic' East along the Rhine. U. Ra'anan, 'Nation and State: Order out of Chaos', in U. Ra'anan, M. Mesner, K. Armes, and K. Martin (eds), *State and Nation in Multi-ethnic Societies: The Breakup of Multinational States* (Manchester: Manchester University Press, 1991), 3–32. On this dichotomy, see also Gledhill, 'Power of Ethnic Nationalism'; F. Meinecke, *Weltbürgertum und Nationalstaat: Studien zur Genesis des deutschen Nationalstaates* (Munich: Oldenbourg, 1908); H. Kohn, *Nationalism: Its Meaning and History* (Princeton, NJ: Van Nostrand, 1955); T. Schieder, 'Typologie und Erscheinungsform des Nationalstaats in Europa', *Historische Zeitschrift*

202(1) (1966), 58–81. For arguments against this dichotomy, see K. Barkey, 'Thinking about Consequences of Empire', in K. Barkey and M. v. Hagen (eds), *After Empire: Multiethnic Societies and Nation-Building* (Boulder, CO: Westview Press, 1997), 108. Even Brubaker later distanced himself from too rigid contrasts between 'ethnic' and 'civic nationalism'; R. Brubaker, *Ethnicity without Groups* (Cambridge, MA: Harvard University Press, 2004).

53. Gosewinkel, *Einbürgern und Ausschließen.*
54. G. Noiriel, *Etat, nation et immigration: Vers une histoire du pouvoir* (Paris: Gallimard, 2001).
55. Marshall and Bottomore, *Citizenship.* For a critical perspective, especially in relation to the developments in the British dominions, see D. Pearson, 'Theorizing Citizenship in British Settler Societies', *Ethnic and Racial Studies* 25(6) (2002), 989.
56. I.C. Fletcher, L.E. Nym Mayhall and P. Levine (eds), *Women's Suffrage in the British Empire: Citizenship, Nation and Race* (London: Routledge, 2000); B. Bader-Zaar, 'Women's Suffrage and War: World War I and Political Reform in a Comparative Perspective', in I. Sulkunen, S.-L. Nevala-Nurmi and P. Markkola (eds), *Suffrage, Gender and Citizenship: International Perspectives on Parliamentary Reforms* (Newcastle: Cambridge Scholars Publishing, 2009), 193–218; S. Dudink, K. Hagemann and A. Clark (eds), *Representing Masculinity: Male Citizenship in Modern Western Culture* (New York: Palgrave Macmillan, 2007); Pierson and Chaudhuri, *Nation, Empire, Colony*; N. Piper, *Racism, Nationalism and Citizenship: Ethnic Minorities in Britain and Germany* (Aldershot: Ashgate, 1998); Y.N. Soysal, *Limits of Citizenship: Migrants and Postnational Membership in Europe* (Chicago, IL: University of Chicago Press, 1994); J. Spinner, *The Boundaries of Citizenship: Race, Ethnicity, and Nationality in the Liberal State* (Baltimore, MD: Johns Hopkins University Press, 1994).
57. For a critique of lop-sided comparisons between the British and Habsburg empires, see Komlosy, 'Habsburgermonarchie', 26f.
58. Burger, *Heimatrecht und Staatsbürgerschaft*; Hirschhausen, 'Von imperialer Inklusion'.
59. On comparison as a historical method or perspective in general, see H. Kaelble, 'Die interdisziplinären Debatten über Vergleich und Transfer', in H. Kaelble and J. Schriewer (eds), *Vergleich und Transfer: Komparatistik in den Sozial-, Geschichts- und Kulturwissenschaften* (Frankfurt am Main: Campus, 2003), 469–93; M. Werner and B. Zimmermann, 'Vergleich, Transfer, Verflechtung: Der Ansatz der Histoire croisée und die Herausforderung des Transnationalen', *Geschichte und Gesellschaft* 28(4) (2002), 607–36; M. Middell, 'Kulturtransfer und historische Komparatistik: Thesen zu ihrem Verhältnis', in M. Middell (ed.), *Kulturtransfer und Vergleich* (Leipzig: Leipziger Universitäts-Verlag, 2000), 7–41; C. Lorenz, 'Comparative Historiography: Problems and Perspectives', *History and Theory* 38(1) (1998), 25–39; H.-G. Haupt and J. Kocka, 'Historischer Vergleich: Methoden, Aufgaben, Probleme: Eine Einleitung', in H.-G. Haupt and J. Kocka (eds), *Geschichte und Vergleich: Ansätze und Ergebnisse international vergleichender Geschichtsschreibung* (Frankfurt am Main: Campus, 1996), 9–45; T. Welskopp, 'Stolpersteine auf dem Königsweg: Methodenkritische Anmerkungen zum internationalen Vergleich in der Gesellschaftsgeschichte', *Archiv für Sozialgeschichte* 35 (1995), 339–67; J. Matthes, 'The Operation Called "Vergleichen"', in J. Matthes (ed.), *Zwischen den Kulturen? Die Sozialwissenschaften vor dem Problem des Kulturvergleichs* (Göttingen: Schwartz, 1992), 75–99; D. Cohen and M. O'Connor (eds), *Comparison and History: Europe in Cross-National Perspective* (New York: Routledge, 2004). A comparative

European analysis of nationality is offered in D. Gosewinkel, 'Staatsangehörigkeit und Nationszugehörigkeit in Europa während des 19. und 20. Jahrhunderts', in A. Gestrich and L. Raphael (eds), *Inklusion/Exklusion: Studien zu Fremdheit und Armut von der Antike bis zur Gegenwart* (Frankfurt am Main: Peter Lang, 2004), 207–27.

60. Miller, 'The Value and the Limits', 19, cf. 23–26; J. Burbank and F. Cooper, *Empires in World History: Power and the Politics of Difference* (Princeton, NJ: Princeton University Press 2010); Kaps and Surman, 'Postcolonial or Post-colonial?'. On the need for comparisons that question the dichotomy between West European and Central/East European empires, see Komlosy, 'Habsburgermonarchie'; McGranahan and Stoler, 'Introduction'; C. Ruthner, '"k.(u.)k. postcolonial"? Für eine neue Lesart der österreichischen (und benachbarter) Literatur/en', in W. Müller-Funk, P. Plener and C. Ruthner (eds), *Kakanien revisited: Das Eigene und das Fremde (in) der österreichisch-ungarischen Monarchie* (Tübingen: Francke, 2002), 93–103, retrieved 9 December 2015 from http://www.kakanien.ac.at/beitr/theorie/CRuthner1.pdf; Barkey and Hagen, 'Conclusion'; B. Gammerl, 'Der Vergleich von Reich zu Reich: Überlegungen zum Imperienvergleich anhand des britisch-habsburgischen Beispiels', in A. Arndt, J.C. Häberlen and C. Reinecke, *Vergleichen, Verflechten, Verwirren? Europäische Geschichtsschreibung zwischen Theorie und Praxis* (Göttingen: Vandenhoeck & Ruprecht, 2011), 221–42; T.R. Weeks, 'Nationality, Empire, and Politics in the Russian Empire and USSR: An Overview of Recent Publications', *H-Soz-Kult* (29 October 2012), retrieved 9 December 2015 from http://hsozkult.geschichte.hu-berlin.de/forum/2012-10-001. Alexander Morrison has put forth an initial empirical study along these lines in: A.S. Morrison, *Russian Rule in Samarkand 1868–1910: A Comparison with British India* (Oxford: Oxford University Press, 2008).

61. A. Thompson, *The Empire Strikes Back? The Impact of Imperialism on Britain from the Mid-Nineteenth Century* (Harlow: Pearson Longman, 2005); A. Burton (ed.), *After the Imperial Turn: Thinking with and through the Nation* (Durham, NC: Duke University Press, 2003); L. Colley, *Captives: Britain, Empire and the World, 1600–1850* (London: Jonathan Cape, 2002).

Chapter 1

NATION-STATES EMERGING ON THE SEMI-PERIPHERY

The Beginnings of a Canadian Nationality: Integration Efforts and Racist Exclusion

The Dominion of Canada was created in 1867 as a confederation of multiple British colonies through the British North America Act. In terms of its domestic affairs, it enjoyed a great deal of independence from the imperial metropolis. For the first time, anglophone Upper Canada (Ontario) and francophone Lower Canada (Quebec) fell under a common federal government. The conflicts between this federal government and those of the individual provinces shaped Canadian politics from the outset. As Canada expanded westward, moreover, this potential for conflict increased. When Manitoba was being incorporated into the Canadian confederation, for example, the so-called Métis, a mostly French-speaking group that had emerged out of the long-standing coexistence of European immigrants and indigenous tribes, rebelled in 1869 and 1885. The Métis demanded political and cultural privileges, and they were partly successful in achieving their goals. Ultimately, however, the federal government suppressed their rebellion. Similarly, the integration of the most western province of British Columbia in 1871 led to numerous conflicts because the provincial and federal governments followed fundamentally different approaches on many issues such as immigration and how to deal with the indigenous population.

Furthermore, the divergent social and economic agendas followed by the alternating Conservative and Liberal governments shaped the contours of Canadian politics before the First World War. At the same time, westward expansion, the construction of the transcontinental railway, the wave of immigration following the discovery of gold in the Klondike and the settlement of the prairies in the 1890s had a decisive impact on Canada's development. During this time, indigenous populations were pushed onto reservations, and the plains between the lakes and the Rocky Mountains increasingly became a purely 'white' area of settlement. From the late nineteenth century onwards, efforts to attract immigrants from the United Kingdom and Western Europe were particularly successful, but this also resulted in social and economic conflicts between older immigrant communities and European newcomers. As a result, the emerging dissonance between imperial and Canadian loyalties continued to grow. On the one hand, the manifestation of a separate national identity was tied to the question of whether Canada should align itself more strongly with the imperial motherland or rather with the United States. On the other hand, the conflict over Irish Home Rule – in large part because of the presence of Irish immigrants – brought arguments tinged with nationalism to Canada. Last but not least, the First World War intensified the contradiction between pro-imperial support of the British war efforts and anti-imperial demands for more autonomy.

Naturalization and the Legal Inclusion of Immigrants

The laws on nationality in Canada were largely defined by British common law, which granted all those born in territories ruled by the British Crown the status of a British subject according to the principle of *ius soli*. Correspondingly, this law automatically integrated second-generation immigrants into the community of British nationals. However, Canada had its own regulations for naturalization that made the inclusion of immigrants easier than in the United Kingdom itself. In comparison to the British Naturalization Act of 1870, the applicable Canadian law passed in 1881 only demanded three years of residency prior to naturalization as opposed to five years.[1] Additionally, the fee of seventy-five cents charged in Canada was much cheaper than the five pounds required in the United Kingdom.[2]

Moreover, Canada's parliament and government were generally in favour of a swift integration of immigrants. They were also willing to advocate the interests of some groups of immigrants such as those from Germany.[3] In 1880, for example, the Canadian government sent along a memorandum to the Colonial Office in London from 'German naturalised subjects in Canada', who were demanding legal equality with the other British subjects: '[A]s citizens of Canada, [we] pay our due proportion of taxes, [and] perform all our various duties as such citizens, including militia service'.[4] The naturalized Germans wanted to be considered as British subjects throughout the empire as a whole. They also demanded permanently valid passports and the assurance of diplomatic protection in Germany.

This memorandum points to the fact that Canadian naturalization did not necessarily confer British subject status across the empire or in the country of a person's origin. The only way to resolve this problem would have been to ensure an empire-wide standard for naturalization laws and to negotiate a corresponding treaty with the foreign country in question – in this case the German Empire. Effectively, this would have entailed extending the residency requirement in Canada to five years in keeping with the UK standard.[5] But the Canadian legislators were not prepared to make naturalization more difficult in the dominion. In the end, the British Foreign Ministry permitted the issuance of permanently valid passports in 1880, but naturalized Britons returning to their countries of origin could not count on British protection against military conscription.

With its easier naturalization process, the Canadian government hoped to make immigration more attractive. Despite all efforts, however, the number of immigrants remained below expectations for the first three decades after 1867. It was not until the last years of the nineteenth century that more immigrants settled in the Canadian prairies, but it must also be noted that the government that came into office in 1896 under Sir Wilfrid Laurier was a strong promoter of immigration (see Fig 1.1).[6]

Yet, not all immigrants benefited from this governmental support. For example, the Canadian government refused to let the migration agency offer the usual premiums to immigrants from Galicia, fearing – as the Habsburg authorities supposed – that increasing 'Galician Immigration' might result in new immigrants outweighing the established immigrant communities.[7] Nonetheless, about 230,000 or more than half of the continental Europeans who migrated to Canada between 1901 and 1910 came from the Habsburg monarchy.

Most of the approximately 750,000 people who moved to Canada from the United States between 1900 and 1914 were remigrants who had migrated from Canada to the United States before returning to Canada.[8] The close connection between immigration and naturalization policies becomes particularly clear when looking at this group. In 1903, Canada introduced an accelerated renaturalization process for individuals who had lost their status as British subjects – for

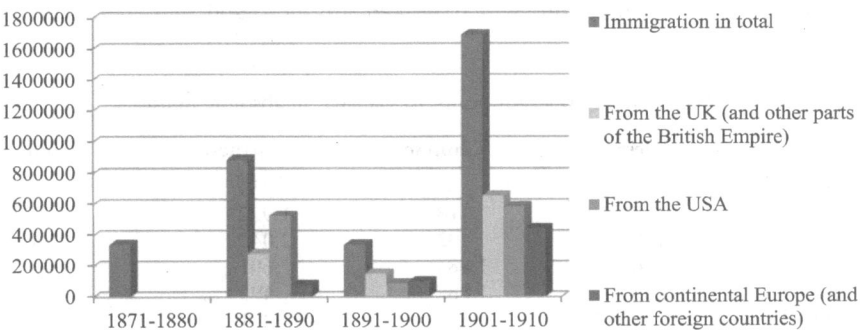

Figure 1.1. Immigrants to Canada according to country of origin, in absolute figures

example, due to having become US-naturalized citizens. These individuals could apply for naturalization after being resident in Canada for just three months.[9]

This simplified renaturalization process contributed to a nationalization of nationality laws because it accelerated the legal integration of all those who were seen as belonging to the proto-national Canadian community. A law passed in August 1914 also reflected this tendency in that it allowed for an accelerated renaturalization process for divorced or widowed women who had lost their British nationality through marriage to a foreigner.[10]

In general, Canadian naturalization policies followed a nation-state model as they aimed to grant all residents the same status as nationals and the same rights of citizenship. All immigrants profited from this approach at first glance, regardless of ethnic identity. However, a closer look at immigration policies reveals that it was above all 'European' immigrants who were to be treated as equal to British subjects within a homogenizing nation-state model that otherwise sought to exclude 'non-whites'.

Migration Policies and the Exclusion of 'Non-Whites'

In the Canadian case, immigration laws primarily determined who was to be integrated into the community of nationals and who was to be excluded. Those denied entry to Canada were likewise excluded from becoming British subjects. While the Canadian authorities promoted the immigration of 'Europeans', they turned other groups away at the border. 'Black' migrants from the United States who wished to cross the forty-ninth degree of latitude to the North were one such group.[11] However, immigrants from Asia, whose number climbed steadily in the early twentieth century, met with the most resistance among contemporaries (see Table 1.1).[12]

Since the 1880s, the province of British Columbia had repeatedly tried to stop the immigration of people from Japan, China and India.[13] The propaganda against 'Asiatic' immigration, which peaked around 1900, also demanded a

Table 1.1. Immigration of 'non-Europeans' to Canada, in absolute figures

Year	'Negro'	'Chinese'	'Japanese'	'Hindoo'
1904/05	5	–	354	45
1905/06	42	18	1,922	387
1906/07	108	92	2,042	2,124
1907/08	136	1,884	7,601	2,623
1908/09	73	1,887	495	6
1909/10	7	2,156	271	10
1910/11	12	5,278	437	5
1911/12	138	6,247	765	3

prohibition against the naturalization of 'Asiatics'.[14] For the most part, however, the debates over the racist exclusion of 'Asians' took place within the context of immigration law. Numerous conflicts erupted between the provincial government of British Columbia and the federal government in Ottawa, especially since the latter sought to retain an ethnically neutral stance on immigration.

After the turn of the century, racist discrimination gained a stronger foothold because the general social climate was increasingly tainted by the xenophobia of the 'white' population.[15] In 1907, the Asiatic Exclusion League in Vancouver sponsored an anti-Asian demonstration that ultimately resulted in riots in which the demonstrators looted Japanese and Chinese shops.[16] The government responded to these incidents by introducing a new regulation in 1908 that only permitted 'Japanese' and 'Indian' immigrants to enter the country if they had travelled directly to Canada from their country of origin. At the same time, informal agreements with the governments in question also made certain that such direct ship connections would not be offered.[17] The figures in Table 1.1 attest to the effectiveness of this strategy.

The Immigration Act passed in 1910 was more decisive in its legal ramifications. It permitted the Canadian government to deny entry to 'immigrants belonging to any race deemed unsuited to the climate or the requirements of Canada'. This law drastically tightened the provisions of its predecessor from 1906, and for the first time explicitly formulated a racist basis for exclusion.[18] These mechanisms are particularly interesting and complex because they also affected the 'Indian' subjects of the British Crown (i.e. people who shared one and the same national status with Canadian Britons). Nonetheless, this policy did not meet with any fundamental resistance in the imperial metropolis. On the contrary, a government commission in London determined in 1914: 'In the early exclusion of Asiatics future historians will perhaps see the most important of all the results secured by the establishment of self-government in the colonies'.[19]

Deterring the Immigration of 'Indian' Subjects

The exclusion of 'Indian' subjects is particularly interesting in terms of the development of British nationality law because it poignantly exemplifies the efforts of the respective dominions to deny immigration even to fellow British subjects on the basis of ethnic identity. Similar exclusionary mechanisms were also in place in New Zealand, Australia and South Africa. The respective laws explicitly sought to bar 'non-white' British subjects from exercising social and political rights that were supposed to be reserved for the 'European' population.[20]

Indeed, these rights were not guaranteed to British subjects throughout the empire, but rather only within certain territories. It was necessary to be a subject of the empire to be entitled to citizenship, but not every subject was deemed worthy of citizenship. Indeed, residence within a specific territory was required for citizenship and not just British subject status. This meant that certain groups of subjects could be excluded from political and social rights by denying them access to specific parts of the British Empire. Typically, the dominions combined ethnically exclusive immigration policies with the simultaneous expansion of citizenship within their territories, resulting in a stratified system of different legal statuses within the community of British subjects. Accordingly, being a subject of the empire did not automatically transfer into a right to citizenship.

As these immigration restrictions were being put into place in the dominions, the central question was whether such racist criteria for exclusion should be explicitly stated or only implicitly included in legislation. By and large, the government in London urged for indirect discrimination between British subjects with different ethnic identities. At least at the official level, it sought to retain a uniform joint community of subjects in order to strengthen the unity of the British Empire and bolster its international prestige. Accordingly, the Canadian government informed the governments in Delhi and London about its proposed ethnically exclusive law. It wrote that it had refrained from such measures in the past 'because of the natives of India being British subjects' and because it did not want to ignore the 'obligations which the British connection involved'.[21] The proposed Canadian law violated these obligations, especially because it legally privileged Japanese nationals over 'British Asiatic subjects' in some respects. This practice, the government in London argued, could damage the international prestige of British subjecthood.[22]

At first, the government in Ottawa sought to deflect this accusation by portraying the exclusion of 'Asiatic subjects' as a protective measure. According to their argument, the wintry climate and the strong competition on the job market made it virtually impossible for these immigrants to successfully establish themselves in Canada. The Indian government, Canada suggested, should therefore protect its subjects by prohibiting their emigration.[23] The government in Delhi, however, rejected this suggestion. According to its information, Delhi claimed, the 'Sikhs and Hindus at present in British Columbia' had been able to acclimate themselves successfully. It further stated that 'it will be impossible in future to urge climatic considerations as a reason for discouraging, on humanitarian grounds, the emigration of Sikhs to British Columbia'.[24] The Indian government's rejection of this law, however, was neither based on a general objection to Canada's exclusionary intentions nor on an insistence on the equality of all British subjects. As long as only marginalized groups were affected and not wealthy people of high social status, the government in Delhi had no objections to the exclusion of 'Indian' subjects. The provisions of the draft law that 'immigrants may be required to possess a prescribed amount of money ... which amount may vary according to the race, occupation or destination of such immigrant' therefore correlated well with Delhi's standpoint.[25]

Whereas the decisive issue for the Indian government was a social one, the government in Ottawa pursued a course of racist exclusion. The draft Canadian law was 'designed to check … any sudden influx of immigrants whose habits of life, or physical or moral characteristics, are repugnant to Canadian ideals'.[26] Furthermore, the government wanted to hinder this immigration because it feared that it would be detrimental to the standard of living of the Canadian population and put a strain on local job markets. In general, social and economic arguments were put forth to justify racist policies of exclusion. Most of these arguments came as no surprise because warnings against the downward pressure on wages were part of the standard repertoire of anti-immigration propaganda. Nonetheless, the idea of a social utopia bound up in these arguments had far-reaching effects.

These links between racist and socio-economic interests reflected the tension between two potential paths of development for the west of Canada in particular. On the one hand, there was the promise of rapid industrial development through the import of cheap labour from Asia. At the same time, however, this influx would potentially create a great divide between rich and poor. On the other hand, as the draft law maintained, racist immigration restrictions could pave the way for the gradual emergence of a mostly egalitarian and agrarian-based society. Following the lines of this argument, Canada's exclusionary policies not only aimed to achieve ethnic homogeneity, but also social homogeneity within the population. In the eyes of some Canadians, it was 'a better thing for the Province of British Columbia that it should develop slowly, under conditions which permitted of [*sic*] the mass of the white population becoming the holders of small properties'; they believed that this was the only way to ensure that the residents had a permanent 'stake in the community'.[27] Ultimately, this argument made the democratic expansion of political and social rights dependent on racist immigration restrictions and the ethnic homogeneity of the population, with a kind of ambivalent elegance.

Furthermore, especially because the Indian government insisted that this ethnically exclusive policy should not lead to measures that 'would publicly identify us with the policy of exclusion of Indians from other portions of the Empire', the effort was made at first only to hinder the immigration of 'Indian' subjects to Canada by unofficial means.[28] As entry into Canada from Asia was only permitted via direct travel routes, only the Canadian Pacific Railway Company could transport people from India to Canada. But the company, in agreement with the government, instructed its representatives to refrain from selling tickets to 'Indians'.[29]

The efforts to conceal the intention to exclude immigrants on the basis of ethnicity were supposed to prevent protests by 'Indian' subjects of the British Crown. In March 1908, however, when the passengers arriving in Vancouver from India aboard the *Monteagle* were supposed to be deported, the Indians residing in Vancouver protested the expulsion of their 'fellow subjects'. They demanded that the British government protect the interests of its Indian subjects across the empire and guarantee them equal rights. Otherwise, they claimed, their 'brothers in India' would not be prepared to tolerate British rule any longer.[30]

Ethnic Differences Within:
French Canadians and Indigenous Populations

In terms of crossing Canada's borders, ethnic differences were relevant to the extent that 'European' immigrants were supposed to be integrated at a rapid pace while 'Asiatic' immigrants were to be denied entry because it was thought that they could not be assimilated.[31] Yet, the issue of ethnic heterogeneity also cropped up within the territory of Canada itself. On the one hand, there was the difference between English and French Canadians. Since 1867, the French-speaking 'minority' within the province of Quebec (they were in fact in the majority) had been granted a great deal of autonomy in its domestic affairs. Additionally, this francophone Catholic population enjoyed certain privileges when it came to language and the organization of education. However, Canadian law construed these privileges as individual rights. Ethnic groups, by contrast, could not collectively claim equal treatment or minority protection.[32]

Whereas the right of French Canadians to cultural difference was generally recognized, the ethnic differences between the 'white' settlers and the indigenous 'Indians' were a different matter. There were four main approaches embodied in Canada's 'Indian policy'. Firstly, the government signed contracts with representatives of the indigenous populations in which the tribes recognized the European claim to the land in exchange for the promise of the protection of the British Crown, the establishment of reservations and regular monetary payments. These agreements resembled international treaties, even though the government repeatedly emphasized that these contracts by no means implied any recognition of indigenous sovereignty. At the same time, because of these contracts, it became necessary to define by law who was an 'Indian' and who was not in order to determine who should be permitted access to the reservations and who should receive the promised payments. This, in turn, led to a kind of internal right of nationality within Canadian law that was referred to as 'Indian status'.[33] Apart from the privileges outlined in these contracts, however, the 'Indians', as British subjects, had the same legal status as 'white' Britons. This was demonstrated in a court decision from 1870 that afforded 'Indians' the right to vote if they fulfilled the property qualifications attached to the right of suffrage.[34]

The second approach to dealing with the indigenous populations can be described as a policy of integration under the auspices of a civilizing mission. Education and Christianization were supposed to 'elevate the red man and place him on a social and intellectual level with his white brother'.[35] The Onward and Upward Club founded by a missionary was one of the institutions dedicated to pursuing this goal. According to its statutes, it sought to 'assist young educated Indians … to engage in those higher and more intellectual pursuits to which as members of a Christian and civilized community, they are both admitted and called' and to 'promote social intercourse, and mutual respect and sympathy between the white and the Indian races'.[36]

More commonly, however, such arguments tended to emphasize the 'racial' inferiority of the 'Indians' as opposed to mutual respect and recognition. Some said that the only way to save the indigenous population from its demise, which was seen as inevitable from a social Darwinist perspective, was to ensure its assimilation into 'white' society. Others maintained that 'the Indian' had to be 'amalgamated with the white population' in order to 'become a source of profit to the country'.[37] To serve this purpose, schooling requirements were introduced in 1884 as well as other compulsory measures, but these continually met with resistance. In 1885, for example, 'Indians' on the western coast of Vancouver Island tied up a teacher and freed two schoolboys who had been retained by him for missing school too often.[38] Nonetheless, this policy of assimilation was partly successful and led to the creation of colonial hybrids (see Illustration 1.1), or rather – in the language of the time – a small group of 'well-educated, enterprising and ambitious Indians who really belong to the life of the nation'.[39]

On the one hand, assimilation necessitated the elimination of indigenous cultural practices, such as 'the abolition of the wasteful and … pernicious Indian feast known as the "Potlach" [and] the heathenish dance called the "Tamanawas",

Illustration 1.1. En route to civilization? 'Group of Indians belonging to the Kwawkewlth Agency, B.C.'. Printed in: Annual Report of the Department of Indian Affairs, Ottawa, 1901, p. 257.

the celebration of which is attended with much that is disgusting'.[40] On the other hand, it also encompassed measures that sought to do away with the special legal privileges associated with 'Indian status'.[41] The so-called 'enfranchisement of Indians' was particularly significant in this respect. It was either based on the acquisition of real estate by assigning tribal land to individual proprietors or the achievement of a university degree.[42] This promise of the 'privileges and responsibilities of full citizenship', and especially the right to vote, was supposed to encourage the 'Indians' to adopt the sedentary lifestyle, notions of private property, and other rules and practices of 'higher civilization'.[43]

It must be said, however, that these assimilating or integrating efforts often contradicted the laws in place in the western provinces and New Brunswick that excluded the 'Indians' from the right to vote solely on the basis of ethnic identity. Moreover, the authorities hardly ever made use of this enfranchisement option, and many of the 'Indians' were not willing to leave their tribes.[44] As attempts were made to compulsorily implement 'enfranchisement' at the beginning of the 1920s, a delegation of the 'Six Nations Indians' successfully protested against these measures in London.[45] In the years prior to 1918, only just over a hundred 'Indians' were accorded full citizenship through 'enfranchisement' in the province of Ontario.[46]

Alongside contracts outlining privileges and policies of integration or assimilation, there was a third, more paternalistic approach to dealing with the indigenous population. The Indian Acts of 1876 and 1880 granted the 'Indians' a special status that exempted them from certain obligations of civil law but also subjected them to criminal provisions, especially in terms of drug consumption and sexual behaviour, that did not apply to the rest of the population.[47] In addition, the acts instituted a particularly autocratic administrative structure for the reserves. In 1885, for example, 'Indians' were required to carry a passport outside of the reserves although there was no legal foundation for this practice.[48] This paternalistic approach, which sought to protect the 'Indians' from the bad influence of the 'European' immigrants, so to speak, led to the establishment of legal mechanisms of discrimination and the 'curtailment of civil liberties'.[49] It rested on a stereotyping of the 'Indians' as passive, naive and helpless. Sometimes, however, this portrayal clashed with everyday experience. In reality, the 'Indians', just like other groups, competed over economic resources, while they were simultaneously aware of how to use the assumption that 'Indians' were passive and in need of assistance to their best advantage. This constellation was quite apparent in the conflicts on the Lower Fraser River between 'Chinese' immigrants and 'Indians', who complained that the newcomers from Asia were stealing their jobs in the fisheries.[50]

Furthermore, the assimilative and paternalistic approaches were closely tied to the self-image of the 'white' Canadians. Especially in comparison to the Indian policy in the United States, which was perceived as inhumane, the Canadian handling of indigenous peoples was supposed to be particularly humane and just. According to these arguments, the policies in the United States sought to eradicate the 'native' populations. Yet, this supposed moral superiority of the Canadian policies towards the 'Indians' has increasingly been contested in recent years. Newer scholarly literature has pointed out that even if the effects of the policies towards the indigenous populations were milder in northern North America than in the south, this did not stem from the humanist principles of Canada's political elites. Rather, these studies argue, the difference must be attributed to varying sets of circumstances such as the more gradual immigration processes in Canada as well as the lower rate of immigration and the thriftiness of the Canadian government in general. The Canadian government mostly pursued a cheaper and more pragmatic path of least resistance. For example, despite its claims to the contrary, it did not intentionally enact education policies with long-term goals – a failure which actually proved to be advantageous for the indigenous population over the long run.[51]

Accordingly, Canada's 'Indian policy' was not necessarily 'humane, just, and Christian', as proclaimed in the Queen's Speech in 1877, but rather shaped by 'sharp social, economic, and spatial distinctions between the dominant and subordinate population' stemming from contractual, assimilative, paternalistic and racist viewpoints.[52] 'Indian status' in fact provided a legal foundation for racist discrimination, although it actually originated in the Indian Acts that largely rested on contractual and paternalistic arguments. It made it possible to assign the indigenous population an underprivileged status, especially through the refusal of the right to vote. The '[a]boriginal people ... were British subjects but not citizens'.[53] Above all, racist arguments bore fruit when the idea that this population could be educated and civilized had been rejected. The minister of the interior put forth just such an opinion in 1904 in a speech in the Canadian House of Commons when he claimed that 'the red man ... lacks the physical, mental or moral set-up to enable him to compete [with the white man]'.[54]

To a certain extent, the contractual, assimilative, paternalistic and racist approaches were interwoven. Social Darwinist notions fuelled assimilation policies while the assumption of indigenous inferiority likewise justified paternalistic approaches. At the same time, however, these four constellations were often contradictory. This was already apparent to contemporaries, who pointed out that 'the very system of banding Indians together on reservations militates against their conversion into citizens'.[55] The paradoxical nature of the Indian Acts fittingly illustrates this problem as the acts first eliminated the theoretical right of the 'Indians' to vote that existed at the time while simultaneously introducing a procedure through which suffrage could be regained.

These contradictions characteristic of the way in which Canada dealt with the indigenous population can be resolved, at least in part, if they are broken down according to location and divided into phases. Around the turn of the twentieth century, the assimilative approach had gained a foothold in eastern Canada while the paternalistic approach was more dominant in the west; the racist paradigm for dealing with the 'Indians' was most prevalent in British Columbia.[56] Chronologically speaking, the approach based on pseudo-international contracts can be said to be the oldest. Around the middle of the nineteenth century, it gave way to assimilative policies that were shortly thereafter accompanied by the paternalism of the Indian Acts in the 1870s and 1880s. As the century came to an end, this model of a 'progressive partnership' between 'Europeans' and 'Indians' failed, ultimately paving the way for the dominance of a racist approach in the early twentieth century.[57]

Just as in the case of the European immigrants, attempts at internal homogenization along the lines of the nation-state approach came into play in Canada's handling of its indigenous population. Originally, assimilation and 'enfranchisement' sought to ensure equal citizenship rights for all British subjects in Canada. Yet this approach lost its footing over time, leaving the field open for an exclusionary approach based on 'racist' criteria. For this reason, in conjunction with the implementation of exclusionary immigration practices, one can speak of an ethnicization of Canadian law after 1900.

The Establishment of an Independent Canadian Nationality

For the most part, Canadian law followed a nation-state pattern in that it sought to close the borders to the outside in an exclusionary way while promoting legal homogeneity within them. Ethnicization, however, also led to the internal exclusion of indigenous populations from citizenship. The 'European' inhabitants of Canada, on the other hand, profited from the general expansion of suffrage and the welfare state. Naturalization policies ensured that even non-British 'Europeans' were integrated into the privileged community of citizens. But the question remains as to whether a process of nationalization also took place in Canada, despite the fact that there was no Canadian nationality as such that distinguished Canadians from other British subjects.

The Canadian nation, as it were, established itself only gradually at first, parallel to the struggles of the Canadian government to gain more independence from the imperial metropolis. These developments resulted in the creation of a Canadian nationality in the wake of the Second World War.[58] The Immigration Law of 1910, however, marked an important milestone along the way. In order to ensure that the restrictive provisions of this law did not apply to individuals who the government saw as belonging to Canada, a certain group was exempted from the strict rules and defined as 'Canadian citizens'. According to law, 'Canadian citizens' were all those born in Canada, all British subjects permanently resident in Canada, and all those naturalized in Canada. Accordingly,

Canadian citizenship was rescinded if British subjecthood was lost or domicile in Canada was abandoned.[59] This law facilitated entry bans and deportations, which sometimes even applied to British subjects. Records show that a 'coloured' seaman, a man from Ceylon and a man naturalized in South Africa – all British subjects, but not Canadian citizens – were deported by the Canadian authorities to the United Kingdom.[60]

These exclusionary mechanisms, including the immigration restrictions against 'Indian' subjects, marked the beginnings of the establishment of an independent Canadian nationality in 1910. Consequently, these measures contradict the prevailing assumption that the British dominions did not legally differentiate between their own nationals and British nationals as a whole.[61] Rather, this distinction had gained a strong foothold as the gradual implementation of a nation-state approach in Canada gained momentum in the early twentieth century.

Hungarian Nationality, Magyarization, and the Nationalization of the Law

The Austro-Hungarian Compromise of 1867 recognized the partial sovereignty of the Kingdom of Hungary under the rule of its Habsburg king who was also the emperor of Austria. Hungary had its own government as well as its own parliament, known as the Reichstag. These bodies were in charge of the country, apart from the matters that fell under the jurisdiction of the Habsburg Empire – namely, foreign affairs, the military and fiscal politics. Within the territory of the Hungarian Crown, the Kingdom of Croatia-Slavonia and Fiume (today Rijeka in Croatia) enjoyed a special constitutional status. Hungary itself was increasingly centralized bureaucratically after 1867, which generated a degree of homogeneity in terms of law and administration.

Different ideas about the extent of the country's independence from the Habsburg Empire dictated Hungarian politics, and the divergent positions on this question defined the party spectrum. Nonetheless, political groups with different opinions were also able to form coalition governments. After the terms of Ferenc Deák and Kálmán Tisza, who was the Hungarian prime minister from 1875 to 1890, the leadership of the government changed hands in quick succession. All the major parties more or less followed an elitist liberal programme. Within the political elite, differences sometimes emerged between aristocratic landowners and bourgeois industrialists. This basic political constellation hardly changed until 1918, despite the fact that the country's social and economic circumstances transformed rapidly. With the exception of a major crisis around 1873, which was also tied to famines and cholera epidemics, the Hungarian gross national product increased during the era of the compromise. Industrialization also expanded and the population grew. As little changed with respect to the extremely unequal distribution of property, this growth prompted a rural exodus and processes of urbanization, as well as waves of emigration to Cisleithania and North America.

The rise of nationalism in the late nineteenth and early twentieth centuries heralded major changes, manifesting itself in the festivities celebrating Hungary's millennial anniversary in 1896 and other public events. Within this context, the national and ethnic differences within the population of the Hungarian state – between 'Magyars' and 'Slovaks', 'Germans' and 'Romanians', 'Serbs' and 'Croats', 'Roma' and 'Jews' – became more significant. The conflicts between the different groups escalated at times, sometimes influenced by co-national movements abroad as in the case of the German-, Serbian- and Romanian-speaking minorities. The agitation against the Jewish and Roma-speaking minorities repeatedly erupted in violence.

By the turn of the century at the latest, the Hungarian government actively pursued a course of Magyarization that promoted the assimilation of non-Hungarian-speaking groups, primarily in the realm of public education. The increasing tensions within the national conflicts contributed to a series of crises that came after 1900. In 1903, a serious conflict broke out with the imperial metropolis over the amendment of the military law. Accompanied by harvest strikes and suffrage demonstrations, it destabilized the political situation and culminated in a general strike in 1913. With the outbreak of war in 1914, the Kingdom of Hungary faced its final, fatal crisis.

The Nationality Law of 1879: Nationalization and Inclusion

Considering the zealousness with which the Hungarian government emphasized the independence of the Hungarian state following the compromise of 1867, it is quite surprising that twelve years passed before the government introduced the draft of a nationality law in the Reichstag. This law drew heavily on its (North) German counterpart from 1870.[62] It regulated the acquisition of nationality through birth according to the principle of *ius sanguinis*, whereby legitimate children inherited the nationality of their fathers.[63] The acquisition of nationality through marriage was likewise regulated in a patriarchal manner. Foreign-born wives automatically acquired the Hungarian nationality of their husbands upon marriage. The third way to become a Hungarian national was through naturalization. The prerequisites for naturalization were legal capacity, a good reputation, the (at least promised) acceptance into a Hungarian municipality, five years of residence in the country, as well as the payment of direct taxes during this period, and the ability to provide for oneself. The Hungarian minister of the interior was responsible for processing applications for naturalization, apart from those in the Kingdom of Croatia-Slavonia where the Ban (i.e. the leader of the Croatian executive) bore this responsibility.

Moreover, the law also regulated the loss of Hungarian nationality. Emigrants could renounce their Hungarian nationality as long as they were not liable to fulfil military service obligations. The authorities could also deprive emigrants of their Hungarian nationality if they failed to return to Hungary upon official request or entered into the service of a foreign state. Ten years of residency outside of Austria-Hungary could also result in the loss of nationality. At the same time, women lost their status as Hungarian nationals through marriage to foreigners. They could, however, regain their Hungarian nationality through a simplified renaturalization process if they divorced or became widowed. This streamlined process was also available to individuals who had lost their Hungarian nationality as minors, either through a ten-year absence or because their fathers had renounced this nationality for the whole family.

On the one hand, the government justified the law on the basis that it needed to be able to determine who was a Hungarian national and who was not in a standard and unambiguous way. Doing so, it claimed, would avoid conflicts with other states and bring the Hungarian laws into line 'with those of Western states, but above all with our neighbouring states'.[64] Furthermore, the law was supposed to take into account the union between Austria and Hungary, without impinging on Hungary's autonomy, and contribute to the 'protection of the interests of the Hungarian state'. According to the government, these interests also included the 'prevention of emigration'. At that moment, it argued, only 'the emigration of the Széklers was of concern', as they were leaving the country for the East 'out of necessity in order to earn their daily bread'. The law threatened to strip these emigrants of their Hungarian nationality. It must be said, however, that this legal status hardly had any meaning for the poor and for those without means in the first place. The government also claimed that the law allowed for the implementation of a specific immigration policy, because it did not impede immigration but still made sure that only 'prospectively useful citizens' could become nationals.[65]

As the law was debated in parliament, its critics generally raised three main points. First of all, they demanded that only the Hungarian minister of the interior be responsible for naturalization, thereby abolishing the special treatment accorded Croatia. In doing so, they were arguing for the elimination of Croatia's rights of autonomy and implicitly calling for the integration of Croatia into the Hungarian state. Secondly, critics wanted Austria to be treated consistently as a foreign country. And, thirdly, they maintained that the provisions regarding the loss of nationality were too strict. According to the delegate Veßter, 'every Hungarian should retain his [right of citizenship] unless he renounces this himself'.[66]

The majority in the Reichstag refused the request to change the constitutional status of the relationship with Croatia. The Hungarian government conceded the second demand in part by treating Cisleithania (i.e. the Austrian half of the empire) as a foreign country in its administrative praxis.[67] The third demand, namely that the loss of Hungarian nationality was only possible upon the request and with the consent of the individual in question, led to more intensive debates.[68] Many Reichstag delegates feared that the government would use the provisions in the draft law to the detriment of its undesirable political exiles. Opponents of the automatic loss of nationality also argued with a strongly nationalist tone. One member urged that 'naturally born citizens' should be exempted from these provisions. Another rejected this rule, 'in particular with respect to the Széklers absent from their fatherland', who were considered to be an ethnic group related to the Magyars.[69]

The proponents of the automatic loss of nationality countered these arguments, pointing to the need to avoid international legal conflicts and to protect the interests of the state. They suggested that it was advisable and natural 'for the state to demand that the absentee proclaim his nationality from time to time; the state must demand this at the very least'.[70] Ultimately, it was agreed that individuals could retain their Hungarian nationality while resident in a foreign country by renewing their passports, among other things, and that the renaturalization of people who had lost their nationality through marriage to a foreigner, for example, would be simplified significantly.[71] Consequently, Hungarian law treated an emigrant as a national, 'as long as some ties still bind him to the country'.[72]

The last provisions deviated quite clearly from the accepted legal norms in Europe at the time. The idea that it should be made easier for women who had lost their nationality through marriage to regain their old nationality upon divorce or the death of their spouse was widespread, but it was seldom enacted. It was justified on the basis that a person's 'innate' nationality did not disappear just because of a legal change in nationality. This inbred national bond was supposed to justify the preferential treatment granted to these women over other foreign women.[73] Similarly, it was argued that an emigrant's sense of national belonging to their home country should be reflected in the law, which should allow them to retain their nationality. Anational arguments that cited the interests of the state, on the other hand, urged that a person who was no longer under the control of the state (e.g. through absence) should be excluded from the community of nationals.

In general, the debates in parliament led to a stronger emphasis on national belonging as opposed to the formal logic of the law and the interests of the state. These nationalizing tendencies, apart from where the Széklers were concerned, were not laced with ethnicity. The idea of the nation that shaped the contours of the law and the debates in 1879 was thus a supra-ethnic one. Everyone was to have equal access to nationality, regardless of ethnic identity, which was effectively demonstrated by the express intention to integrate immigrants according to the letter of the law.

Magyarization Policies and the Ethnicization of the 'Nation'

Alongside the flooding of the Tisza River and the national assistance efforts for Szeged, 'the most Hungarian of all the Hungarian cities', the law that introduced mandatory instruction in Hungarian in public schools ensured for rigorous debate in the year in which the Nationality Act of 1879 was passed.[74] This law marked the beginning of a conflict-ridden process in which the Magyars (defined as an ethnocultural group) would come to define the 'nation', while all the other 'ethnic' populations in Hungary were to be assimilated or marginalized. After 1879, the national, state-building aspects of Hungary's policies on education and nationalities became more pronounced.[75] Some scholars even speak of a 'move to forced Magyarization'.[76] This policy of assimilation dictated the way in which the Hungarian government dealt with ethnic heterogeneity from then on. Its effects can be seen in the growth of the Hungarian-speaking percentage of Hungary's population (excluding Croatia) between 1880 and 1910 from 44.9 per cent to 54.6 per cent; the percentages of German, Slovakian, Romanian, Ukranian, Croatian and Serbian speakers, however, either decreased or remained constant during this time.[77]

This tendency towards Magyarization was particularly predominant among Hungarian Jews.[78] In the case of the Jews, cultural assimilation ran parallel to legal emancipation. As of 1867, the Jews were by and large treated as equal citizens of Hungary, but full emancipation only ensued in 1895.[79] However, neither assimilation nor equality hindered the eruption of anti-Semitic sentiments. In 1882, for example, the murder of a servant girl in the village of Tisza-Eszlár led to accusations of ritual murder and anti-Semitic riots. The acquittal of the 'Jewish' suspect in August 1883 also unleashed protests in Budapest.[80]

The implementation of Magyarization meant a departure from the notion of the supra-ethnic nation that had dominated the constitutional debates of 1848, the nationalities law of 1868 and the Nationality Act of 1879.[81] An ethno-cultural understanding of the nation effectively took its place in the late nineteenth century.[82] Such ethnicization processes also impacted non-Magyar nationalities, who started to organize politically and to offensively advocate their national interests.[83]

An 1886 law on the 'mass repatriation of the Csángó-Magyars from Bukovina' supports this ethnicization thesis. The law affected the so-called Széklers, whose return migration and settlement was being promoted politically. It made it easier for them to become nationals, 'without respect to when they or their ancestors emigrated', by dropping the costs and conditions otherwise attached to (re-)naturalization.[84] Through this law, it became possible to extend claims to Hungarian nationality backward for an unlimited stretch of time on the basis of a shared language and descent, which was reflected in the short and uncontroversial parliamentary debates on the subject.[85] In this sense, the law established a kind of positive discrimination based on ethnic criteria, as it granted an ethnically defined group legal privileges.

The Readmission of Former Nationals and the Politics of Migration

The nationalization and increasing ethnicization of the boundaries demarcating the Hungarian community of nationals was also reflected in the administrative praxis regarding the so-called repatriation of former Hungarians who had been resident in Austria. In some cases, it was not entirely clear whether the individuals belonged to the Cisleithanian or Transleithanian half of the empire. The following example of the Singer family demonstrates just how complicated these cases could be.[86]

In August 1888, a wandering girl was picked up by the police in Rohrbach in the district of Lilienfeld. Investigations proved that the girl in question was Julia Singer, the illegitimate daughter of Anna Singer, born in July 1878 at a maternity home in Vienna. Shortly beforehand, the girl had been 'turned over' to the seamstress Sedlaczek in Hernals, from whom she had run away. In order to clarify where Julia Singer should be 'put' and which municipality should provide for her welfare in the future, it first had to be determined which municipality was 'responsible' and where she enjoyed the right of domicile.[87] This right of domicile was a kind of municipal membership that was exclusively based on the principle of *ius sanguinis* at the time. Individuals had a right of domicile in the municipality in which their father or unmarried mother enjoyed this right.

Three potential home municipalities of the father of Julia Singer's unmarried mother, Michael Singer, were involved in the protracted negotiations over who was responsible for the girl; two of them were located in Hungary and one in Lower Austria. Michael Singer had worked for years as a distiller in a Hungarian municipality, and married Franziska Kanpi who was officially resident there. His daughter Anna had presented a certificate of domicile issued by the Israelite Community of this town when she went to the maternity home in Vienna; the Hungarian authorities, denied the validity of this document because religious communities were not authorized to issue certificates of domicile. Michael Singer had also worked for several years in another Hungarian municipality, where he had been living since 1887 with his son, who enjoyed the right of domicile there.

In Lower Austria, moreover, Michael Singer had run a drinking establishment for almost twenty years, and his trade license identified Singer as having a right of residence in the town. The Cisleithanian authorities had also conscripted Hanns Salomon Singer, one of Michael's sons, to serve in the military in Lower Austria. The Austrian government, however, contested the conclusiveness of these facts, citing that Hanns Singer had only been drafted as a foreigner with the permission of the respective Hungarian authorities. This was then, in turn, disputed by the

Hungarian officials. The Austrians also pointed out that Michael Singer had been convicted of fraud in 1886 and deported to Hungary, proving that he did not possess a right of domicile in any Austrian municipality.

The Cisleithanian and Transleithanian authorities fought over the right of domicile and nationality of the Singer family for years, ultimately over who would pay the money that had already been spent on the care of the seven illegitimate grandchildren of Michael Singer who had been born in Vienna. In the end, the Hungarian Ministry of the Interior recognized Michael Singer and his descendants as Hungarian nationals. This example illustrates how complex it could be to determine where individuals legally belonged if they changed their place of residence and thereby crossed administrative borders such as those between Hungary and Austria. It also demonstrates the differing interests of municipal and national authorities, some of which were contradictory, especially given the key issues of military service and welfare provision.

The number of such ambiguous cases increased after 1889 because Hungarians lost their nationality after residing in Austria for ten years according to the law passed in 1879. If these individuals did not attain Austrian citizenship, they became stateless. This prompted an agreement between the Cisleithanian and Transleithanian governments in 1894. Hungary was supposed to 'take back' those who had become stateless if requested to do so by the Austrian authorities in cases in which questions had arisen as to the provision of welfare, or when these men could not be conscripted into the military because of their statelessness.[88] There were at least twelve such cases prior to 1899. Although the Hungarian authorities tried to get out of paying for welfare provisions in several cases, they only denied readmission in one case, citing the fact that it was uncertain whether the person in question was originally a Hungarian national.[89]

The number of readmission requests as well as the number of refusals increased between 1900 and 1918.[90] During this period, women in particular were denied reintegration into the Hungarian community of nationals because they had attained their Hungarian nationality 'merely' through marriage to a Hungarian before they had subsequently lost it again. The purpose of the 1894 agreement, according to the Hungarian Ministry of the Interior, was that only those individuals who were 'originally' citizens of the state in question should be readmitted as nationals to their country of origin.[91] In another instance, a widowed woman was not readmitted because her 'original (descent-based) Hungarian citizenship' could not be proven beyond doubt.[92] Generally speaking, the acquisition of Hungarian nationality through marriage was irrelevant within administrative praxis because descent was seen as the only 'real way' to define national belonging.

The debates over the Emigration Acts of 1903 and 1909 further exemplify the simultaneous nationalization and ethnicization of Hungarian law.[93] The main goal of these laws was to control and reduce overseas emigration in order to 'still the national loss of blood'.[94] An official ordinance prohibiting emigration to

Brazil issued at the end of 1900 was one of the most radical measures taken in this regard, but it was the laws of 1903 and 1909 that created the legal framework for such restrictions.[95]

However, it is questionable whether such prohibitions could in fact be implemented. The flow of emigrants increased significantly around the turn of the century. While the average number of Hungarian nationals emigrating to the United States per year was not over forty thousand before 1900, it more than tripled for the years between 1901 and 1911.[96] For this reason, it became all the more important to promote their return. According to an official document from 1901, such an undertaking had a great deal of potential, especially when it came to 'Hungarians', because they 'had the closest ties to their home country'. The situation was different, however, for 'the Slavic nationalities …, whose members relatively quickly lost their allegiance to their fatherland, led astray by quite lively pan-Slavic agitation'.[97]

The lack of an internal sense of belonging to the Hungarian nation was thus cited here as the reason for the lower number of returning emigrants among the non-Magyar nationalities. But, the ethnically differentiated remigration policies of the Hungarian or the joint government might also have been a factor. In 1905, the Foreign Ministry of Austria-Hungary declared that the costs for the return of poor Hungarians to Hungary would only be paid by the government if the migrants in question could prove their Hungarian nationality. For Magyar-speakers, merely 'the knowledge of the language' was evidence enough, whereas non-Magyar-speaking Hungarians had to provide documents.[98] Additionally, the demands in the Reichstag to send more teachers and pastoral workers to counsel the emigrants and imbue them with the 'Hungarian spirit' further speak to the fact that the country's emigration policies rested on an ethnocultural understanding of national belonging.[99]

The emigration laws themselves, however, did not differentiate on the basis of ethnicity. In addition to establishing the framework for emigration restrictions and promoting the return of emigrants, the laws sought to improve the situation of all Hungarian emigrants abroad by 'providing them with work, setting up accommodation and caring for their religious and spiritual needs'.[100] The one hundred thousand copies of an informational brochure printed by the 'Hungarian Assistance Agency' in New York in 1910 attest to the fact that at least sometimes these support services for emigrants made an effort to treat all Hungarian nationals equally, regardless of ethnic identity. It suggested that immigrants should 'make inquiries as to the authorized agents of the Hungarian asylum … before reaching the shores of Ellis Island' as these trustworthy agents could protect them against 'being led astray, cheated or exploited … by unscrupulous people'. This information was provided in the brochure in Hungarian as well as in German, Slovakian, Romanian, Serbian, Croatian and Ruthenian (see Illustration 1.2).[101]

Given this partially state-funded assistance for emigrants, the Hungarian emigration policies were seen as exemplary by Austrian organizations that demanded

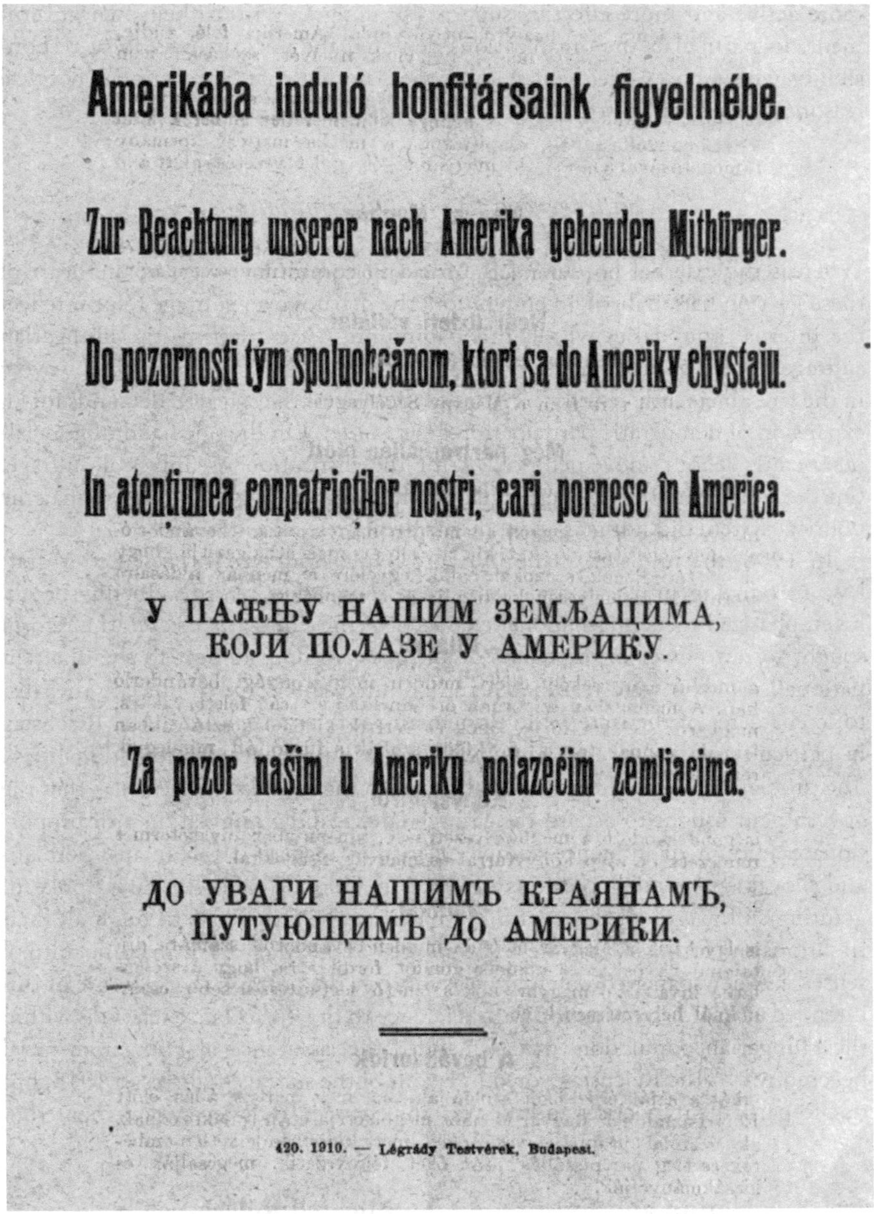

Amerikába induló honfitársaink figyelmébe.

Zur Beachtung unserer nach Amerika gehenden Mitbürger.

Do pozornosti tým spoluokčanom, ktorí sa do Ameriky chystaju.

In atenţiunea conpatrioţilor nostri, cari pornesc în America.

У ПАЖЊУ НАШИМ ЗЕМЉАЦИМА, КОЈИ ПОЛАЗЕ У АМЕРИКУ.

Za pozor našim u Ameriku polazećim zemljacima.

ДО УВАГИ НАШИМЪ КРАЯНАМЪ, ПУТУЮЩИМЪ ДО АМЕРИКИ.

420. 1910. — Légrády Testvérek, Budapest.

Illustration 1.2. The Hungarian nation abroad as a multilingual community (Hungarian, German, Slovakian, Romanian, Serbian, Croatian and Ruthenian). Cover of an informational brochure for Hungarian emigrants to the United States, 1910. From: Vienna, HHStA, MdÄ, Admin. Reg., F 15, Auswanderung, Ktn. 31.

more active and more effective support for emigrants from their own government. In particular, the organizations deplored the unclear division of responsibility within the Cisleithanian ministries, noting that 'for national political reasons', only the Ministry of the Interior was involved in Hungary.[102]

Suffrage and Ethnic Discrimination

Whereas the external borders of the national community were at the heart of these laws on nationality and emigration, the debates over suffrage reform reflect the internal boundaries within this community. According to the Hungarian suffrage census, approximately 6 per cent of the population was entitled to vote in the late nineteenth century.[103] Around the turn of the century, demands for an expansion of democratic participation grew louder. On the one hand, the social-democratic labour movement called for the institution of universal suffrage. On the other hand, non-Magyar nationalities increasingly complained that the political system did not guarantee them adequate representation.[104]

In 1908, the minister of the interior, Gyula Andrássy Jr, presented a draft law introducing universal male suffrage among other reforms. In his speech, he emphasized the supra-national character of the Hungarian state. The reform sought to put power in the hands of all those 'without respect to the different nationalities' who were reasonable and cultured and could appreciate the 'historic character of the state'. The Romanian-speaking delegates to the Reichstag in particular reacted to this with 'noise from the benches of the nationalities'. The problem was – as the statistics attached to the draft law indicated – that the government sought to accord the Hungarian-speaking population a disproportionate amount of influence compared to the German-, Romanian-, Serbian- and Slovakian-speaking portions of the population. When Andrássy spoke of granting suffrage to all those who 'were tied to the fatherland through all their traditions and feelings', what he really meant was the Magyars in an ethnocultural sense.[105] A newspaper commentary was more to the point in that it wrote of this intended ethnic discrimination with reference to the 'special race relations within the Hungarian population' that demanded the 'assurance of Hungarian racial hegemony'.[106] The Reichstag voted in favour of the suffrage reforms in 1913, but due to parliamentary crises and the war, the changes were never implemented.

Nation and Empire: A Complicated Relationship

The legal developments related to nationality and citizenship in Hungary and Canada resembled one another. In both cases, a nation-state approach triumphed in the end. The privileged treatment accorded to women married to foreigners in Hungary who were legally no longer nationals but effectively considered to be part of the nation, for example, attested to this in the Hungarian case. In both countries, migration policies sought to sharpen the borders of the nation-state. In Hungary, where emigration was prevalent, inclusive mechanisms came into play, while in Canada, where immigration was paramount, exclusive mechanisms were implemented. Moreover, Canada as well as Hungary extended equal citizenship to ever-larger portions of their populations. In terms of this equalization, however, Transleithania, with the emancipation of the Jews but a lack of more extensive suffrage reforms, lagged behind Canada where more and more people had come to enjoy the same political and social rights.[107]

Nonetheless, in both the Hungarian and Canadian contexts, one can speak of an ethnicization of the nation after the turn of the century. Anational arguments that emphasized the interests of the state or the empire gave way to ethnically exclusive and discriminatory measures. The debates over the law of 1879 and the assimilating policies of Magyarization exemplify this transition from, briefly put, arguments based on a statist rationale to nationalistic impulses. In Canada, on the other hand, the process of integration into the nation-state was accompanied by increasing discrimination against the indigenous 'Indians' and the rejection of 'Asiatic' immigrants. For this reason, as well as divergent interests with regard to naturalization policies, the dominion repeatedly found itself embroiled in conflicts with the imperial metropolis.

Similarities and Differences:
Sub-metropolitan and Semi-peripheral Spaces

These conflicts reveal that the general imperial constellation had a greater influence on legal developments in Canada than in Hungary. Whereas Hungary was in a position to define its own community of nationals, a corresponding independent Canadian nationality as such first appeared around 1910. The majority of the Canadian population shared not only the same national status, but also a similar cultural identity with fellow British subjects in the United Kingdom and the other dominions. Largely because of these British ties, the developments in Canada were more tightly linked to overarching imperial tendencies. The triumph of an imperialistic approach in other parts of the British Empire in the early twentieth century, for example, boosted racist discrimination in Canada.

Canada's position as a country of immigration, moreover, put the spotlight on the integration of 'European' immigrants and their legal equality. The intended goal, at least in theory, was to overcome social differences as well. Whereas ethnically exclusive measures in Canada were justified with reference to this integrative nationalism, Hungarian nationalism was more separatist in nature. In Hungary, national self-determination played a more important role than the integration of the population. The lack of social and legal equalization processes can also be explained through the ethnicized notion of the nation that emerged around 1900.[108] A large proportion of Hungary's political elite harboured the hope that this could – unlike the older, multi-ethnic concept of the nation – bind the marginalized masses to the state without having to accord them comprehensive political and social rights.

Why did the development of nationality and citizenship laws in both these cases ultimately follow the same nation-state approach, despite the aforementioned differences? One way to approach this question is to look at the specific positions of Canada and Hungary within their respective empires. Both were non-metropolitan territories that can be described as semi-peripheral on the basis of their relative political autonomy.[109] The legislative manoeuvring room afforded Hungary by the 1867 Compromise, and Canada by the British North America Act, established the foundation for the implementation of a nation-state approach below the imperial level. It is therefore not surprising that this process began to take shape in Hungary shortly after 1867, especially given the long tradition of demands for autonomy that preceded the compromise. The fact that this process of nationalization vis-à-vis the law had set in by 1900 in Canada at the latest questions the widespread assumption that the First World War was the major catalyst behind the formation of a Canadian nation.[110] The sub-metropolitan and semi-peripheral 'in-between' position of Canada and Hungary (i.e. a position between privilege and disadvantage in a constitutional-political sense) ultimately paved the way for the triumph of a nation-state approach in both cases. On the periphery and in the metropolis, the relationship between concepts of the nation and imperial structures thus took on different forms.

The Metropolis and the Semi-periphery: 'Imperial Nation' versus 'Colonial Nationalism'

Whereas imperialist asymmetries and the metropolis as such were rather weak in the Habsburg Empire, the United Kingdom enjoyed a clearly privileged position as the metropolis within the global British Empire. The UK parliament in London alone made all the important decisions, despite the fact that the subjects in the dominions and the colonies had no influence over who sat on the benches. Several different perspectives were reflected in the debates over this colonial structure. Some argued that this imperialistic asymmetry was absolutely necessary for the continued existence of the empire, while others criticized its injustice and compulsory nature.[111] Two solutions were proposed in response to these critiques that can be summarized under the rubric of 'colonial nationalism' on the one hand, and the 'imperial nation' on the other. Both these forms prove to be particularly insightful when looking at the relationship between the empire and the nation. Instead of siding clearly with pro- or anti-imperialistic arguments, both of these approaches were ambivalent in terms of their sometimes confrontational and sometimes cooperative relationship with imperial formations.

Along the lines of Richard Jebb's 'colonial nationalism', the dominions primarily populated by 'European' immigrants were to gradually leave the imperial union as national states.[112] Since, in Jebb's eyes, the ethnic homogeneity of the population was essential for the successful formation of a nation-state, the regulation of intra-imperial migration stood at the heart of his approach. In particular, the dominions were supposed to prohibit the immigration of 'Indian' subjects and deport those who had already immigrated to their territory. Only by means of this exclusion, Jebb maintained, could the empire fulfil its own existential purpose, namely the 'promotion and protection of nation-states'.[113] However, Jebb basically ignored the problematic presence of indigenous peoples in the dominions when it came down to establishing ethnic homogeneity. The goals of colonial nationalism clearly contradicted the idea of the equality of all British subjects. Only when 'non-whites' were subjugated within imperialistic asymmetries, according to this line of thought, could the dominions become independent nation-states. These notions shaped Canada's migration policies, which were criticized by those who advocated stronger imperial cohesion because of the centrifugal tendencies inherent within 'colonial nationalism'.

These opponents favoured a concept that can be described as 'imperial nationalism'. This approach proposed the institution of a kind of 'imperial citizenship' that would include all British subjects, thereby having a centripetal effect. J.R. Seeley was the main proponent of this idea. He wanted to turn the British Empire into a nation-state within which all subjects enjoyed the same rights of political participation at the imperial level. Seeley, however, had no answer to the question of whether the 'non-white' population should also come to enjoy the privileges of equal citizenship.[114] In 1892, Albert Shaw used a similar argument when he proposed adopting the United States' federalist model of political organization for the British Empire. With this approach, Shaw wanted to herald in the 'universality of citizenship' and pave the way for an empire 'consisting of self-governing groups of Britishers, in which each individual one of "God's Englishmen" would have rights as extensive as any of his fellows'.[115] Quite apparently, however, 'non-white' British subjects had no place in this imperial federation; Shaw never mentions their position within the proposed imperial community of citizens, not even as a problem.[116] The notion of 'imperial citizenship' did not seek to establish equal citizenship for all British subjects, but rather aimed to integrate 'white' British subjects into an imperial nation from which the 'non-whites' were supposed to be excluded.

Ultimately, this notion of imperial citizenship rested on the same kind of ethnic exclusion and legal discrimination characteristic of colonial nationalism. Whereas the 'colonial nationalism' coming out of the dominions and relying on the territorial subdivisions of the British Empire developed centrifugal tendencies, the concept of an imperial nation emphasized the 'racial' identity of individuals as the primary criteria for membership. Its advocates wanted to bring the 'white' British subjects in the different parts of the empire together in a legally homogeneous polity in order to strengthen the cohesion of the empire. Beginning in 1887, 'colonial nationalism' came to play a role in the 'colonial' (later 'imperial') conferences between the governments of the dominions and that of the United Kingdom. This cooperation at least partly paved the way for the indirect participation of voters in the 'white' colonies in politics at the imperial level. The full realization of the concept of 'imperial citizenship', on the other hand, would have led to the complete loss of the privileged position of the British parliament and its voters in the United Kingdom, which is one of the main reasons why imperial nationalism never gained a real foothold.

The relationship between notions of the nation and imperial interests in the metropolis with those in the semi-peripheral zones of the British Empire remained ambiguous until the end of the First World War. The dominions vacillated between cooperation and confrontation, which resulted in tensions between the retention of imperialistic asymmetries of power, the inclusion of the 'white' British subjects in a legally homogeneous polity and the centrifugal aspirations of colonial nationalism. In the end, the third option won out in 1931 with the so-called Statute of Westminster that granted the dominions substantial autonomy. Ultimately, this move further propelled the gradual disintegration of the British Empire.

Peripheries: Independence, Autonomy and Equality

The ambivalent attitude of the British metropolis towards nationalist ideas was doubtlessly rooted in the national conflict between Great Britain and Ireland within the United Kingdom itself. Its influence on contemporary debates about the empire and the nation cannot be overestimated.[117] Irish nationalism also oscillated between confrontation and cooperation, but unlike in the dominions, the emerging Irish nation was denied the same kind of autonomy under the rubric of 'Home Rule'.[118] Ireland was unable to employ a nation-state approach until it finally gained independence at the end of the First World War. It must be said, however, that British law did not fully recognize an independent Irish nationality until well into the twentieth century.

Czech nationalism enjoyed a similar status within the Habsburg context as Irish nationalism in the British Empire.[119] National self-determination was in this case also first achieved after 1918. However, the Moravian Compromise of 1905, among other measures, had already granted the emerging Czech – or, as it was referred to officially, 'Bohemian' – nation partial autonomy. This

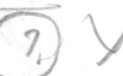

compromise both enabled and forced the demarcation of national communities within the existing imperial structure.[120] The relationship between Czech nationalism and the empire was shaped by both confrontation and cooperation, whereby its centrifugal tendencies – due to the complex constitutional structure of Austria-Hungary – were largely directed against the Cisleithanian government and less against the Habsburg Empire as a whole.[121]

Irish and Czech nationalism developed in politically homogeneous entities, namely in the United Kingdom and in Austria. In both cases, representatives could be sent to the respective parliaments in London and Vienna, whose decisions were valid for the entire realm of state. Therefore, the position of the Irish and the Czechs compared to the semi-peripheral position of the Canadians and Hungarians was less legally autonomous. Nonetheless, the Irish and Czech attitudes towards imperial unity also vacillated between cooperation and confrontation. In particular, the partial autonomy granted to the Czechs under the thumb of the Cisleithanian state was indicative of this ambivalence.

The formation of the Indian nationalist movement, in contrast, was heavily influenced by clear imperialist asymmetries and India's decidedly peripheral position. Alongside the semi-peripheral examples mentioned above, as well as the nationalism that formed within the metropolises themselves, the case of India points to a third possible constellation between the nation and the empire within imperial formations. Although the Indian nationalist movement called for autonomy and 'Home Rule', it also emphatically pointed to the all too often promised but never implemented entitlement of all British subjects to equal rights, without regard to ethnic identity. These appeals were directed at the imperial metropolis, thereby confirming the paramount position of the UK parliament. They resulted out of the imperialist discrimination that Indian subjects had faced, especially in the dominions.[122] Such pronounced colonial disadvantages indicate the central difference between India on the one hand and Canada and Hungary or Ireland and the Czechs on the other. Despite these factors, however, the nationalist movement in India also wavered back and forth between a cooperative and a confrontational attitude towards the empire.

Nation and Empire:
Alternatives to the Narrative of National Emancipation

This brief overview of the different constellations of nation and empire reveals that nationalization processes were quite dependent on the specific position of the emerging nation within the imperial structure. Correspondingly, the different types of nationalization must be distinguished from one another as well. The widespread narrative tracing a path from imperial dependence to national emancipation cannot adequately describe the variety of ways in which nationalism was articulated and expressed. This model of emancipation assumes that, within the context of an ethnically and politically heterogeneous imperial formation, the combination of internal homogenization and an exclusive tightening of external borders along the lines of the nation-state will inevitably lead to the gradual secession of the nation from the empire. As a result, according to this narrative, advocates of imperial cohesion sought to quell any nation-state aspirations emerging within the empire.[123]

Whereas this portrayal accurately reflects certain phenomena, it is by no means the only explanation. The cases of Hungary and Canada, for example, clearly demonstrate that nation-state structures could be established below the imperial level that could coexist with overarching imperial structures.[124] Although these processes eventually led to national autonomy in Canada and Hungary, it was not clear to contemporaries if and when such a development might come. In a certain sense, it can be said that the specific positions of Canada and Hungary within their respective imperial contexts fostered nationalization processes in both countries.

Consequently, the claim that nationalization processes were inherently indicative of tendencies towards imperial disintegration can be misleading. A more nuanced approach is necessary to adequately describe the development of nationalism in intra- and sub-imperial contexts.[125] Such a perspective needs to differentiate between cooperative and confrontational attitudes towards imperial unity as well as whether national belonging was based on territorial or personal criteria, and whether the nation itself was defined in multi-ethnic inclusive or ethnically exclusive terms. It must also appreciate the significance of whether nationalist demands came from the colonial periphery, a sub-metropolitan position or from within a politically homogeneous part of the empire. The specific imperial structure, moreover, shaped the contours of emerging nationalist movements and steered them in certain directions by fostering or blocking different paths.

This more differentiated way of thinking about the relationship between nation and empire speaks to the calls within historical research for a revision of the assumption linked to the narrative of emancipation that the disintegration of imperial formations was inevitable in the era of nationalism. It stresses the importance of imperial powers of cohesion on the one hand, and argues that the coexistence of national identities and imperial loyalties was indeed possible on the other.[126] This notion of coexistence could be found in all the cases of intra- and sub-imperial nationalism discussed in this chapter. Likewise, cooperative and confrontational attitudes towards imperial unity appeared in different constellations. The ambivalence between these two poles was particularly apparent in the demands for supra-ethnic equality that were being voiced in India. In a paradoxical way – with the narrative of emancipation in mind – a peripheral colonial nationalist movement advocated measures that could potentially have strengthened imperial unity. The autonomy granted to ethnonational groups in

Cisleithania likewise points to the potential for coexistence between the nation and the empire. The next chapter delves into this co-dependency by directing its gaze at India and Austria. Although these two territories occupied different positions within their respective imperial formations, did they steer a similar course when it came to handling ethnic heterogeneity within their borders?

Notes

1. London, PRO, CO 383/23. See also A. Howell, *Naturalization and Nationality in Canada: Expatriation and Repatriation of British Subjects; Aliens their Disabilities and their Privileges in Canada* (Toronto: Carswell & Co., 1884), 60f.
2. London, PRO, FO 881/2306. In a report dated 15 October 1872, the Canadian minister of agriculture, Pope, determined that it was 'not expedient … to make the naturalization of aliens … more difficult' if the goal was to continue to attract German immigrants. The fee in the United Kingdom was roughly equivalent to a twentieth of the average annual wage of a worker, while the fee in Canada was roughly equivalent to a six-hundredth.
3. Day, *Multiculturalism*, 136f.
4. London, PRO, FO 83/799. On German emigration to Canada, see J. Wagner, *A History of Migration from Germany to Canada, 1850–1939* (Vancouver, BC: UBC Press, 2006).
5. London, PRO, FO 83/799, Colonial Office to Foreign Office, 5 January 1881. See also London, PRO, FO 881/2306, Colonial Office to Foreign Office, 27 May 1873.
6. The figures come from W.D. Scott, 'Immigration and Population', in A. Shortt and A.G. Doughty (eds), *Canada and its Provinces: A History of the Canadian People and their Institutions by One Hundred Associates*, vol. VII, *The Dominion: Political Evolution* (Toronto: Glasgow, Brook & Company, 1914), 520–24. The total number of immigrants as a percentage of the total population (at the beginning of each period) amounted to 9.8% from 1871–1880, 20.6% from 1881–1890, 7% from 1891–1900, and 31.6% from 1901–1910.
7. Vienna, HHStA, MdÄ, Adm. Reg., F 15, Ktn. 7, *Memorandum über Auswanderungsfragen*, May 1901; cf. Day, *Multiculturalism*, 124f.
8. V. Knowles, *Forging our Legacy: Canadian Citizenship and Immigration, 1900–1977* (Ottawa: Citizenship and Immigration Canada, 2000), 3, 7f.
9. Canada, *An Act to Amend the Acts Relating to Naturalization and Aliens* (1903).
10. This amendment was passed with the consent of the government in London; London, PRO, HO 45/14522, Colonial Office to the Canadian Government, 20 August 1914.
11. Knowles, *Forging our Legacy*, 10.
12. Scott, 'Immigration and Population', 526. See also Roy, *A White Man's Province*, 270; Day, *Multiculturalism*, 116; M. Harper and S. Constantine, *Migration and Empire* (Oxford: Oxford University Press, 2010), 31.
13. London, IOR, Mss. Eur. D 819. See also K. Fedorowich, 'The British Empire on the Move, 1760–1914', in S. Stockwell (ed.), *The British Empire: Themes and Perspectives* (Malden, MA: Blackwell, 2008), 90.
14. In 1902, a court upheld the discriminatory practice of denying British subjects of Chinese descent the right to vote. See Roy, *A White Man's Province*, XVI, 21f.
15. Ibid., 91f., 154.

16. Knowles, *Forging our Legacy*, 36f.; Roy, *A White Man's Province*, 191.
17. Roy, *A White Man's Province*, 212. See also Knowles, *Forging our Legacy*, 38.
18. Knowles, *Forging our Legacy*, 32f.; P.S. Li, 'Chinese Diaspora in Occidental Societies: Canada and Europe', in D. Hoerder, C. Harzig and A. Shubert (eds), *The Historical Practice of Diversity: Transcultural Interactions from the Early Modern Mediterranean to the Postcolonial World* (New York: Berghahn Books, 2003), 137, speaks of 'institutional racism' in the Canadian context. See also J. Belich, *Replenishing the Earth: The Settler Revolution and the Rise of the Anglo-World, 1783–1939* (Oxford: Oxford University Press, 2009), 465.
19. London, IOR, Mss. Eur. E 267/213, p. 120.
20. This practice was particularly clear to see in the case of New Zealand, which was considered to be the frontrunner in terms of the establishment of political and social citizenship rights as well as the exclusion of 'non-European' immigrants. H.H. Lusk, *Social Welfare in New Zealand: The Result of Twenty Years of Progressive Social Legislation and its Significance for the United States and Other Countries* (London: Heinemann, 1913); W.P. Reeves, *Das politische Wahlrecht der Frauen in Australien*, trans. R. Grazer (Leipzig: Dietrich, 1904); United Kingdom, *Report of the Inter-departmental Committee Appointed to Consider the Doubts and Difficulties which Have Arisen in Connexion with the Interpretation and Administration of the Acts Relating to Naturalization* (London, 1901), 120. See also S. Banerjee, *Becoming Imperial Citizens: Indians in the Late-Victorian Empire* (Durham, NC: Duke University Press, 2010), 20f.
21. London, IOR, L/PJ/6/888, file 3168, report by Mackenzie King, March 1908.
22. London, IOR, L/PJ/6/864, file 1371, confidential memo by Mackenzie King.
23. London, IOR, L/PJ/6/864, file 1371, Mackenzie King to Morley, 14 April 1908. See also London, IOR, L/PJ/6/888, file 3168, confidential memo by Mackenzie King, May 1908.
24. London, IOR, L/PJ/6/864, file 1371, Governor-General to the Colonial Office, 7 January 1909.
25. In this part, section 37, the term 'class' was quite consciously replaced with 'race'. London, IOR, L/PJ/6/864, file 1371, explanatory remarks on the draft law. See also London, IOR, L/PJ/6/864, file 1371, note about a conversation with Mackenzie King, March 1908.
26. London, IOR, L/PJ/6/864, file 1371, explanatory remarks on the draft law.
27. London, IOR, L/PJ/6/888, file 3168, report by Mackenzie King, March 1908. See also Pearson, 'Theorizing Citizenship', 993; Banerjee, *Becoming Imperial Citizens*, 20f.
28. London, IOR, L/PJ/6/864, file 1371, Indian Government to the India Office, 20 May 1909. See also ibid., India Office to the Colonial Office, 9 March 1910.
29. London, IOR, L/PJ/6/888, file 3168. On a failed, likewise unofficial, plan to ship 'the indigent unemployed East Indians in British Columbia' to British Honduras, see London, IOR, L/PJ/6/864, file 1371.
30. London, IOR, L/PJ/6/864, file 1371, Mdayran to Morley, 23 March 1908. See also London, IOR, L/PJ/6/888, file 3168, confidential memo by Mackenzie King, 10.
31. On the problematic aspects of the integration of 'European' immigrants, see Knowles, *Forging our Legacy*, 19, 35 and passim.
32. P. Macklem, *Indigenous Difference and the Constitution of Canada* (Toronto: University of Toronto Press, 2001), 62f. On the continuing conflicts between anglophone and francophone Canadians, see, for example, D. Morton, 'Divided Loyalties? Divided

Country?', in W. Kaplan (ed.), *Belonging: The Meaning and Future of Canadian Citizenship* (Montreal: McGill-Queen's University Press, 1993), 56f.

33. D.G. Smith (ed.), *Canadian Indians and the Law: Selected Documents, 1663–1972* (Toronto: McClelland, 1975), XVII, XXV; J. St. Germain, *Indian Treaty-Making Policy in the United States and Canada, 1867–1877* (Lincoln, NE: University of Nebraska Press, 2001), 11f., 23. See also the text of the Royal Proclamation from 1763 in I.A.L. Getty and A.S. Lussier (eds), *As Long as the Sun Shines and Water Flows: A Reader in Canadian Native Studies* (Vancouver: University of British Columbia Press, 1983), 29–38.

34. B. Slattery and L. Charlton (eds), *Canadian Native Law Cases*, vol. 2, *1870–1890* (Saskatoon: University of Saskatchewan, Native Law Centre, 1981), 565f. It must be noted, however, that the Indian Act of 1876 practically denied all 'status Indians' the right to vote in that it turned them into collective owners of the tribal properties and thereby made it impossible for them to fulfil the private property qualifications necessary to attain suffrage.

35. Canada, Annual Report of the Department of Indian Affairs (Ottawa, 1890), IX.

36. Ibid., 22f.

37. Ibid., 165; cf. S. Carter, *Aboriginal People and Colonizers of Western Canada to 1900* (Toronto: University of Toronto Press, 1999), 116; Smith, *Canadian Indians*, XVII; St. Germain, *Indian Treaty-Making Policy*, 44.

38. Canada, Annual Report of the Department of Indian Affairs (Ottawa, 1885), LVIII; cf. St. Germain, *Indian Treaty-Making Policy*, 103f., 106f.; R.L. Nichols, *Indians in the United States and Canada: A Comparative History* (Lincoln, NE: University of Nebraska Press, 1998), 225f., 232f.

39. D.C. Scott, 'Indian Affairs, 1867–1912', in A. Shortt and A.G. Doughty, *Canada and its Provinces: A History of the Canadian People and their Institutions by One Hundred Associates*, vol. VII, *The Dominion: Political Evolution* (Toronto: Glasgow, Brook & Company, 1914), 622f.

40. Canada, Annual Report (1885), LV. See also Smith, *Canadian Indians*, XVIIf.

41. For example, 'Indian' women who married 'Europeans' lost their 'Indian status'; see Carter, *Aboriginal People*, 116f.

42. Canada, The Indian Act (1876); Smith, *Canadian Indians*, 111f. See also Howell, *Naturalization and Nationality*, 10; Scott, 'Indian Affairs', 619f.; Day, *Multiculturalism*, 112.

43. Canada, Report of the Department of the Interior for 1875, cited in St. Germain, *Indian Treaty-Making Policy*, 44. See also ibid., 40, 83, 111f.; Nichols, *Indians*, 212.

44. Scott, 'Indian Affairs', 620; S.L. Harring, *White Man's Law: Native People in Nineteenth-Century Canadian Jurisprudence* (Toronto: University of Toronto Press, 1998), 214.

45. J.R. Miller, 'Petitioning the Great White Mother: First Nations' Organizations and Lobbying in London', in *Reflections on Native–Newcomer Relations: Selected Essays* (Toronto: University of Toronto Press, 2004), 217–41. See also Nichols, *Indians*, 208, 212.

46. R.J. Brownlie, '"A Better Citizen than Lots of White Men": First Nations Enfranchisement – An Ontario Case Study, 1918–1940', *Canadian Historical Review* 87(1) (2006), 34.

47. Canada, Annual Report (1885), LXI, LXIV. See also Scott, 'Indian Affairs', 618f.; Smith, *Canadian Indians*, XVII; St. Germain, *Indian Treaty-Making Policy*, 100.

48. Harring, *White Man's Law*, 107, 263–65; Nichols, *Indians*, 207.

49. Smith, *Canadian Indians*, XXIII.
50. Canada, Annual Report (1885), LX.
51. St. Germain, *Indian Treaty-Making Policy*, 3f., 6, 110, 121, 165; Harring, *White Man's Law*, 7; Nichols, *Indians*, XVI, 209f.; D. Leighton, 'A Victorian Civil Servant at Work: Lawrence Vankoughnet and the Canadian Indian Department, 1874–1893', in I.A.L. Getty and A.S. Lussier (eds), *As Long as the Sun Shines and Water Flows: A Reader in Canadian Native Studies* (Vancouver: University of British Columbia Press, 1983), 107.
52. St. Germain, *Indian Treaty-Making Policy*, 165. Carter, *Aboriginal People*, 102f.
53. Carter, *Aboriginal People*, 117; Smith, *Canadian Indians*, XVIII; Harring, *White Man's Law*, 107, 215.
54. Stifton in the Canadian House of Commons, 18 July 1904; as quoted in D.J. Hall, 'Clifford Stifton and Canadian Indian Administration 1896–1905', in I.A.L. Getty and A.S. Lussier (eds), *As Long as the Sun Shines and Water Flows: A Reader in Canadian Native Studies* (Vancouver: University of British Columbia Press, 1983), 126.
55. Canada, Annual Report (1890), 165; Harring, *White Man's Law*, 11, 107.
56. St. Germain, *Indian Treaty-Making Policy*, 6; Harring, *White Man's Law*, 214f.
57. Carter, *Aboriginal People*, 13, 150f. See also Scott, 'Indian Affairs', 593; Smith, *Canadian Indians*, XIX; G.F.G. Stanley, 'As Long as the Sun Shines and Water Flows: An Historical Comment', in I.A.L. Getty and A.S. Lussier (eds), *As Long as the Sun Shines and Water Flows: A Reader in Canadian Native Studies* (Vancouver: University of British Columbia Press, 1983), 13; Hall, 'Clifford Stifton', 125; St. Germain, *Indian Treaty-Making Policy*, 3 f.; Harring, *White Man's Law*, 11; Nichols, *Indians*, 211f., 245, 250f.; Day, *Multiculturalism*, 9.
58. W. Kaplan (ed.), *Belonging: The Meaning and Future of Canadian Citizenship* (Montreal: McGill-Queen's University Press, 1993), 7.
59. London, IOR, L/PJ/6/864, file 1371, Indian emigration to Canada, 1908–1910. 'Canadian domicile' was automatically acquired after three years of residency, but it was lost upon the establishment of residency outside Canada.
60. London, PRO, HO 144/22959; cf. Harper and Constantine, *Migration*, 322.
61. Pearson, 'Theorizing Citizenship', 994. Like this study, apart from citing divergent dates (ibid., 1000f.), Pearson generally differentiates between three processes in the development of the law in the dominions, namely the creation of a distance to the indigenous minorities ('aboriginalization'), then the exclusion of the 'Asiatic' immigrants ('ethnicization'), and finally the distinction between native and immigrant Britons ('indigenization').
62. Hungary, GA L from 1879; S. Berényi, *Der Erwerb und der Verlust der ungarischen Staatsbürgerschaft*, trans. I. Schwartz (Leipzig: Duncker & Humblot, 1906). See also E. Milner, *Die österreichische Staatsbürgerschaft und der Gesetzesartikel L:1879 über den Erwerb und Verlust der ungarischen Staatsbürgerschaft* (Tübingen: F. Fues, 1880), 3; E. v. Polner, 'Das Staatsrecht des Königreichs Ungarn und seiner Mitländer', in A. v. Berzeviczy (ed.), *Ungarn: Land und Volk, Geschichte, Staatsrecht, Verwaltung und Rechtspflege, Landwirtschaft, Industrie und Handel, Schulwesen, wissenschaftliches Leben, Literatur, bildende Künste* (Budapest: Verlag des Franklin-Vereines, 1917), 234.
63. According to §19, the principle of place of birth applied to 'those born in Hungary and foundlings' in so far as no other nationality could be determined. See also Hirschhausen, 'Von imperialer Inklusion', 13f.

64. *Pester Lloyd*, 10 October 1879, Abendausgabe. *Pester Lloyd* was a liberal German-language daily newspaper that reported, sometimes word for word, on the debates in the Reichstag. On the debates over the law of 1879, see also A. Csizmadia, 'Die Entwicklung des ungarischen Staatsbürgerschaftsrechts', in H. Lentze and P. Putzer (eds), *Festschrift für Ernst Carl Hellbling* (Salzburg: Fink, 1971), 109f.

65. *Pester Lloyd*, 10 October 1879, Abendausgabe. The law of 1879 was much less restrictive in respect to naturalization than its predecessor of 1847/48, which was never implemented. Csizmadia, 'Staatsbürgerschaftsrecht', 105f.

66. *Pester Lloyd*, 19 October 1879.

67. Accordingly, Hungarians could lose their nationality by living in Austria for ten years.

68. Veßter, Szederkényi, Mocsáry and Simonyi argued along these lines in *Pester Lloyd*, 29 October 1879 and 4 November 1879.

69. Szederkényi and Veßter in *Pester Lloyd*, 29 October 1879 and 5 November 1879.

70. Szilágyi in *Pester Lloyd*, 5 November 1879.

71. Hungarian nationality was not lost if: (a) one of the domestic authorities was informed of the wish to retain this nationality; (b) individuals were registered with one of the Austro-Hungarian consulates; or (c) they renewed their passports.

72. Berényi, *Staatsbürgerschaft*, 109.

73. Polner, 'Staatsrecht', 234, speaks of a national duty of repatriation. On parallels with the German debates on nationality law, see Gosewinkel, *Einbürgern und Ausschließen*, 178–90, 278–302.

74. A. Freifeld, *Nationalism and the Crowd in Liberal Hungary, 1848–1914* (Washington, DC: Woodrow Wilson Center Press, 2000), 241f.

75. J. v. Puttkammer, *Schulalltag und nationale Integration in Ungarn: Slowaken, Rumänen und Siebenbürger Sachsen in der Auseinandersetzung mit der ungarischen Staatsidee 1867–1914* (Munich: Oldenbourg, 2003), 34; cf. A.C. Janos, *The Politics of Backwardness in Hungary, 1825–1945* (Princeton, NJ: Princeton University Press, 1982), 126f.

76. Freifeld, *Nationalism*, 244. P.M. Judson, 'Constructing Nationalities in East Central Europe: Introduction', in P.M. Judson and M.L. Rozenblit (eds), *Constructing Nationalities in East Central Europe* (New York: Berghahn Books, 2005), 2, speaks of 'aggressive nationalizing policies'.

77. H. Fischer and K. Gündisch, *Eine kleine Geschichte Ungarns* (Frankfurt am Main: Suhrkamp, 1999), 138f. For a critique of the thesis that Magyarization was successful, see R.A. Kann, 'Zur Problematik der Nationalitätenfrage in der Habsburgermonarchie 1848–1918', in A. Wandruszka and P. Urbanitsch (eds), *Die Habsburgermonarchie 1848–1918*, vol. 3, *Die Völker des Reiches*, Part 2 (Vienna: Verlag der Österreichischen Akademie der Wissenschaften, 1980), 1319. See also V. Kárády, 'Egyenlötlen elmagyarosodás, avagy hogyan vált Magyarország magyar nyelvü országgá: Történelmiszociológiai vázlat', *Századvég* 6(2) (1990), 5–37; L. Kontler, *Millennium in Central Europe: A History of Hungary* (Budapest: Atlantisz Publishing House, 1999); E. Babejová, *Fin-de-Siècle Pressburg: Conflict & Cultural Coexistence in Bratislava 1897–1914* (New York: Columbia University Press, 2003).

78. The percentage of Hungarian-speaking 'Jews' within the 'Jewish' population in Hungary in general grew steadily after 1880, from 55.3 per cent in 1880 to 62.6 per cent in 1890, 70.3 per cent in 1900 and 75.7 per cent in 1910. P. Haber, Die Anfänge des Zionismus in Ungarn, 1897–1904 (Cologne: Böhlau, 2001), 139.

79. Ibid., 149f.; T. Ungvári, *The 'Jewish Question' in Europe: The Case of Hungary* (Boulder, CO: Social Science Monographs, 2000); cf. Janos, *The Politics of Backwardness*, 116f.

80. Freifeld, *Nationalism*, 246f. On the lack of intensive and harmonious integration of 'the Jews', see also G. Schöpflin, 'Jewish Assimilation in Hungary: A Moot Point', in B. Vago (ed.), *Jewish Assimilation in Modern Times* (Boulder, CO: Westview Press, 1981), 75–88.

81. G. Kövér, 'Inactive Transformation: Social History of Hungary from the Reform Era to World War I', in G. Gyáni, G. Kövér and T. Valuch (eds), *Social History of Hungary from the Reform Era to the End of the Twentieth Century* (Boulder, CO: Social Science Monographs, 2004), 208f. On the national conflicts within the context of 1848, see A. Gerö, *The Hungarian Parliament (1867–1918): A Mirage of Power*, trans. J. Patterson and E. Koncz. New York: Columbia University Press, 1997. 92. See also L. Gumplowicz, *Das Recht der Nationalitäten und Sprachen in Oesterreich-Ungarn* (Innsbruck: Wagner, 1879), 227; Janos, *The Politics of Backwardness*, 122; Péter, *Hungary's Long Nineteenth Century*, 183–98, 343–54.

82. Z. Szász, 'Die Ziele und Möglichkeiten, der ungarischen Regierungen in der Nationalitätenpolitik im 19. Jahrhundert', in F. Glatz and R. Melville (eds), *Gesellschaft, Politik und Verwaltung in der Habsburgermonarchie* (Stuttgart: Steiner, 1987), 332f.; L- Gogolák, 'Ungarns Nationalitätengesetze und das Problem des magyarischen National- und Zentralstaates', in A. Wandruszka and P. Urbanitsch (eds), *Die Habsburgermonarchie 1848–1918*, vol. 3, *Die Völker des Reiches*, Part 2 (Vienna: Verlag der Österreichischen Akademie der Wissenschaften, 1980), 1207–303. On the so-called *Lex Apponyi* of 1907, see Puttkammer, *Schulalltag*, 136.

83. G. Schoedl, *Alldeutscher Verband und deutsche Minderheitenpolitik in Ungarn 1890–1914: Zur Geschichte des deutschen 'extremen Nationalismus'* (Frankfurt am Main: Lang, 1978), 10. See also Freifeld, *Nationalism*, 294f.; F. Veliz, *The Politics of Croatia-Slavonia 1903–1918: Nationalism, State Allegiance and the Changing International Order* (Wiesbaden: Harrassowitz, 2012).

84. Hungary, GA IV from 1886; Berényi, *Staatsbürgerschaft*, 66.

85. *Pester Lloyd*, 19 February 1886.

86. See also Burger, *Heimatrecht und Staatsbürgerschaft*, 93–95.

87. On the Singer case, see Vienna, AVA, MdI, Allg., 8, Ktn 353, 23148–1896, 32285–1896 and 3844–1898.

88. Vienna, AVA, MdI, Allg., 8, Ktn 353, 3340–1894, correspondence between the k.k. Ministry of the Interior and the k.u.k. Ministry of the Interior, January 1894.

89. Vienna, AVA, MdI, Allg., 8, Ktn 353, Letters A-St. Six cases involved questions of military service and the other six cases involved the provision of welfare for those involved. In a few cases, the documentation on the final decision has not survived.

90. There were nineteen requests for repatriation by people whose last names began with the letters 'A' or 'N'. Of these nineteen, seven cases were related to military service and twelve to the provision of welfare. In a few cases, the request was withdrawn or a final decision was never reached. Hungary denied readmission in three cases. Vienna, AVA, MdI, Allg., 8, Ktn. 144 and 176, letters 'A' and 'N'.

91. Vienna, AVA, MdI, Allg., 8, Ktn. 144, 75805–1917 and 74069–1917, Marie Adam.

92. Vienna, AVA, MdI, Allg., 8, Ktn. 144, 11005–1917 and 6265–1917, Elisabeth Arthofer.

93. Hungary, GA IV from 1903 and II from 1909. See Vienna, HHStA, Adm. Reg., F 15, Ktn. 31, Ungarisches Auswanderergesetz.

94. Member of the Reichstag Hock as quoted in *Pester Lloyd*, 14 November 1908, 4.

95. Vienna, HHStA, Adm. Reg., F 15, Ktn 31, 106399–1900, k.u. Ministry of the Interior to k.u.k. Ministry for Foreign Affairs, 15 November 1900.
96. See B. Bolognese-Leuchtenmüller, *Wirtschafts- und Sozialstatistik Österreich-Ungarns*, vol. 1, *Bevölkerungsentwicklung und Berufsstruktur, Gesundheits- und Fürsorgewesen in Österreich 1750–1918* (Vienna: Verlag für Geschichte und Politik, 1978), 135f. Between 1876 and 1910, 1,422,205 Hungarian nationals emigrated to the United States, 6,056 to Canada, 264,460 to Argentina and 8,500 to Brazil. T. Horvath and G. Neyer (eds), *Auswanderungen aus Österreich: Von der Mitte des 19. Jahrhunderts bis zur Gegenwart* (Vienna: Böhlau, 1996), 35.
97. Vienna, HHStA, MdÄ, Adm. Reg., F 15, Ktn. 7, Memorandum on questions of emigration, May 1901.
98. Vienna, HHStA, MdÄ, Adm. Reg., F 8, Ktn. 140, 34813–1905, Zirkularerlass, 1 May 1905.
99. Madaráß in *Pester Lloyd*, 13 and 14 November 1908.
100. Hungary, GA IV from 1903, §35.
101. Vienna, HHStA, MdÄ, Adm. Reg., F 15, Ktn. 31, 53313–1910 and 48793–1910.
102. Vienna, HHStA, MdÄ, Adm. Reg., F 15, Ktn. 31, österreichisch-ungarische Kolonialgesellschaft to k.u.k. Ministry for Foreign Affairs, 31 August 1917.
103. Z. Szász, 'Inter-Ethnic Relations in the Hungarian Half of the Austro-Hungarian Empire', *Nationalities Papers* 24(3) (1996), 395f.; Fischer and Gündisch, *Geschichte Ungarns*, 130; Gerö, *The Hungarian Parliament*, 50.
104. Gerö, *The Hungarian Parliament*, 46f.; Janos, *The Politics of Backwardness*, 126. On the earlier suffrage debates, see Gerö, *The Hungarian Parliament*, 52.
105. All quotes: *Pester Lloyd*, 11 November 1908. See also Gerö, *The Hungarian Parliament*, 9f., 53f.
106. P. Balogh, 'Die Wahlbezirke und die Nationalitäten', *Pester Lloyd*, 8 November 1908, 2.
107. On processes of equalization and contrary tendencies in Hungary, see Kövér, 'Inactive Transformation', 26f., 36, 127, 152f.
108. Janos, *The Politics of Backwardness*, 92, 102, 163–65. See also S. Zimmermann, *Divide, Provide, and Rule: An Integrative History of Poverty Policy, Social Policy, and Social Reform in Hungary under the Habsburg Monarchy*, trans. J. Harbord (Budapest: CEU Press, 2011).
109. Cf. Pearson, 'Theorizing Citizenship', 995; Berger and Miller, 'Nation-Building', 318.
110. J. Darwin, 'Imperial Twilight, or When Did the Empire End?', in P. Buckner (ed.), *Canada and the End of Empire* (Vancouver: UBC Press, 2005), 15–24.
111. Cf. B. Stuchtey, *Die europäische Expansion und ihre Feinde: Kolonialismuskritik vom 18. bis in das 20. Jahrhundert* (Munich: Oldenbourg, 2010), 216–18; N. Owen, *The British Left and India: Metropolitan Anti-Imperialism, 1885–1947* (Oxford: Oxford University Press, 2007).
112. R. Jebb, *Studies in Colonial Nationalism* (London: E. Arnold, 1905). On Jebb and his concept, see also Gorman, *Imperial Citizenship*, 146f.
113. R. Jebb, 'The Imperial Problem of Asiatic Immigration', *Journal of the Royal Society of Arts* 56(2892) (1908), 594f.
114. J.R. Seeley, *The Expansion of England: Two Courses of Lectures*, rev. edn (Leipzig: Tauchnitz, 1884).
115. A. Shaw, 'An American View of Home Rule and Federation', *Contemporary Review* 62 (September 1892), 305–18. See also A.V. Dicey, 'A Common Citizenship for the

English Race', *Contemporary Review* 71 (April 1897), 457–76; Pearson, 'Theorizing Citizenship', 994.

116. Shaw, 'American View'. See also Dicey, 'Common Citizenship'. For a disconcerting reproduction of such implicit and silent exclusions of 'non-white' subjects in a recent academic publication, see Gorman, *Imperial Citizenship*, 68, 100.

117. See J. Regan-Lefebvre, *Cosmopolitan Nationalism in the Victorian Empire: Ireland, India and the Politics of Alfred Webb* (Basingstoke: Palgrave Macmillan, 2009), 6. Some Irish proponents of Home Rule even referred to Hungary's autonomy as a model. See ibid., 122.

118. E.F. Biagini, *British Democracy and Irish Nationalism 1876–1906* (Cambridge: Cambridge University Press, 2007); N. Canny, 'Foreword', in K. Kenny (ed.), *Ireland and the British Empire* (Oxford: Oxford University Press, 2005), ix–xix; P. Hart, *The IRA at War: 1916–1923* (Oxford: Oxford University Press, 2003).

119. P. Wassertheurer, 'Deutscher und tschechischer Nationalismus im österreichischen Kaiserreich', in H. Timmermann, E. Voráček and R. Kipke (eds), *Die Beneš-Dekrete: Nachkriegsordnung oder ethnische Säuberung: Kann Europa eine Antwort geben?* (Münster: Lit, 2005), 41–53; J. Kořalka, *Tschechen im Habsburgerreich und in Europa 1815– 1914: Sozialgeschichtliche Zusammenhänge der neuzeitlichen Nationsbildung und der Nationalitätenfrage in den böhmischen Ländern* (Vienna: Verlag für Geschichte und Politik, 1991); P. Haslinger, 'Staatsrecht oder Staatsgebiet? Böhmisches Staatsrecht, territoriales Denken und tschechisches Emanzipationsbestreben 1890–1914', in D. Willoweit and H. Lemberg (eds), *Reiche und Territorien in Ostmitteleuropa: Historische Beziehungen und politische Herrschaftslegitimation* (Munich: Oldenbourg, 2006), 345–58; J. Kwan, 'The Austrian State Idea and Bohemian State Rights: Contrasting Traditions in the Habsburg Monarchy, 1848–1914', in L. Eriksonas and L. Müller (eds), *Statehood before and beyond Ethnicity: Minor States in Northern and Eastern Europe, 1600–2000* (Brussels: P.I.E. Lang, 2005), 243–73.

120. According to Judson, 'Introduction', 4f., this constellation resulted in the emphasis on language within Czech nationalism.

121. J. Štaif, 'The Image of the Other in the Nineteenth Century: Historical Scholarship in the Bohemian Lands', in N.M. Wingfield (ed.), *Creating the Other: Ethnic Conflict and Nationalism in Habsburg Central Europe* (New York: Berghahn Books, 2003), 81–100.

122. N.S. Bose, *Racism, Struggle for Equality and Indian Nationalism* (Calcutta: KLM, 1981), 1.

123. Rudolph, 'Nationalism and Empire'; Emerson, *From Empire to Nation*; Tilly, 'How Empires End', 7; A.J. Motyl, 'From Imperial Decay to Imperial Collapse: The Fall of the Soviet Empire in Comparative Perspective', in R.L. Rudolph and D.F. Good (eds), *Nationalism and Empire: The Habsburg Empire and the Soviet Union* (New York: St. Martin's Press, 1992), 15–43; C. Taylor, *Reconciling the Solitudes: Essays on Canadian Federalism and Nationalism*, ed. G. Laforest (Montreal: McGill-Queen's University Press, 1993), 43f. With regards to the Habsburg case, see also S. Wank, 'The Habsburg Empire', in K. Barkey and M. v. Hagen (eds), *After Empire: Multiethnic Societies and Nation-Building* (Boulder, CO: Westview Press, 1997), 45–57. O. Jászi, *The Dissolution of the Habsburg Monarchy* (Chicago, IL: University of Chicago Press, 1929) is somewhat less sceptical as to the possibility of a supra-national state entity.

124. On the centripetal effects of national rights of autonomy within imperial formations, see Rudolph, 'Nationalism and Empire', 3f.; D. Rusinow, 'Ethnic Politics in the Habsburg Monarchy and its Successor States: Three "Answers" to the National Question', in R.L.

Rudolph and D.F. Good (eds), *Nationalism and Empire: The Habsburg Empire and the Soviet Union* (New York: St. Martin's Press, 1992), 243–67.

125. Berger and Miller, 'Nation-Building', 317; G.B. Cohen, 'Nationalist Politics and the Dynamics of State and Civil Society in the Habsburg Monarchy, 1867–1914', *Central European History* 40(2) (2007), 241; Miller, 'The Value and Limits', 22; Barkey, 'Consequences of Empire', 100; Veliz, *Politics*, 65, 68; Argast, *Staatsbürgerschaft*, 20, 17f., 26.

126. J. Leonhard and U. v. Hirschhausen, 'Does the Empire Strike Back? The Model of the Nation in Arms as a Challenge for Multi-ethnic Empires in the Nineteenth and Early Twentieth Century', *Journal of Modern European History* 5(2) (2007), 196–223; L. Cole and D.L. Unowsky (eds), *The Limits of Loyalty: Imperial Symbolism, Popular Allegiances, and State Patriotism in the Late Habsburg Monarchy* (New York: Berghahn Books, 2007); Cohen, 'Nationalist Politics', 244; Canny, 'Foreword'; I. Deák, *Beyond Nationalism: A Social and Political History of the Habsburg Officer Corps 1848–1918* (New York: Oxford University Press, 1990); idem, 'The Fall of Austria-Hungary: Peace, Stability, and Legitimacy', in *The Fall of Great Powers: Peace, Stability, and Legitimacy*, ed. G. Lundestad (Oslo: Scandinavian University Press, 1994), 81–102; A. Maxwell, *Choosing Slovakia: Slavic Hungary, the Czechoslovak Language and Accidental Nationalism* (London: I.B. Tauris, 2009); M. Prokopovych, *Habsburg Lemberg: Architecture, Public Space, and Politics in the Galician Capital, 1772–1914* (West Lafayette, IN: Purdue University Press, 2009), 288; Belich, *Replenishing the Earth*, 465.

Chapter 2

STATIST APPROACHES

From Ethnic Neutrality to a Politics of Recognition in Austria

In Austria, Cisleithania or – as referred to in the official language of the day – the kingdoms and lands represented in the Reichsrat (Imperial Council), the year 1867 heralded in a new era of liberal politics. But this was not a liberal victory along nationalist lines as in Hungary; rather, it marked the triumph of liberalism over neo-absolutism in a political and constitutional sense. The constitution of 1867 guaranteed all citizens certain fundamental civil rights and established a constitutional monarchy with the Reichsrat as its parliament. Yet, some neo-absolutist elements remained in place after 1867, including the centralized administration with directors of the gubernatorial districts (*Bezirkshauptmänner*) and the governors (*Statthalter*) of the fifteen Crown lands. This administration was headed by the Imperial-Royal government in Vienna and the Austrian emperor. Alongside this bureaucratic hierarchy, Cisleithania had its so-called autonomous administration, organized around the largely self-governing municipalities (*Gemeinden*) and executive bodies at the district and Crown land levels (*Bezirks- und Landesausschüsse*). The latter, in cooperation with the diets (*Landtage*), were responsible for the domestic affairs of the Crown lands. The judiciary, which was bolstered by the establishment of the Imperial Court and the Higher Administrative Court in 1867, ensured that the constitution and the law were upheld.

Most of the Crown lands were ethnically heterogeneous or multilingual (Bohemia, Moravia, Silesia, Galicia, Bukovina, Styria, Carinthia, the Austrian

Littoral and Tyrol); only a few were mostly homogeneous in terms of language, such as Upper and Lower Austria, Salzburg and Voralberg (German), Dalmatia (Croatian) and Carniola (Slovenian). Given this administrative constellation, it was impossible for the empire to avoid heated debates regarding ethnic heterogeneity over the course of the long nineteenth century, especially in light of the simultaneous rise of nationalism. Moreover, an increase in migration within the empire further intensified this multicultural diversity. Like the other significant waves of migration, such as seasonal migration to the German Empire and emigration to North and South America, this migration within the Empire was driven primarily by economic interests, and it brought large portions of the rural population to the industrial and urban centres, most especially Vienna.

In the early phase of the dual monarchy, Austria-Hungary experienced an economic boom during the so-called *Gründerzeit* that came to an abrupt and catastrophic end with the market crash in 1873. Beginning in the late 1870s, the economy revived and continued to grow relatively steadily until the outbreak of the First World War. However, despite this upward trend, the empire experienced widespread hunger, poverty and suffering throughout the constitutional era. Many contemporaries saw these phenomena as the products of capitalist exploitation, which in turn spurred the growth of the labour movement in the last few decades of the nineteenth century. Yet, although the Austrian social democratic party made its way into parliament and diets, it still did not attain any kind of executive power. At first, the government was largely controlled by the German-speaking liberals. In 1879, the conservative 'Iron Ring' took over the reins. It strengthened the position on the non-German-speaking nationalities and initiated the first sociopolitical reforms. In 1897, the Badeni crisis sparked a period of intensive conflicts between the different nationalities, in which various governments, most following in short succession, sought to dampen the fires of nationalism.

The early twentieth century saw the advent of universal male suffrage and rights of social citizenship. These developments went hand in hand with the emergence of mass media and broadening democratic structures that furthered the establishment of the Christian-socialist party as well as diverse nationalist parties, who influenced political debates with their nationalistic and sometimes anti-Semitic propaganda. Concurrently, the conflicts between national groups and anti-Semitic sentiments increasingly erupted in violence on the streets. The outbreak of the First World War brought an end to this constitutional era. Authoritarian government structures were reintroduced at first, but ultimately the Habsburg monarchy collapsed. Against this backdrop, this chapter queries whether Austrian nationality and citizenship laws were shaped by nation-state, statist or imperialist tendencies. Such a perspective is particularly relevant for the ongoing scholarly debate about whether it was national and centrifugal forces or pan-national and centripetal forces that prevailed in Austria during this period.[1]

CITIZENSHIP?

Nationality Laws Immune to Nationalization

During the constitutional era, nationality laws in Austria did not change. Although the constitution of 1867 indicated that a law on the acquisition and loss of Austrian nationality was supposed to come, no amendment was ever made. This is quite surprising, especially given the fact that nationality laws were often used as an instrument to include or exclude certain ethnic groups elsewhere. Why did nothing change in Cisleithania, despite the fact that the question of national belonging became all the more controversial during this time? Why did this field of law in particular prove to be immune to the general nationalization of politics, or rather why was it purposely left out?

By and large, the *Allgemeines Bürgerliches Gesetzbuch* (ABGB, General Civil Code) from 1811 regulated Austrian nationality law until 1918.[2] The Austrian law rested on *ius sanguinis*, the principle of descent, which meant that children inherited the nationality of their fathers or unmarried mothers. According to this principle, children born to immigrants residing within the country were not integrated into the community of nationals, but children born to emigrants abroad retained their parents' nationality. In both respects, however, Austrian law also deviated from this principle of descent. On the one hand, the ABGB dictated that Austrian nationality (the law itself spoke of '*Staatsbürgerschaft*', which is usually translated as 'citizenship', but in fact referred to nationality as defined for the purposes of this book) was automatically acquired by an individual who formally took up a trade or public office, or who had resided within the country for ten years. In particular, the last provision – the so-called 'principle of domicile', which dictated that a person should belong to the state in whose territory he was permanently resident – integrated immigrants and their descendants into the community of nationals, regardless of *ius sanguinis*. By 1867, however, all these grounds for the acquisition of nationality had been abolished.[3]

Consequently, as of 1867, there was no longer any legal regulation that automatically integrated immigrants and their descendants into the Austrian state. This meant that legal inclusion was only possible through naturalization. According to the ABGB, naturalization was the purview of the political authorities, who were to assess 'the property, employability and moral conduct of the applicant', and then, when a municipality had indicated that the candidate could become a member of its community, issue a certificate of naturalization.[4] It is rather conspicuous that a certain period of domicile within the country – usually five years in keeping with the international standard – was not outlined as a prerequisite in Austria. In this respect, naturalization was comparably inclusive. Moreover, the reform of the residency laws in 1896 simplified the Austrian naturalization process by making it easier for individuals to become official members of a municipal community.

Austrian law also deviated from *ius sanguinis* in its treatment of emigrants. On the one hand, the ABGB stated that Austrian nationality was automatically rescinded after ten years of residency abroad. On the other hand, according to the Emigration Patent of 1832, nationality was lost upon emigration itself (i.e. by crossing the border with no intention of returning).[5] The children of emigrants, however, enjoyed certain legal privileges that made it possible for them to reacquire their Austrian nationality immediately upon return to the country.[6] The patent also declared that an Austrian woman lost her Austrian nationality upon marriage to a foreigner. However, these women were denied any kind of simplified repatriation as the Emigration Patent stated that they could only regain their original nationality after the death of their spouse and through the normal naturalization procedure.[7] Similarly, in 1833, it was also determined that a foreign-born woman acquired the nationality of her Austrian husband. In fact, this was the only legal basis for the automatic acquisition of Austrian nationality that remained in place until 1918.

This last point, namely the question of the nationality of married women, was hardly discussed in Austria prior to 1918. This silence is quite remarkable, especially given the fact that the right to an independent national status for married women played a decisive role in the amendment of the respective British laws in 1914 as well as those in the German Empire in 1913.[8] In both cases, advocates of women's rights demanded that a woman should be entitled to a nationality that was not tied to that of her husband. They argued that women were just as closely bound to their respective nations as men, which meant that it was unjust to strip a woman of her nationality upon marriage to a foreigner. At the very least, they suggested, special regulations should apply to women who returned to their country of birth as divorcees or widows. In discussions surrounding the reform of the Austrian ABGB in 1908 and 1913, however, the publications of the women's movement did not even mention the matter.[9] Only a review of a book published by an international women's organization pointed to the discrimination against women in nationality law, stating that this injustice seemed to be rather bearable, if compared to the drastic provisions of §591.[10] Section 591 of the ABGB denied women, as well as members of religious orders, minors and 'the insane, the blind, the deaf or the mute' the right to serve as witnesses to last wills and testaments.[11] Prior to the ABGB amendment, the different strands of the Austrian women's movement engaged in heated discussions about guardianship, marriage, inheritance and contract laws as well as the duty of fathers to pay for illegitimate children, but they hardly concerned themselves with the question of whether nationality laws adequately reflected women's sense of national belonging. In fact, the nationality issue was only mentioned in a single publication that dealt with the legal status of women in an international comparison.

Thus, demands for the independent nationality of married women – crucial for the nationalization of the law in other countries – were hardly voiced in Cisleithania. While certain women's organizations in Austria did not shy away from using nationalist arguments in other contexts, they refrained from doing so as far as nationality law was concerned. When discussing the reform of the AGBG, however, they emphasized female emancipation and equality between the sexes instead. This hints at the fact that the nation-state pattern in general did not figure prominently in Austrian debates about nationality, and that concepts of the nation hardly affected the development of the law. Rather, a statist approach prevailed that sought to accord Austrian nationality to all members of the resident population in an ethnically neutral fashion.

Emigration: The Primacy of Military Interests and the Principle of Ethnic Neutrality

Unlike the nationality of married women, the legal exclusion of emigrants was a matter of intense public debate, especially when it came to overseas emigration. Arguments were made against the automatic loss of nationality through a ten-year absence to the effect that, 'in the interests of the state and the nations', the ties that bind an emigrant to his homeland should not be loosened.[12] Above all, this argument emphasized the aim of the multinational state to establish 'Austrian colonies' and achieve the 'colonization of foreign states through its own people'.[13] At the beginning of 1914, the Austro-Hungarian Colonial Society, the 'only non-confessional and non-national welfare society for emigrants', argued along similar lines. It noted that since Austria had to make do without 'state colonization', it had to 'pursue economic [colonization] overseas'.[14] The Colonial Society demanded, among other things, that it should be easier to retain Austrian nationality abroad. Citing the economic interests of the Austrian state, it claimed that such policies would promote the investment of emigrants' savings in Austrian bonds, and make it cheaper and safer for Austrians living abroad to send money home, while also fostering the expansion of overseas exports. For these reasons, according to the Colonial Society, the emigration movement should not be sacrificed in the name of military interests, with all due respect to the legitimate insistence on the proper fulfilment of military service. In contrast, it recommended easing the draft obligations for those who had moved abroad for economic reasons, and it suggested – shortly after the Balkan Wars and before the First World War – an 'amnesty for conscripts who had left their home country' without having previously obtained official permission to do so.[15]

These arguments bring us to the crux of the matter at hand: the idea of granting amnesty to returning emigrants who had failed to fulfil their military service obligations had already been brought up in the Reichsrat some years prior, but it was repeatedly put down by the government.[16] Not surprisingly, the Imperial and Royal Ministry of War opposed this notion 'in the interests of the army' in the discussions about the emigration act among the different ministries. It also argued vehemently against measures that would add to the appeal of emigration, which included making it easier to retain Austrian nationality abroad. Instead, it demanded clear limitations on emigration. As a result of these competing interests, the first attempt to draft an emigration act failed in 1904.[17] In the end, the restrictive standpoint of the War Ministry prevailed in 1913, which meant that no legislative changes were made that affected the exclusion of emigrants between 1867 and 1918.[18]

Interestingly, both sides in these conflicts argued in the interests of the state, citing economic interests on the one hand and military interests on the other. Neither side, however, sought the inclusion or exclusion of specific ethnic groups. The 'national ties' binding emigrants to their homelands were supposed to be strengthened, but within the context of the 'nations' and not a singular 'nation'. Rather than privileging one of the national groups within the Austrian population, the idea was that all nationalities should be treated equally. Nationality law in Austria, therefore, continued to be shaped by the interests of the state within a framework of ethnic neutrality.

Immigration and the Rejection of Ethnically Exclusive Measures

Issues surrounding the legal status of immigrants were also discussed during the constitutional era. Experts cited the 'rise of the notion of the state' as the reason for eliminating the automatic acquisition of nationality.[19] As nationality was increasingly coupled with the rights and duties of citizenship, they claimed, becoming a national needed to be a conscious act rather than just a consequence of establishing residency. In their opinion, the state also had to be able to determine who belonged and who did not.[20] The simple application of *ius sanguinis*, they maintained, was the way to properly control the national status of the population.[21] That said, however, following a strict principle of descent hindered the legal integration of large portions of the resident population. This, as their arguments noted, brought certain disadvantages because these people enjoyed the protection of the state and specific rights, but they were not obligated to serve in the military. Accordingly, they demanded that at least the children of immigrants should be forced to adopt Austrian nationality. Citing the British example, one jurist suggested that second-generation immigrants should acquire nationality on the basis of *ius soli*.[22] The state was also at the heart of these arguments because Austria had a vested interest in achieving congruence between its resident population and the community of its nationals whose ethnic identities were irrelevant. Such a perspective resulted in an openness to immigration as well as a commitment to the legal integration of immigrants

Rather than emphasizing the needs of the state, those in favour of halting immigration countered these arguments by claiming that immigration restrictions would protect domestic workers against wage competition. Most of the proposed prohibitions were directed at certain ethnic groups. In 1898, for example, a member of the Reichsrat named Prochazka advocated a 'Prohibition against the Immigration of Chinese Coolies to Austria'. The proposition noted that 'through the expansion of the Trans-Siberian railway the danger' was approaching 'that Chinese workers, the so-called coolies, encouraged by unscrupulous and greedy major capitalists … might be prompted to emigrate to Austria', which meant that 'Austria's labour force' had to be protected.[23] With its conjunctive wording, this proposal hints at the virtual nature of the danger that it sought to avoid pre-emptively. Nonetheless, Prochazka, hoping to tap into racist fears, brought up the proposal twice more, but he met with little success.

Demands for the exclusion of another ethnic group, however, found a broader base of support. At the end of the 1880s, several petitions reached the Reichsrat that demanded a prohibition against the 'immigration and settlement of foreign Israelites in Austria'. Over two thousand submissions were made, stemming from initiatives in almost all the Crown lands, with a total of 37,068 signatures.[24] As a result, several Reichsrat members motioned for an immigration prohibition directed at 'foreign Jews' 'coming mostly from Russia'.[25] These proposals reflected the popularity and prevalence of anti-Semitic sentiments around the turn of the century and thereafter. Ultimately, however, they were never politically successful as the Reichsrat dismissed them all. Yet, neither the state-centred, generally immigrant friendly and ethnically neutral stance nor the anti-Semitic, anti-immigration and ethnically exclusive demands led to legislative changes. Not only was the exclusion of specific groups never achieved, but also the naturalization process remained the cornerstone of the legal inclusion of immigrants.

The Principle of Ethnic Neutrality and Naturalization in Practice

In order to assess naturalization practice, information about immigrants, applicants and naturalized individuals is needed. For it is only possible to determine whether naturalization policies actually achieved a general congruence between the resident population and the community of nationals or whether it excluded a major group of immigrants when all three groups are taken into account. Moreover, this information allows for an analysis of the role ethnic differences played in these processes. Exact figures are available for the period between 1885 and 1903. During this time, an average of approximately 3,350 people became naturalized Austrians each year. After the turn of the century, this number increased significantly, with 6,444 naturalizations in 1903.[26] If these figures are compared to the number of immigrants living permanently in Austria, it becomes quite clear that the majority of the foreign resident population was not naturalized. The census of 1880 counted 350,014 persons who were born abroad. This number rose continually, to 631,515 in 1910. This means that the share of foreign-born persons in the total population increased from 1.0 per cent in 1880 to 2.2 per cent in 1910.[27] Naturally, some of these figures may be slightly skewed because it may have been in the interests of those counted to keep their nationality a secret by providing a foreign place of birth in order to avoid military conscription. In addition, not everyone born abroad was necessarily a foreigner. Yet these figures nevertheless show clearly that the number of naturalizations was far too low to ensure the integration of immigrants into the Austrian citizenry. At the beginning of the century, approximately one in every fifty inhabitants of Cisleithania was not an Austrian national and the number of non-naturalized immigrants remained noticeably high. This indicates that the administration did not actually try to strive for congruence between the resident population and the community of nationals. At the same time, the rising number of naturalizations after 1900 reflects an increased effort to integrate immigrants.

Given the lack of data on the total number of applications submitted, it is difficult to tell which criteria the authorities used to determine whether to approve or refuse naturalization requests. The following analysis draws primarily on the files of the Imperial-Royal Ministry of the Interior. This ministry only dealt with naturalization issues in special cases, which means that these documents cannot provide a wholly representative overview. That said, however, the subordinate administrative authorities generally followed the guidelines set by the ministry in processing applications, so the records of the ministry are generally indicative of the key principles that guided the naturalization process.[28]

First of all, the role of ethnic difference vis-à-vis naturalization can be gleaned from these sources as the information that immigrants and naturalized citizens provided about their respective countries of origin also speaks to their ethnic identities. More detailed information is only available for those individuals naturalized between 1893 and 1902. Of the naturalized individuals, 60 per cent came from Hungary, 26.2 per cent from the German Empire (mostly from Prussia, Bavaria and Saxony), 4.7 per cent from Russia, 3.4 per cent from Italy and 1 per cent from Switzerland. The rest came from Turkey and south-east European states (2.3 per cent), Western Europe (0.8 per cent) and the USA (0.4 per cent).[29] As these statistics indicate, most immigrants came from states located directly on Austria's borders. It can therefore be supposed that the group of naturalized Austrians was just as ethnically heterogeneous as the populations of the major countries of origin, namely Hungary, the German Empire and the Russian Empire.

The calls for an immigration prohibition against Jews suggest that this group might very well have been subjected to exclusive mechanisms. For many years, the proportion of Jews among those naturalized was relatively high. In 1888, for example, Jews represented 35 per cent (see Fig. 2.1).[30] In comparison to the percentage of Jews in the population as a whole, as well as the number of naturalized Jews in other countries and especially in the German Empire, the Austrian

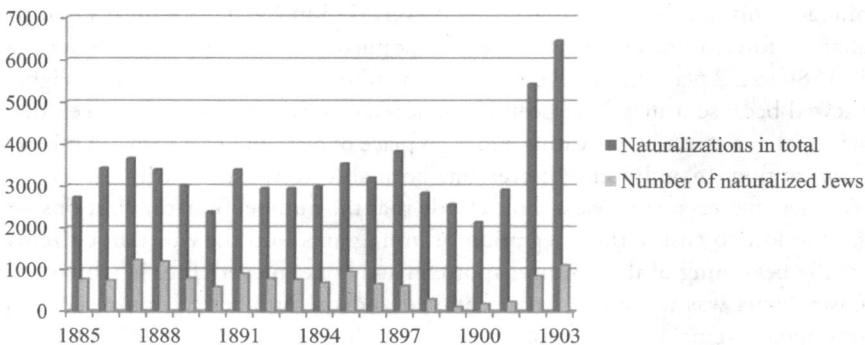

Figure 2.1. Naturalizations in Austria and number of naturalized Jews, in absolute figures

authorities approved naturalization for an unusually large number of Jews.[31] Given this phenomenon, it seems highly unlikely that anti-Semitic sentiments had a decisive influence on the naturalization process.

The statistics also show that the percentage of Jews among the total number of naturalizations at the turn of the century sank significantly, but began to climb again in 1902. A look at the geographic distribution of Jewish naturalizations reveals that these diminishing numbers were without a doubt the result of changing naturalization policies in Lower Austria: 420 Jews were naturalized there in 1897, and this number rose to 536 in 1902; but in the four years in between, a total of only 377 Jews were naturalized.[32] It can therefore be surmised that the naturalization process in Lower Austria, which included the city of Vienna, was influenced by anti-Semitism during these four years. The records of the Imperial-Royal Ministry of the Interior correlate this fact. In 1898, for instance, the Moravian governor's office refused the naturalization request of a Jewess who had been living in Vienna her whole life, but had been denied official membership in the municipality by the Viennese city council. Within this context, the governor's office complained about the 'huge number of applications [for naturalization] by complete strangers with absolutely no ties to the crown land of Moravia ..., who ... had been promised official membership by one of the Jewish municipalities in Moravia'. According to the authorities in Brno (now part of the Czech Republic), the governor's office in Lower Austria should actually have been responsible for the naturalization of these individuals. Quite apparently, many Jews sought to circumvent the exclusive policies in place in Vienna by submitting their naturalization requests in Moravia.[33]

Apart from such cases, the records do not indicate that any anti-Semitic guidelines for handling naturalization requests had been put in place. Jewish applicants were denied naturalization on the basis that their applications were not sufficiently justified, or they had been convicted of a crime, or there was a danger that they might become a burden to the public welfare system – but not because they were Jews.[34] In one case in which an applicant had accused the authorities of having 'falsified the facts simply because of his Jewish faith', the Interior Ministry ordered a re-evaluation of his application in order to deflect the accusation that anti-Semitism had played a role in the decision.[35] At the most, these records indicate that non-Jewish applicants were assessed less strictly than their Jewish counterparts when it came to their respective financial situations.[36] However, it cannot be surmised that there was an established pattern of ethnic exclusion, especially because the available evidence cannot be seen as indicative of the general situation.[37]

With respect to Italian applicants, ethnocultural criteria and language skills in particular were more relevant. In these cases, it was necessary to establish whether applicants could be considered 'assimilated' – for example, because they had an Austrian mother or did not speak Italian.[38] One applicant was denied naturalization because 'he could be identified as an Italian immediately, based on how he spoke'.[39] These kinds of criteria became all the more significant after the outbreak of the First World War. Before the war, the authorities treated the requests of Italians sceptically, but only refused them on ethnocultural grounds if the applicant 'felt a sense of Italian national belonging' or was a member of an Italian nationalist association.[40]

Political activities that raised doubts in the eyes of the authorities as to the loyalty of an applicant also led in a few cases to the denial of naturalization requests submitted by social democrats. For instance, the Hungarian national Dr Hugo Stark, born in Prague in 1870, was not naturalized because the mayor of the town in which he lived described him as a socialist agitator.[41] Integrity was another criterion that the authorities took seriously. In 1898, they denied the naturalization request of Johann Martinek, born in 1841 in Hungary and resident in Vienna since 1895, because he had been sentenced to three days in jail in 1881 for drinking four glasses of beer but only paying for two. The Interior Ministry recommended upholding the decision to deny his application because his 'moral conduct' was not in keeping with that of an Austrian national.[42]

One of the most significant criteria was 'the assets [and] employability' (i.e. the financial situation) of the respective applicant. Take, for example, the case of Felix Schwarzfischer, a young novice in a Benedictine monastery near Innsbruck and a Bavarian national, who submitted a naturalization application in 1897. The authorities were willing to approve his request, because Schwarzfischer's father had promised to 'pay 5,000 florin for the upkeep of his son in the event that the latter becomes unemployable'.[43] The clockmaker Josel Salmon Schächter, however, met with less success. Born in 1869 in Russia, he later moved to Przemyśl (now part of Poland) and applied for naturalization in 1894 at the governor's office in Lemberg (now Lviv in Ukraine). According to the information provided by the Israelite religious community, Schächter had an annual income of 600

Kronen and additional assets of 3,000 Kronen. The metalworkers' cooperative society also confirmed that he could support himself and his family with the proceeds of his business. Additionally, two municipal councillors affirmed the fact that Schächter had clocks valued at approximately 2,000 Kronen in his workshop. The authorities, however, determined that his business capital listed in the tax registers only amounted to 90 Kronen. In the end, they denied his application, citing the lack of 'sufficient income in the event that he was not able to work anymore', and that he could 'not prove that he was in the possession of 1,000 florins in capital'.[44]

There was no strict rule as to how much capital or the amount of assets an applicant had to have to be considered for naturalization – in the case cited here, the bar was set comparably high – but in general, many naturalization requests were denied due to a lack of financial means. The local municipalities also took a good look at the financial situation of an applicant before guaranteeing any kind of right of domicile, because they naturally had a vested interest in acquiring wealthy members, and also desired to avoid having to pay for impoverished members.[45] It must be noted, however, that the reform of the right of domicile in 1896 did away with this particular mechanism of exclusion because it proscribed the automatic acquisition of membership in a municipality after ten years of residency. This reform made it easier for poorer applicants to successfully apply for naturalization after the turn of the century.

In general, the Interior Ministry added another administrative hurdle to the existing legal criteria of integrity and employability, namely residence in Austria. In 1869, for instance, it was relatively easy for Abramo Azam to acquire Austrian nationality for himself and his three brothers. The Azams were Greek Catholics and lived as well-to-do businessmen in Egypt. They sought to gain the protection of the local Imperial and Royal consulate by acquiring Austrian citizenship. 'Austrian nationality was granted to the four Azam brothers; they were accepted because they donated a large sum of money to the municipality of Baden'.[46] With reference to this case, the Foreign Ministry stated that cases in which naturalization was bought were not in the best interests of the state, and that such occurrences could easily lead to international complications.

The Interior Ministry later emphasized that applicants for naturalization must be resident within the country, as can quite clearly be seen in the case of the naturalization of the Persian national Leon Mackertich. In 1893, the Lower Austrian governor's office allowed for the naturalization of Mackertich, who had been born in 1850 in Isfahan and was living in Smyrna (now Izmir in Turkey), as were his wife and two daughters, after the municipality of Stockerau guaranteed his admittance. In response, the ministry decreed that the naturalization of individuals who were not resident in Austria, 'but rather saw the acquisition of Austrian nationality as a means to ensure the protection of the Austro-Hungarian consulate in Turkey … was nothing less than undesirable'. In the future, it declared, the authorities were supposed to assess such 'sham naturalizations' harshly in order to find sufficient reason to dismiss them.[47] Despite these tightened guidelines, there was still no particular period of residence required before an application for naturalization could be submitted.

In sum, as has already been demonstrated for the period before 1867, language, religion and culture did not generally play a significant role in the approval of naturalization requests after 1867, with only a few exceptions.[48] Apart from the anti-Semitic discrimination that appeared in Lower Austria at the turn of the century, and the treatment of Italian applicants after 1914, ethnic criteria were not decisive when it came to the acquisition of Austrian nationality. Rather, the focus was clearly on the financial and political interests of the state, which meant that naturalization in Austria was governed by a statist approach.

Citizenship and the Recognition of Difference in the Moravian Compromise

Up to now, this chapter has only provided scant evidence attesting to the relevance of ethnic differences in the Cisleithanian context. The question remains, however, as to whether the same applies to the development of laws regulating access to citizenship rights within this period. At the outset, laws on citizenship were by and large indifferent in terms of ethnic belonging, being predominantly shaped by a notion of equality. The Josephine reforms around the turn of the nineteenth century, which also influenced the ABGB, emphasized civic equality over the inequality between aristocrats and commoners.[49] However, this principle of equality was later imbued with a new spirit, reinterpreted and adapted in light of the evermore important national question. The constitution of 1867, for example, brought the notion of cultural identity to the forefront in Article 19: 'All the races of the state shall have equal rights, and each race shall have the inviolable right of maintaining and cultivating its nationality and language. The state recognizes the equality of the various languages in the schools, public offices, and in public life'.[50]

This article drew on considerations that had already played a role in the constitutional debates of 1848, and it lent ethnocultural differences legal relevance.[51] Essentially, the state declared that it would not interfere in matters of cultural identity and it guaranteed every individual the right to be taught and heard in her own language.[52] 'Races of the state' – the term used in the original is *Volksstamm* – could, however, also be interpreted as defining ethnocultural groups as collective legal entities that were a constitutive element of the state itself.[53] This transfer of the legal relevance of ethnic difference from the cultural realm where individuals spoke and listened to the political sphere where collectives acted had a decisive impact on the gradual development of Austrian laws on citizenship. Over the course of this process, ethnocultural groups turned into nationalities or nations as they made their way onto the political stage.

Citizens' rights to the recognition of their ethnocultural identities and the judicial enforcement of these rights led to a flood of legal conflicts, especially with regard to schooling and official administrative languages.[54] Many of these lawsuits reached the highest courts. Within this context, a number of questions emerged that the courts had to resolve: how could the ethnocultural identity of a person be defined or determined? When is a language considered to be a 'national language'? Are the Jews a separate '*Volksstamm*'? The judgements passed by the Higher Administrative Court and the Imperial Court therefore laid the legal foundation for the later legislative implementation of mechanisms that recognized different ethnic identities.[55] Simultaneously, national identification came to play a more significant role, especially following the Badeni crisis of 1897 and within the context of the relationship between the Czechs and the Germans. In street protests and shop boycotts as well as conflicts involving schools and other cultural institutions, nationalist pressure to adhere to a single ethnic identity grew by leaps and bounds.[56] These processes made it more difficult for individuals to choose between different identities depending on the situation at hand or to refrain from clearly identifying with one particular group at all.[57] Correspondingly, the structures of settlement, migration, education and social welfare became all the more important, as did the degree to which the respective national groups mobilized themselves politically.[58]

At first, it was primarily the social and cultural elites of the non-hegemonic nationalities who demanded cultural recognition and actively sought to unify and homogenize the respective national collective.[59] These processes of nationalization effectively destabilized the statist ideal of supra-ethnic neutrality because this neutrality was implicitly dependent on the hegemony of the German-speaking population. Moreover, the advocates of the supra-national character of the state also fell under the wheels of the nationalization movement.[60] This dynamic ultimately pushed the cultural and individual right to the recognition of ethnic difference into the realm of politics.

In other words, around the turn of the century, the right to cultural and national difference was politicized. It was no longer understood as an individual entitlement, but rather it was defined collectively in terms of national groups and their demands for more autonomy.[61] The so-called Moravian Compromise of 1905 is the most prominent example of this process.[62] Essentially, the compromise led to the division of the Moravian electorate into Czechs – or in the terms of the compromise itself, Bohemians – and Germans. Candidates and voters were divided according to their nationality, which meant that the election resulted in two national constituencies sending delegates to the Moravian diet. The third, non-national constituency of the diet consisted of the large landowners, who were by far the smallest group of voters but elected a fifth of the delegates to the Moravian diet. Despite the introduction of a universal class of electors, the unequal system of class-based suffrage remained in place. Moreover, through a system of qualified majorities, each of these three constituencies basically had a veto right when it came to central issues to be dealt with by the diet.[63] The idea was that this compromise would guarantee equality for both nationalities by recognizing these two national groups as well as preventing the political outvoting of the minority, thereby resolving the nationalist conflicts.[64] At the same time, the compromise also preserved the privileged position of the large landowners. Both these aspects were interrelated in that the attempt to deflate nationalist conflicts was tied up in the debate over the introduction of equal, universal suffrage and the elimination of estate-based privileges. This complex constellation resulted in class-based or nationally defined groups that pursued divergent agendas.

For the most part, it can be said that the Moravian Compromise succeeded because it allowed several of the parties involved to prevent what they saw as the worst-case scenario. The large landowners were able to retain their privileged position while the German delegates were able to avoid being outvoted by the Czech fractions when it came to decisive issues. Furthermore, the stabilization of the existing order and the avoidance of revolutionary change also gave conservative Czech groups and the entire elite reason to support the compromise. The so-called young Czechs and radical-nationalist German groups, on the other hand, opposed the pact.[65] Outside the political spectrum of the diet itself, the social democrats tolerated the compromise, even though they still organized a large demonstration demanding equal, universal suffrage in 1904.[66] In many respects, the Moravian Compromise actually resembled the Austro-Marxist suggestions for resolving the problem of the different nationalities in Austria.[67]

The question as to whether the Moravian Compromise should be seen as an anti-democratic project sponsored by social elites or as a successful attempt to resolve the nationalities conflict ignores a central aspect of the compromise that points to a blind spot in these arguments. Whereas some believed that nationality-based constituencies were the only way to put a damper on these conflicts, others claimed that only equal, universal suffrage could oust the 'phantom of nationalist thought' from the political stage.[68] In a quite striking way, the idea of proportional representation hardly played a role in these debates, despite the fact that it would have ensured for the political representation of minority nationalities without carving certain privileges or ratios into stone.[69] This blind spot illustrates quite clearly that neither the recognition of ethnic difference among voters nor equal, universal suffrage were advocated on their own accord; rather these notions were used by certain actors as a means through which to pursue their own economic, social and political interests. The Moravian Compromise can therefore be seen as a prime example of how suffrage could be shaped by forms of ethnic differentiation that were dependent on specific local constellations, offering a fruitful comparative perspective on similar schemes discussed or established in other parts of Austria as well as in Hungary, India and East Africa.

In the Cisleithanian context, the Moravian Compromise, as well as the later compromises in Bukovina in 1910 and Galicia in 1914, defined national identity at the level of individuals.[70] Instead of defining distinct national territories, the population was divided into ethno-national groups on an individual basis, irrespective of where people lived or where they were born. The compromises therefore accorded different legal statuses to specific individuals – for example, as a Czech or as a German – within one single territory. In the case of the Moravian Compromise, this meant that suffrage throughout the country was divided according to separate Czech and German constituencies. For the twenty mandates within the general electorate, this resulted in an electoral map with two layers (see Map 2.1)

The compromise also led to the formation of a system of national lists and registers that made it possible to specify the national identity of each person.[71] Within the context of the Moravian Compromise, the Austrian Marxists Karl Renner and Otto Bauer also suggested a solution to the nationality problem that rested on personal criteria.[72] However, they sought to combine this division of individuals according to nationality with a territorial, supra-national, state-based structure. Renner suggested 'throwing two nets over the map of the country, one economy-based and the other ethnic', and to 'organize the population twice, once according to nationality and once along the lines of the state'.[73] In doing so, he sought to combine two contradictory ways of resolving the problem of the nationalities, namely the so-called 'Austrian-governmental' or German-centric approach, which reflected Renner's state- or economy-based structure, and an 'ethnic standpoint'.[74]

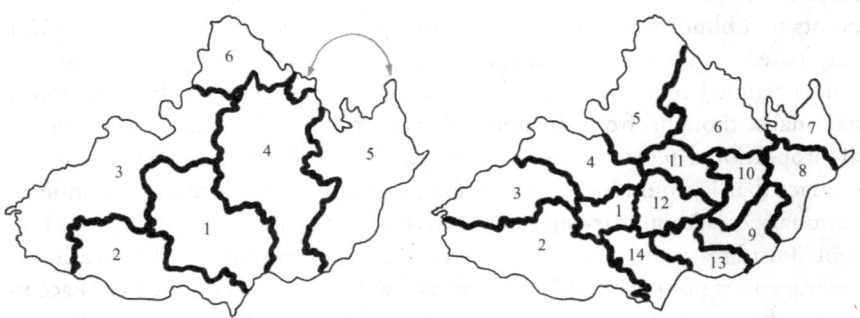

Map 2.1. The ascription of ethnonational identities to individuals: 'The Moravian Compromise of 1905: 6 German and 14 Czech voting constituencies'. Based on: *Sudetendeutscher Atlas*, 2nd edn, Munich 1955, p. 26 (courtesy of Sudetendeutscher Rat).

A third approach that was also put forward worked from a territorial principle that drew boundaries between ethnically homogeneous areas. This variant played a significant role in the introduction of universal male suffrage for the Cisleithanian Reichsrat in 1907, where the attempt was made to create ethnically homogeneous constituencies.[75] Ideas that suggested moving further towards autonomy for the different nationalities based on a territorial framework often drew on the idea of a federation of ethnically homogeneous Crown lands. According to this notion, the borders of the Crown lands were supposed to be shifted to match the settlement areas of the different nationalities.[76] It is quite clear that these territorial and federal notions of national autonomy would have had a much more detrimental effect on the unity of the Austrian state than the approach suggested by the Austrian Marxists, which distinguished between nationalities at the level of individuals, but also emphasized an anational, state entity on a territorial level. The coexistence of these individual and territorial-based principles begged the question to what extent the unity of the Austrian state should and could be preserved in light of the growing nationalization of the political sphere.

Social Citizenship Rights and Ethnic Neutrality

The recognition of ethnic difference increasingly gained a foothold in the realm of cultural rights after 1867, as well as in terms of suffrage after 1900. Did the same apply to social citizenship rights? Differentiation according to nationality did not play a role in protective labour legislation, the health and accident insurance for workers instituted in 1888/89 or the pension scheme for employees introduced in 1906.[77] The health and accident insurance categorized the working population according to sectors, but independent of their ethnic identities and regardless of whether they were considered to be foreigners or nationals according to the law. At the most, the exclusion of agricultural and forestry workers in this social welfare insurance scheme might have implicitly discriminated against those nationalities that were mostly settled in agricultural areas, such as the Polish or Ukrainian populations.[78] That said, however, the question was never raised in the public or parliamentary debates as to whether certain nationalities were overrepresented or underrepresented in the tenth of the Austrian population that benefited from health insurance in 1901.[79] Even the statements of legal experts regarding these sociopolitical reform plans emphasized that an adequate social security system had to guarantee the free movement of those insured, which implicitly meant that all insured individuals were to be treated equally, regardless of their respective ethnic identities.[80] A few isolated commentaries did point out – mostly in a polemic way – that the financial burdens and benefits were unequally distributed among the different national groups.[81] Similarly, nationalist interests also sometimes influenced who was chosen for certain offices within the insurance institutions.[82] In general, however, the differences between the economic sectors and the distinction between employers and employees dominated the debates over these social welfare initiatives. The provision of a modern system of social security was thus seen as one of the tasks of an ethnically neutral state.

The situation was somewhat different with older welfare structures such as poor laws. As the municipalities were responsible for assisting the poor, only those who had a right of domicile in a particular municipality were entitled to welfare assistance. Official membership or the right of domicile was acquired, like nationality, on the basis of *ius sanguinis* (i.e. through birth or naturalization). This stipulation meant that many migrants who remained in the country but lacked a formal right of domicile where they actually lived could not take advantage of local poor relief. Consequently, when these individuals became needy, they were deported to the municipality in which they enjoyed a right of domicile. As of 1863, the municipalities were also free to approve or deny requests to join them at their own discretion. Did they in fact try to exclude certain ethnic groups from becoming part of their official communities? For the periods 1870–1880 and 1890–1900, this question can be examined on the basis of those cases in which it came to ministerial appeals or trials at the administrative courts. In such cases, the refusal of the right of domicile to individual applicants must have been important enough to the local municipalities that they were willing to risk a great deal of administrative effort as well as significant sums of money to fight the case at hand.[83]

In both these decades, the question of which municipality was responsible for the welfare costs of an individual was the most prevalent reason for conflicts over the right of domicile. There were fewer battles over the issue of whether a person had to fulfil military service in a municipality or which municipality was supposed to issue certificates of residence or other documents. Between 1870 and 1880, most of the cases involved German-speaking individuals whose right of domicile was contested. Between 1890 and 1900, on the other hand, members of different national groups were equally affected. No particular pattern can be detected for either decade to the effect that municipalities with German-speaking majorities, for example, refused to admit Czech-speaking immigrants. Rather, an analysis of these cases provides a varied picture. The municipality of Kaltenbrunn in Bohemia (today Studánky in the Czech Republic) fought against the admission of the 'deaf and dumb lunatic' Eleonora Ruderstein. The municipality of Radkersburg in Styria (today Radgona in Slovenia) insisted that Graz (today in Austria) was responsible for a man named Franz Richter. There was also a fight over whether Leopold Ragani possessed a right of domicile in Neufelden or in Weitersfelden, both of which were municipalities in Upper Austria, and over whether Franz Foremny belonged to Polanka or Gorajowice, both of which were located in Galicia (today in Poland). And, the city of Vienna protested the assignment of Gustav Feilhauer to its municipal community. This list could go on forever, but what is clear in all these cases is that financial concerns were primary for the municipalities involved. Regardless of the ethnic identity of a person, they sought to avoid potential welfare cases.

The amendment of the law on the right of domicile in 1896 also led to a decisive change within the poor relief laws. As the new law granted a right of domicile after ten years of residence in a municipality, it was no longer possible to deport the needy without further reason.[84] The intention of the amendment was to relieve some of the financial burden on the rural communes in which most of the domestic migrants had a right of domicile, which meant that they bore the brunt of the costs for poor relief. According to the arguments behind this move, it was unfair that the large industrial municipalities who benefited from the work of these immigrants were not financially responsible for their welfare.[85] Many migrants automatically attained a right of domicile in the city of Vienna as a result of this legal change.[86] At the outset of the twentieth century, this led to some cases in which Viennese authorities sought to deny Czechs in particular formal admission to the municipal community. In 1902, for example, a Bohemian Reichsrat member, Dr Plaček, complained to the Imperial-Royal Ministry of the Interior that the magistrate in Vienna refused to process applications submitted in the 'Bohemian language'. In these files, Bohemian municipalities petitioned the city of Vienna to recognize the right of domicile of migrants from Bohemia who had settled in Vienna.[87]

It is quite probable, especially considering the political context in which these cases were embedded, that the city of Vienna made a concerted effort to exclude 'non-German' Austrians from acquiring the right of domicile in the city.[88] According to a municipal statute put in place in 1900, anyone who wanted to be naturalized in Vienna had to pledge to uphold 'the German character of the city'.[89] Dr Plaček's interpellation in the Reichsrat as well as the anti-Semitic outlook of the majority in the city council of Vienna at the turn of the century also point to the fact that it was 'Czechs' and 'Jews' who were most affected by these exclusionary measures.[90] This strategy also explains the significant decrease in the number of naturalizations of Jews in Lower Austria at the beginning of the twentieth century. If the Viennese magistrate refused to guarantee 'Jewish' applicants formal admission into the municipal community, then they could not be naturalized. That said, however, the authorities never explicitly cited the ethnic identity of the individual in question as the reason for the dismissal of an application. In the files related to the right of domicile in Vienna in 1901 and 1902, mostly social criteria as well as financial considerations were provided as the official reasons for refusals.[91] Even the civil servants in the Imperial-Royal Ministry of the Interior came to the conclusion that the 'practices described … were understandably directed against the poorer levels of the population'.[92]

Despite the explicitly social nature of these refusals, ethnic criteria undoubtedly played a significant, yet implicit role.

The Viennese authorities, however, only pursued this ethnically exclusive course for a few years. In 1903 and 1904, the percentage of 'Jews' formally admitted to the municipal community of Vienna amounted to 5.4 and 7.1 per cent respectively, which was close to and even above the average percentage in a number of Cisleithanian states at 6.1 and 6.5 per cent respectively.[93] The fact that this ethnically exclusive practice was not put in place permanently had to do with the intervention of the superordinate state authorities who were not willing to tolerate these kinds of measures because they defied the ethnically neutral and socially just intentions of the amendment to the law on the right of domicile from 1896. Accordingly, the Imperial-Royal Ministry of the Interior informed the governors and other officials in 1900 that they should fiercely oppose municipal attempts to hinder the acquisition of the right of domicile by immigrants who were legally entitled to it. To enforce this policy, the ministry advised, the authorities should employ all the administrative power they possessed or, if these failed, they should exercise their influence in more informal ways.[94]

Officially, however, the interpretation of the legal stipulations did not lie in the hands of the ministry, but rather it fell under the jurisdiction of the courts. In 1906, the Higher Administrative Court passed its final judgement on the questions that had been raised. It also disapproved of the measures adopted by the Viennese administration, and emphasized that in the interests of the free movement of citizens and a just distribution of the burden of poor relief, the municipalities were required to grant formal admission to those automatically entitled to domicile. According to the court, the municipalities in question had no right to overrule this stipulation.[95] In terms of the right of domicile, therefore, the superordinate state authorities and courts enforced an ethnically neutral and non-exclusive approach to municipal membership that sometimes went against the wishes of the respective municipal administrations.[96] As of 1906 at the latest, poor relief as well as the social welfare system were governed by a principle of ethnic neutrality.

Promises of Equality, a Politics of Recognition and Racist Discrimination in India

Following the Indian rebellion or war against the British East India Company in 1857, the government in London took over direct control of much of the south Asian subcontinent in 1858. Upon acquiring sovereignty over the territory, the government guaranteed the realm's new Indian subjects – 'of whatever race or creed' – 'equal and impartial protection of the law' in the Queen's Proclamation.[97] At the time, the most established of the existing structures of governance were the supposedly ethnically neutral British-Indian systems of law and administration in the presidencies of Bengal, Madras (now Chennai) and Bombay (now Mumbai), the oldest bastions of rule under the British East India Company. Over the course of the eighteenth and nineteenth centuries, the British East India Company had brought the rest of the subcontinent under its control. Only the territories of the so-called Indian princely states remained officially autonomous. After 1858, however, even politics in these territories fell under the thumb of British agents.

In 1876, Queen Victoria was crowned Empress of India, effectively expressing the British claim to supremacy in all of India; the Crown not only asserted its direct rule over British India, but also its indirect control over the princely states. The British-Indian government itself also pursued a course of territorial expansion. To the north-west, this prompted military conflicts in Afghanistan as well as a rivalry with the Russian Empire; and to the east, it led to the annexation of Burma in 1886. Within British India, the government sought to consolidate its administration. Not least because of the allegedly excellent administration on the subcontinent, fans of the empire referred to India as the 'jewel in the crown' of the British Empire. The Indian Civil Service was a significant factor in this regard. This corps of civil servants, mostly recruited from the United Kingdom, held the top offices in the Indian administration. The government of British India was headed by a governor-general who bore the title of viceroy and was appointed by the government in London. The India Office in the capital sought to exercise control over the Indian government, at least to the extent allowed considering the vast distance between the two. Ultimately, the parliament in London acted as the supreme legislative body and determined the political structure of India.

The British cited two main justifications to legitimize their rule in India. Whereas one approach emphasized the difference between 'natives' and 'Europeans' in an orientalist sense, the other sought to eliminate this difference by 'civilizing' the Indian population. Advocates of the first position justified British rule with the right of conquest or with the dire need to fill the vacuum of power that had resulted at the end of the Mogul Empire. The proponents of the 'civilizing mission', in contrast, argued that the Indian population would advance politically, culturally and economically under British rule so that it could then govern itself. The contradiction inherent within this supposedly liberal paradigm that justified British rule with its imminent end, as well as the fundamental juxtaposition between these two approaches, shaped the contours of British politics and administration in India.

Alongside these ideological conflicts, economic and military interests also defined British policies in India. On the one hand, India was seen as a market for British goods as well as a depot for British investment capital; at the same time, however, it was seen as a supplier of raw materials and labour migrants; these 'indentured labourers', however, were very much at the mercy of their employers.

In terms of military interests, the Indian army was the focal point because it was financed by the taxes raised in India and was paramount to upholding the power of the British Empire in imperial conflicts. Simultaneously, the army was also the foundation of the autocratic administration. India repeatedly experienced rebellions and food riots and, after the turn of the century, anarchistic and nationalistic uprisings as well. The colonial authorities diffused these situations with violence and reacted with increasingly repressive countermeasures, none of which would have been possible without military control.

In a social and cultural sense, the British sought to impose a European model in India, which contributed to the delineation of different social and ethnic groups. For example, the Permanent Settlement of 1793 set large landowners apart from the common population, and the Code of Criminal Procedure distinguished between 'Europeans' and 'natives'. However, these categories and hierarchies were often challenged by hybrid groups such as 'European vagrants', 'Anglo-Indians' and British-educated 'Indians'. Many of the 'Indians' with British educational backgrounds played a pivotal role in the emergence of the Indian nationalist movement that demanded political participation and ultimately voiced demands for a separate, self-governing parliament for India after the turn of the century.

The Reforms of 1918–19 and Ethnic Differences in the Electorate

If the question of the legal and administrative treatment of ethnic heterogeneity in India is approached from the end of the period examined in this book, the so-called Montagu–Chelmsford reforms come to mind first. With this reform project, the government – partly in response to the Indian nationalist movement – sought to continue its careful course of expanding the rights of political participation in which ethnic differences among the Indian population played a decisive role. The reform agenda, named after the Secretary of State for India at the time, Edwin Montagu, and the viceroy Lord Chelmsford, was based on the notion 'that India could be reshaped in the image of England' and 'that responsible government ... should be extended to India'.[98] The deliberations over these plans began in 1916. During this time, India's great financial and military contributions to the British war effort meant that the demands for more political participation weighed heavily in the debates.[99] The discussions circled around two main points. On the one hand, there was the question of what would make for a suitable mix of democratic government and autocratic-colonial administration. On the other hand, there were disagreements over the details of who was to be entitled to vote and the introduction of ethnically defined electorates.

The Government of India Act of 1919 ultimately determined that 105 of the 144 members of the new legislative assembly for India would be elected and the

Table 2.1. Distribution of the elected members of the legislative assembly across the provinces and electorates according to the Government of India Act of 1919

Electorates Provinces	General	Muslim	Sikh	Large Landowners	Europeans	Indian Chambers of Commerce	Total
Madras	10	3	–	1	1	1	16
Bombay	7	4	–	1	2	2	16
Bengal	6	6	–	1	3	1	17
United Provinces	8	6	–	1	1	–	16
Punjab	3	6	2	1	–	–	12
Bihar and Orissa	8	3	–	1	–	–	12
Central Provinces	4	1	–	1	–	–	6
Assam	2	1	–	–	1	–	4
Burma	3	–	–	–	1	–	4
Delhi	1	–	–	–	–	–	1
Ajmer Merwara	1	–	–	–	–	–	1
Total	**53**	**30**	**2**	**7**	**9**	**4**	**105**

other members would be appointed by the government. The 105 elected seats were distributed across the provinces and different electorates (see Table 2.1).[100] According to the tax census, 900,000 people were entitled to vote, which was roughly equivalent to 0.5 per cent of the entire population.[101] Women, men under the age of 21, 'persons of unsound mind' and foreigners were denied suffrage according to the law.[102]

The exclusion of women met with a wave of resistance. '[N]umerous petitions from women of the educated classes' demanded equality or at least suffrage for women with university degrees. The Chief Commissioner of Assam, in contrast, advocated only the enfranchisement of 'European women'. The committee in charge of the franchise issue spoke out against suffrage for women, citing the traditional division of the male and female spheres as well as the 'social condition' of women in India. The only member of the committee in favour of women's suffrage was Sir Sankaran Nair.[103]

In the end, the new suffrage regulations differentiated between individuals on the basis of social as well as ethnic criteria; chambers of commerce and large landowners were guaranteed 'special representation' while Muslims and Sikhs were granted 'communal representation'. Akin to the Moravian Compromise, these reforms incorporated a mix of social and ethnic criteria that drew lines between different groups. Apparently, however, British contemporaries were not aware of these parallels – or they consciously chose not to refer to the Austrian case: '[Responsible government] appeared only when the territorial principle had vanquished the tribal principle … The solitary examples that we can discover of opposing principle are those of Austria, a few of the smaller German states, and Cyprus. It is hardly necessary to explain why we dismiss these as irrelevant or unconvincing.'[104]

The question of which groups were to be entitled to or denied 'communal representation' figured prominently in the negotiations.[105] The representation of Muslims in particular was a major issue in terms of the elections for the provincial councils as well as the Indian legislative assembly at large.[106] Earlier reforms had already introduced separate Muslim electorates, contributing to the transformation of the religious difference between Muslims and Hindus into what increasingly came to be seen as an ethnic difference.[107] Simultaneously, the political significance of the Muslim League kept growing. Its representatives demanded 'Home Rule' for India at the end of 1916, together with the Indian National Congress, and they presented a joint reform proposal. According to the league's suggestion, a certain number of electoral seats were supposed to be reserved for Muslims, amounting to 30 per cent in the Legislative Council of the United Provinces and a third of the Indian Legislative Assembly.[108] This reform proposal was one of the most influential of the many drafts that circulated during the deliberations.

The establishment of the Muslim electorates was not very controversial. Almost all of the provincial governments supported this suggestion.[109] Montagu and Chelmsford's report, however, emphasized that the special treatment of ethnic groups within the franchise should be considered an exception to the rule.[110] The representatives of the Indian National Congress from the United Provinces pointed out in return that 'communal representation' should be replaced as soon as possible with a system of proportional representation that would also guarantee the political representation of minorities.[111] Ultimately, Muslim electorates were established in almost all of the provinces, and 23 per cent of the seats in the United Provinces were reserved for Muslim delegates.[112]

There were also other groups that demanded separate electorates. In Punjab, for example, the reforms granted the Sikhs 'communal representation'.[113] The 'Europeans', on the other hand, were less successful in their efforts. Citing the fact that they were the only ones already familiar with the system of 'responsible government', they demanded 'a separate electorate and representation in proportion to their importance rather than their numerical strength'.[114] Among others, Chelmsford was opposed to this move because he did not want to offer the 'racialist attitude of the European community' any kind of political stage.[115] Consequently, the 'European' representatives in the Legislative Assembly were not elected by a 'white' electorate, but rather by the 'European' chambers of commerce and plantation owners. 'European British subjects' were only granted communal representation in a few provincial councils. In the United Provinces, for example, where 'Europeans' made up less than 0.1 per cent of the population, they were given one of the 118 seats.[116]

Not least because of their loyalty to the British-Indian government, the 'Anglo-Indians' also demanded their own electorate.[117] This group, with its 'intermediate position between the races of the East and West', was only afforded 'communal representation' in the provincial councils of Madras and Bengal; in the other provinces, the delegates nominated by the government represented their interests.[118] The 'Indian Christians' were dealt with in a similar manner in that they only received a separate electorate in the province of Madras.[119]

Alongside such ethnic, 'racist' and religious differences, social differences also played a decisive role in the suffrage debates. The category of 'Panchamas', for example, was based on the stratification within the Indian caste system. In Madras, communal representation was demanded for the so-called untouchables because many people were convinced that the representation of their interests had to be guaranteed by law as they would otherwise have little access to the political sphere due to their low social status and lack of education.[120] In this case, the government took on a protective position and sought to increase the number of nominated representatives for this group.[121] Likewise, nominations were supposed to account for the interests of the 'depressed classes' and the population of the 'backward tracts' in the provincial councils.[122] This is by no means the complete list of the groups for which the committee discussed special forms of representation. The 'Mahishyas of Bengal and Assam, the Marwaris of Calcutta, the Bengali domiciled community of Bihar and Orissa, the Ahoms of Assam, the Mahars of the Central Provinces, the Uriyas of Madras and the Parsis of Bombay' as well as others failed in their attempts to attain communal representation.[123] The length of this list illustrates just how much these different groups associated the acquisition of their own electorate with prestige as well as the recognition of their political relevance.

All told, there were two main positions put forth in the debates on suffrage reform. One side sought to establish a uniform electorate for all of India that was to be divided territorially into constituencies. From this point of view, communal representation was only supposed to be a temporary measure used only on an exceptional basis. This approach was favoured by the Indian Minister, Montagu, who at least theoretically strove to achieve the modernization and democratization of the political system in India on the basis of supra-ethnic interests and the 'greater welfare of the whole'.[124] Similar to the debates in Austria, there were also some in India – especially within the nationalist movement – who believed that the creation of a single electorate would overcome the conflicts between the different ethnic, religious and social groups. A new 'feeling of nationality', according to this argument, would strengthen the conviction that each subject was 'as much a citizen of the country as any other', and weld everyone together in a single 'body-politic'.[125]

In contrast, opponents claimed that the ethnic and social heterogeneity of India made special forms of representation that took into account the differences within the population indispensable.[126] Proponents of this approach included the majority of the Indian government as well as the so-called Southborough Committee, which was responsible for working out the details of the franchise reforms. Although the committee did express the hope that 'it will be possible at no distant date to merge all communities into one general electorate', it nevertheless underscored the differences between groups with its decision to provide representation for different interests in the form of either separate electorates or nominated appointments to the legislative bodies.[127] The Southborough Committee generally preferred communal representation for the established native and colonial elites in particular.[128] The Indian government, in contrast, favoured nominations – not least because it would then be responsible for the appointments itself – and depicted itself as the guarantor of the interests of all disadvantaged groups.[129]

Unlike in Austria, proportional representation also played a role in the debates in India. However, the suggestion that 'in a country like India, inhabited as it is by people of various castes and religions, Proportional Representation is the only means by which it is possible adequately to secure electoral justice to the divergent elements that constitute the nation,'[130] found little support. In general, the Montagu–Chelmsford reforms clung to the British system of majority representation in which each territorially defined constituency elected just one representative. Plural constituencies were only established in Madras and Bombay in which the top two or more candidates receiving the most votes could win a seat in the assembly.[131] This model, which was similar to that of proportional representation, guaranteed political representation for minorities within a homogeneous electorate.

In sum, one can say that the statist principle of recognizing differences based on ethnic criteria stood at the heart of the attempt to ensure political representation for minorities in India. The Indian administration in particular saw itself as a supra-ethnic, neutral arbitrator. At the same time, the over-representation and privileged status afforded 'Europeans' reflects elements of a more discriminatory imperialist approach. Consequently, the mechanisms of recognition that were put in place can be seen as a strategy designed to prevent – under the classic motto of 'divide and conquer' – internal homogenization along the lines of a nation-state, which was the goal of the Indian nationalist movement.

The Status of India and Indian Subjects in the Empire: Nationalist Perspectives

In the debates over the protection of minorities, members of the nationalist movement repeatedly touted that a single Indian nation – *une et indivisible* – would herald the elimination of all differences. Yet the nationalist movement itself was not unified and indivisible. A split emerged between the moderate and radical fractions within the movement in the early twentieth century. The two sides fought over what they perceived as the proper mix of democratic participation and colonial autocracy within the context of the Montagu–Chelmsford reforms. They questioned how power should be divided among London, the government of British India and the provincial administrations controlled by elected councils. Montagu and Chelmsford suggested a dyarchy model that would gradually shift sovereignty from London to the democratically legitimized Indian government.[132] In doing so, they touched on the issue of national self-determination, which was discussed internationally at the end of the First World War. The Indian national-ist movement called upon the Allies to uphold the principles that they themselves demanded of their opponents: 'That which they claim for Poland, for Bohemia, for Italia Irredenta, for Alsace-Lorraine, for Serbia, for Montenegro, for Bosnia, for Herzegovina, they must claim also for Ireland and for India'.[133]

Three main positions were put forth in terms of how independent India was supposed to become. The governors of the Indian provinces in particular demanded dictatorial powers for themselves within the dyarchy. A strengthening of the colonial executive, they argued, would help to protect the Indian popula-tion at large against autochthonous oligarchs.[134] The Anglo-British Association also supported this position because it was concerned about the preservation of British economic interests in India.[135] The second, intermediary position was that of the moderate nationalists. They advocated keeping sovereignty in the hands of London as a counterbalance to the power of the colonial administration. At the same time, they also called for more extensive powers for the provincial gov-ernments that were controlled by the councils, especially in terms of budgetary matters, so that they could effectively fight 'the increasing poverty of India'.[136] In principle, the moderates were willing to work within the framework of the reforms. The radicals, on the other hand, actually refused to collaborate with the reform programme proposed by Montagu and Chelmsford. They criticized the suggested reforms as 'insufficiently progressive', and demanded the complete transfer of power to democratic institutions on the provincial level as well as a partial transfer of power on the central level.[137]

Parallel to the question of Indian independence, there were also lively debates over the legal status of individual Indian subjects within the empire. The key issue at hand was the supposed equality of all British subjects and the concept of reciprocity by which Indian subjects in other parts of the empire should be entitled to the same rights enjoyed by British subjects from the rest of the empire in India.[138] In particular, the debates circled around the legal discrimination against Indian migrants in the dominions.[139] '[W]hat is the status of us Indians in this Empire?', questioned Gopal Krishna Gokhale in 1910 in light of Natal's politics of immigration in the legislative council in Delhi, and with reference to the obligation of the government in London 'to ensure to us just and humane and gradually even equal treatment in this Empire'.[140] From the turn of the century, Indian representatives in the council had begun to complain even more about the treatment of Indian immigrants, in particular in South Africa. The Indian government repeatedly promised to do its best to advocate for equality for Indian subjects.[141] Yet, the words of Viceroy Minto reveal just how ambivalent the government in Delhi was when it came to the idea of equality: 'Important classes of the population' in India, according to Minto in 1910, 'are learning to realise their own position ... and to compare their claims, for an equality of citizenship, with those of a ruling race'.[142]

Whereas Minto linked the notion of legal equality with certain positions within a racist hierarchy, thereby stripping it of its real meaning, Indian representatives in the council drafted a concept of equality that had nothing to do with 'racist' differences; they spoke of 'rights as citizens of the British Empire, solemnly and permanently secured to them [the Indian subjects] by the noble Proclamations by their beloved Sovereigns'.[143] Another member of the council rhetorically questioned: 'Shall British citizenship be a by-word among the nations of the earth or a reality under which British Indians enjoy equal rights with other subjects of His Majesty the King-Emperor?'[144] These arguments in fact contributed to the addition of clauses to the Emigration Act of 1910 that allowed for emigration prohibitions if 'the Governor General is dissatisfied with the treatment of free Indians' in the territory in question.[145] In 1911, emigration to the colony of Natal was indeed prohibited on this basis. During the First World War, however, the viceroy hindered further attempts to exert pressure on the dominions.[146] But, in 1917, the military authorities pushed through a general emigration prohibition in order to prevent the exodus of men who could be called to military service.[147] Although it was ultimately impossible to enforce the statist principle of ethnic neutrality and to achieve equality between 'Indian' and 'European' subjects of the British Crown, these debates in the early twentieth century nonetheless brought the notion of equal citizenship within the empire to the forefront of political debate for the first time.[148]

Prior to 1900, discrimination against Indian labour migrants and the so-called indenture system – which was condemned as a form of slavery in 1910 – attracted much less critique.[149] During this time, emigration laws only ensured for the health, the contractual rights and the return of Indian migrants. The protective paternalist intent of these laws was clearly reflected in a decree issued in 1886 that at least one baby soother per every five hundred migrants had to be carried aboard an emigrant ship.[150] In the last decades of the nineteenth century, the demands of the Indian nationalist movement concentrated less on equal rights for Indian migrants within the empire; rather it was focused on the Native Volunteer Movement and the right of Indian subjects to bear arms, as well as the Ilbert Bill debate and the elimination of differential treatment for 'Europeans' and 'natives' within the Code of Criminal Procedure.[151]

The Ilbert Bill Debate in 1883–84 and Imperialist Discrimination

The Indian Code of Criminal Procedure emphasized the equality of all before the law, regardless of ethnic identity, but it also contained two stipulations that differentiated between 'whites' and 'non-whites'. Unlike 'natives', for example, 'European British subjects' who had been accused of a crime had to be brought before a justice of the peace. This office, moreover, could only be held by a 'European'. Furthermore, 'European' defendants had a right to a trial by jury in which at least half of the members were also 'white'.[152] The main purpose of these stipulations was to prevent 'Indians' from having a right to pass legal judgement over 'Europeans'.[153] The first attempt to weaken this racist discrimination in the criminal code failed in 1872. At the same time, however, it was possible for 'Indians' to preside in court over 'Europeans' in the Presidencies. Particularly in the country's interior, referred to as 'mufassil', where the courts were often considered to be unreliable, there was a strict adherence to the idea that a 'native judge' could not pass judgement over a 'European' defendant. This discrepancy, as well as the lack of qualified personnel in the Indian Civil Service, made it difficult to ensure that a 'European' judge presided in every case against a 'European', which in turn led to its own set of problems. Ultimately, this situation unleashed a new wave of debates over racist discrimination within the Code of Criminal Procedure.[154]

In February 1883, Courtenay Ilbert presented a draft law on behalf of the Indian government that was intended to eliminate 'race distinctions, which are as invidious as they are unnecessary'.[155] He later back-pedalled on this statement, claiming that the goal was merely the 'removal … of race-disqualifications' for judges, not the complete eradication of race-based distinctions within the Code of Criminal Procedure.[156] That said, however, Ilbert portrayed the abolition of ethnic differences within the law and the creation of a homogeneous legal sphere as one of Britain's long-term political goals in India, citing both the Charter Act of 1833 as well as the Queen's Proclamation of 1858. He claimed that the administration of justice had since then been modernized and standardized to such an extent that the judicature and the career tracks for 'native' and 'European' judges could now be unified, the distinction between 'Presidency Towns' and the 'mufassil' could be removed, and the equality of all before the law could now be put in place.[157] The racist distinctions within the Code of Criminal Procedure, according to Ilbert, were an anomaly and contradicted the notion that the British Empire was an 'Empire of law'.[158] The majority of the council supported the draft law in the hope that it would promote 'good feeling and cordiality between European and Native Civilians which are indispensable to their working together',[159] and 'assist them [the Natives of India] in their onward progress'.[160] Indian representatives in the council likewise hoped that the amendment would succeed in 'raising the weak and lowly to the level of the strong and high, and making equal law and equal justice the basis of political paramountcy in the world'.[161]

The opponents of the proposed law pointed to the objections of the non-official 'Europeans' in India against the provisions. Moreover, they claimed in a paternalistic way that the 'Indians' themselves were not interested in legal equality as they had only been talked into thinking that it was a good idea.[162] The Chambers of Commerce also feared that the changes would lead to the withdrawal of British capital invested in India.[163] Additionally, opponents argued that there was no 'European' public that controlled the justice system in the hinterlands as there was in the Presidencies, which meant that only the existing legal privileges protected 'European' defendants against having to stand before a judge 'alien in thought and moral standard, and ignorant of the manners, customs and habits of the accused', and being convicted on the basis of scurrilous accusations made by 'natives'.[164] The cultural difference between 'Indians' and 'Europeans', they also maintained, could not be overcome through an English education – 'unless Christianity is a sham, and the belief in national character a delusion'.[165] Based on the assumption of innate differences, these racist arguments were supposedly affirmed in the example of a murderer, who 'wholly unprovoked, ripped open a child, tore out its entrails, devoured them before the eyes of his still living victim, was apprehended actually red-handed, attempted no denial, and pleaded only the deliberate fulfilment of a vow to a goddess', and was then only sentenced to three years in prison by an 'Indian' judge.[166]

A further objection was made in relation to Ilbert's reference to the 'empire of law', which opponents countered with the slogan 'empire of prestige'. The rhetorical question of whether 'there ever [was] a nation that maintained its supremacy by the righteousness of its laws', was dismissed by the proposed law's critics who asserted that law in India had always rested on military power:[167]'[The Government of India] is essentially an absolute Government founded not on consent, but on conquest.'[168] Yet another argument against the Ilbert Bill did not question the rule of law itself, but rather called upon Magna Carta as the embodiment of an old and honoured tradition of law: 'Every Englishman carries with him the feeling that it is his birth-right to be tried by his peers, a right given to him by Magna Charta ... The Englishman feels that if tried by a Native he will not be tried by "legale judicium parium suorum"'.[169] In a sense, this argument transferred the status of equality enjoyed among aristocrats and commoners – the peers of Magna Carta – onto the notion of the equality shared among the members of one 'race'. This argument therefore implicitly equated the heritability of social status within the feudal system with the inheritance of 'racial' identity within the colonial hierarchy. In a paradoxical way, however, this argument drew on a document that was considered to be the basis for the 'rights of Englishmen' and therefore the concept of equal citizenship in order to justify 'racial' discrimination. Ilbert commented on this rather dubious stretch of the imagination in a historical sense, noting 'that Magna Charta has as much to do with the Bill now before us as Domesday Book has to do with the Permanent Settlement.'[170]

The Ilbert Bill also led to widespread political debates outside the Legislative Council in India as well as in London.[171] After all, the whole conflict was sparked in the British capital. On 5 February 1883, three days after the draft bill was proposed, *The Times* in London predicted the 'intense unpopularity' of the amendment and claimed that the elimination of the racist privileges for 'Europeans' was akin to the relinquishment of British rule over India. It was not until the next day that the papers in Calcutta turned the Ilbert Bill into a big issue.[172] In turn, this led to numerous assemblies and demonstrations in favour of and against the bill in India.[173] In March, the 'European and Anglo-Indian Defence Association', financed by British-Indian entrepreneurs, was founded to organize the protests. A large portion of the British civil service, and the majority of 'Anglo-Indians', supported the opposition to the bill led by the non-official 'Europeans'.[174] Gender differences also played a key role in these debates. On the one hand, opponents pointed out the potential dangers faced by 'European' women in order to win support for their cause, often objecting to the 'policy of placing Englishwomen under the criminal jurisdiction of polygamists'.[175] On the other hand, they decried the arguments for the bill as unnatural by emphasizing their nationalist-emancipatory, anti-colonial and feminist elements. In doing so, those opposed to the bill sought to reinforce the 'racial hierarchy' by linking it to the 'supposedly more natural gender hierarchy'.[176]

The attempt to drum up opposition to the bill in the heartland of the empire, however, met with little success. For example, the parliamentary committee of the English Trades Union Congress expressly refused to support the bill's opponents.[177] Moreover, the British government took sides against the critics of the Ilbert Bill.[178] The position maintained by the government in London made it possible for the Indian government to save face while also negotiating a compromise that did not entirely do away with the principle of legal equality. In its final form, the draft bill allowed for high-ranking 'Indian' judges to preside over cases involving 'Europeans', but it also extended the right of 'Europeans' to a trial by a jury in which at least half of the jurors were 'European'.[179] It must also be noted, though, that as of 1884, there were only three 'Indian' judges who were high-ranking enough to preside over the trials of 'Europeans'. In his statement on this compromise, the viceroy expressed his displeasure with the methods and arguments used by the opposition, and he reaffirmed his commitment to legal equality as a long-term goal.[180] Despite his declaration, a renewed attempt to expand legal equality in 1898 and extend the right to a trial by jury to 'natives' also failed.[181] Opponents to this move maintained that a trial by jury only made sense within an ethnically uniform society because such a procedure necessitated 'a homogenous people' – in the sense of uniform and united – 'who make their own laws, and are determined that those laws shall be enforced'.[182]

Accordingly, they claimed, the 'non-European' population in India did not fulfil this requirement.

The debate over the way to handle ethnic differences in the Code of Criminal Procedure was shaped by fundamentally different principles. The mostly conservative opponents of legal equality, especially within the 'European' public and on the lower levels of the Indian administration, stressed the irreconcilable nature of the racial differences between 'Europeans' and 'natives'. At the same time, they also highlighted the necessarily violent character of colonial rule, thereby making the case for imperialist mechanisms of discrimination. Those who spoke out for a more liberal position within the upper ranks of the British-Indian government and in the Indian nationalist movement, on the other hand, focused on education, progress and the chance to fill the gaps in a civilizing sense. Therefore, they promoted legal equality and ethnic neutrality along statist lines.[183] In the end, however, legal equality was not achieved during the more liberal 1880s, nor in the more conservative 1890s. Rather, the difference between 'natives' and 'Europeans' increasingly took on racist overtones, thereby strengthening the strains of imperialist discrimination at work in India.

The Ambivalent Legal Status of the Nationals of the Indian Princely States

Another group that met with legal discrimination encompassed the members of the pseudo-sovereign Indian princely states or 'Native States'. This group was defined according to purely official criteria. Unlike most inhabitants of British India, they were not British subjects as they had only been accorded the less privileged status of 'British protected persons'.[184] Whereas these protected persons fell wholly under the jurisdiction of the princely states, British subjects enjoyed the protection of British jurisdiction even within the princely states. The authorities were particularly interested in ensuring this privilege for the 'European British subjects of Her Majesty', who were not to be subject to local jurisdiction.[185]

After 'white' Britons, either in the service of the East India Company or the Crown, were permitted to enter and settle within the princely states for the first time in 1858, the question emerged at the beginning of the twentieth century as to whether their privileged legal status as British subjects could be passed from generation to generation *ad infinitum* within the princely states that were considered to be foreign countries for the purposes of the nationality law. According to the provisions then in force, it was only possible to pass British subjecthood over two generations. Theoretically, the great grandchildren of the first 'European' immigrants could no longer claim to be treated as British subjects.[186] In order to permanently guarantee the privileges of 'European' subjects in the princely states, the administration suggested allowing for the perpetual inheritance of

British subject status abroad. However, this move met with scepticism because it would have guaranteed the descendants of 'Indian' British subjects an unlimited claim to the protection of the British state abroad as well.[187] For this reason, the India Office suggested refraining from issuing an official legal regulation and offered an administrative solution instead. In cases 'relating to a great grandson of an European British subject in a native state', it advised the authorities, 'if the man was to all practical intents and purposes what would ordinarily be called a European', to simply ensure by informal intervention that the individual in question be tried before a British court as opposed to the 'native courts'. A similar procedure was already employed in cases concerning non-British 'Europeans'.[188] In doing so, the official legal distinction between British subjects and the members of the Indian princely states was turned into a 'racial' distinction between 'Europeans' and 'natives' that was mostly enforced by ad hoc administrative decisions. This created a grey area for the administration where they could afford privileges to 'whites' and refuse them to 'non-whites', irrespective of whether the persons involved were British subjects or not.

Ultimately, the lack of a clear distinction between the status of subjects and protected persons made it possible to manipulate the administrative handling of these matters. Consequently, the British authorities ran into trouble when it came to explaining or clarifying these differences as soon as the residents of the Indian princely states applied for naturalization. As protected persons, these individuals were neither nationals nor foreigners, but rather something in between. When they sought naturalization in the UK, however, the problem of their nationality in terms of the law had to be resolved: they were either subjects, which meant that naturalization was irrelevant, or they were aliens who had to be naturalized in order to become British subjects. At the end of 1889, for example, a 23-year-old single surgeon, Kuman Bhabendra Narayan, who was living in London, applied for British subjecthood as a 'natural-born Subject of the State of His Highness the Maharajah of Kuch Behar'.[189] The Home Office, which more or less supported his application, consulted the India Office on how to proceed. The officials in the India Office conceded that '[i]t seems to be somewhat unfortunate, just now, that subjects of native states should be allowed to fall between two stools', but it nonetheless requested that the application be refused and that no official reasons should be given. According to the India Office, it was not a smart move to firmly clarify the status of the subjects of the Indian princely states. The India Office therefore forbade 'any allusion in refusing his application to the question of his Foreign or British Nationality'.[190] The Home Office found the explanations from the India Office somewhat confusing, so it asked for clearer directions on how to proceed in such cases. However, this request was retracted 'after discussion in committee and semi-official correspondence with India Office'. The semi-official character of these negotiations is highlighted by the fact that a couple of pages have been removed from the file.[191]

Quite obviously, the India Office sought to avoid clarifying the legal status of the subjects of the Native States. This ambiguity afforded the authorities a maximum amount of leeway when it came to determining who should be granted or denied certain rights. To this extent, discriminatory practices based on 'racial' criteria were hidden behind this inclusive exclusion of 'protected persons' in a grey zone between nationals and foreigners.

Immigration and Naturalization in India

The question still remains, however, as to whether and how ethnic differences played a role in immigration and naturalization policies in India. The legal status of immigrants was determined by the Foreigners Act of 1864. This act allowed for the deportation of foreigners and required them to register with the police.[192] At first, these provisions mainly affected 'European' immigrants. It was not until the end of the nineteenth century that immigration from non-European countries became more significant, especially as Chinese immigration to Burma increased. Within this context, the US government inquired as to the regulations affecting 'Chinese immigration' in the British Empire. The Indian government replied that there were 'no such regulations in existence'.[193] In fact, there is no mention of any other kinds of immigration regulations, not least any ethnically exclusive immigration policies, in the sources for this period all the way up to the First World War.

A look at the files related to naturalization also confirms that the Indian authorities by and large maintained a practice of ethnic neutrality. According to a law from 1852, 'any person whilst actually residing within British India' could apply for naturalization. Only 'a short statement as to the origin and residence of the applicants and the purposes for which the applications were made' had to be provided.[194] In general, the legislature as well as the administration had little to do with questions of naturalization. This was tied to the fact that attaining the status of a British subject in India did not really accord any kind of citizenship rights until the end of the First World War. Naturalization was therefore only relevant for economic elites or those who sought to attain a position in the administration.[195] In comparison to Canada, for example, the number of immigrants was also considerably lower. It was not until the early twentieth century that the government in London began to take an interest in naturalization in India as it began deliberations over a standard empire-wide policy on naturalization. Within this context, the Indian naturalization statistics for 1905 to 1907 were recorded in London.[196]

During this period, ninety-nine applications were made, and eighty-five of them were approved. The largest number of applicants (twenty-four) came from the Ottoman Empire whereas eighteen came from China (and had settled in

Burma), fourteen from Persia, eight from Germany, and seven from Russia and the Indian princely states, respectively; an additional four came from Romania, three from Greece and two each from Italy, Austria-Hungary, Denmark and Goa. There was also one applicant each from Afghanistan, Bahrain, Kuwait, Switzerland, Bulgaria and Abyssinia. This geographic distribution was roughly equivalent to that of immigration to India in general. Most immigrants to India came from the Near East, the Far East and central Asia. The few non-British Europeans who settled permanently in India were more likely to apply for naturalization. The authorities denied naturalization to four applicants from the Ottoman Empire, three from Persia, two from the Indian princely states, one each from Germany, Russia, Greece, Goa and Abyssinia. In most cases, the reason given for the refusal was that the intent of the individual to reside permanently in India seemed rather dubious. No specific pattern of inclusion or exclusion can be detected in the distribution of the refusals, which largely correlates to the distribution of the applications across the different countries of origin. There were Christians and Muslims, Jews and Arabs, Chinese and Europeans among those naturalized, as well as among those whose requests were denied. Therefore, an ethnically defined pattern of inclusion or exclusion did not affect naturalization in India.

Rather, ethnic neutrality and a statist approach reigned supreme. These principles were also to be found among the proponents of the Ilbert Bill as well as in the claims of the Indian nationalist movement for legal equality. The elements of recognition associated with a statist approach, moreover, also bore fruit in the Montagu–Chelmsford reforms. Yet the ethnic differentiation within these measures can be seen as an attempt to stall internal processes of homogenization along the lines of the nation-state. The reforms of 1918–19 also revealed discriminatory tendencies. The laws on criminal procedure, however, were clearly informed by imperialist notions. In the case of India as a whole, the imperialist and statist approaches were both coexistent and influential. This simultaneity and ambivalence was most thoroughly expressed in the Indian government's vacillation between promises of equality, policies of neutrality with regards to the ethnically heterogeneous population, and guarantees of 'European' privileges.

The Formation and Determination of Ethnic Identities

In Austria, the matter was less ambiguous. The development of nationality and citizenship laws was clearly shaped by statist notions. The military and economic interests of the state were paramount in the mostly ethnically neutral policies put in place. Nationalist and anti-Semitic demands for ethnic exclusion never gained a foothold in Cisleithanian policies concerning nationality and citizenship. In terms of suffrage as well as cultural autonomy, mechanisms that recognized difference emerged after the turn of the twentieth century. These were intended to quell the tides of conflict between the different nationalities. From this perspective, the late Habsburg monarchy was less marked by an unavoidable conflict between centripetal and centrifugal forces than it was by the theoretically successful attempt to adapt an older statist model to deal with the rising challenge of ethnonational identities and differences in the early twentieth century.

Similarities and Differences:
Bureaucratic Reactions to Ethnization Processes

In Austria as well as India, the strength of the statist approach and seemingly rational adherence to the interests of the state in opposition to racist and nationalist demands rested on similar administrative traditions that ensured the proper functioning – at least in their own opinion – of irreplaceable and perfectly organized bureaucratic apparatuses.[197] In India, the administration drew on the Queen's Proclamation of 1858 as well as utilitarian and liberal notions that adhered to a long-term goal of overcoming ethnic differences and establishing legal equality for all.[198] The course of ethnic neutrality pursued within the Austrian bureaucracy, on the other hand, could be traced back to the era of enlightened absolutism and the reforms of Joseph II.[199] Utilitarianism as well as Josephinism both justified a somewhat ruthless experimentation with administrative techniques in the name of achieving an efficient, rational and just machinery of government. In this sense, both the Austrian and Indian bureaucracies sought to bind their ethnically heterogeneous populations into unified states with a uniform legal framework. At first glance, the creation of ethnically defined electorates such as in the Moravian Compromise of 1905 or in the Montagu–Chelmsford reforms of 1918–19 appears to contradict these homogenizing impulses. Yet, these manifestations of a politics of recognition should more aptly be seen as an attempt to counteract the tendencies towards ethnization and nationalization that emerged in the early twentieth century without having to completely abandon the principle of ethnic neutrality. Both the Austrian and the Indian governments sought to stage themselves as benevolent supra-ethnic referees seeking to guarantee equality among the different ethnonational groups.

These efforts met with much less success in India than they did in Cisleithania. The failed attempt to erase the discriminatory distinctions between 'Europeans' and 'natives' in terms of the Code of Criminal Procedure, as well as the privileges accorded 'European' voters in the reforms of 1918–19, demonstrate how imperialist discrimination often clouded statist intentions. The utilitarian and liberal perspectives that justified British rule as a civilizing mission with the end goal of universal equality in the future, on the other hand, were ultimately entangled with conservative arguments that stressed the rights of conquest in a colonial context. Despite these contradictions, both positions often led to similar results in the realm of practice. In fact, imperialist as well as statist approaches influenced the developments in India in a kind of contradictory simultaneity.

This inconsistency was by and large the result of India's colonial-peripheral position within the British Empire. Although the government in Delhi repeatedly tried to boost its prestige within the empire, and to insist on the same status as that of the governments in the dominions, the debate over the discrimination against Indian subjects in South Africa and other parts of the empire point to the failure of these undertakings. Even within India itself, the government did not manage to assert itself over the 'European' public, who insisted on keeping their 'racist' privileges. Such strong colonial asymmetries did not exist in Cisleithania, which made it easier for the statist approach to spread its wings in a more consistent way. Moreover, the varying ways in which ethnic differences and identities were formed and determined in India and Austria also paved the way for divergent developments with respect to nationality, citizenship and ethnic diversity.

Concessions, Sidestepping Tactics and the Formation of Ethnic Differences

If ethnic differences do not simply exist, but are rather social constructs embedded in a historical context, the question remains as to how they are created. Scholars often distinguish between identity-building processes from above and those from below. For example, the formation of the identities of 'the Muslims' and 'the Hindus' in opposition to each other, which increasingly took on an ethnic dimension, was shaped by processes coming from below: the eruption of violent conflicts, the establishment of specific celebrations, religious reform movements, the differentiation between the written languages of Hindi and Urdu, political rivalries at the communal level and arguments over the protection or slaughter of cows.[200] In Austria, riots and social unrest as well as initiatives to establish museums, theatres and even choirs, reading clubs and sport clubs pushed the process of nationalization forward 'from below'.[201] On the other hand, the political and administrative elite also played a key role in the construction of ethnic differences in that it produced anthropological and ethnographic knowledge about cultural and 'racial' difference, founded schools with different languages of instruction and introduced ethnically defined electorates. With such measures that recognized ethnic difference, the respective administrations deviated from the statist principle of ethnic neutrality in an attempt to make concessions while also simultaneously sidestepping the demands of the evermore influential nationalist movements. This is not to say, however, that the elites only reacted to 'naturally' growing ethnicization and nationalization processes coming from below. Rather, both dynamics – from above and below – were so entangled in their mutual reciprocity that one can ask the proverbial question of which came first, the chicken or the egg.[202] Just as the administrative and political elites unleashed the very processes that they believed to be reacting to, grass-roots dynamics informed the development of the laws that in turn shaped them.

The idea of making concessions while sidestepping the issue is meant to express the fact that the administration only partly conceded to ethnonational demands in that it almost always pursued its own agenda under the table. For example, the Moravian Compromise secured the privileges of the large landowners as a class, but also avoided the introduction of universal, equal suffrage through the creation of ethnically defined electorates. The government's intention to skirt around the suffrage issue also explains why proportional representation was largely absent in the debates. After all, proportional representation would have guaranteed the rights of ethnic minorities, but it would have been much more compatible with further measures leading towards equal citizenship rights.

The Indian government used a similar circumvention manoeuvre with an element of 'divide and conquer' in the hope that a split between Hindus and Muslims would weaken the Indian nationalist movement.[203] Moreover, the intensified ethnonational conflicts within the Indian population that resulted from the government's policies of recognition continually provided new arguments for refusing claims for political self-determination. According to these arguments, democratic structures along 'European' lines could not be established in India because of the pre-existing ethnic conflicts and traditional forms of communalism.[204] In addition, by acknowledging ethnic differences in terms of the franchise, the government also created a way to strengthen and increase the privileges accorded to 'Europeans'.

The Determination of Ethnic Identities in Censuses

Regardless of the intentions behind the recognition of ethnic differences, these governments first had to find a way to determine the ethnicity of a person in an official way. Legal distinctions between ethnic groups could only be effective if it had been established who was a 'European' or a 'native' or a Czech or a German. Censuses played a key role in the establishment of corresponding criteria for determining ethnicity.[205]

In India, the census employed ethno-religious categories (see Map 2.2 and 2.3) as well as 'racial' classifications. Over the course of the four censuses taken between 1881 and 1911, the interest of the statisticians in fine-tuning racial distinctions grew. Even prior to 1900, the census distinguished between 'Europeans', 'Eurasians' and 'Natives' within the Christian population. The intermediary category of 'Eurasians' – which was sometimes referred to as a 'mixed race' – pointed to the difficulties in making a clear distinction between

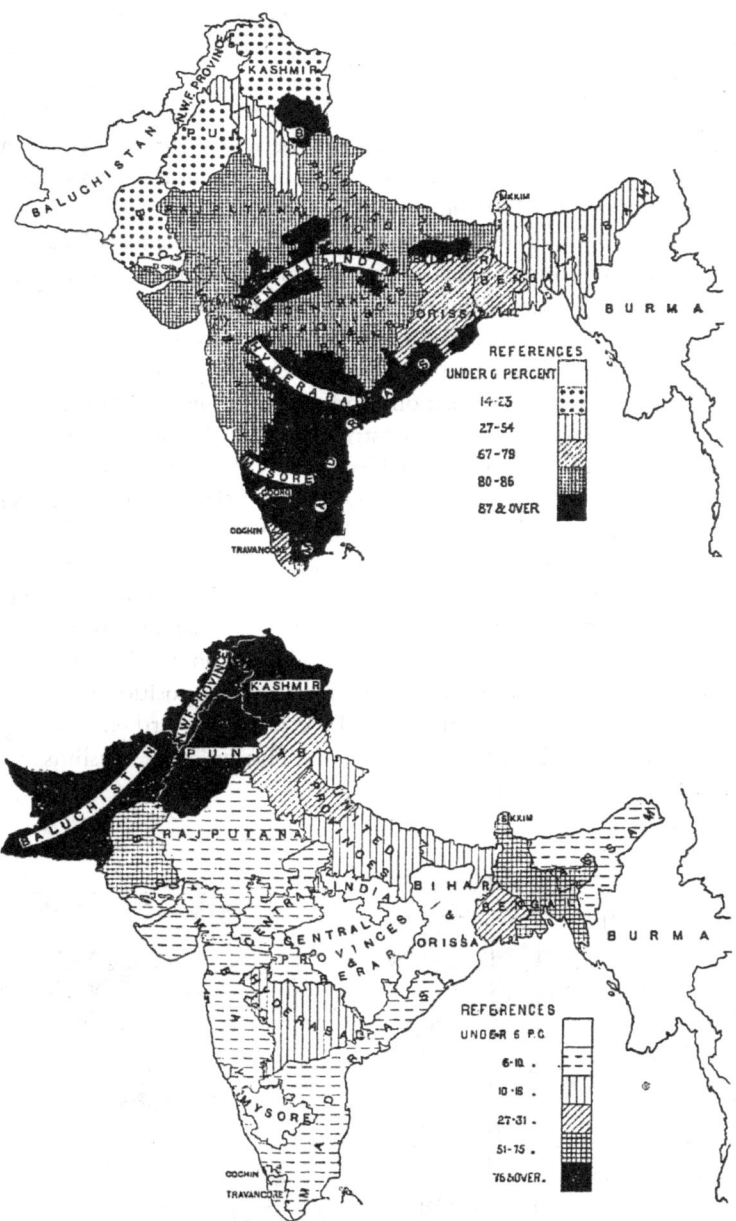

Maps 2.2 and 2.3. The territorial distribution of ethno-religious differences: 'Maps showing the distribution of Hindus and Muhammadans'. Extracted from: Census of India, 1911, vol. 1, Report, Calcutta 1913, pp. 119 and 128.

'whites' and 'non-whites'.[206] Later census reports divided the Indian population according to seven 'racial' types that were supposed to be defined according to the varying intensity of blue skin pigmentation.[207]

In part, the increasing relevance of 'racial' categories resulted from the attempt to transfer the imperialist asymmetry of power between 'Europeans' and 'natives' into a racial hierarchy, and thus to turn this asymmetry into what appeared to be a natural phenomenon.[208] At the same time, however, the racial hierarchization of the Indian population also rested on the desire of the statisticians to classify the population according to encyclopedic definitions that attempted to map the social ranks of the caste system onto different degrees of 'Aryan descent'.[209] The British colonial authorities believed that more accurately dividing the population into groups would make it easier to govern the country. However, this supposedly standard system of identification produced nothing but confusion. On the one hand, the different categories obstructed a consistent assessment; on the other, the administrative desire to establish order collided with the interpretative ambiguity that could be used by those who were being categorized. Therefore, rumours had the power to distort the counts because word had spread, for example, that the censuses were supposed to be used for a military draft, assessing taxes or finding 'two virgins' who were to fan Queen Victoria from dawn to dusk. Such suspicions certainly impacted the ways in which people answered the questions.[210] Similarly, different groups within the Indian population took advantage of the colonial categories in order to better their social position within the new hierarchy.[211] Despite their ambiguities, the censuses nevertheless strengthened the lines demarcating the differences between 'Hindus' and 'Muslims' as well as between 'Europeans' and 'natives'.

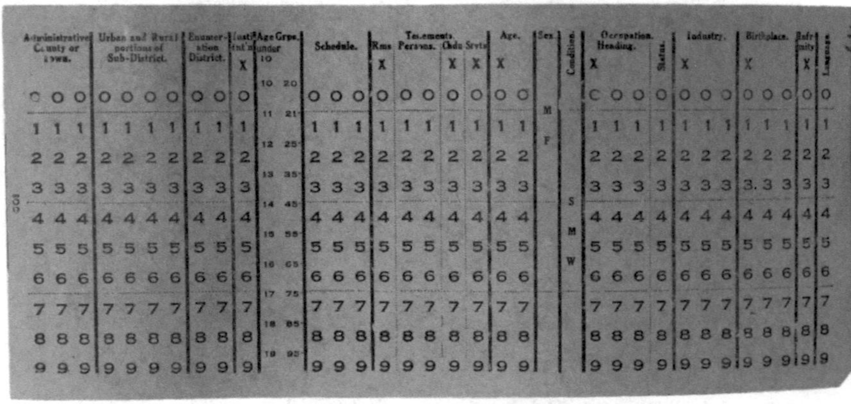

Illustration 2.1. Making the census more precise: A machine-readable census card from the United Kingdom, 1911. From: London, PRO, RG 27/7.

Not only in India, but also across the empire, censuses came to focus more and more on the 'racial' difference between 'whites' and 'non-whites'. The surveys done in the nineteenth century, however, still used contradictory categories. In 1871, for instance, the residents of Canada were classified as being of 'English', 'Welsh' or 'Scotch … nationality', whereas the population of the 'West African settlements' was identified as 'white' or 'black and coloured'; the population of the United Kingdom, in contrast, was comprised of 'Angles or Saxons, Scandinavians, and Celts, all of the Aryan stock' in the eyes of the statisticians.[212] The surveys then distinguished between 'natives of the United Kingdom' and the rest of the colonial populations in the decades thereafter.[213] In 1907, the Statistical Society of London demanded a more precise categorization according to 'racial' criteria as well as more detailed data about the 'British and other white population' in the colonies in particular.[214] These demands were met in the census report of 1911 that included a table indicating the 'population distributed according to certain races' using the following categories: 'Europeans (or Whites)', 'Native Races', 'Half-Castes (or Mixed Races)', 'Indians', 'Chinese', 'Other Coloured Races' and 'Race not Stated'. In addition, the census for the UK recorded the 'natives of India and Ceylon of Asiatic origin … separately from those of European parentage', and differentiated between 'Europeans' and 'Asiatics' within the non-indigenous population of East Africa.[215] Pressed to do so by academic circles, the empire-wide censuses increasingly accentuated the distinction between 'white' and 'non-white', and established an intermediary category with the rubric 'Asiatics'. Simultaneously, the criteria employed to determine this classification shifted from the territorially defined 'natives of the United Kingdom' to the qualification of 'European parentage' that referred rather to individuals.[216]

In contrast, the Austrian censuses focused on language in determining nationality or '*Volkszugehörigkeit*' (ethnicity). The International Statistical Congress in St Petersburg played a critical role in that it recommended in 1872 that collecting data on language should be obligatory in all censuses.[217] In 1846, the Austrian census had used some 'racial' criteria in that it differentiated between 'Slavs', 'Romance-language speakers', 'Germans' and 'members of "Asiatic tribes" (Magyars, Jews, Gypsies and Armenians)'.[218] In the second half of the nineteenth century, the focus of attention turned towards the question of whether language alone was enough to determine the ethnic identity of a person, and which language – the colloquial language, the family language or the mother tongue – was best suited for this purpose. 'Racial' classifications did not become meaningless, but, if at all, they were only addressed via language.[219] As 'race' was difficult to determine objectively, one expert even suggested that the ethnic identity of the person in question should be based on his or her 'profession of national belonging', or other subjective identification.[220] Such a voluntaristic criterion was even further separated from a supposedly innate and unchangeable 'racial' identity than language, which could be acquired.

The general equation of language with nationality in the Habsburg Empire led to a number of problems. For one, this approach contradicted the Hungarian notion of a multilingual nation.[221] Secondly, it also raised the question of which languages should be recognized as forming a 'nation'. The Austrian census distinguished between speakers of German, Bohemian-Moravian-Slovakian, Polish, Ruthenian, Slovenian, Serbo-Croatian, Italian-Ladin, Romanian and Magyar.[222] The official establishment of these nine categories effectively prevented the formation of additional ethnonational identities.[223] In particular, the authorities refused to count Yiddish among the languages recognized as delineating a separate nationality, despite the fact that representatives of the Jewish community stressed that the Jews had such a pure line of descent, the likes of which no other ethnic group could claim.[224] Lastly, since each person had to specify just one of the above-named languages, polyvalent and polyglot identities seemed to disappear. In fact, the censuses increasingly became arenas of nationalist conflicts in which the 'battle for national supremacy' was waged.[225] Every nationalist movement sought to increase the number of speakers of 'its' language, because the results of the census were crucial for determining whether a language counted as being commonly used within a certain region. They were also decisive for calculating a nationality's proportional representation in the appointment of civil servants, judges and teachers.

For this reason, the political significance of the question of which languages should be officially recognized continued to grow. Whereas the registration of 'mother tongues', which was advocated by Czech nationalists for instance,[226] concealed processes of assimilation, using 'colloquial languages' veiled over the existence of minority languages. Consequently, some statisticians suggested that registering the 'family language' spoken within the home was perhaps the most precise way to proceed.[227] Nonetheless, the government continued to insist on using colloquial language as the main criterion.[228] The answer to the question of the census takers as to which language was spoken everyday therefore increasingly became a more fundamental decision in which an individual was forced to identify with one nationality as opposed to others. This development, however, frustrated the intentions of the census authorities, who sought to use language to reach an objective assessment of the ethnic composition of the population. In practice, the censuses became more like declarations of subjectively defined ethnonational preferences.[229]

Legal Recourses, Administrative Decisions and the Ethnic Identities of Individuals

Whereas these subjective dimensions came to play a stronger role in census counts, the bureaucratic-legal assessment of the ethnic identities of individual people moved in the opposite direction. Measures that recognized difference, such as the establishment of separate ethnonational electorates, necessitated the official determination of each person's ethnicity. At first, this was done primarily on the basis of language and the self-assigned national confession of the individual.[230] Around the turn of the century, however, supposedly objective criteria began to play a more significant role, especially because it was feared that people would consciously provide false information in order to infiltrate the electorates of other nationalities. For this reason, the determination of ethnonational identities came to rest on the descent of an individual alongside language and other verifiable indicators of a national ethos, such as involvement in national associations, public statements or the schools attended by a family's children.[231] In Moravia, the compromise of 1905 accelerated this move to objectify the determination of ethnonational identities. The administration instituted national registries and a legally regulated procedure for determining ethnicity. In practice, the local authorities divided the population into a German and a Czech list, and then everyone was entitled to make objections as to his or her own categorization or that of others. As the elections for the Reichsrat approached in 1907, the Moravian authorities received no less than three thousand complaints in this regard. Some complainants even took their cases to the Imperial Court because they disagreed with the decisions of the administration and the lower courts. In order to minimize administrative and judicial complications in the future, the governor's office issued an official catalogue of questions that tried to assess and determine an individual's ethnonational identity on the basis of objectively verifiable facts.[232]

Whereas the determination of ethnonational identities was regulated through complex legal parameters in Austria, the British authorities in India dealt with the matter differently. Rather than focusing on the personal attributes of a given person, such as a self-assigned national confession, political engagement or language, the decisive criteria in the British case was the territorial origin of individuals (i.e. their place of birth or residence). Not the least, this preference for a territorial-based classification system was related to the importance of the principle of *ius soli* in British law. Even the definition of 'European British subjects' in the Indian Code of Criminal Procedure rested on territorial criteria, and encompassed all 'subjects of Her Majesty, born, naturalized or domiciled in the United Kingdom of Great Britain and Ireland, or in any of the European, American, or Australian Colonies or Possessions of Her Majesty, or in the Colony of New Zealand, or in the Colony of the Cape of Good Hope or Natal', as well as the children and grandchildren of these individuals.[233] Therefore, what mattered most was having a geographic origin located in one of the territories of the British Empire inhabited primarily by 'whites'. Due to the increasing migration between India and these territories, however, a growing number of 'non-white' subjects began to fulfil the requirements of this strictly territorial definition. In part due to these changing circumstances, the Montagu–Chelmsford Reforms of 1918–19 sought to make 'European descent' a prerequisite for becoming a 'European' in the eyes of the law in British India, which effectively introduced the use of 'racial' categories.[234]

Apart from these official legal regulations, however, the question remains as to how the authorities actually determined the ethnic identity of an individual in practice. The distinction between 'European' and other jurors outlined in the Code of Criminal Procedure, for example, rested on a list that was compiled by the district collector who determined whether 'the person belongs to either of the races'.[235] This list was published and, as in Austria, individuals could object to the classification or absence of an individual in these registries. However, the appeal process was comparably simple in India: 'Any order of the Collector … in preparing or revising the list shall be final'.[236] Furthermore, it was up to the complainant to provide evidence, and not the authorities.[237] Ultimately, the decisions made by the local officials mattered most. The same applied to the division of the population into the ethnically defined electorates in the years 1918–19. The declaration of a voter that he was 'European or Anglo-Indian' was supposed to be accepted by the 'officer charged with the preparation of the electoral roll', 'unless he is satisfied that the declaration is not made in good faith'.[238] Underneath the veneer of the territorial principle within British law, ad hoc decisions by individual officers made it possible to categorize the population according to personal and 'racial' criteria, whereby officials almost always relied on the supposedly apparent differences between 'whites' and 'non-whites'. 'This made claims to European status by Indian-looking persons difficult to prove or disprove.'[239]

The determination of the ethnic identities of individual people functioned quite differently in Austria compared to in India. Whereas complex legal parameters were decisive in Cisleithania, local decisions based primarily on appearance counted most in India. These different methods corresponded to the dominance of linguistic criteria in Austria as opposed to the 'racial' categories used in India. The bipolar distinction between 'white' and 'non-white' in India thus clearly expressed the imperialist pattern of discrimination and the colonial asymmetry of power.

The two poles were also asymmetrical in that the status of a 'non-white' was defined in a primarily negative way with respect to membership in the positively defined group of 'whites'.[240] Further distinctions within the category of 'non-whites', such as that of 'Asiatics', did not destabilize this bipolar asymmetry as long as the indivisibility of the 'white' identity was not called into question. But grades of differentiation that went a step further, including the creation of the intermediary category of 'Anglo-Indians', could in fact undermine the asymmetrical character of the distinction between 'whites' and 'non-whites'. They made it easier to form positive identities on the side of the divide that had previously only be defined in negative terms. And this plethora of differentiations ultimately threatened the primacy of the 'whites'. The move from the dichotomous separation of 'Europeans' and 'natives' in the nineteenth-century Code of Criminal Procedure to the multipolar distinctions outlined in the reforms of 1918–19 exemplify this very process. The 'Europeans' continued to be a privileged group in the early twentieth century, but they were increasingly only one group among many.

In contrast, a multipolar system of difference shaped the contours of the Cisleithanian case from the very beginning. Since language was the decisive factor in determining ethnonational identities in Austria, the different potential identities were all defined positively. A distinction was not made between 'Germans' and 'non-Germans', but rather between Germans, Czechs, Italians, etc. The fact that these identities were constructed along the same lines also made it difficult for imperialist measures of discrimination to gain a foothold in Cisleithania as they had in India. Moreover, colonial asymmetries were by and large absent in the Austrian case because Bosnia was the only territory in the Habsburg Empire whose relationship to the metropolis resembled that of a colony. Did Bosnia prove to be an exception in the Habsburg case? How did legal parameters and administrative praxis develop within this colonial context? These are the questions that will be discussed in the next chapter.

Notes

1. Stourzh, *Die Gleichberechtigung der Nationalitäten*; J. King, *Budweisers into Czechs and Germans: A Local History of Bohemian Politics, 1848–1948* (Princeton, NJ: Princeton University Press, 2002); T. Zahra, *Kidnapped Souls: National Indifference and the Battle for Children in the Bohemian Lands, 1900–1948* (Ithaca, NY: Cornell University Press, 2008); P. Judson, *Guardians of the Nation: Activists on the Language Frontiers of Imperial Austria* (Cambridge, MA: Harvard University Press, 2006).
2. J. Ulbrich, *Das Staatsrecht der österreichisch-ungarischen Monarchie* (Freiburg im Breisgau: Mohr, 1884), 34f.; H.-J. Seeler, *Das Staatsangehörigkeitsrecht Österreichs*, 2nd edn (Frankfurt am Main: Metzner, 1966), 104; H. Burger, 'Passwesen und Staatsbürgerschaft', in W. Heindl and E. Saurer (eds), *Grenze und Staat: Paßwesen, Staatsbürgerschaft, Heimatrecht und Fremdengesetzgebung in der österreichischen Monarchie 1750–1867* (Vienna: Böhlau, 2000), 168; Gosewinkel, *Einbürgern und Ausschließen*, 33–41.
3. Seeler, *Das Staatsangehörigkeitsrecht Österreichs*; Burger, 'Passwesen und Staatsbürgerschaft'.
4. Österreich, ABGB, §30; Ulbrich, *Staatsrecht*, 35; Seeler, *Das Staatsangehörigkeitsrecht Österreichs*, 104.
5. Milner, *Die österreichische Staatsbürgerschaft*, 56f.
6. Seeler, *Das Staatsangehörigkeitsrecht Österreichs*; Burger, 'Passwesen und Staatsbürgerschaft'.
7. F. Karminski, *Zur Codification des österreichischen Staatsbürgerschaftsrechtes: Eine staatsrechtliche Studie* (Vienna: Manz, 1887), 104f.

8. Gosewinkel, *Einbürgern und Ausschließen*, 194–303; A. Dummett and A. Nicol, *Subjects, Citizens, Aliens and Others: Nationality and Immigration Law* (London: Weidenfeld and Nicolson, 1990).

9. F. Winter, 'Die Reform des bürgerlichen Rechtes', *Arbeiterinnen-Zeitung* 17(7–10) (1908), Pts. 1 to 4; 'Die Reform des Allgemeinen Bürgerlichen Gesetzbuches', *Der Bund* 3(1) (1908), 1–3; M. Spitzer, 'Zur Reform des bürgerlichen Gesetzbuches', *Der Bund* 3(2) (1908), 4–5, Pts. 1 and 2; ibid. 4(8) (1909), 1–3; E. von Fürth, 'Die Teilnovelle zum allgemeinen bürgerlichen Gesetzbuche', *Der Bund* 9(9) (1914), 1–5; H. Herzfelder (H. H.), 'Die Novelle zum allgemeinen bürgerlichen Gesetzbuche', *Zeitschrift für Frauenstimmrecht* 4(8) (1914), 2; H. Herzfelder, 'Die Stellungnahme der Frauen zum Reformentwurf des bürgerlichen Gesetzbuches', *Der Bund* 8(4) (1913), 13–14. See also M. Healy, 'Becoming Austrian: Women, the State, and Citizenship in World War I', *Central European History* 35(1) (2002), 13f.

10. 'Die Stellung der Frau im Rechte der Kulturstaaten', *Arbeiterinnen-Zeitung* 21(25) (1912), 2–3. The problem is also mentioned in L. Caro, *Auswanderung und Auswanderungspolitik in Österreich* (Leipzig: Duncker & Humblot, 1909); Karminski, *Codification*.

11. Cf. B. Bader-Zaar, 'Gaining the Vote in a World of Transition: Female Suffrage in Austria', in B. Rodríguez-Ruiz and R. Rubio-Marín (eds), *The Struggle for Female Suffrage in Europe: Voting to Become Citizens* (Leiden: Brill, 2012), 203.

12. Caro, *Auswanderung*, 217f., 229f. See also Karminski, *Codification*, 3f., 44f.; Caro, *Auswanderung*, 11, portrays the Hungarian emigration laws from 1903 and 1909 as role models.

13. Caro, *Auswanderung*, 181.

14. Vienna, HHStA, MdÄ, Adm. Reg., F 15, Ktn. 10, 4161–1914, Kolonialgesellschaft to k.u.k. Außenministerium, 16 January 1914. On this colonial society founded in 1894, see E. Kolm, *Die Ambitionen Österreich-Ungarns im Zeitalter des Hochimperialismus* (Frankfurt am Main: Lang, 2001), 25f., 34.

15. Vienna, HHStA, MdÄ, Adm. Reg., F 15, Ktn. 10, 24768–1914, Kolonialgesellschaft to k.u.k. Außenministerium, 28 March 1914. See also Caro, *Auswanderung*, 230.

16. Interpellations of the delegate Zore, 1 October 1897 and 28 April 1898, and the delegate Biankini, 18 October 1898 and 22 November 1899, in the Austrian Reichsrat.

17. Vienna, HHStA, MdÄ, Adm. Reg., F 15, Ktn. 31, 42289–1908 and 85266–1911, Auswanderungsgesetz.

18. Vienna, HHStA, MdÄ, Adm. Reg., F 15, Ktn. 31, 72264–1913.

19. Milner, *Die österreichische Staatsbürgerschaft*.

20. A. Groedel, *Die Ersitzung der Staatsangehörigkeit* (Greifswald: J. Abel, 1894), 18, 41. Ibid., 34, cites the Hungarian law of 1879 as a model.

21. Ibid., 41.

22. Ibid., 43f.

23. Austria. Abgeordnetenhaus des österreichischen Reichsrats: *Stenographische Protokolle der Sitzungen des Abgeordnetenhauses des Reichsrats* (Vienna, 14th Session, 1898), Supplement No. 334.

24. Abgeordnetenhaus des österreichischen Reichsrats, *Protokolle*, Index (10th Session, 1891). See also M. John, 'National Movements and Imperial Ethnic Hegemonies in Austria, 1867–1918', in D. Hoerder, C. Harzig and A. Shubert (eds), *The Historical Practice of Diversity: Transcultural Interactions from the Early Modern Mediterranean to the Postcolonial World* (New York: Berghahn Books, 2003), 87–105.

25. 1891 by Hauck; 1897, 1900 and 1901 by Schönerer; 1898, 1899, 1900 and 1901 by Prochazka; and 1905 by Fresl. Abgeordnetenhaus des österreichischen Reichsrats, *Protokolle*, Index (11th Session, 1897), (13th Session, 1898), (14th Session, 1898), (15th Session, 1899), (16th Session, 1900), (17th Session, 1907).
26. J. Thon, *Die Juden in Oesterreich* (Berlin: Lamm, 1908), 49.
27. Bolognese-Leuchtenmüller, *Wirtschafts- und Sozialstatistik*. In 1869, 44 per cent of the population born in a foreign country came from Hungary, rising to 52 per cent in 1880. In the later censuses, those born in Hungary were not counted separately. Some of these immigrants may have had Austrian parents, which would have made them nationals and not foreigners, but this group could hardly have been large enough to skew the figures in such a way as to negate this argument.
28. The files analysed for the period from 1870 to 1899 can be found in Vienna, AVA, MdI, Allg., 8, Ktn. 353, 354, 355 and 356 (Letters A–Z), and for the period from 1900 to 1918 in ibid., Ktn. 144 and 176 (Letters A and N). This collection contains 111 naturalization cases.
29. Thon, *Die Juden in Oesterreich*, 53.
30. Cf. ibid., 49.
31. Ibid., 50, 53; Burger, *Heimatrecht und Staatsbürgerschaft*, 79. On the German case, see Gosewinkel, *Einbürgern und Ausschließen*, 233–77.
32. Thon, *Die Juden in Oesterreich*, 51.
33. Vienna, AVA, MdI, Allg., 8, Ktn. 356, 26481–1898. See also Karminski, *Codification*, 35f.
34. Vienna, AVA, MdI, Allg, 8, Ktn. 144, 30667–1914, 3539–1906, 55660–1902, 25584–1905 and 49974–1905.
35. Ibid., 35544–1908 and 29787–1908.
36. Ibid., 54075–1906, 45367–1906 and Ktn. 176, 51923–1906.
37. On the neutral treatment of Jewish naturalization applications, see also Hirschhausen, 'Von imperialer Inklusion', 9f.; Burger, *Heimatrecht und Staatsbürgerschaft*, 77–83.
38. Vienna, AVA, MdI, Allg, 8, Ktn. 144, 71200–1917, 66273–1917, 8075–1916 and 3725–1916.
39. Ibid., 36098–1914. See also Hirschhausen, 'Von imperialer Inklusion', 17f.
40. Vienna, AVA, MdI, Allg, 8, Ktn. 144, 13459–1914, 19115–1911, 28423–1909 and 51078–1903.
41. Vienna, AVA, MdI, Allg., 8, Ktn. 353, 32097–1897. On this case, see also Burger, *Heimatrecht und Staatsbürgerschaft*, 92f.
42. Vienna, AVA, MdI, Allg., 8, Ktn 353, 11473–1898 and 18693–1898.
43. Ibid., 23599–1897 and 25129–1897. 5,000 Gulden amounted to 10,000 Kronen. The average weekly wage of a worker at this time was about 20 Kronen.
44. Ibid., 13653–1898.
45. Burger, *Heimatrecht und Staatsbürgerschaft*, 33. On the significance of economic and financial criteria for naturalization, see also Hirschhausen, 'Von imperialer Inklusion', 11.
46. Vienna, HHStA, MdÄ, Adm. Reg., F 57, Ktn. 9, Kanzlei Kafka to k.u.k. Außenministerium, 10 August 1870.
47. Vienna, AVA, MdI, Allg., 8, Ktn 353, 9815–1894. On the Turkish critique against these naturalizations, see J. Berchtold, *Recht und Gerechtigkeit in der Konsulargerichtsbarkeit: Britische Exterritorialität im Osmanischen Reich 1825–1914* (Munich: Oldenbourg, 2009), 229.

48. Burger, 'Passwesen und Staatsbürgerschaft', 172.
49. P.H.R. v. Harrasowsky, *Geschichte der Codification des österreichischen Civilrechtes* (Vienna: Manz, 1868); R.H. v. Herrnritt, *Nationalität und Recht dargestellt nach der österreichischen und ausländischen Gesetzgebung* (Vienna: Manz, 1899), 43. See also B. Bader-Zaar, 'Foreigners and the Law in Nineteenth-Century Austria: Juridical Concepts and Legal Rights in the Light of the Development of Citizenship', in A. Fahrmeir, O. Faron and P. Weil (eds), *Migration Control in the North Atlantic World: The Evolution of State Practices in Europe and the United States from the French Revolution to the Inter-War Period* (New York: Berghahn Books, 2003), 138f.; F.L. Fillafer, 'The "Imperial Idea" and Civilising Missions', *Historyka: Studia Metodologiczne* 42 (2012), 42; R.J.W. Evans, *Austria, Hungary, and the Habsburgs: Essays on Central Europe c. 1683–1867* (Oxford: Oxford University Press, 2006).
50. 'Fundamental Law Concerning the General Rights of Citizens: The Austrian Constitution of 1867', in W.F. Dodd (ed.), *Modern Constitutions: A Collection of the Fundamental Laws of Twenty-Two of the Most Important Countries of the World, With Historical and Bibliographical Notes* (Chicago, IL: The University of Chicago Press, 1909). See also Baier, *Sprache und Recht*.
51. Stourzh, *Die Gleichberechtigung der Nationalitäten*.
52. Baier, *Sprache und Recht*.
53. 'Fundamental Law Concerning the General Rights of Citizens'.
54. V. Russ, *Der Sprachenstreit in Oesterreich: Ein Beitrag zur sprachlichen Ordnung in der Verwaltung* (Vienna: Konegen, 1884); Baier, *Sprache und Recht*; Stourzh, *Die Gleichberechtigung der Nationalitäten*; H. Burger, *Sprachenrecht und Sprachengerechtigkeit im österreichischen Unterrichtswesen: 1867–1918.* (Vienna: Verlag der Österreichischen Akademie der Wissenschaften, 1995); Zahra, *Kidnapped Souls*.
55. E. Melichar, 'Die Rechtslage der Nationalitäten in Zisleithanien nach der Dezember-Verfassung 1867 im Lichte der Judikatur des Reichsgerichtes (1869–1918)', in L. Holotik and A. Vantuch (eds), *Der österreichisch-ungarische Ausgleich 1867: Materialien (Referate und Diskussionen) der internationalen Konferenz in Bratislava 28.8.–1.9.1967* (Bratislava: Verlag der Slowakischen Akademie der Wissenschaften, 1971), 451–74. See also Stourzh, *Die Gleichberechtigung der Nationalitäten*.
56. N.M. Wingfield (ed.), *Creating the Other: Ethnic Conflict and Nationalism in Habsburg Central Europe* (New York: Berghahn Books, 2003); eadem, *Flag Wars and Stone Saints: How the Bohemian Lands Became Czech* (Cambridge, MA: Harvard University Press, 2007); E. Winkler, *Wahlrechtsreformen und Wahlen in Triest 1905–1909: Eine Analyse der politischen Partizipation in einer multinationalen Stadtregion der Habsburgermonarchie* (Munich: Oldenbourg, 2000); P. Ther, *In der Mitte der Gesellschaft: Operntheater in Zentraleuropa 1815–1914* (Vienna: Oldenbourg, 2006); Cohen, 'Nationalist Politics', 259f.; King, *Budweisers*; J. Schmid, *Kampf um das Deutschtum: Radikaler Nationalismus in Österreich und dem Deutschen Reich 1890–1914* (Frankfurt am Main: Campus Verlag, 2009); M. Moll, *Kein Burgfrieden: Der deutsch-slowenische Nationalitätenkonflikt in der Steiermark 1900–1918* (Innsbruck: StudienVerlag, 2007); T.M. Kelly, *Without Remorse: Czech National Socialism in Late-Habsburg Austria* (Boulder, CO: East European Monographs, 2006).
57. Some studies emphasize, in contrast, that most of the population remained nationally indifferent despite these nationalist movements. See Zahra, *Kidnapped Souls*; Judson, *Guardians of the Nation*; Cohen, 'Nationalist Politics', 260.

58. Koralka, *Tschechen*; D.L. Unowsky, 'Peasant Political Mobilization and the 1898 Anti-Jewish Riots in Western Galicia', *European History Quarterly* 40(3) (2010), 412–35.

59. M. Hroch, *Social Preconditions of National Revival in Europe: A Comparative Analysis of the Social Composition of Patriotic Groups among the Smaller European Nations*, trans. B. Fowkes (Cambridge: Cambridge University Press, 1985).

60. On the debate over German as the national language, see Herrnritt, *Nationalität*, 135; Gumplowicz, *Nationalitäten*, 122f.; Baier, *Sprache und Recht*, 32f.; Stourzh, *Die Gleichberechtigung der Nationalitäten*, 84f.

61. Stourzh, 'The Multinational Empire Revisited'; King, *Budweisers*, 5, speaks of 'sub-citizenships' within this context. In Hungary, however, this right to the recognition of ethno-national difference was not collectivized in the same way. Péter, *Hungary's Long Nineteenth Century*, 344–50. On the significance of the Irish case for the Austrian debates, see G. Strakosch-Graßmann, *Das allgemeine Wahlrecht in Österreich seit 1848* (Leipzig: Deuticke, 1906), 97.

62. A. Freiherr v. Skene, *Der nationale Ausgleich in Mähren 1905* (Vienna: Konegen, 1910); R.H. v. Herrnritt, 'Die Ausgestaltung des österreichischen Nationalitätenrechts durch den Ausgleich in Mähren und in der Bukowina', *Österreichische Zeitschrift für öffentliches Recht* 1(5–6) (1914); H. Glassl, *Nationale Autonomie im Vielvölkerstaat: Der Mährische Ausgleich* (Munich: Sudetendeutsche Stiftung, 1977), 15–21; J. Malíř, 'Der mährische Landtag', in H. Rumpler (ed.), *Die Habsburgermonarchie 1848–1918*, vol. 7, *Verfassung und Parlamentarismus*, Part 2, *Die Regionalen Repräsentativkörperschaften* (Vienna: Verlag der Österreichischen Akademie der Wissenschaften, 2000), 2057–103; Burger, *Heimatrecht und Staatsbürgerschaft*, 124.

63. R. Luft, 'Politischer Pluralismus und Nationalismus: Zu Parteienwesen und politischer Kultur in der tschechischen Nation vor dem Ersten Weltkrieg', *Österreichische Zeitschrift für Geschichtswissenschaften* 2(3) (1991), 72–87.

64. Skene, *Der nationale Ausgleich*.

65. R. Luft, 'Die Mittelpartei des mährischen Großgrundbesitzes 1879 bis 1918: Zur Problematik des Ausgleichs in Mähren und Böhmen', in F. Seibt (ed.), *Die Chance der Verständigung: Absichten und Ansätze zu übernationaler Zusammenarbeit in den böhmischen Ländern 1848–1918* (Munich: Oldenbourg, 1987), 187–243; Glassl, *Nationale Autonomie*, 10f., 15f.; W. Freißler, 'Der mährische Ausgleich', *Deutschradikales Jahrbuch mit Zeitweiser für 1913* 1 (1912), 209f. See also T. Tönsmeyer, 'Der böhmische Adel zwischen Revolution und Reform, 1848–1918/21: Ein Forschungsbericht', *Geschichte und Gesellschaft* 32(3) (2006), 364–84; E. Glassheim, 'Between Empire and Nation: The Bohemian Nobility, 1880–1918', in P.M. Judson and M.L. Rozenblit (eds), *Constructing Nationalities in East Central Europe* (New York: Berghahn Books, 2005), 61–88.

66. N. Leser, 'Die Arbeiterbewegung: Solidarität der Sozialisten?', in F. Seibt (ed.), *Die Chance der Verständigung: Absichten und Ansätze zu übernationaler Zusammenarbeit in den böhmischen Ländern 1848–1918* (Munich: Oldenbourg, 1987), 101–15; Glassl, *Nationale Autonomie*, 10; K. Ucakàr, *Demokratie und Wahlrecht in Österreich: Zur Entwicklung von politischer Partizipation und staatlicher Legitimationspolitik* (Vienna: Verlag für Gesellschaftskritik, 1985).

67. R. Springer [K. Renner], *Der Kampf der österreichischen Nationen um den Staat: Theil 1: Das nationale Problem als Verfassungs- und Verwaltungsfrage* (Leipzig: Deuticke, 1902); O. Bauer, *Die Nationalitätenfrage und die Sozialdemokratie* (Vienna: Brand, 1907); Leser, 'Die Arbeiterbewegung'.

68. V. Adler, *Das allgemeine, gleiche und direkte Wahlrecht und das Wahlunrecht in Oesterreich* (Vienna: Bretschneider, 1893), 48. See also Strakosch-Graßmann, *Wahlrecht*, 21, 56, 59.

69. Bauer, *Nationalitätenfrage*, 356, was one of the few who mentioned proportional representation as a possible solution.

70. On the attempts to compensate at the local level, see King, *Budweisers*, 137f.; H. Hein-Kircher, 'Jewish Participation in the Lemberg Local Self-Government: The Provisions of the Lemberg Statute of 1870', *Simon-Dubnow-Institute Yearbook 10* (2011), 237–54.

71. E. Bernatzik, *Über nationale Matriken: Inaugurationsrede* (Vienna: Manz, 1910). On the nationality registers, see also G. Stourzh, 'Ethnic Attribution in Late Imperial Austria: Good Intentions, Evil Consequences', in R. Robertson and E. Timms (eds), *The Habsburg Legacy: National Identity in Historical Perspective* (Edinburgh: Edinburgh University Press, 1994), 67–83.

72. Bauer, *Nationalitätenfrage*, 357f.; Springer, *Kampf*.

73. R. Springer [K. Renner], *Grundlagen und Entwicklungsziele der Österreichisch-ungarischen Monarchie* (Vienna: Deuticke, 1906), 208.

74. Gumplowicz, *Nationalitäten*, 122, 125. See also Herrnritt, *Nationalität*, 135.

75. See Strakosch-Graßmann, *Wahlrecht*, 80f.; Ulbrich, *Staatsrecht*, 16; Ucakar, *Demokratie und Wahlrecht*; Winkler, *Wahlrechtsreformen*.

76. A.C. Popovici, *Die Vereinigten Staaten von Groß-Österreich: Politische Studien zur Lösung der nationalen Fragen und staatsrechtlichen Krisen in Österreich-Ungarn* (Leipzig: Elischer, 1906). See also Gumplowicz, 123; Herrnritt, *Nationalität*, 43–45.

77. H. Konrad (ed.), *'Daß unsre Greise nicht mehr betteln gehn!': Sozialdemokratie und Sozialpolitik im deutschen Reich und in Österreich-Ungarn 1880 bis 1914* (Vienna: Europaverlag, 1991), 33; H. Hofmeister, 'Landesbericht Österreich', in P.A. Köhler and H.F. Zacher (eds), *Ein Jahrhundert Sozialversicherung in der Bundesrepublik Deutschland, Frankreich, Großbritannien, Österreich und der Schweiz* (Berlin: Duncker & Humblot, 1981), 485, 533f.; 562f.; 596f.

78. J. Kaan, 'Die Arbeiter-Unfallversicherung in Oesterreich', in Special-Comité für Socialökonomie, Hygiene und öffentliches Hilfswesen (ed.), *Sociale Verwaltung in Österreich am Ende des 19. Jahrhunderts*, vol. 1, *Socialökonomie* (Vienna: Franz Deuticke, 1900), 22; Hofmeister, 'Landesbericht Österreich', 549, 601f., 621.

79. Special-Comité für Socialökonomie, Hygiene und öffentliches Hilfswesen (ed.), *Sociale Verwaltung in Oesterreich am Ende des 19. Jahrhunderts: Aus Anlass der Weltausstellung Paris 1900*, 2 vols (Vienna: Deuticke, 1900); Hofmeister, 'Landesbericht Österreich', 611f.

80. F. Gärtner, 'Der Ausbau der Sozialversicherung in Oesterreich', Ph.D. dissertation (Heidelberg: Ruprecht-Karls-Universität Heidelberg, 1909).

81. A. Schubert, *Das Deutschtum im Wirtschaftshaushalte Österreichs*, vol. II, *Die Abgabenleistungen d. Deutschen in Österr. an den Staat* (Reichenberg: R. Gerzabek & Co., 1906), 109.

82. Interpellation of the delegate Prade, 1891, Abgeordnetenhaus des österreichischen Reichsrats, *Protokolle*, Index (11th Session, 1897).

83. Vienna, AVA, MdI, Allg., 11/4, Ktn. 413 and 414, Heimatrecht. See also Burger, *Heimatrecht und Staatsbürgerschaft*, 88–92.

84. Austria, RGBl. 1896, No. 105. See Seeler, *Das Staatsangehörigkeitsrecht Österreichs*, 114.

85. Abgeordnetenhaus des Reichsrats, *Protokolle*, Motivenbericht zur Heimatrechtsnovelle (11th Session, 1894), Supplement No. 969.

86. Vienna was already home to around 100,000 people who were not members of the municipal community in 1884. Russ, *Der Sprachenstreit*, 9.

87. Vienna, AVA, MdI, Allg., 11/4, Ktn 433, 10597–1902. See also ibid., 35733–1907.

88. John, 'National Movements', 90, 97f. See also S. Hahn, 'Inclusion and Exclusion of Migrants in the Multicultural Realm of the Habsburg "State of Many Peoples"', *Histoire Sociale / Social History* 33(66) (2000), 307–24.

89. Stourzh, *Die Gleichberechtigung der Nationalitäten*, 113.

90. S. Walz, *Staat, Nationalität und jüdische Identität in Österreich vom 18. Jahrhundert bis 1914* (Frankfurt am Main: Lang, 1996); J.W. Boyer, *Karl Lueger (1844–1910): Christlichsoziale Politik als Beruf*, translated by O. Binder (Vienna: Böhlau, 2010), 123–78.

91. Vienna, AVA, MdI, Allg., 11/4, Ktn 433, 40861–1901, 40862–1901 and 5787–1901.

92. Ibid., 6982–1900, Interner Vermerk zu einem Bericht der niederösterreichischen Statthalterei über die Heimatrechtspraxis der Gemeinden, 17 February 1900.

93. Thon, *Die Juden in Oesterreich*, 58.

94. Vienna, AVA, MdI, Allg., 11/4, Ktn 433, 6982–1900.

95. Ibid., 52534–1906.

96. On a similar conflict in Breslau, see T. v. Rahden, *Jews and Other Germans: Civil Society, Religious Diversity, and Urban Politics in Breslau, 1860–1925*, trans. M. Brainard (Madison, WI: University of Wisconsin Press, 2008), 202–5.

97. Proclamation by the Queen to the Princes, Chiefs, and the People of India, 1 November 1858. See also A.B. Keith (ed.), *Speeches & Documents on Indian Policy 1750–1921*, vol. 1 (London: Milford, 1922), 382f.

98. Report by Montagu and Chelmsford, quoted in T.R. Metcalf, *The New Cambridge History of India*, vol. 3.4, *Ideologies of the Raj* (Cambridge: Cambridge University Press, 1994), 225f.

99. Estimates suggest that approximately 60,000 'Indian soldiers' were killed in the First World War. S. Bose and A. Jalal, *Modern South Asia: History, Culture, Political Economy* (Delhi: Oxford University Press, 1997), 98f.

100. V.P. Menon, *Montagu-Chelmsford Reforms* (Bombay: Bharatiya Vidya Bhavan, 1965), 53. The members of the second chamber, the Council of State, which was to be established according to the law of 1919, was also structured along similar lines.

101. Menon, *Montagu-Chelmsford Reforms*, 144. See also P.G. Robb, *The Government of India and Reform: Policies towards Politics and the Constitution, 1916–1921* (Oxford: Oxford University Press, 1976), 109.

102. London, IOR, V/26/261/1, Report of the Franchise Committee, 1918–19, Calcutta 1919, p. 3.

103. London, IOR, L/PJ/3/695, 5th Dispatch, p. 2. See also A. Roy, *Gendered Citizenship: Historical and Conceptual Explorations* (New Delhi: Orient Longman, 2005), 36–77.

104. *The Montagu-Chelmsford Reform Proposals. With a Foreword by Annie Besant* (Madras: Sons of India, n.d., ca. 1918), 35. See E.W. Parker, *Outlines of Constitutional Law – India: Containing a Summary of the Statutes of Parliament Relating to the Government of India, Including the Indian Councils Acts, 1861–1909, and the Regulations made thereunder* (Allahabad: Pioneer Press, 1910), 164.

105. London, IOR, V/26/261/1, Report of the Franchise Committee, p. 1.

106. Due to the lower census figures, the number of enfranchised individuals for the election of the provincial councillors was greater than that of those entitled to vote for the

legislative assembly. London, IOR, V/26/261/1, Report of the Franchise Committee, p. 52. See also Menon, *Montagu-Chelmsford Reforms*, 25.

107. Metcalf, *Ideologies*, 224; Bose and Jalal, *Modern South Asia*, 104; Galanter, *Competing Equalities*, 25. On the continued significance of syncretist hybrids of Muslim and Hindu identities, see M. Juneja and M. Pernau, 'Einleitung', in M. Juneja and M. Pernau (eds), *Religion und Grenzen in Indien und Deutschland: Auf dem Weg zu einer transnationalen Historiographie* (Göttingen: V&R unipress, 2008), 23. On earlier franchise regulations, see F. Robinson, *Separatism among Indian Muslims: The Politics of the United Provinces' Muslims 1860–1923* (Delhi: Oxford University Press, 1993).

108. *A Scheme for Reforms: Passed by the National Congress on Dec 29 1916, and by the All-India Muslim League on Dec 31 1916* (Adyar: Commonweal Office, 1917), 1 and 4. On the so-called Lucknow Pact between the Muslim League and the National Congress, see Metcalf, *Ideologies*, 225; Bose and Jalal, *Modern South Asia*, 128f.; Robb, *Government*, 70f.

109. London, IOR, V/26/261/1, Report of the Franchise Committee, p. 7.

110. *The Montagu-Chelmsford Reform Proposals*, XLIXf., 37, 133f.

111. London, IOR, V/26/261/2, Evidence taken before the Reforms Committee (Franchise), vol. 1, Calcutta 1919, p. 110.

112. London, IOR, V/26/261/1, Report of the Franchise Committee, p. 7, 45 and 58f.

113. *The Montagu-Chelmsford Reform Proposals*, XLIXf., 37f.; London, IOR, V/26/261/1, Report of the Franchise Committee, p. 7.

114. London, IOR, L/PJ/3/695, Dispatch on the Montagu-Chelmsford-Report, p. 2. See also London, IOR, V/26/261/2, Evidence taken before the Reforms Committee (Franchise), vol. 1, Calcutta 1919, p. 99f.

115. Robb, *Government*, 37. See also *The Montagu-Chelmsford Reform Proposals*, 37f.

116. London, IOR, V/26/261/1, Report of the Franchise Committee, p. 7f., 45 and 58f.

117. London, IOR, V/26/261/2, Evidence taken before the Reforms Committee (Franchise), vol. 1, Calcutta 1919, p. 116.

118. *The Montagu-Chelmsford Reform Proposals*, 37f., 112; London, IOR, V/26/261/1, Report of the Franchise Committee, p. 7, 45 and 58f.

119. Ibid.

120. London, IOR, L/PJ/3/695, 5th Dispatch, p. 5 and 10f.; London, IOR, V/26/261/1, Report of the Franchise Committee, p. 7f. See also Robb, *Government*, 112f.

121. London, IOR, V/26/261/1, Report of the Franchise Committee, 7; London, IOR, L/PJ/3/695, 5th Dispatch, p. 5 and 10f. See also *Gordon*, 445.

122. London, IOR, V/26/261/1, Report of the Franchise Committee, p. 3 and 5. See also ibid., p. 58f.; Menon, *Montagu-Chelmsford Reforms*, 48; Galanter, *Competing Equalities*, 26.

123. London, IOR, V/26/261/1, Report of the Franchise Committee, p. 7.

124. *The Montagu-Chelmsford Reform Proposals*, 37, XLII.

125. The Presidential Address, p. 6 and 7. See also London, IOR, L/PJ/3/695, Minute of dissent by Nair.

126. London, IOR, V/26/261/1, Report of the Franchise Committee, p. 3 and 6. London, IOR, V/26/261/2, Evidence taken before the Reforms Committee (Franchise), vol. 1, Calcutta 1919, p. 99f.

127. London, IOR, V/26/261/1, Report of the Franchise Committee, p. 8. See also B.S. Cohn, *India: The Social Anthropology of a Civilization* (New Delhi: Oxford University Press, 2000), 107.

128. London, IOR, V/26/261/1, Report of the Franchise Committee, p. 8 and 14; London, IOR, L/PJ/3/695, Dispatches on Indian Constitutional Reforms, Dispatch on the Montagu-Chelmsford Report, p. 39.

129. London, IOR, L/PJ/3/695, Dispatches on Indian Constitutional Reforms, 5th Dispatch, 1. See also Metcalf, *Ideologies*, 190.

130. Neo-Fabian Society, *Problems of Reform in the Government of India* (Madras: Neo-Fabian Society, 1919), 79.

131. London, IOR, V/26/261/1, Report of the Franchise Committee, 6. See also *The Montagu-Chelmsford Reform Proposals*, 39; Neo-Fabian Society, *Problems of Reform*, 38.

132. London, IOR, L/PJ/3/695, Dispatch on the Montagu-Chelmsford Report, p. 5. See also Robb, *Government*, 80.

133. A. Besant, *India's Hour of Destiny. Being the Address of the Chairman of the Reception Committee of the Special Madras Provincial Conference, Aug 3 1918* (Adyar: Commonweal Office, 1918), 1f. On the connection between Indian and Irish calls for 'Home Rule', see Metcalf, *Ideologies*, 129; Regan-Lefebvre, 136–42; Banerjee, *Becoming Imperial Citizens*, 55–74.

134. London, IOR, L/PJ/3/695, Minutes by Chelmsford, p. 2f.; ibid., Dispatch on the Montagu-Chelmsford Report, 37; ibid., Minute of dissent by Nair, p. 4.

135. Robb, *Government*, 101f.

136. London, IOR, L/PJ/3/695, Minute of dissent by Nair, p. 1f., 5 and 18.

137. Robb, *Government*, 100.

138. London, IOR, V/26/261/1, Report of the Franchise Committee, p. 91.

139. Metcalf, *Ideologies*, 216.

140. Indian Legislative Council: (Abstract of the) Proceedings of the Council of the Governor General of India, assembled for the purpose of making laws and regulations, vol. 48 (Calcutta, 25 February 1910), 239. See also R. Sturman, 'Indian Indentured Labor and the History of International Rights Regimes', *American Historical Review* 119(5) (2014), 1463.

141. Indian Legislative Council, Proceedings of the Council, vol. 45 (18 January 1907), Inquiry by Nahab Baadur Khwaja Salimulla of Dacca and Anser from Finlay. See also London, IOR, L/PJ/5/462.

142. Indian Legislative Council, Proceedings of the Council, vol. 48 (25 January 1910), 48.

143. Ibid. (25 February 1910), 251, Gokhale.

144. Ibid., 260, Subba Rao. See also ibid., vol. 48 (25 February 1910), 239, Sachchidananda Sinha. On the use of the term 'citizen' in the Indian context, see also M. Pernau, *Ashraf into Middle Classes: Muslims in Nineteenth-Century Delhi* (New Delhi: Oxford University Press, 2013).

145. Indian Legislative Council, Proceedings of the Council, vol. 48 (23 March 1910), 575, (25 February 1910), 261. See also India, Act 14 of 1910, Emigration.

146. India, Regulation No. 2366–8, 1 April 1911. Robb, *Government*, 42.

147. Ibid., 42f.

148. Metcalf, *Ideologies*, 219. See also Banerjee, *Becoming Imperial Citizens*, 1, 3; Sturman, 'Indian Indentured Labor', 1462f.

149. Indian Legislative Council, Proceedings of the Council, vol. 48 (25 February 1910), 239, Gokhale. See also Metcalf, *Ideologies*, 215f. On the system of indenture, see D. Northrup, *Indentured Labor in the Age of Imperialism, 1834–1922* (Cambridge: Cambridge University Press, 1995); R. Mahase, '"Plenty a Dem Run Away": Resistance

by Indian Indentured Labourers in Trinidad, 1870–1920', *Labor History* 49(4) (2008), 465–80; Banerjee, *Becoming Imperial Citizens*, 78.

150. India, Regulation No. 94-E, 18 March 1886. General Rules and Orders under Enactments in force in British India. Calcutta 1907. See also India, Act 6 of 1869, Emigration; India, Act 7 of 1871, Indian Emigration. See also B. Daviron, 'Mobilizing Labour in African Agriculture: The Role of the International Colonial Institute in the Elaboration of a Standard of Colonial Administration, 1895–1930', *Journal of Global History* 5(3) (2010), 484f.; Sturman, 'Indian Indentured Labor', 1445f.

151. Over the course of these conflicts, the Indian National Congress came into being in 1885. See M. Sinha, *Colonial Masculinity: The 'Manly Englishman' and the 'Effeminate Bengali' in the Late Nineteenth Century* (Manchester: Manchester University Press, 1995), 69f.; E. Hirschmann, *'White Mutiny': The Ilbert Bill Crisis in India and Genesis of the Indian National Congress* (New Delhi: Heritage, 1980), 3.

152. India, Act 25 of 1861, Code of Criminal Procedure, ch. 2, sec. 25 and 39ff. plus ch. 23, sec. 323.

153. On the resulting problem that cases against 'Europeans' were often dismissed because of mishandling by 'Indian' officials, see R.G. Sanyal (ed.), *The Record of Criminal Cases: As between Europeans and Natives for the Last Hundred Years*, 2nd edn (Calcutta: Sanyal & Co. 1896); E. Kolsky, *Colonial Justice in British India: White Violence and the Rule of Law* (Cambridge: Cambridge University Press, 2010).

154. Hirschmann, *'White Mutiny'*, 23, 39. In 1881, a high-ranking 'non-white' judge was recalled from his post outside the Presidencies after the local 'whites' demanded that he should be transferred. London, IOR, L/PJ/6/44, file 1038. See also Metcalf, *Ideologies*, 204f.; Hirschmann, *'White Mutiny'*, 25; Sinha, *Colonial Masculinity*, 36.

155. Indian Legislative Council, Proceedings of the Council, vol. 22 (2 February 1883), 42.

156. Ibid., vol. 23 (4 January 1884), 4. See also Hirschmann, *'White Mutiny'*, 37f.

157. Indian Legislative Council, Proceedings of the Council, vol. 23 (4 January 1884), 5f., 15. See also London, IOR, V/27/140/3, p. 18; Metcalf, *Ideologies*, 37.

158. Indian Legislative Council, Proceedings of the Council, vol. 23 (4 January 1884), 16, 21.

159. Ibid., vol. 22 (9 March 1883), 139, Quinton.

160. Ibid. (7 January 1884), 48f., Sir A. Colvin. See also ibid., 49, 50f.; Hirschmann, *'White Mutiny'*, 26f., 80.

161. Indian Legislative Council, Proceedings of the Council, vol. 22 (9 March 1883), 141, Kristodas Pal. On references to the promises of equality, see also Hirschmann, *'White Mutiny'*, 58.

162. Indian Legislative Council, Proceedings of the Council, vol. 23 (7 January 1884), Evans.

163. Ibid., vol. 22 (9 March 1883), 144, Miller.

164. Ibid. (9 March 1883), 155f., Evans. See also London, IOR, L/PJ/102, file 1253.

165. Indian Legislative Council, Proceedings of the Council, vol. 22 (9 March 1883), 155f., Evans.

166. Ibid., vol. 23 (7 January 1884), 44f., Thomas.

167. Ibid. (7 January 1884), 45, Thomas.

168. Letter to the Editor by the former member of government Stephen in *The Times*, 1 March 1883, as quoted in Sinha, *Colonial Masculinity*, 39.

169. London, IOR, L/PJ/102, file 1253, Advocate General in Bombay, John Marriot, to India Office, 19 June 1883. See also Indian Legislative Council, Proceedings of the Council, vol. 23 (7 January 1884), 38, Evans.

170. Ibid. (4 January 1884), 16, Ilbert. See also ibid. (7 January 1884), 57f. On racist readings of the Magna Carta, see also Young, *English Ethnicity*, 20.
171. Hirschmann refers to the agitation against the bill as 'white mutiny'. On the emergence of the structures of a political public in India and the polarization between 'white' and anti-colonial discourses resulting from the Ilbert Bill debates, see Sinha, *Colonial Masculinity*, 23, 33f.
172. Hirschmann, 'White Mutiny', 41f. In the UK, *The Englishman* in particular took sides with the opponents while the *Pall Mall Gazette* favoured the proponents.
173. Ibid., 52f., 63, 107f., 231f., 239; Sinha, *Colonial Masculinity*, 55.
174. Hirschmann, 'White Mutiny', 75, 109f., 144f., 174. See also London, IOR, L/PJ/6/100, file 1049, Memorial of Eurasian and Anglo-Indian European British subjects, 1883.
175. Sinha, *Colonial Masculinity*, 52. See also London, IOR, L/PJ/6/102, file 1262; ibid., L/PJ/6/100, file 1049, Memorial of Ladies resided in Bihar, 1 June 1883; Metcalf, *Ideologies*, 211f.
176. Sinha, *Colonial Masculinity*, 33f. See also K. Ballhatchet, *Race, Sex and Class under the Raj: Imperial Attitudes and Policies and their Critics, 1793–1905* (London: Weidenfeld and Nicolson, 1980), 48f.
177. Hirschmann, 'White Mutiny', 192f., 196f. On anti-imperialist discourses in the UK, see also Stuchtey, *Expansion*; Owen, *The British Left*.
178. Hirschmann, 'White Mutiny', 185, 195, 244.
179. India, Act 3 of 1884, Code of Criminal Procedure. See also Indian Legislative Council, Proceedings of the Council, vol. 22, 611f., Statement of the Governor General. See also Sinha, *Colonial Masculinity*, 33, 245f.; ibid., 37.
180. Indian Legislative Council, Proceedings of the Council, vol. 23 (7 January 1884), 57f., 69, Lord Ripon.
181. Ibid., vol. 36 (12 March 1898), 321, Rai Bahadur Charlu. See also ibid. (15 October 1897), 358, Sir Henry Prinsep. India, Act 5 of 1898, sec. 443f.
182. Indian Legislative Council, Proceedings of the Council, vol. 37 (12 March 1898), 324, Chalmers in the name of the government.
183. Metcalf, *Ideologies*, 203f.
184. Parker, *Outlines*, 152; UK, 53&54 Vict ch. 37, Foreign Jurisdiction Act (1890), sec. 15.
185. Regulation No. 178-J, 23/09/1874. General Rules and Orders in British India, 1907.
186. London, IOR, L/PJ/6/731, file 2469, Indian government to India Office, 27 July 1905.
187. London, IOR, L/PJ/6/731, file 2469.
188. London, IOR, L/PJ/6/702, file 2977, India Office Memo, 10 February 1905, Sir Dennis Fitzpatrick and Mr H.H. Shepard.
189. London, PRO, HO 144/316/B7560.
190. London, PRO, HO 144/316/B7560, Home Office note from January 1900. See also the file memo from the India Office in London, IOR, L/PJ/6/269, file 160 (29 January – 8 May 1890).
191. London, PRO, HO 144/316/B7560.
192. India, Act 3 of 1864, Foreigners.
193. London, IOR, L/PJ/6/172, file 431.
194. London, IOR, L/PJ/6/249, file 616 and L/PJ/6/899, file 3884.
195. London, IOR, L/PS/18/D139.
196. London, IOR, L/PJ/6/899, file 3884.
197. D. Cannadine, *Ornamentalism: How the British Saw their Empire* (Oxford: Oxford University Press, 2001), 43; Lindström, *Empire*, 16–104.

198. K.K. Raman, 'Utilitarianism and the Criminal Law in Colonial India: A Study of the Practical Limits of Utilitarian Jurisprudence', *Modern Asian Studies* 28(4) (1994), 739–91; Banerjee, *Becoming Imperial Citizens*, 22f.

199. Herrnritt, *Nationalität*, 43; Bader-Zaar, 'Foreigners', 138f.; Fillafer, 'The "Imperial Idea"', 42; Evans, *Austria*; J.-P. Himka, 'Nationality Problems in the Habsburg Monarchy and the Soviet Union: The Perspective of History', in R.L. Rudolph and D.F. Good (eds), *Nationalism and Empire: The Habsburg Empire and the Soviet Union* (New York: St. Martin's Press, 1992), 79–93. On the role of Josephinism, see also J. Deak, *Forging a Multinational State: State Making in Imperial Austria from the Enlightenment to the First World War* (Stanford, CA: Stanford University Press, 2015).

200. Cohn, *India*, 55; idem, *The Census, Social Structure and Objectification in South Asia*, Reprint (Copenhagen: Soertryk, 1984), 27f.; Bose and Jalal, *Modern South Asia*, 108; F. Robinson, 'Municipal Government and Muslim Separatism in the United Provinces, 1883 to 1916', in J. Gallagher, G. Johnson and A. Seal (eds), *Locality, Province and Nation: Essays on Indian Politics, 1870 to 1940* (Cambridge: Cambridge University Press, 1973), 73, 89f.

201. K. Struve, 'Gentry, Jews, and Peasants: Jews as the Others in the Formation of the Modern Polish Nation in Rural Galicia during the Second Half of the Nineteenth Century', in N.M. Wingfield (ed.), *Creating the Other: Ethnic Conflict and Nationalism in Habsburg Central Europe* (New York: Berghahn Books, 2003), 103–26; Wingfield, *Flag Wars*; Cohen, 'Nationalist Politics'; Judson, *Guardians*; Unowsky, 'Peasant'; Hroch, *Social Preconditions*; Moll, *Kein Burgfrieden*.

202. As Barkey and Hagen argue in their conclusion (187), it makes little sense to talk of a typical West European form of nationalization 'from below' as opposed to an East European form 'from above'.

203. M. Mann, '"Torchbearers upon the Path of Progress": Britain's Ideology of a "Moral and Material Progress" in India. An Introductory Essay', in H. Fischer-Tiné and M. Mann (eds), *Colonialism as Civilizing Mission: Cultural Ideology in British India* (London: Anthem, 2004), 15; M. Waligora, 'What Is Your "Caste"? The Classification of Indian Society as Part of the British Civilizing Mission', in H. Fischer-Tiné and M. Mann (eds), *Colonialism as Civilizing Mission: Cultural Ideology in British India* (London: Anthem, 2004), 143; Bose and Jalal, *Modern South Asia*, 106, 118; Metcalf, *Ideologies*, 186, 222; Cohn, *India*, 106. Scholars disagree as to the extent to which the British colonial administration consciously sought to create a divide between 'Hindus' and 'Muslims'; see Robinson, *Separatism*, 345f.; Cohn, *The Census*, 38f.

204. H. Fischer-Tiné, 'National Education, Pulp Fiction and the Contradictions of Colonialism: Perceptions of an Educational Experiment in Early Twentieth-Century India', in H. Fischer-Tiné and M. Mann (eds), *Colonialism as Civilizing Mission: Cultural Ideology in British India* (London: Anthem, 2004), 247.

205. Jenkins, *Rethinking Ethnicity*, 69f.

206. London, IOR, V/15/18, Report of the Census of British India, 1881, 39; ibid., V/15/33, General Report of the Census of India, 1891, 495f. 1881 distinguished between English-speaking and 'purely British' individuals in assessing language knowledge; ibid., 223f.

207. London, IOR, V/15/89, Report of the Census of India, 1911, p. 383f. See also ibid., V/15/18, Report of the Census of India, 1901. See also Cohn, *India*; idem, *The Census*; S. Bayly, *Caste, Society and Politics in India from the Eighteenth Century to the Modern Age* (Cambridge: Cambridge University Press, 1999).

208. Mann, 'Torchbearers', 22; Sinha, *Colonial Masculinity*, 1; E.M. Collingham, *Imperial Bodies: The Physical Experience of the Raj, c. 1800–1947* (Cambridge: Polity, 2001), 8.
209. Cohn, *The Census*, 43. See also Waligora, 'What Is Your "Caste"?', 149f.; Mann, 'Torchbearers', 23; Bayly, *Caste*, 127; Juneja and Pernau, 'Einleitung', 41f.
210. Cohn, *The Census*, 37.
211. Ibid., 44; Bose and Jalal, *Modern South Asia*, 108; Bayly, *Caste*, 122; Waligora, 'What Is Your "Caste"?', 143.
212. London, PRO, RG 30/4, Census for England and Wales, 1871, vol. IV, p. IX, LXXVIf. and 303.
213. London, PRO, RG 30/5 (1881); ibid., RG 30/6 (1891); ibid., RG 30/7 (1901).
214. London, PRO, RG 19/45, Memorandum of the Statistical Society in Preparation of the Census of 1911, p. 122f. 'The omission (of the distinction of white and coloured) is the more significant as it represents a concession to racial sentiment of comparatively recent development, whether connected with the Ethiopian movement or not, does not, of course, appear in the reports'. Ibid.
215. London, PRO, RG 30/8 (1911), p. 216, 292 and 370f.
216. See also the minutes of two conferences held in preparation of the empire-wide censuses in London, PRO, RG 19/45 and RG 19/5.
217. E. Brix, *Die Umgangssprachen in Altösterreich zwischen Agitation und Assimilation: Die Sprachenstatistik in den zisleithanischen Volkszählungen 1880–1910* (Vienna: Böhlau, 1982), 83. See also ibid., 24 and 27f.; Gumplowicz, *Nationalitäten*, 247–69.
218. Brix, *Umgangssprachen*, 75.
219. Russ, *Der Sprachenstreit*, 5; Brix, *Umgangssprachen*, 16, 28. On the role of ethnography in the production of difference, see R. Bendix, 'Ethnology, Cultural Reification, and the Dynamics of Difference in the Kronprinzenwerk', in N.M. Wingfield (ed.), *Creating the Other: Ethnic Conflict and Nationalism in Habsburg Central Europe* (New York: Berghahn Books, 2003), 149–66. The first census to explicitly use the concept of 'race' took place in the First Republic in 1923. W. Pircher, 'Von der Population zum Volk: Biopolitik und Volkszählung in Österreich', in M. Stingelin (ed.), *Biopolitik und Rassismus* (Frankfurt am Main: Suhrkamp, 2003), 106.
220. Brix, *Umgangssprachen*, 96f. See also Gumplowicz, *Nationalitäten*, 189–92, 205; Herrnritt, *Nationalität*, 79.
221. Brix, *Umgangssprachen*, 14, 80.
222. Stourzh, *Die Gleichberechtigung der Nationalitäten*, 82; Walz, *Staat*, 141; Brix, *Umgangssprachen*, 100; Cohen, 'Nationalist Politics'.
223. Russ, *Der Sprachenstreit*, 8. See also Brix, *Umgangssprachen*, 110.
224. As cited in Stourzh, *Die Gleichberechtigung der Nationalitäten*, 79f. See also Walz, *Staat*, 131, 142; Burger, *Heimatrecht und Staatsbürgerschaft*, 121f.
225. Brix, *Umgangssprachen*, 14f., 29, 41. Gumplowicz, *Nationalitäten*, 239.
226. Brix, *Umgangssprachen*, 63, 89, 100. See also Herrnritt, *Nationalität*, 80.
227. Brix, *Umgangssprachen*, 74. On censuses and the issue of language, see also Judson, *Guardians*.
228. Brix, *Umgangssprachen*, 98f. See also Pircher, 'Population', 104.
229. Along these lines, it was suggested that the colloquial language be registered, like votes, independently and secretly. Brix, *Umgangssprachen*, 52f.
230. Stourzh, *Die Gleichberechtigung der Nationalitäten*, 203; Brix, *Umgangssprachen*, 29, 48.
231. Baier, *Sprache und Recht*, 72; Stourzh, *Die Gleichberechtigung der Nationalitäten*, 206f.

232. Stourzh, 'Ethnic Attribution', 74f.; Brix, *Umgangssprachen*, 50f.
233. India, Act 10 of 1871, ch. 7, sec. 71. See also Indian Legislative Council, Proceedings of the Council, vol. 22 (9 March 1883), 135; Sinha, *Colonial Masculinity*, 63.
234. London, IOR, V/26/261/1, Report of the Franchise Committee, 1918–19, p. 91.
235. India, Act 25 of 1861, ch. 23, sec. 329ff.
236. Ibid.
237. India, Act 10 of 1872, ch. 2, sec. 83.
238. London, IOR, V/26/261/1, Report of the Franchise Committee, 1918–19, p. 91.
239. Hirschmann, *'White Mutiny'*, 7. See also Sinha, *Law of Citizenship*, 75f.; McGranahan and Stoler, 'Introduction', 10; Kolsky, *Colonial Justice*.
240. See H. Amesberger and B. Halbmayr, 'Race/"Rasse" und Whiteness: Adäquate Begriffe zur Analyse gesellschaftlicher Ungleichheit?', *L'Homme* 16(2) (2005), 136; H. Sippel, 'Die Klassifizierung "des Afrikaners" und "des Europäers" im Rahmen der dualen Kolonialrechtsordnung am Beispiel von Deutsch-Südwestafrika', in A. Eckert and J. Müller (eds), *Transformationen der europäischen Expansion vom 16. bis zum 20. Jahrhundert* (Rehburg-Loccum: Evangelische Akademie Loccum, Protokollstelle, 1997), 154–70. On the dialectic asymmetry of oppositions, see F. Fanon, *Black Skin, White Masks*, trans. C.L. Markmann (New York: Grove Press, 1967).

Chapter 3

IMPERIALIST DISCRIMINATION IN COLONIAL CONTEXTS

National Belonging, Migration and the Recognition of Difference in Bosnia

Bosnia and Herzegovina were the Habsburg Empire's only colonial possessions. At the Congress of Berlin in 1878, the great powers of the time sought to reconcile their interests vis-à-vis the Balkan territories that had belonged to the Ottoman Empire. The ensuing treaty allowed for the Austro-Hungarian occupation of these two formally Turkish provinces. According to the agreement reached in 1879 between the government in Vienna and the Ottoman Empire, the sultan officially retained his sovereignty over Bosnia and Herzegovina, but Austria-Hungary took over the actual administration of the territory. This international blessing for the occupation, however, should not gloss over the fact that the populations of both territories resisted the advent of Austro-Hungarian rule. The Habsburgs did not have an easy time taking over the reins thanks to the efforts of Bosnian partisan-like groups, and resorted to the use of brute force as necessary. Thus, from the very beginning, the Austro-Hungarian administration of Bosnia was marked by violence. The military was called upon again in 1881 and 1882 to put down uprisings against military conscription. Similarly, the organized settlement of mostly German-speaking Hungarians in Bosnia and Herzegovina later reinforced the elements of violent conquest that had come to be associated with Habsburg rule.

Despite considerable resistance, the Imperial and Royal troops were ultimately able to establish Austro-Hungarian supremacy and ensure peace, order and security. The military administration was then gradually replaced by civil administrative structures. The joint Ministry of Finance took control of the

---

Notes for this chapter begin on page 154.

Bosnian government. It sought to establish an efficient bureaucracy, stimulate the economy, build up the country's infrastructure – including its schools – and implement a tax system that was to pay for all these measures. Benjámin von Kalláy, the Imperial and Royal Minister of Finance in office from 1882 to 1903, justified the occupation as a civilizing mission. He was convinced that Hungary as a hinge between East and West had a duty to introduce Bosnia's eastern population to the 'modern' Western world. The mostly autocratic administration was supposed to be responsible for this task; it was to modernize the country in a technical as well as an economic sense, while suppressing (at least at first) the impulses of social and cultural modernization.

As a result, the Habsburg administration was strongly conservative in its sociopolitical outlook. By clinging to the pseudo-feudal agricultural order and taking over large portions of Ottoman law, it effectively perpetuated the existing socio-confessional structure of the population in which a mostly Muslim elite presided over a generally Catholic or Orthodox lower and middle class. Simultaneously, the authorities squelched political activities through censorship and the prohibition of assemblies, while also introducing a strict system of passport and migration controls to limit the mobility of the population. As part of these efforts to bring about a controlled modernization of the country, the authorities also sought to construct and entrench a notion of supra-confessional Bosnian nationality that was supposed to overcome the differences between Muslims, Catholics and Orthodox Christians. Accordingly, the equal treatment of all Bosnians, regardless of confession, was a key element of Habsburg rule.

Meanwhile, the attitude of the indigenous population towards the government vacillated between cooperation and resistance, although it must also be said that emigration – many Muslims left for Turkey while Serbs and Croats headed to the United States – presented a third option. Despite the efforts to create a supra-confessional Bosnian nation, a gradual ethnicization of the confessional differences between Muslim Bosniaks, Orthodox Serbs and Catholic Croats began to take place after the turn of the twentieth century. As the government loosened some of its restrictions in 1903, it unleashed a wave of politicization across much of the population that resulted in the establishment of separate ethno-confessional reading societies, choirs and political parties. The increasingly heated public political debates often circled around the demands of the different religious communities for political autonomy. In 1909, the government finally granted Muslims the right to regulate their own domestic affairs.

Just one year prior to this, Austria-Hungary had annexed Bosnia and Herzogovina and thereby taken the country fully out of the hands of the sultan. Over the course of the annexation, the government declared its intention to introduce elements of constitutional rule. It lived up to its promise in 1910 by issuing statutes for Bosnia that granted the Bosnian parties political representation in the *Landtag* (akin to a regional diet). At the same time, however, nationals of Bosnia and Herzegovina were denied the right to participate in the political decisions made at the imperial level, despite the fact that, at least theoretically, Austrian and Hungarian nationals were represented through the delegations deputized by the Cisleithanian and Transleithanian parliaments, respectively. In addition, the Bosnian diet – unlike the diets of the Austrian Crown lands – was not autonomous, as it was still subject to the control of the Imperial and Royal Ministry of Finance along with the rest of the Bosnian government apparatus. Despite these constitutional steps, Habsburg rule in Bosnia still rested on an asymmetrical imperialist balance of power in which the nationals of Bosnia and Herzegovina occupied a less privileged position.

Not surprisingly, therefore, international tensions and the wars in the Balkans increased the potential for conflict inherent in this situation. Disagreements erupted more frequently both inside and outside the constitutional organs as a result. Anarchists and terrorists increased their activities, forcing the government to declare a temporary state of emergency in 1913. The outbreak of the First World War only served to exacerbate these problems. Most countrymen unwillingly fulfilled their military obligations, but a portion of the population actually supported the enemy forces. Simultaneously, the Habsburg military intensified the violence by which it held onto rule though internments, expulsions and even executions.

Contested Sovereignty

The occupation of Bosnia in 1878 brought with it a rather complex legal question as to how Bosnians at home and abroad should be dealt with in terms of their official nationality. At first, the fact that the sultan retained sovereignty ensured for confusion. Whereas the Austro-Hungarian government claimed 'de facto sovereignty' on the basis of its 'effective rule', this position was weakened by a convention signed in 1879 that conceded 'certain official rights' to the sultan in order to attain approval for the Habsburg occupation of the Sanjak of Novi Pazar.[1] Moreover, the Austro-Hungarian authorities recognized the Turkish nationality of those Bosnians who had emigrated to the Ottoman Empire when the occupation ensued in 1878, despite the fact that the Treaty of Berlin, which governed the occupation of Bosnia, did not grant the inhabitants of Bosnia a right to choose for themselves.[2] All other Bosnians, however, were supposed to lose their status as Turkish subjects.[3] Accordingly, the Bosnian government decreed on 13 November 1881 that Bosnian nationals in Turkey should fall under the jurisdiction of the Imperial and Royal consulate. As a result, Bosnians were to be treated akin to the nationals of the monarchy in international affairs.[4] In practice, however, the situation was much more ambiguous.

First of all, the Foreign Ministry in Vienna was not able to completely assert its sovereignty over the people of Bosnia and Herzegovina vis-à-vis the Turkish authorities until well into the 1880s.[5] On 17 'Zi'l-Hidsche' 1303 (i.e. according to the Gregorian calendar on 16 September 1886), a decree issued by the Turkish Ministry of the Interior, which had reached the Imperial and Royal Foreign Ministry via secret intelligence, declared that the nationals of the provinces of Egypt, Bosnia and Herzegovina, Tunisia, Cyprus, Bulgaria, Eastern Rumelia, Creta and Lebanon had not forfeited their Ottoman nationality in the eyes of the 'Sublime Porte', as the Ottoman government was called.[6] Based on this stipulation, the Turkish authorities continued to issue passports to Bosnians, which allowed them to acquire land in the Ottoman Empire, for instance. The Imperial and Royal Minister of Finance, in contrast, repeatedly stressed that it would not recognize the validity of Turkish documents issued to Bosnians.

The case of the former Egyptian Minister of Finance, Mohammed Hafiz Pascha, clearly illustrates the issues surrounding these conflicts over nationality. In 1880, the Imperial and Royal Ministry of Finance recognized Hafiz as a Bosnian national and issued him a passport. Hafiz then used this document to claim the protection of the Imperial and Royal embassy in Egypt. The Imperial and Royal ambassador quite obviously doubted Hafiz' claims to Bosnian descent, especially given that Hafiz as well as his father were born in Egypt, and his mother was 'even … a fellah'; the ambassador suspected that Hafiz had only acquired a Bosnian passport in order to escape his tax obligations in Egypt by obtaining the protection afforded Imperial and Royal subjects.[7] The Bosnian authorities, on the other hand, insisted that Hafiz was Bosnian. When the Egyptian authorities later decided that Bosnian nationals in Egypt should still be treated as Turkish subjects, given the fact that Egypt still officially belonged to the Ottoman Empire, Hafiz became an Austrian citizen.[8] In the end, however, this move did not afford Hafiz the protection of the Habsburg Empire that he so desired, because the Egyptian authorities determined that he had never lost his Egyptian nationality.[9]

There were also conflicts about the sovereignty over individuals from Bosnia with other states whose territories had formerly been part of the Ottoman Empire. For instance, when Bulgaria sought to impose military conscription in the 1880s, some residents sought the protection of the Imperial and Royal authorities, citing their right to do so as Bosnians. The Imperial and Royal ambassador interpreted the indignant reaction of the Bulgarian government to these arguments as an attack on the prestige of the Habsburg monarchy, and decided, in the name of his government, to extend the protection of the empire to all Bosnians and Herzegovinians in Bulgaria.[10] In the case of Salomon A. Pinto, the Imperial and Royal government enforced this claim; at the same time, however, it directed its officials to proceed with extreme caution in determining the 'supposed Bosnian nationality' of individuals applying for passports in the future.[11]

Initially, the Bosnian administration also reacted ambivalently in such cases. It stressed that it alone had the right to determine the official nationality of Bosnians living abroad.[12] Concurrently, it also instructed local authorities to proceed strictly and with extreme caution in issuing passports to 'Spanish Jews residing in Bulgaria'.[13] As a result, many applicants were not recognized as nationals and therefore denied passports. Moreover, when those affected by the directive then sought 'repatriation in their Bosnian homeland' in 1885, the government denied their requests. The authorities based their refusals on the fact that many of the applicants had forfeited their claims to Bosnian nationality because 'most had emigrated to Bulgaria 50 to 60 years ago, had not left behind any property, were not counted in any census registers or the membership lists of the Israelite community, they did not pay any communal or religious community fees, and lastly, they had not fulfilled their military obligations since compulsory service had been introduced for the occupied territories in 1882'. The only way for them to be granted naturalization was if 'all their male members born between 1862 and 1865' belatedly served their time in the military in Bosnia.[14] This argument illustrates quite clearly the extent to which military and fiscal interests shaped the policy of the Bosnian administration.

Yet the case of Luka Zrnić, who emigrated from Bosnia in 1881 and worked as a teacher at a Serbian secondary school, indicates just how indiscriminate the authorities could be in pursuing these interests. In 1896, the Bosnian authorities stopped Zrnić at the border on the way back from a visit to Bosnia, took away his passport and sent him for a military medical examination. In return, the government in Belgrade demanded his release as a Serbian national. The Bosnian authorities, however, insisted that Zrnić fulfil his military obligations in Bosnia because 'according to the regulation in place for Bosnia-Herzegovina, long-term absence did not equate the forfeiture of Bosnian-Herzegovinian nationality'.[15] The Habsburg authorities were only willing to recognize the Serbian nationality of Bosnians who emigrated to Serbia immediately following the occupation in 1878 and not that of those such as Zrnić who had not left until 1881. Towards the end of the nineteenth century, the different powers ruling over the Balkans were thus engaged in a tough competition over individual military conscripts that they fought on the terrain of nationality law.

How ambiguous nationality issues were sometimes reconciled is also demonstrated by the case of approximately 90 'Turkish gypsies' who requested financial assistance as Bosnian nationals from the Imperial and Royal Consulate in Cairo in 1906. The Habsburg authorities recognized the Bosnian origins of 'these people', but stressed that they had already been living abroad for 40 years. Only a few of them had been 'sent from Tangier to Bosnia' in 1902, where they had 'declared that they should not be considered Bosnian nationals because they, or rather their ancestors, had left Bosnia so long ago'. At the time, the Bosnian authorities had granted their request, issuing them papers that allowed them to leave the country for Turkey. However, the Imperial and Royal Ministry of Foreign Affairs now instructed all the consular authorities to strip the 'Turkish gypsies' of these papers and to deny them any kind of support in the future.[16]

At first glance, these examples demonstrate the inconsistent way in which the Bosnian government dealt with the matter of nationality. Whereas, in the case of the 'Spanish Jews' from Bulgaria and the 'Turkish gypsies', the authorities claimed that Bosnian nationality had been lost by living abroad for a long time, they did an about-face when it came to Zrnić and Hafiz. Ethnic criteria quite obviously played a role in deciding who was to be considered a national, especially given the conscious exclusion of the Bulgarian 'Sephardic Jews' and the 'gypsies'. It must be noted, though, that the risk of international complications also lessened the interest of the authorities in upholding an inclusive policy towards the 'Spanish Jews'; likewise, the 'gypsies' lack of financial means made them unattractive as potential nationals. Moreover, bribery was definitely at work in some cases, and quite possibly in that of Hafiz. In general, however, the decisions of the Bosnian authorities were guided by the country's interest in achieving the largest number of taxpayers and potential military conscripts.

The Unclear Regulations on the Acquisition and Loss of Bosnian Nationality

Alongside nationality conflicts with other states, the occupation of Bosnia also prompted the question of whether its residents were to be considered Austrian or Hungarian nationals within the imperial context. Since the dualistic structure of the Habsburg Empire made a compromise impossible, the authorities created a separate nationality status for the occupied territories of Bosnia and Herzegovina.[17] As early as 1880, the government drafted rules for the acquisition of Bosnian nationality, but these were not anchored in law until the Bosnian Constitution was issued in 1910.[18] In outlining these rules, the three joint ministries maintained different standpoints shaped by their respective interests: the Ministry of Finance advocated the legal integration of immigrants in order to promote the settlement of 'foreign colonists in the country'; the Foreign Ministry wanted to firmly establish sovereignty over the people of Bosnia as well as over its territory; and the Ministry of War sought to eliminate foreign consular protection for residents of Bosnia in order to be able to fully enforce military conscription – it also wanted to make it easier to deport 'agitators' who polemicized against the Habsburg occupation.[19]

The naturalization praxis that resulted from these negotiations made the acquisition of nationality contingent upon the forfeiture of the previous nationality as well as the employability and the 'respectability and morality' of the applicant.[20] In terms of emigration and the forfeiture of nationality, however, the authorities did not make any further stipulations.[21] According to the commission's report, limitations on emigration from Bosnia to Austria or Hungary were not necessary 'because such individuals are not lost to our army'. It also stated that no clarification was needed as to the legal status of 'indigenous Bosniaks ...', who went to one of the neighbouring principalities, acquired their nationality and then returned to the country'. In this case, it noted, 'the national government can make use of the right accorded every government to expel politically undesirable foreigners'.[22]

Another aspect of nationality was completely ignored at the time, namely the acquisition of nationality by birth. This issue was first regulated in the constitution of 1910 because the Habsburg authorities had to share sovereignty over the people of Bosnia with the Turkish sultan until annexation.[23] For all intents and purposes, the constitution established the principle of *ius sanguinis* and also declared that all children born or found in Bosnia were nationals, as long as 'there is no evidence suggesting another nationality'. Earlier provisions regarding the acquisition and loss of nationality also remained in place.[24]

Essentially this meant that, until 1910, all 'Bosnian-born' individuals did not have a clear legal status. Officially, they were still subjects of the sultan, but in practice they were treated as nationals by the Habsburg authorities. Their claim to Habsburg nationality, however, lacked a legal foundation. At first glance, this might seem to be just splitting hairs, but it effectively meant that native Bosnians were pushed into a legal grey zone in which they were at the mercy of the whims of the Habsburg authorities. Officials were in a very strong position vis-à-vis almost all the inhabitants of Bosnia, as well as those Bosnians who like Luka Zrnić had emigrated after 1878. They could either expel them as foreigners because their claims to Bosnian nationality could not be proved, or they could force them to serve in the army, as it was equally impossible for them to claim that they had forfeited Bosnian nationality. Thus, in addition to the goal of strengthening the Bosnian economy through immigration, the military interest in potential soldiers and the desire to retain the ability to expel politically undesirable individuals shaped the contours of the ambiguous ways in which the authorities dealt with the matter of Bosnian nationality.

Opening the Doors for Immigration

Following the occupation, the Bosnian authorities initially sought to implement a rational settlement scheme. One of their goals was to resettle the 100,000 to 250,000 Christian refugees who had left Herzegovina during the rebellion against Ottoman rule in 1875.[25] In 1891, for instance, the authorities proudly announced an increase in the number of 'repatriation attempts of Herzegovinian refugees in Montenegro', which they primarily attributed to the better economic situation in Herzegovina as opposed to Montenegro.[26] In reality, however, the majority of the refugees who had fled in 1875 had not returned home even ten years after the occupation. Bosnia also sought to attract 'foreign colonists'.

'[A]round 9,660 European [sic] colonists, whom the administration had invited', settled permanently in Bosnia.[27] The authorities granted these colonists tax privileges and helped them to attain land under attractive conditions.[28] In addition to these economic goals, the Habsburg government also had plans for settlement that were motivated by strategic military interests. In the end, though, their settlement attempts were just as unsuccessful as the one undertaken by Tiroleans in 1882.[29] The most prominent achievement of this Habsburg policy was the colony of Franzjosefsfeld, where German-speaking Protestants from Hungary settled in the 1880s.[30] The lack of success of most of these settlement projects was partly due to administrative and financial difficulties, but also to the fact that Bosnia and Herzegovina were not uninhabited, despite what many contemporaries seemed to think. In reaction to a letter from a German-speaking village that wanted to resettle in Bosnia in 1879, a Hungarian newspaper pointed out to its readers that it was false to assume that Bosnia was full of free land that could be scooped up by colonists.[31]

According to official statistics, the population of Bosnia and Herzegovina grew by 739,880 (almost 64 per cent) between 1879 and 1910 (see Table 3.1).[32] This increase resulted less from the growth of the autochthonous population and the relatively insignificant immigration of some ten thousand colonists than it did from the influx of civil servants, employees, soldiers and tradespeople, some of whom only temporarily relocated to Bosnia. Furthermore, as Table 3.1 shows, the Jewish community grew quite remarkably under Habsburg rule. Bosnia also became home to Greek-Catholic, Protestant and Reformed Church diasporas. This ethno-religious heterogeneity suggests that the Bosnian immigration policies were largely free of ethnically exclusive mechanisms.

Rather, social criteria and financial considerations seem to have shaped how the Bosnian authorities dealt with immigration, as they were definitely not interested in increasing the number of poor people in the country.[33] As long as immigrants were able to provide for themselves, they did not face any major bureaucratic hurdles. The naturalization cases that can still be found in the files of the Imperial-Royal Ministry of the Interior even indicate that Bosnian officials actually ignored the military-based objections of the Cisleithanian authorities when it came down to making it easier for farmers to settle in the country. Two candidates were naturalized without further ado, for example, despite the fact that they had circumvented military conscription in Austria as well as Russia

Table 3.1. Population and religious-confessional groups in Bosnia and Herzegovina

Year	Total population	Serbian Orthodox	Muslim	Roman Catholic	Other	'Israelite'	Greek Catholic	Protestant
1879	1,158,164	42.9%	38.7%	18.1%	0.3%	(counted	as	others)
1910	1,898,044	43.5%	32.2%	22.9%	–	0.6%	0.4%	0.3%

by emigrating from Galicia to Russia in the late 1870s as teenagers, only to resettle in Bosnia in the 1890s.[34]

Closing the Doors to Emigration

The emigration policies pursued by the Bosnian authorities, in contrast, were definitely more restrictive. The military service law of 1882 largely prohibited the emigration of those 'subject to the draft'. In fact, it was one of the main tasks of the Bosnian administration to 'prevent the emigration of draftees', and they could put a stop to the emigration of entire families whose sons were obligated to serve in the military. In one case, a man who wanted to follow his family who had already emigrated was caught as he tried to cross the border illegally.[35] Regardless of these military considerations, the Bosnian authorities tried to prevent the emigration of the Muslim population in particular as of the early 1890s. They only issued emigration papers in exceptional cases.[36] People who were suspected of trying to help Bosnians to emigrate were either expelled or sometimes kept under surveillance by the Imperial and Royal consulate in Constantinople. The Bosnian government even had reason to suspect official Turkish authorities of supporting this emigration of Muslims.[37] Investigations undertaken by the consulate in Turkey, however, did not confirm their suspicions. Rather, they indicated that the Turkish government had been secretly opposed to immigration from Bosnia since the late 1880s because the initial wave of well-to-do immigrants in 1878 and 1879 was followed by a wave of poorer immigrants, whose welfare and settlement caused major problems for the Ottoman administration.[38]

A 'Report on the Political Situation' from 1891 reveals why the Bosnian government was so interested in limiting the emigration of its Muslim population. It pointed to the 'true Oriental character inherent within the Bosnian population, like all other Balkan populations', that made them 'stubbornly' believe the rumour that the imminent transfer of the Sanjak of Novi Pazar to Russia threatened the Muslims.[39] Furthermore, the report highlighted the economic motives for emigration. In particular, it noted, small landowners were leaving the country because the modernization of the economy was endangering their existence. However, this exodus was judged to be rather harmless because 'it was not a great loss to the country if elements that do not want to come to terms with the new economic situation decide to leave, because they do not possess the necessary determination to fight the battle for their existence with their own two hands'.[40] Therefore, the desire to restrict Muslim emigration did not arise out of mercantile interests, but rather was politically motivated. The 'Mohammedan emigration' weakened, according to the report, 'a well-meaning element' of the population in political terms, and further strengthened 'the already existing Serbian recrudescence'.[41] Based on such assessments, the report recommended 'continually improving the legal and material situation of the population' as well as promoting the 'peaceful cultural work …, [the] development of sources of financial aid … [and] intellectual progress' in order to counteract the trend towards emigration.[42] Although the Bosnian government sought to influence the ethnic composition of the Bosnian population to suit its interests through such efforts and by closing the doors to emigration, approximately sixty thousand Muslim Bosnians left the country between 1878 and 1918.[43]

The Transition to Closed-Door Migration Policies

By referring to the 'Serbian recrudescence', the report touched upon a development that was quite unsettling for the Bosnian authorities. The intensification of the activities of political groups opposed to Habsburg rule prompted the government to crack down on the access of Serbian nationals to the territory of Bosnia in the early 1890s. In 1892, for example, it expelled the Serbian theatre director Folije Iličić because he had held 'inflammatory speeches'. The Serbian ambassador in Vienna repeatedly contested such expulsions – usually without much success – and complained that Serbian nationals were being denied entry to Bosnia on the basis of flimsy excuses.[44] Similar restrictions applied to oppositional Muslims. The authorities often used an administrative trick in such cases. They declared politically undesirable Bosnians, after they had left the country, to be illegal emigrants and then denied them re-entry.[45] Over time, the Bosnian government intensified its use of this praxis. In 1911, for example, it sent fifty-five lists to the Imperial and Royal embassy in Constantinople with the names of people who had left Bosnia 'with or without permission', and who would not be allowed to re-enter Bosnia.[46]

After the outbreak of the First World War, this praxis became even more restrictive. On 21 September 1916, the Bosnian government decreed that all those 'individuals who had fled abroad' and had not returned to Bosnia by the end of October would be stripped of their Bosnian nationality. Those affected by this decree then lost any official entitlements, positions and rights in Bosnia.[47] In general, the Bosnian government closed the doors of its formerly open-door migration policies during the war. Political suspicions directed against emigrants were omnipresent. In 1916, when the Imperial and Royal Ministry of War called for 'a general return of nationals who had emigrated from Bosnia and Herzegovina to lands overseas, especially the United States of North America', the Bosnian government and the Imperial and Royal Ministry of Finance replied that their remigration 'was not desirable because of political considerations', considering that these emigrants were 'in part Orthodox Serbs, in part Catholic Croats who had largely succumbed to south Slavic propaganda, which meant that the return of these less than loyal elements … was certainly not desirable'.[48]

As could be expected during a time of war, military conscription played a predominant role alongside such political considerations. Even before the war, the Bosnian authorities had tried to force two nationals on a visit to Bosnia who had been naturalized in the United States to serve in the army in 1913. Although this move obviously violated international agreements, the Bosnian government was only deterred from seeing this through by massive pressure exerted by Washington and Vienna.[49] In 1916, the Bosnian administration demanded a sweeping emigration prohibition for all male nationals up to the age of fifty, which was supposed to remain in place even after the war was over. This request not only rested on the interest in 'strengthening the army', but also – in a reversal of the argument used in the report of 1891 – on the economic goal to 'retain the population classes engaged in farming and business'.[50] In the period leading up to the end of the First World War, the Bosnian government increasingly tried to clamp down on immigration as well as emigration. But how did it intend to deal with the ethnic heterogeneity of its virtually confined population?

Identity Construction, Conversions and Dealing with Ethno-religious Differences

At first, the Bosnian government generally adopted a principle of ethnic neutrality. It treated Muslims, Orthodox Serbs and Catholic Croats equally, and stressed the importance of tolerance.[51] This statist approach corresponded closely to the rational and authoritarian self-image of the administration, which the Imperial and Royal Minister of Finance, Benjámin von Kállay, put into words in 1895, noting 'that the Austro-Hungarian Empire had been given the task of bringing civilization to the peoples of the East' and that this 'cultural mission' would be achieved through 'rational administration'.[52] This administrative rationality culminated in the attempt to construct a supra-confessional national identity in which the different groups were supposed to fuse into a Bosniak national consciousness. To this end, the Bosnian government standardized language and writing, founded a national museum in 1888 and published the journal *Nada*, almost as if it was familiar with quite recent scholarship on nation building.[53] In turn, the individual, quasi-sectarian ethno-religious identities were to be banned from the public sphere and from associational life.[54] One could almost go so far as to say that political passivity was expected of the population in return for the economic fruits of modernization.[55] However, this late manifestation of enlightened absolutism failed in part due to the fact that portions of the population did not want to submit to becoming a passive and malleable tool of the state. It also fell victim to an internal contradiction: on the one hand, the government wanted to regulate everything down to the last detail, but on the other hand, it promised to remain neutral and to refrain from interfering in the internal affairs of the different religious communities such as confessional schools and religious jurisdiction.[56]

Furthermore, in the late nineteenth century, the authorities resorted more often to the tactic of playing one ethno-religious group against another. For example, they sought to strengthen the position of the Bosnian Muslim community to turn it into a viable political player. As a result, by 1900 at the latest, the difference between Muslims, Orthodox Serbs and Catholic Croats became increasingly significant, not only for the government but also for the different groups themselves, who developed a sense of internal belonging and of external demarcation (Illustration 3.1).[57]

Even in the late nineteenth century, it was clear that this enlightened absolutist strategy would fail to overcome ethnic differences. The Muslims insisted on Turkish as the official language of the Sharia courts, special treatment for Muslim soldiers that allowed them to follow dictates of their religion, and the separation of Christian and Muslim female pupils and workers.[58] At the same time, the government observed an 'increased self-consciousness' among the Orthodox Serbs, whose evermore vehement demands made the somewhat fearful Muslims all the more insistent on their 'religious stubbornness' and on defending their

Illustration 3.1. Visual differences? Ethnographic sketches: 'Mostar: Muslim women' (Rudolf von Ottenfeld) and 'Sarajevsko Polje: The orthodox' (Ladislaus Batakn). Published in the so-called *Kronprinzenwerk: Die österreichisch-ungarische Monarchie in Wort und Bild*. Bosnien und Hercegovina, Vienna: k.k. Hof- und Staatsdruckerei, 1901, pp. 323 and 319. From: http://phaidra.univie.ac.at/o:12994.

'religious-national sphere of jurisdiction'. This made it even more difficult, the government noted, to keep the population as quiescent as it had been in the past.[59]

The debates over converts, and the question of how the transition to a different religious community was to be regulated, reveal just how much the mutual drawing of boundaries between different religious and confessional groups as well as the competition between them fed into their gradual transformation into ethnonational communities. In 1879, the Bosnian government prohibited officials from meddling in issues related to conversion because such matters were considered part of the internal affairs of the religious communities.[60] Shortly thereafter, the district government in Visoko declared that 'the Mohammedans who wanted to convert to Christianity were legally not allowed to do so', which sparked heavy protests among Catholics.[61] In response, the Cisleithanian government stressed that it saw 'the authorities' avoidance of meddling in the relationships between the religions and confessions that coexisted in Bosnia … as the only means to maintain civil attitudes towards one another and allow for the peaceful development of these relationships'.[62]

The authorities, however, did not adhere to this policy of non-intervention over the long run. The missionary practices pursued by the Catholic archbishop of Sarajevo, Josip Stadler, as well as the growing protests of Muslim groups against supposedly forced baptisms and kidnappings of female Muslims willing to convert, drove the government to issue an official resolution.[63] According to the regulations governing conversions from 1891, only individuals over twenty-three years of age were entitled to change their religion, and a clergyman from their previous faith had to confirm that the decision to convert had been made of their own free will.[64] However, this decree did nothing to quiet the situation. Under pressure from the Catholic hierarchy, the Vatican and the Imperial and Royal government, the Bosnian government announced in 1893 that it would continue to tolerate the conversion of those over the age of fourteen, which once more sparked protests from the Muslim side. A case from 1903 in which the authorities violently removed a Muslim widow who wanted to convert to Catholicism with her two daughters speaks to the stereotypes that were reinforced by these conflicts. The widow later supposedly appealed to Archbishop Stadler to free her from a harem, which made the matter a topic of discussion at the imperial level.[65] Although conversion was never really a mass phenomenon in Bosnia – only approximately five hundred Muslims converted to Christianity between 1878 and 1918 – individual cases such as this one fired the flames of aggression between the religious communities.[66] A compromise that was amenable to all sides could not be found until 1918.

In addition to the matter of conversions, demands for cultural and religious autonomy played a decisive role in adding ethnonational dimensions to existing religious and confessional differences. There were in fact two different processes at work at the time. Initially, the Habsburg government sought to keep religious communities separated, at least in an organizational sense, from their centres of power located outside the country. In particular, it wanted to retain the right to appoint religious leaders who would hold office within the Habsburg territories. The official Orthodox and Catholic churches were reorganized along these lines in 1880 and 1881.[67] For the most part, the Muslim hierarchy in Bosnia also loosened its ties to Constantinople in 1882 and submitted to Habsburg control.[68] Later, however, the representatives of the different religious communities pushed for independence from the Bosnian government. In 1905, the Orthodox Serbs were granted autonomy in terms of schooling and organizational matters. Four years later, in 1909, autonomy took effect for the Muslims following extensive negotiations.[69]

Autonomy for Muslims was especially problematic for two reasons. On the one hand, the Bosnian Muslims demanded the right of the Sheikh-ul-Islam in Constantinople to be involved in the appointment of the head of the Bosnian Muslims, the Reis-ul-ulema. In the end, the Bosnian authorities agreed to this request.[70] On the other hand, the Muslims argued that 'Islam did not recognize the jurisdiction of unbelievers over its religious organizations'.[71] Consequently, the Bosnian Muslims sought to ensure their autonomy by organizing themselves as a voluntary association. The constitution of 1909, however, established a different structure that closely resembled that of the so-called autonomous or self-governing administration in the Austrian Crown lands. The autonomous organization of the Muslims was subdivided over four levels. At the lowest level, all members (at least theoretically) elected representatives who then sent delegates to the next level up. The national assembly in Sarajevo then stood at the top. It was part of its mandate 'to supervise schools, select textbooks, direct the management of vakuf properties, prepare an annual budget, and otherwise administer Islamic affairs'.[72]

All together, these conflicts and developments fostered the political organization of ethnonational groups. A Muslim national or peoples' party (MNO) was founded in 1906, and a Serbian party (SNO) followed in 1907. A Croatian party (HNZ) was also established in 1908, which meant that 'each ethnic group was represented by at least one party'.[73] It is rather questionable, however, whether the Bosnian government actually managed 'to channel political activism in pro-Imperial directions' as it gradually removed the prohibitions against ethnonational organizations.[74]

Ethno-religious Diversity and the Bosnian Constitution of 1910

With the Bosnian Constitution of 1910, the diet created a public forum for the new ethnonational parties. Whereas the political rights of citizenship were linked to mechanisms that recognized difference, those regulating social welfare privileges as well as military conscription did not take ethnicity into consideration. This applied to older poor relief structures as well as to the 1909 law on the obligatory workers' health insurance, which largely resembled its Austrian forerunner. It must be noted, though, that social citizenship rights were largely devoid of practical relevance prior to the First World War.[75] The case was quite different in terms of military service because the Bosnian authorities had a vested interest in conscription. Ethno-religious differences played a marginal role in terms of the draft, cropping up in issues such as exemptions for clergymen, the oath of service and everyday life in the military.[76] In general, the legal and administrative framework of the draft aimed to conscript all those eligible, equally and without regard to ethnic identity.

Yet, the actual implementation of the draft was linked to a form of legal discrimination that brought disadvantages for Bosnian nationals as opposed to their Austrian and Hungarian counterparts. Although Bosnians were obligated to serve in the joint army, they were denied participation in the political decision-making processes at the imperial level. Austrians and Hungarians, in contrast, were, at least theoretically, represented by means of the respective parliamentary delegations. Simultaneously, the Bosnian diet, unlike the Reichsrat in Vienna and the Reichstag in Budapest, had no influence when it came to important laws. For example, imperial decrees governed the laws on military service in Bosnia in a quite absolutist way. Moreover, in principle, the laws passed in Bosnia were dependent on the approval of the Imperial and Royal government as well as the Austrian and Hungarian governments.[77] At its core, the relationship between Bosnia and Austria-Hungary was colonial in nature, even after the annexation of 1908, although the extension of complete Habsburg sovereignty over Bosnia and Herzegovina was justified by the goal of achieving a constitutional order as well as 'a clear and unambiguous legal status' for Bosnia.[78]

The constitution, which was imposed in February 1910, bore a strong resemblance to its Cisleithanian counterpart. Article 2 of the Bosnian Constitution mandated the equality of all nationals before the law, and declared the supraethnic neutrality of the law as one of its fundamental principles. It also contained provisions that recognized difference, such as Article 8, which granted freedom of religion and officially recognized 'the Islamic, the Serbian Orthodox, the Roman and Greek Catholic, the Protestant, the Augsburg and the Helvetic confession and the Israelite' religious communities. Article 9 granted these communities the right to govern their own internal affairs. Article 11 clearly resembled Article 19 of the Austrian Constitution of 1867 in that it guaranteed all Bosnians the right to preserve their 'national character and language'.[79]

The most clearly articulated mechanisms for recognizing difference were found in the electoral code that was imposed along with the constitution and regulated the composition of the Bosnian diet.[80] All male nationals over twenty-three years of age were granted active voting rights. The franchise, however, was spread over three constituencies. In the first constituency, large landowners (1st class voters) – women could vote via male proxies – as well as major taxpayers, university degree holders, the clergy, civil servants, and non-duty officers (2nd class voters) elected eighteen delegates. The second constituency, represented by twenty delegates, was composed of the other enfranchised voters from city districts. The third constituency, with thirty-four delegates, represented the rural communities. The constitution thus instituted a system of universal, unequal suffrage. All three con-stituencies were further subdivided according to ethno-confessional criteria, and 'the mandates were divided across the three main confessions according to the ratio of their percentages of the population'. Of the seventy-two elected delegates of the Bosnian diet, the 'Catholics' elected sixteen, the 'Islamites' twenty-four, and the 'Serbian-Orthodox' population thirty-one. 'Additionally, one mandate was awarded to the Israelites in the second constituency.'[81] Twenty so-called virilists were also members of the Bosnian parliament on the basis of the offices they held. They included the head rabbi of Sarajevo, the muftis of Sarajevo and Mostar, the four Orthodox and three Catholic bishops, and the two heads of the Franciscan Order.[82] The Bosnian government chose not to give in to the request to grant the colonists two mandates as well.[83]

The electoral code thus established ethnically based electorates and subdivided these in the second and third constituencies into territorial, single-member elec-toral districts. The allocation was done – much like in Moravia – through lists that were compiled and published by district officials. The Bosnian government decided who was to be recorded or not recorded on a specific list when com-plaints were made. Furthermore, in terms of parliamentary decisions, all three groups basically had a veto when it came to religious issues.[84] But, this recogni-tion of differences proved to be a failure in praxis. The diet elected in 1910, for instance, was plagued by increasingly aggressive debates during the Balkan Wars. After declaring a state of emergency in July 1912 and May 1913, respectively, the government shut down the diet because it had not been able to come to an agreement regarding the budget or the language question. In addition, the del-egates became increasingly vocal in their demands for a government that would be controlled by the diet, which effectively meant that they postulated extensive autonomy from Habsburg rule. After the assassination of the Crown prince in July 1914, the diet was closed for a third time and finally dismissed completely in February 1915.[85]

The Law and Racist Discrimination in British East Africa

When it took over the administration of British East Africa from the British East Africa Company in 1895, the British government in London brought a heterogeneous territory under its control that was politically as well as ethnically complex. On the one hand, different African groups occupied and ruled over the equatorial area in the east of the continent. On the other hand, the coast and the offshore islands were governed by the Arabian Sultan of Zanzibar, and an influential group of Indian traders had also settled there. The British interest in East Africa, which had originally been piqued by missionaries, researchers and big game hunters, grew as a result of the efforts to clamp down on the slave trade in the Indian Ocean as well as the 'scramble for Africa' among the European powers. By 1890, the German Empire and the United Kingdom had come to an agreement over the boundaries of their spheres of interest in East Africa. They officially recognized the sovereignty of the sultan over the islands and a ten-mile-wide stretch of the coast. Consequently, it is a bit misleading to say that the government in London brought this territory under its control with the establishment of the British East Africa Protectorate in 1895. The government only indirectly controlled the sultanate of Zanzibar, which was declared to be a British Protected State in 1890, together with the locally resident Arab elites. Plus, structures for effective control were lacking in most of the sprawling and largely untapped mainland territory.

Initially, the primary focus of the political and economic interests in the colonial acquisition of land lay in Uganda, which was far away from the coast. A railway was built between 1895 and 1901 that ran right through the East Africa Protectorate, connecting Lake Victoria in the interior to the coast. This construction project brought thousands of workers from India to East Africa, some of whom stayed as railway employees and traders once the tracks were finished. At the same time, many 'European' settlers arrived who set up farms in the highlands of Kenya in particular. In 1905, the Colonial Office took over the reins of the protectorate from the Foreign Office. The colonial administration gradually intensified its rule, sometimes resorting to violence. It pushed 'African' tribes such as the Maasai and the Nandi from their land so that it could offer property to European colonists. Moreover, by instituting a hut tax, the administration forced the 'African' inhabitants of the protectorate to pay for colonial rule and drove many to take up wage work, which often resembled forced labour. The uprisings against and resistance to these measures were put down by the British military. Parallel to this strategy, the British colonial authorities ensured the support and cooperation of the local elites, which effectively strengthened their control over the population.

At the same time, the British government only slowly formalized its own administrative structures. An executive council was appointed to assist the governor in 1906, followed by a legislative council in 1907. From then on, the 'European' settlers, who had organized themselves politically at an early stage, continually competed with the colonial administration for influence and power. The latter vacillated between sympathy with the demands of the 'Europeans' and its role as the paternalist protector of the 'African' people. In part, one can differentiate between the rather pro-'African' position of the Colonial Office in London and a rather pro-'European' position within the government in Mombasa and Nairobi. Furthermore, conflicts built up between the 'European' and the 'Indian' immigrants, whose representatives and organizations became increasingly vocal in their demands for equality and political participation. The colonial officials more or less positioned themselves as a neutral referee between the two groups. The major bones of contention were the immigration restrictions that applied to 'Indians', the exclusion of 'non-European' landowners from the highlands, and the introduction of a franchise system.

The 'African' tribes did not really participate in these conflicts as they were primarily interested in preventing the loss of their land through military and legal means, as well as improving their working conditions through strikes. Until 1914, however, these efforts were only poorly coordinated at best. During the First World War, East Africa became a battleground between British and German troops. The colonial administration mobilized the entire population, which in turn intensified the conflicts over the legal status of the different ethnic groups as well as the distribution of power in Kenya.

Nationality, Birth Registers, and Discrimination against the Indigenous Population

An analysis of nationality laws in the East African context necessitates determining to what extent the establishment of the British protectorate in 1895 changed the legal status of the population. The British authorities themselves only dealt with the formal legal dimensions of this issue in a few isolated cases. In 1901, for instance, the British law officers issued a statement in response to the question as to whether the children born to a Bulgarian missionary and his English wife in the protectorate could acquire British subjecthood on the basis of *ius soli*. They noted that the answer to this question depended on whether 'His Majesty … exercise[s], in fact, dominion and sovereignty'. Along the stretch of coast that nominally belonged to the Sultan of Zanzibar, which was legally considered to be a foreign country, they argued, British *ius soli* did not apply, nor had it taken effect in the hinterlands, because '[i]t has not yet been thought expedient to confer the status of British subjects upon the natives of Protectorates'.[86] At the same time, however, the 'African' inhabitants were not considered to be foreigners, which made for a quite precarious and ambivalent status in terms of the law.

When members of the Maasai tribe submitted a formal complaint to the colonial administration in 1913, the East African High Court was forced to deal with the issue. According to the terms of a bilateral agreement, the Maasai had been resettled on two reserves in 1904, and the British had guaranteed them the use of these territories 'so long as the Masai [*sic*] as a race shall exist'. When the administration pushed through a new agreement in 1911 and dissolved one of the reserves, some of the Maasai brought the case to the High Court.[87] But, the court dismissed the matter without dealing with the actual issue at hand. Rather, it simply determined that the Maasai could not make their case before a British court of law because 'British East Africa was not actually British territory, and therefore the Maasai were not British subjects'.[88] At the same time, the court judged that they were 'protected foreigners, who, in return for that protection, owe obedience'.[89]

Although the 'African' population was denied British subject status and the privileges that went along with it, they were nevertheless obligated to be obedient, which was diametrically opposed to the symmetry of the rights and duties of citizenship otherwise anchored in the European legal tradition. In fact, the East African administration turned this idea upside down in that the 'African' inhabitants were granted fewer rights than 'European' British subjects, despite the fact that they had many more obligations when it came to matters such as taxes. The High Court justified this situation by claiming 'that the Protectorate is over a country in which a few dominant civilised men have to control a great multitude of the semi-barbarous', making it necessary 'to secure the safety of the [white population]'.[90] The court's statement clearly illustrates just how much British rule in East Africa rested upon 'race and class supremacism'.[91] Not least because of the way it legitimized racist discrimination, this judgement was criticized by legal experts in East Africa and the United Kingdom.

The dominant legal opinion that those born in the East Africa Protectorate did not acquire British subject status based on *ius soli* effectively meant that the great-grandchildren of the immigrants who came from the United Kingdom were at risk of losing their British nationality because it could only be passed along abroad for two generations. In order to circumvent this problem, the British Nationality and Status of Aliens Act from 1914 removed this two-generation restriction for those born in British protectorates. Drawing on both *ius soli* and *ius sanguinis*, the law stipulated that British subjects could pass their nationality from generation to generation ad infinitum 'where the Crown exercises jurisdiction over British subjects'. At first, this provision was formulated in an ethnically neutral way. It even made it possible for the great-great-grandchildren of Indian immigrants to acquire British nationality. But whether those in question were actually able to take advantage of this clause depended on local administrative praxis. For example, only those who were officially registered at birth could provide the documentation required for acquiring British subjecthood.

De facto, however, 'non-white' British subjects were denied the right to acquire British nationality because, as of 1914, the authorities only permitted a birth to be registered if 'either one or both parents are of European or American origin or descent'.[92] A look at the birth registers also reveals that 'whites' were

Table 3.2. Births registered in the East Africa Protectorate, listed according to the ethnicity and 'race' of the parents

Year	'Whites'	Indians	Arabs and Somalis	'Swahili'	Africans	Total number of registered births
1905	63.1%	12.3%	9.6%	4.1%	10.9%	73
1910	43.3%	5.2%	12.9%	19.6%	19.0%	194
1915	100%	0%	0%	0%	0%	89

always proportionately over-represented. Table 3.2 shows the effects of the law of 1914 on the registers, which, as of 1915, no longer recorded the births of 'non-white' children; this practice therefore denied all those children who were not registered the proof required to claim British nationality.[93] In this case, day-to-day administrative praxis transformed an ethnically neutral law into a mechanism of racist discrimination.

The naturalization policies – if one can actually speak of any policy given the fact that naturalizations were very rare in East Africa – followed a similar pattern. Only the documentation for a single case between 1867 and 1918 has survived. The single and childless Persian national Henry Plummer Ishmael, son of David and Bhanu Ishmael, was born in Shiraz but resident in Mombasa. He had been working in the East African Customs Office of the British Crown for eleven years when in 1906 he applied to acquire British subject status at the age of twenty-three.[94] His application was processed by the Home Office in London because '[n]o machinery has as yet been established by means of which an alien can become naturalized in the British East Africa Protectorate'.[95] Given the lack of a formal policy, Captain Cowie, one of the representatives of the 'European' settlers, suggested in 1909 that a procedure should be implemented for the naturalization of foreigners. In response, the Crown Advocate pointed out that such a move was impossible because British East Africa was not really a colony.[96] Moreover, he noted, British subject status was not associated with any material rights of note in the East Africa Protectorate, so naturalization was rather senseless.

As the significance of the material and legal privileges associated with British subjecthood increased, the question of naturalization also became more pressing. In May 1917, the committee appointed to prepare an electoral code recommended to the Legislative Council that 'every adult male British subject whether by birth or naturalisation of European origin' should have the right to vote, whereby it defined 'European origin' as 'whole blooded descent from European ancestors'. These provisions were designed to deny suffrage to British subjects from India as well as 'natives'. At the same time, it was supposed to become possible for non-British 'Europeans' to attain the right to vote: 'If the right to vote is restricted to British subjects it is felt that means should be provided whereby foreigners of European origin in the Protectorate may be enabled to become naturalised British subjects'.[97] Rather than differentiating between subjects and aliens in terms of nationality, the committee suggested drawing a racial distinction between 'Europeans' and 'non-Europeans'. It thus sought to use naturalization as a way to preserve the privileged position occupied by all 'Europeans' as opposed to the rest of the population of the protectorate.

Migration Politics: Excluding 'Asiatics' and Welcoming 'Europeans'

The nationality of migrants hardly played a role in the immigration laws that applied to East Africa; rather, it was the ethnic identity of immigrants that mattered. The authorities sought to uphold the notion of Kenya as a 'white man's country' by denying the entry of 'non-white' immigrants. This process was only gradual at first. Early on, economic factors primarily motivated immigration policies. The administration aimed to spur economic growth by bringing in immigrants from regions such as Punjab. The railway connecting Mombasa on the coast with Nairobi and Lake Victoria (known as Nyanza as well), for example, was mainly built by workers who had come to East Africa as part of the Indian indenture system. Of the estimated thirty-two thousand migrants who came, approximately six thousand remained in the country after the project had been completed.[98] In the early twentieth century, the government also wanted to attract 'Indian' farmers to East Africa, and it built two villages for this purpose. This settlement project failed, however, mostly because the East African authorities were not able to find enough 'Indian' settlers who they believed were capable of becoming successful farmers.[99] Plans to sponsor the immigration of Finns and 'Eastern European Jews' – in 1902, the British colonial secretary, Chamberlain, suggested creating a 'Jewish National Home in East Africa' – also failed.[100] Instead of such strategies, a course of action was later adopted that promoted the immigration of 'European' settlers and banned the immigration of other groups. At the same time, the pressure on the autochthonous population to take up wage work was increased to make up for the loss of immigrant labourers.

One of the first suggestions for an immigration law was proposed in 1903 by the British agent in Zanzibar, who was in charge of the administration of the East African Protectorate at the time. He was of the opinion that 'the influx of destitute aliens … should … be checked'. Initially, the primary intention was to exclude poor immigrants, regardless of ethnic identity. The main concern was that their welfare would put a strain on the coffers of the colonial administration. Consequently, those indentured labourers from India who wanted to stay in East Africa after their so-called contracts had expired had to pay a deposit that could be used to finance their return to India 'in the event of their failing to obtain suitable and lucrative employment'.[101] These migration policies, which were ethnically neutral at the core, aligned with the position maintained by the Foreign Office as well as the demands voiced by the India Office 'that the restrictions were applied to all immigrants alike, and did not involve any discrimination against Asiatics as such'.[102] Moreover, by prohibiting the entry of impoverished immigrants, deportations within the British Empire were also supposed to be prevented. '[O]ne British Colony can hardly expel undesirables into another', because – as all the members of the Cabinet in London agreed – this would challenge the cohesion of the whole empire.[103] Nonetheless, such deportations continued to occur. In 1904, for example, the government in Zanzibar shipped 'a batch of no less than sixteen Europeans', who could not prove their supposed Italian or Austrian nationality, to Bombay after they had been observed 'begging from natives'.[104] As this example illustrates, the exclusion of impoverished 'whites' was also racially motivated in that their presence did not mesh with the narrative of supremacy that was used to legitimize colonial rule.

Generally speaking, the government in London did not object to the exclusion of immigrants on the basis of 'racial' criteria as long as the laws and regulations in question did not explicitly state these criteria. Within the corresponding debates, the Colonial Office pointed to the 'common practice [of the] Colonial Governments to resort to ... restricting the immigration into the Colonies of undesirables of various kinds, whether alien or not'.[105] At the same time the Colonial Office praised the exemplary nature of a law passed in Natal in 1897 that hid racially exclusive practices behind a veneer of ethnic neutrality by denying entry to everyone 'who, when asked to do so by any officer ..., shall fail to himself write out and sign, in the characters of any language of Europe, an application'.[106] Local officials decided which language – German, English, Swedish or others – the immigrants had to prove that they knew. Thus, on a case-by-case basis, the officials could make sure that immigrants could be denied entry if they were considered to be undesirable for 'racial' reasons.

The Foreign Office distanced itself from the 'drastic and illiberal character' of this practice, choosing then to institute – following the model of the United States – medical-based criteria for exclusion and a right of asylum for those persecuted for political reasons.[107] Yet it did little to hinder the transfer of the racially exclusive immigration practices of Natal to the East African context. In doing so, the Foreign Office paved the way for the exclusion of 'Asiatics', 'whether alien or not', which also potentially affected British subjects from India. According to the East African Immigration Regulation issued in 1906, all immigrants had to prove that they possessed sufficient financial means or pay a deposit that could be used to finance their deportation if necessary. In order to avoid interfering with trade in Zanzibar, this regulation did not apply to 'natives of Persia, Arabia (exclusive of the Levant), of the British, Italian, German, and Portuguese Protectorates on the East Coast of Africa, and of the islands adjacent thereto, including Madagascar'. 'Indian' immigrants had to pay a deposit of 50 rupees, while 'Europeans' had to pay 750 rupees. Moreover, 'any person deemed by the Immigration Officer to be an undesirable immigrant' could be denied entry.[108]

Working from these ethnically neutral phrased regulations defined by fiscal interests, the administration in the protectorate, which had been under the leadership of the Colonial Office since 1905, gradually put ethnically exclusive policies into place that fostered the immigration of 'Europeans' but hindered that of 'non-Europeans'. In 1909, the governor of East Africa spoke out against 'any system of State-aided Indian immigration'.[109] A year later, the representative of the 'European' settlers in the Legislative Council, Lord Delamere, called for more extensive measures to prevent 'the settlement of Asiatics in this country'.[110] In 1910, the government also eased the restrictions on the entry of 'whites' to the country by reducing the required deposit in half, making it only 375 rupees. It also gave these immigrants six months to find employment in East Africa, whereas all other immigrants only had a week to do so.[111] Some of the regulations were tightened even further during the First World War. In 1915, for example, 'Somalis' were prohibited from immigrating to the protectorate.[112] That same year, the government required the Uganda Railway Company to pay for the repatriation of the families of its 'Indian' employees.[113] A year later, in 1916, the government called upon local officials to be stricter in enforcing the immigration regulations. In particular, those entering the country were to pay their deposits before they were permitted on land.[114] It also made it easier to deport illegal immigrants, and raised the required deposit for 'non-whites' to 100 rupees in 1918.[115]

The decisive factor feeding into these developments and the evermore resolute exclusion of 'Asiatics' was the racism of the 'European' settlers who imagined East Africa as a colony in which 'whites' ruled over the 'black' population, and where there was no room for a third 'race'.[116] This vision collided with the economic interests of those who advocated the import of cheap labour from Asia. In the 'Native Labour Commission' of 1912–13, both sides fought over the best way to resolve the lack of a sufficient labour force in East Africa. The representatives of the 'European' settlers in the highlands wanted to put a stop to the recruitment of 'Asiatic' workers within the indenture system. Instead, the 'indigenous' population was supposed to be forced to take up wage labour. The idea was to 'get them [the natives] trained and willing to work; so that we may be able to get our work easily done, and they at the same time may learn to become useful citizens'.[117] In contrast, the businessmen and plantation owners along the coast, as well as most of the administrative officials, were in favour of recruiting 'Asiatic' labourers. Despite their differing opinion on imported labour, these men were no less racist than their opponents. They claimed, for example, that '[t]he results obtained from the imported Chinese had been … superior to the African', or that 'one Indian equalled ten Kikuyu'.[118] Ultimately, the majority of the commission came to the conclusion that indentured labourers were only to be brought to East Africa in exceptional cases and only as long as their repatriation was guaranteed. The permanent presence of the 'Asiatics', they argued, had a 'deteriorating effect morally upon the natives of the country'.[119] Although the government increasingly put a stop to the influx of 'Asiatics' and sought to attract 'European' immigration,[120] the number of 'Europeans' lagged behind that of other immigrant groups. According to government statistics, the number of 'European' residents rose from 506 in 1901 to 2,654 in 1910 and 5,438 in 1914, while that of 'Indians, Arabs and Others' dropped from about 35,000 in 1901 to 20,986 in 1911, but then increased again to 22,118 in 1916.[121] Consequently, the administration tried to provide 'European' settlers with even more cheap land, which necessitated expropriating land from indigenous tribes and resettling them. At the same time, the introduction of taxes was supposed to force the 'Africans' to find jobs, which would have basically tied them legally to their employers according to the Masters and Servants Ordinance issued in 1906.[122] In 1912, moreover, the government stipulated that 'natives' were only allowed to leave the reserves to work or to look for employment. In 1915, it also ordered the registration of all 'natives' with personal descriptions, fingerprints, registration numbers and identity documents. These measures were intended to supply the 'European' settlers with a tightly controlled, cheap 'African' labour force that was largely stripped of any rights.[123]

Territorial Segregation and Discrimination According to 'Racial' Criteria

One of the results of these policies was the territorial segregation of the population according to 'racial' criteria. The Land Committee, which met in 1904–5 under the leadership of Lord Delamere, proposed 'segregating the races in the towns, reserving the highlands exclusively for Europeans, and confining Indian agricultural settlement to the lowlands'.[124] The colonial administration sometimes followed this suggestion hesitantly, but at other times it was quite willing to go along with such plans.[125] It violently cracked down on the freedom of movement enjoyed by the 'indigenous' population, forcing the tribes onto reserves.[126] At the same time, 'non-European' immigrants were prohibited from acquiring land in the highlands that was considered to be particularly well suited for the settlement of 'Europeans'. This discrimination according to ethnic criteria within the context of civil law was principally rejected by the Liberal government that came to power in London at the end of 1905, but the East African administration was nonetheless granted 'reasonable discretion' when it came to governing the protectorate.[127]

Accordingly, the Crown Lands Ordinances of 1909 and 1915 prohibited granting Crown lands to 'Asiatics or Natives' and gave the governor a right to veto the sale of land, which was supposed to prevent 'non-Europeans' from acquiring property in the highlands.[128] With reference to these ordinances, for example, Dhanpat Nand Lal was informed in 1917 that he would be 'required to vacate his present premises, and that no permission will be granted to him to re-erect his mill for his own use in any part of the European area'.[129] By adopting these policies, the administration effectively created strictly separate areas of settlement for the different 'races'.

After the First World War, this territorial segregation had ramifications for nationality issues. In 1920–21, the East Africa Protectorate was divided into the Colony and Protectorate of Kenya. Whereas all children born in the colony were to acquire British subject status based on *ius soli*, those born in the protectorate were only to be granted the less-privileged status of a 'British protected person'. As all of the areas of the highlands reserved for 'Europeans' belonged to the colony, but the coastal areas primarily inhabited by 'non-Europeans' were declared to be part of the protectorate, this territorial segregation led to the privileging of 'whites' in terms of nationality.[130] Yet this was the rather unintended, if not actually hoped for, consequence of policies that sought to uphold the widespread desire to create separate spaces for different 'races' in the early twentieth century.

The different ethnic groups were not only segregated between the highlands and the coast, but also within the developing urban centres.[131] In this process, medical and hygienic arguments played an increasing role: Governor Northey noted, in 1919: '[I]t looks as if, in time, residential qualifications should be rather educational and hygienic than racial'.[132] This tendency was also reflected in the plan for the 'commercial and residential segregation of races' in Nairobi that William Simpson from the London School for Tropical Medicine developed in 1913 on behalf of the East African government. Simpson was convinced 'that segregation and demolition of the Indian bazaar were necessary to eliminate a "continual menace to the community"'.[133] The Nairobi City Council, however, opposed this radical idea and instead decided 'that both residential and commercial segregation of the three communities be achieved gradually by controlling future sale and lease of land'.[134]

Simpson was also involved in the drafting of the Public Health Bill of 1918, which the government depicted as an ethnically neutral measure justified on the basis of 'pure matters of health ... [and] public peace'. It was argued that due to the 'incompatibility of character', the 'different susceptibility of different races to disease' and the different 'standards of living of Europeans, Asiatics and Natives', each community had 'a natural desire as far as possible to live among its fellows and not to be mixed up with members of other races'. Moreover, the law did not make 'invidious distinctions between one race and another', but rather it made it 'equally unlawful for a European to live in an Indian area ... as it would be for an Indian or Asiatic to live in a European area'.[135] The hypocrisy within these arguments exemplifies the strong link between spatial separation and racist hierarchies in everyday life under apartheid. There were hotels, restaurants and clubs reserved solely for 'whites', as well as separate schools, train compartments, hospitals and even cemeteries for the different 'races'. Consequently, an omnipresent spatial structure existed that permanently reproduced the hierarchy between 'Europeans', 'Arabs', 'Asiatics' and 'Africans' in social praxis.[136]

The concept of 'racial' inequality also pervaded the legal sphere. In addition to the discriminatory measures regarding the acquisition of land and mobility, the code of criminal procedure also rested on racial inequality. As in India, cases against 'whites' were only heard by the upper courts and juries 'composed of Europeans or Americans'.[137] These regulations explain the clemency that 'European' defendants came to count upon. For instance, a settler who had murdered one of his 'boys' was only sentenced to two months hard labour in 1908.[138] In another case from 1911, a 'European' who had shot an 'African' was acquitted by the jury, against the recommendation of the judge. This case provoked an indignant response among the British public. The *Manchester Daily Guardian* wrote that '[s]ome of the white colonists in British East Africa badly need to be taught that they are subjects, not kings'.[139] Equality before the law was neither guaranteed in theory nor in practice in East Africa. Rather, the colonial legal system turned this principle upside down.

Racist discrimination was also at work in areas that affected the core idea of civic equality. Contrary to liberal legal traditions that coupled fiscal and military duties with political rights, duties were almost exclusively placed upon the 'natives' in East Africa, whereas the 'rights' were primarily reserved for the 'Europeans'. The protectorate officials only collected direct taxes from the 'natives', for example; all the others were at most obligated to pay municipal taxes.[140] Correspondingly, the attempt to extend the poll tax to the 'non-African' residents of the protectorate met with vehement opposition among the 'Indian' and 'European' representatives in 1912. They called upon the slogan of the American Revolution, 'no taxation without representation', and refused to pay any direct taxes as long as they were not allowed to elect representatives for the Legislative Council, which only comprised appointed members at the time. Yet they did not even bother to mention the fact that this coupling of fiscal duties and political rights should not apply for 'Africans'.[141]

A similar pattern was also to be found in the regulations affecting the military and military service obligations. Initially, British rule in East Africa was upheld militarily, and especially through the Indian army troops who were stationed there alongside the King's African Rifles, which was composed of professional 'African' soldiers. In 1905, self-run volunteer corps were also created that elected their own officers and whose members had to be 'of European parentage'. 'Eurasian British subjects' and 'Goanese or Parsis' were only allowed to join if they formed their own 'non-European' troops subject to the command of 'European' officers appointed by the government.[142] When the military draft was introduced at the outbreak of the First World War, however, it initially only applied to 'natives'. The 'Ordinance to provide for the Recruitment of Native Carriers for the Military Forces now operating in the Protectorate' from August 1915 obligated those 'headmen' appointed by the administration 'to provide from their Reserves the number of men required'.[143] It was not until the end of 1915 that 'every male person between the ages of 18 and 45' was obligated to fulfil 'compulsory military and other service'. Simultaneously, the government stressed that this general service obligation would not be demanded of 'Europeans' as long as a sufficient number of them joined the volunteer corps.[144] Apparently, the colonial administration wanted to avoid the equal treatment of all 'racial' groups when it came to military service because forcing 'whites' to serve did not mesh well with imperialist notions. Moreover, the 'Compulsory Service Ordinance' coupled military service with political participation rights in the case of the 'Europeans' in that elected 'European' representatives were incorporated in the East African 'War Council'.[145] However, political consequences were not drawn for any other ethnic group on the basis of military duties.

The enforcement of these service obligations was not uniform across the population because some groups were treated differently. The government did not even decide to insist that 'Europeans' fulfil their service obligations until the beginning of 1917. Despite this increased pressure, it was still possible for some of them to avoid recruitment.[146] 'African' residents of the protectorate who tried to get out of having to serve in the military, on the other hand, were treated harshly. In August 1918, for example, the Maasai refused to put up more recruits when requested to do so by the government. In response, the government sent in troops to enforce the fulfilment of compulsory military service. This endeavour ended in violence. Two women and several animals were killed in an 'unfortunate affair at a Masai [*sic*] Village where the troops, owing to a misunderstanding, fired without orders'.[147] The Maasai then attacked the 'recruiting camp', and fourteen of the attackers lost their lives in the process.[148] The recruitment war that then ensued cost the 'natives' numerous lives and did not come to an end until June 1919.[149]

Suffrage and Racial Discrimination

Although the 'Europeans' were far less consistently compelled to serve in the army, they were the only group supposed to be rewarded with political rights after the war. On the other hand, the 'African' population, which could claim 23,869 dead, and the 'Indian' immigrants who also had to serve in the army, were still to be deprived of such citizenship rights.[150] From the very beginning, the racial hierarchy shaped the debates over suffrage in British East Africa. Whereas the 'Europeans' wanted elected representatives to advocate their interests, they also demanded the exclusion of the 'Indian' population from the franchise. 'Indian' representatives opposed such a discriminatory policy and advocated the supra-ethnic equality of all British subjects instead. The exclusion of the 'African' population from political rights, on the other hand, was hardly mentioned by anyone. 'African' interests were only supposed to be represented in the Legislative Council by appointed officials or missionaries.[151]

The Legislative Council had been established in 1907 and comprised members appointed by the governor, including six government officials and two 'European' settlers. An 'Indian' delegate was first appointed to the council in 1909. That said, however, this position often remained vacant in the years that followed because the government could not find a candidate whom it found suitable.[152] In response to the repeated demands of the 'Europeans' for elected, as opposed to appointed, representation in the council, the government set up a committee in 1917 to draft a bill to this effect. From the outset, the committee was supposed to distinguish between 'European non-official members', who were to be elected, and the 'representation ... of the Asiatic, Arab and Native communities' by appointed delegates.[153] In May, the committee recommended that suffrage should be granted to 'every adult male British subject whether by birth or naturalisation of European origin'. In order to ensure the political participation of all 'whites', the committee dismissed the idea of 'any property or educational qualification'. Furthermore, only a year of residency within the protectorate was required to be included on the list of voters. The council itself was supposed to decide whether 'white' women should be granted suffrage.[154] The committee also recommended the establishment of ten constituencies that would reflect the different economic interests of the highland and coastal residents. There was also supposed to be a separate constituency for the 'Dutch' settlers who had come from South Africa.[155]

The debates over the committee's suggestions were primarily shaped by the opposition between the 'Europeans' and the 'Indians'. On the one hand, Lord Delamere, the most prominent representative of the 'white' settlers of the highlands, coupled suffrage with the 'Europeans'' claims to autonomy and the right to govern their domestic affairs in the future, independent of the government in London, as was the case with the dominions. In his eyes, matters pertaining to the rest of the population were supposed to remain under the thumb of the Colonial Office. In other words, Delamere demanded nothing less than the creation of two spheres of sovereignty, separating the inhabitants of the East African territory along 'racial' lines. From this point of view, the 'Europeans' were supposed to govern themselves in a constitutional manner, while the 'non-European' population was to remain subject to the absolute rule of 'white' officials. Along these lines, moreover, the admission of a nominated 'Indian' representative to the council should 'never be allowed to entrench one iota on the rights of Britons to govern a British Colony'.[156]

The contraposition was put forth by the 'Nairobi Indians' at the beginning of 1918 in a statement addressed to the British king as well as several influential people in India. They promised to continue to support the British war effort and called for the appointment of a governor who would be 'sympathetic towards Indian aspirations and ... strong enough to hold the scales even between the various communities'. In addition, they demanded at least two elected representatives in the new Legislative Council.[157] Above all, the 'Indians' placed their hopes in the hands of a strong, ethnically neutral administration that would be able to uphold equality against the discriminatory demands voiced by the 'Europeans'. The Indian government and the India Office in London supported this position and sought to prevent an all too explicit mechanism of discrimination with respect to the vote.[158] The Colonial Office and the East African government, on the other hand, took sides with the 'Europeans' and maintained the opinion that a 'British European preponderance in the Government ... [is] essential', and the 'contention put forward by prominent Indians that they should be given equal representation ... [is] untenable'.[159]

In the end, the Legislative Council officially adopted most of the committee's suggestions – which reflected the wishes of the 'European' settlers – in April 1919. The only demand that was not fulfilled was that only one 'Indian' representative would serve in the council. The majority of the Legislative Council insisted on two nominated 'Indian' council members. At the same time, the council also decided to raise the number of 'European' mandates by one to eleven. A petition to grant suffrage to 'non-Europeans possessing certain educational qualifications', on the other hand, was denied by a large majority. In contrast, with just a scant majority, the council instituted universal active and passive suffrage for 'European' women.[160] The Legislative Council Ordinance with these changes took effect in the middle of 1919.[161] With respect to social and gender differences, suffrage in East Africa was quite inclusive. Yet this inclusiveness only applied to the 'European' population, as the very same regulations were clearly tinged with racism.

Furthermore, the new ordinance did not bring about the end of the suffrage debates. As early as 1920, the British government, under pressure from the India Office, introduced suffrage for the 'Indian' population.[162] There were two potential ways to implement this directive: either through a system of communal representation with ethnically defined electorates along the lines of the Montagu–Chelmsford reforms of 1918–19, or through the integration of 'Indian' voters in the voting lists that had been reserved for 'Europeans'. Essentially, a different notion of supra-ethnic equality stood behind each of these options. A conversation that took place in London between the colonists' representative, Lord

Delamere, and the Secretary of State for India, Peel, in April 1923 illustrates the heart of the problem:

> Delamere: We feel that one of the difficulties is that if we admit Indians to any form of equality …
> Peel: *Any* form of equality?
> Delamere: Can you have qualified equality?
> Peel: That is what I am asking.[163]

Initially, Delamere argued the 'Indian' subjects of the British Crown, and even more so the 'Arabs' and the 'natives', would be overburdened if – according to the principle of supra-ethnic equality – they were placed on an equal footing with the 'Europeans' in terms of suffrage. It was, he claimed, 'very hard on them to mix them up in the white man's politics if it means that they have a vote on a common electoral roll'. In response, Peel suggested implementing a multi-tiered system of suffrage. On the one hand, he recommended that suffrage could be tied to an 'education test' for 'non-European' voters, 'so that they would be, I will not say on a level with the white man, but on a respectable intellectual level'. On the other hand, he proposed that the 'non-whites' should be guaranteed 'representation on a communal basis'. Delamere rather reluctantly took up with this recommendation, conceding that it might be conceivable in the future to grant 'non-Europeans' the right to vote 'on a limited communal basis'. Nonetheless, he explicitly distanced himself from the notion that 'you should ever give them representation according to their numbers, or anything like that'.[164] As the arguments raised on both sides illustrate, the recognition of ethnic differences within the franchise could have a discriminatory effect, especially if it was informed by notions of 'racial' inequality as opposed to legal equality.

Difference, Discrimination and Racism

A comparison of the Bosnian electoral code of 1910 and the East African Legislative Council Ordinance of 1919 reveals a fundamental difference between these two contexts. Although both territories occupied a colonial-peripheral position within their respective imperial constellations, the developments in Bosnia leaned towards statist policies of recognition, whereas an imperialist pattern of discrimination was established in East Africa. Apart from this distinction, there are a number of interesting similarities. For instance, the unclear regulations on the loss of nationality in Bosnia as well as the ambivalent legal status of the protectorate residents in East Africa created a precarious zone between nationals and non-nationals. Those situated in these grey areas could be burdened with duties, while the authorities could still deny them any citizenship rights.[165] Moreover, this intermediary zone gave the respective administrations more room to manoeuvre, strengthening the absolutist-authoritarian nature of their rules, especially in terms of immigration in East Africa and emigration in Bosnia. A contemporary hinted at this parallel when he described Bosnia as akin to 'a Crown colony ruled by dictatorial force'.[166] That said, however, the Bosnian constitution provided a path for the entire population to move away from such a dependent relationship, but in East Africa it was primarily the 'whites' who profited from the greater autonomy of the local government and the establishment of constitutional structures.

As this difference shows, the principle of legal equality was more heavily entrenched in Bosnia than in East Africa. The introduction of universal male suffrage in 1910, as well as the unease among Habsburg legal experts and civil servants regarding the less-privileged status of the Bosnians with respect to Austrian and Hungarian nationals, underscores this point.[167] While the discrimination against Bosnians was considered to be an unavoidable consequence of the legal complexity of the dual monarchy that actually went against accepted norms, the legal discrimination against the 'African' and 'Indian' populations in East Africa were justified on the basis of a supposed lack of civilization, or 'racial' inferiority.

With such racist arguments, the politically influential 'European' settlers were able to substantiate their demands for the creation of a 'white man's country'.[168] Their representatives played a decisive role in the implementation of imperialist policies of discrimination, sometimes against the will of the protectorate administration and the government in London. A comparable group that put forth such an offensively racist position did not exist in Bosnia. Even though settlers were brought into Bosnia following the Habsburg occupation, these immigrants could by no means claim the same kind of privileges as the 'European' settlers in East Africa. Additionally, the Bosnian colonists could not risk open conflicts with the seemingly all-powerful administrative authorities due to their own political and economic marginality. The administration itself leaned towards the Josephinist ideas of equality before the law and supra-ethnic neutrality as opposed to taking sides with its mostly German-speaking 'tribesmen'.[169] The racist convictions of the 'European' settlers as well as portions of the protectorate administration were the key that opened the doors for imperialist discrimination within the law and administrative praxis in East Africa. Is it fair to say in reverse that such racist views were not prevalent in the Habsburg colony of Bosnia and did not shape policies there? Or is it rather more fitting to distinguish between different forms of racism that manifested in their own particular ways in Bosnia and in East Africa?

Transcontinental and Inner-European Racism

Most modern notions of 'racial' order draw on concepts that emerged in the eighteenth century. One of the most influential factors was Carl von Linné's classification of humans according to the pigmentation of their skin, which differentiated between the 'red' *homo americanus*, the 'white' *homo europaeus*, the 'yellow' *homo asiaticus* and the 'black' *homo africanus*. The 'hairy' *homo ferus* and the *homo monstrosus*, which included 'deviant forms from several regions' under the same miscellaneous rubric, rounded out Linné's classification scheme.[170] Another influential thinker was Johann Friedrich Blumenbach, who divided humans according to the shapes of their skulls into 'Caucasian', 'Ethiopian', 'Mongolian', 'Malaysian' and 'American' types.[171] Other classification schemes based on characteristics such as eye colour, hair, and nose shape were less popular.[172] By the beginning of the nineteenth century at the very latest, these 'racial' classifications were increasingly coupled with the idea that one 'race' was superior to the others.[173]

These race-based ranking orders were as tightly linked to transcontinental colonialism as earlier enlightened-encyclopedic constructions of 'racial' categories. On the one hand, the colonizers brought 'the booty that fueled the mania for classification' back to Europe; on the other hand, the system of slavery established within the Caribbean plantation societies contributed significantly to the establishment of a racial hierarchy.[174] This combination of factors resulted in a form of transcontinental skin-colour racism that emphasized the superiority of the 'white' colonial rulers over the 'non-white' colonial slaves, and ultimately shaped the hierarchy between 'Europeans', 'Indians' and 'Africans' that played such a central role in East Africa.[175] The distinctions between these 'races' were mostly based on the assumption of clearly visible phenotypic differences. In turn, this made it easier for local administrations to enforce these hierarchies because officials believed that they could determine who should be privileged and who should be discriminated against with a quick glance.

Mistakes, however, did happen, as in the case of a certain Archibald Washington Jackson who was sentenced by a court in Greenwich, London in 1907 for 'wandering abroad to beg and gather alms'. He claimed that his father was an 'American negro' and his mother an 'Indian squaw', who had given birth to him in 'Gurandeville Indian Territory near Texas, USA'. The authorities thus treated him as a national of the United States and deported him there after he had served his sentence at the government's expense. Almost thirty years later, Jackson, who had taken on the name James Lone Hawk van Waalke, was taken into custody by US immigration officials as he tried to enter the state of Washington from Canada. The US authorities identified him as Charles Stanley Jarvis, born in Sydenham, London to an Irish father and a Scottish mother. As a birth certificate that had been discovered confirmed these details, the government in London accepted the British subject status of Jarvis, alias Jackson, alias van Waalke, and paid for his return to the United Kingdom. A London police officer noted in his file that Archibald or James or Charles must have had 'remarkable looks' in order to be able 'to pass as half negro – half Indian'.[176]

Whereas colonial racism based on skin colour trusted in the fact that such mistakes were quite exceptional, inner-European forms of racism, such as anti-Semitism or antiziganism, were completely preoccupied by the fear that 'racial' others could hide like parasites, unbeknownst among the general population. Despite numerous and supposedly precise attempts to clearly distil the phenotypic differences between 'Jews', 'Slavs', 'Aryans' and others, this fear was still omnipresent; time and time again, the 'enemy' had to be rooted out of the 'healthy body of the people'. These fear-driven aspirations to achieve racial purity also influenced the writings of Guido von List and Jörg Lans von Liebenfels, to name just a few of the racist authors who were milling about Vienna in the early twentieth century.[177]

The supposed problem of the invisible differences between 'races' was closely linked to the fact that inner-European forms of racism were more strongly based on language differences as in the case of the 'Slavs', or religious differences as in the case of the 'Jews', as opposed to transcontinental racial hierarchies that were purportedly based on unalterable physical differences.[178] This contrast should not be formulated too strongly, however, because inner-European forms of racism could also be radicalized on a biological foundation.[179] The exclusion of 'Spanish Jews resident in Bulgaria' and 'Turkish gypsies' by the Habsburg Bosnian authorities, for example, leaned in this direction.[180] Sometimes contemporaries even drew their own parallels between transcontinental and inner-European forms of racism, referring to Bosnia as 'our European India' in one case.[181] Moreover, it cannot be said that racist notions were not popular in Bosnia, or that they did not affect policy decisions. Similarly, such a distinction between a global form of skin-colour racism and a regional version of cultural racism can help to clarify why the enforcement of legal inequality required less administrative effort in East Africa because it was based on the assumption of visible physical differences; that said, however, it can by no means explain why imperialist discrimination gained a foothold in East Africa whereas the statist recognition of difference shaped laws and administrative praxis in Bosnia.

Savagery, Superiority, Hygiene and Racial Hierarchies

Distinctions between different forms of racism can also be made on the basis of whether they differentiated between groups according to the level of 'civilization', notions of 'racial' supremacy or medical-hygiene theories. The 'civilizing' paradigm treated 'natives' akin to children, who could gradually achieve the next level of development under the strict supervision of 'white' instructors who considered themselves to be more civilized. Only when these 'indigenous peoples' had achieved the necessary level of maturity, the argument went, could they be treated as legal equals. The irrational brutality, sexual licentiousness and unproductive laziness of 'natives' were, in particular, seen as proof of their savagery and their dire need to become more civilized.

Instruction in industriousness played a major role in the East African context. Governor Belfield determined in 1917 that the government's intention was 'to make of the native a useful citizen', and that 'the best means of doing so is to induce him to work ... by humane and properly regulated pressure'.[182] Two years later, his successor wrote in a similar way that 'the native' had to be taught that 'cooperation between the European and himself will be beneficial to both'. He also claimed that 'the native' had to learn 'to live in better and more sanitary surroundings ... [and] to be proud of his proper place in the world and ashamed of his former idleness'.[183] Consequently, the teaching of emotions such as pride, shame, peaceableness and ambition, was an integral component of the civilizing mission in East Africa. The colonists and government officials repeatedly stressed that it was not enough to introduce 'the natives' to European knowledge and modern technology; rather, they claimed, these efforts at rational education ignored the matter of moral values, and had led to the problem in India that the 'non-white' population no longer knew and accepted its 'proper place'.[184]

In general, the 'European' advocates of the civilizing mission did not have a high opinion of the 'Indians' in the East African context because, in a way, both groups were competing over who would teach the 'natives'. When the proposal to turn German East Africa into an Indian colony was discussed after the end of the First World War, the 'European' majority in the Legislative Council spoke out against this move because it claimed that only 'white' colonial rulers could lay the foundation 'for Christianity and for Western Civilization', and therefore the 'whites' had to protect the 'natives' against the damaging influences of such a quasi-oriental colonial administration.[185] In contrast to the 'Europeans', they also claimed, the 'Indians' were 'a poor class of petty traders', and therefore by no means productive themselves as they were 'entirely parasitic on the native who grows the produce'.[186] Consequently, in their eyes, it was 'white men's' duty to protect the 'natives' from Indian exploitation. A positive counter-image of the 'European' colonial rulers was also implicitly anchored within these arguments. This opposition allowed the 'Europeans' to legitimize a racist hierarchy on the basis of the civilizing mission that accorded them superiority over the 'Indians' as well as the 'natives'.

These paradigms in which progress and education could raise the 'backward' to their teachers' level of civilization over the long term had the potential to make both groups equal in a sense. The claims that based 'European' rule on 'racial' superiority, by contrast, were based on the idea of a permanent, insurmountable gap between those who were to command and those who were to obey. This argument not only perpetuated the racial hierarchy ad infinitum, but also led some to the social Darwinist conclusion 'that the Masai [*sic*] and many other tribes must go under', because 'white mates black in a very few moves'.[187] Although this hierarchical model supposedly based on biology contradicted the idea of a civilizing mission, it was relatively easy to reconcile these two strains of thought. The governor of the Cape Colony, Lord Milner, for example, declared that political equality was impossible because '[t]he white man ... is elevated by many, many steps above the black man; steps which it will take the latter centuries to climb, and which it is quite possible that the vast bulk of the black population may never be able to climb at all'.[188]

These racist strategies of legitimization were complemented by medical-eugenic theories that focused on 'racial hygiene' in terms of the separation and inequality of biologically defined 'races'.[189] Most of these theories suggested that each group should be assigned to a habitat reflective of their respective needs that would improve their health and capacity to work. The plans of William Simpson and the East African Public Health Bill of 1918, for instance, followed this line of thought. Although in terms of intellectual history as well as the history of science, these three legitimization strategies were broadly associated with different periods in history – the civilizing paradigm was at the forefront in the first half of the nineteenth century, the superiority thesis in the second half of the nineteenth century, and 'racial hygiene' after 1900 – the East African example illustrates that, in praxis, it was possible for all three strategies to coexist in the colonial exercise of power.

In Bosnia, on the other hand, only elements of a civilizing rhetoric can be detected – for example, when the authorities claimed to 'raise the human dignity of the population', to 'cultivate culture and prosperity' and to do away with the 'squalidness' that characterized Bosnia.[190] As this idea of progress at least theoretically aimed at equality in the future, it suited the equalizing structures of Austro-Hungarian dualism and the statist focus on neutrality and recognition much better than the assumption of an unchangeable hierarchy or medical-hygienic segregation. In the case of British East Africa, in contrast, the structure of the empire itself was based on inequality and therefore actually strengthened racist strategies of legitimization.[191] It was thus quite easy for the privileging of the 'European' settlers and the discrimination against the 'non-white' population to dominate the law as well as administrative praxis.[192] At the same time, the preponderance of a statist-egalitarian approach in the colonial context of Bosnia, despite the fact that the rule of a Christian empire over a largely Muslim population had the potential to develop into a discriminatory hierarchy, cannot be attributed to the idea that racist notions were irrelevant in the Habsburg context. Rather, the clearly less asymmetrical imperial structures, as well as the specific type of justification for the colonial exercise of power, stood in the way of imperialist patterns of racist discrimination in Bosnia – contrary to the developments in East Africa.

Notes

1. Abgeordnetenhaus des österreichischen Reichsrats, *Protokolle* (9th Session, 16 January 1880), Supplement No. 119, 1f. See also R.J. Donia, *Islam under the Double Eagle: The Muslims of Bosnia and Hercegovina, 1878–1914* (New York: East European Quarterly, 1981), 10f.
2. Austria, RGBl., 1879, No. 43, Bosnia. Vienna, HHStA, MdÄ, Adm. Reg., F61, Ktn 20, 45127–1896, k.u.k. Ministry of Finance to k.u.k. Ministry for Foreign Affairs, 2 October 1896.
3. Vienna, HHStA, MdÄ, Pol. Arch., XXXX., Ktn 210, Schutzrecht über Bosnier und Herzegowiner im Auslande, 1879–1882.
4. V. Heuberger, 'Politische Institutionen und Verwaltung in Bosnien und der Hercegovina 1878 bis 1918', in H. Rumpler (ed.), *Die Habsburgermonarchie 1848–1918*, vol. 7, *Verfassung und Parlamentarismus*, Part 2, *Die Regionalen Repräsentativkörperschaften* (Vienna: Verlag der Österreichischen Akademie der Wissenschaften, 2000), 2383–425, 2393.
5. Vienna, HHStA, MdÄ, Adm. Reg., F61, Ktn 20, 7607–1884, 1228–1886 and 63226/7–1911.
6. Vienna, HHStA, MdÄ, Adm. Reg., F61, Ktn 20, 31127–1886. 'Zi'l-Hidsche' refers here to Dhū l-Hiddscha, the twelfth month of the Islamic calendar.
7. Ibid., 23287/7–1880, Embassy in Kairo to k.u.k. Ministry for Foreign Affairs, 5 December 1880.
8. Ibid., Embassy in Kairo to k.u.k. Ministry for Foreign Affairs, 9 February 1881 and 30 July 1881. According to the Egyptian authorities, the British consulate dealt with the Cypriots in the same way. The British occupation of Cyprus was also governed by the Treaty of Berlin in 1878.
9. Ibid., Embassy in Kairo to k.u.k. Ministry for Foreign Affairs, 8 May 1881 and 6 September 1881.
10. Vienna, HHStA, MdÄ, Adm. Reg., F61, Ktn 20, 1228/7–1882, Ambassador in Sofia to k.u.k. Ministry for Foreign Affairs, 1 January 1882.
11. Ibid., 16190–1882, k.u.k. Ministry for Foreign Affairs to Consulate in Varna, 27 August 1882.
12. Ibid., 22890–1882, Note from the k.u.k. Ministry for Foreign Affairs on a letter from the k.u.k. Ministry of Finance.
13. Ibid., 4295–1884, Weisung Z 896 I/BH, 18 February 1884.
14. Ibid., 29430–1886, Report of the Bosnian Government, 5 January 1886.
15. Vienna, HHStA, MdÄ, Adm. Reg., F61, Ktn 20, 45127–1896, k.u.k. Ministry of Finance to k.u.k. Ministry for Foreign Affairs, 2 October 1896.
16. Vienna, HHStA, Konsulatsarchiv Jerusalem, Ktn 140, 43515–1906, Erlass des k.u.k. Ministry for Foreign Affairs, 18 June 1906.
17. D. Juzbašić, 'Die Annexion von Bosnien-Herzegowina und die Probleme bei der Erlassung des Landesstatutes', *Südost-Forschungen* 68 (2009), 263.
18. Juzbašić, 'Annexion', 291.
19. Vienna, HHStA, MdÄ, Adm. Reg., F61, Ktn 20, 16581–1880, Protokoll der Sitzung zur Regelung der Ein- und Auswanderungsbedingungen in Bosnien und der Herzegowina, 21 August 1880.
20. Ibid., Protokoll und Entwurf einer Instruction über die Erwerbung der Landesangehörigkeit in Bosnien und der Herzegowina.

21. Ibid., k.u.k. Ministry of Finance to k.u.k. Ministry for Foreign Affairs, 26 August 1880.
22. Ibid., Kommissionsbericht.
23. Turkish subjects could not be naturalized in Bosnia because they were not considered to be foreigners. Ibid., 17782–1880, k.u.k. Minsitry of Finance to k.u.k. Ministry for Foreign Affairs, 15 September 1880.
24. §§ 3 and 4; E. Bernatzik (ed.), *Die österreichischen Verfassungsgesetze*, mit Erläuterungen, 2nd edn (Vienna: Manz, 1911), 1037f. See also P. Vrankić, *Religion und Politik in Bosnien und der Herzegowina (1878–1918)* (Paderborn: Schöningh, 1998), 31.
25. M. Velikonja, *Religious Separation and Political Intolerance in Bosnia-Herzegovina* (College Station, TX: Texas A&M University Press, 2003), 118; Donia, *Islam*, 9, 32.
26. Vienna, HHStA, MdÄ, Adm. Reg., F61, Ktn 20, k.u.k. Ministry of Finance to k.u.k. Ministry for Foreign Affairs, 23 October 1891, vertraulicher Bericht zur Lage in Bosnien und der Herzegowina.
27. T. Bittiger, *An Elite in Transition: The Muslims of Bosnia and Hercegovina under Austro-Hungarian Rule, 1878–1914* (Berlin: Osteuropa-Institut der Freien Universität Berlin, 2001), 18f. On the perception of Bosnia as a non-European territory, see Koller, 'Bosnien', 199f.
28. J.K. Heimfelsen, *Die deutschen Kolonien in Bosnien* (Vienna: Gerold & Co., 1911), 11, 113f. and passim.
29. J. Milojković-Djurić, *The Eastern Question and the Voices of Reason: Austria-Hungary, Russia, and the Balkan States 1875–1908* (New York: Columbia University Press, 2002), 70.
30. Milojković-Djurić, *The Eastern Question*, 72f. See also Heimfelsen, *Die deutschen Kolonien*.
31. *Pester Lloyd*, 3 January 1879.
32. The numbers come from Vrankić, *Religion und Politik*, 2.
33. Vienna, HHStA, MdÄ, Adm. Reg., F61, Ktn 20, k.u.k. Ministry of Finance to k.u.k. Ministry for Foreign Affairs, 22 April 1881.
34. Vienna, AVA, MdI, Allg., 8, Ktn 353, 24321–1897, 24380–1897, 39975–1897 and 25301–1897.
35. Vienna, HHStA, MdÄ, Adm. Reg., F61, Ktn 20, 15830–1889 and 5790–1889.
36. Vienna, HHStA, MdÄ, Adm. Reg., F61, Ktn 20, 15830–1889, 46620–1892 and 51163–1901. On the emigration of Bosnian Muslims, see also Koller, 'Bosnien', 210f.
37. Ibid., 42400–1891, k.u.k. Ministry of Finance to k.u.k. Ministry for Foreign Affairs, 29 November 1891.
38. Ibid., 7006–1892, Vertraulicher Bericht des k.u.k. Botschafters Baron Calice aus Konstantinopel, 15 February 1892.
39. Vienna, HHStA, MdÄ, Adm. Reg., F61, Ktn 20, 23 October 1891, vertraulicher Bericht zur Lage in Bosnien und der Herzegowina.
40. Ibid.
41. Ibid.
42. Ibid.
43. Bittiger, *Elite*, 27; Donia, *Islam*, 30; Velikonja, *Religious Separation*, 127.
44. Vienna, HHStA, MdÄ, Adm. Reg., F61, Ktn 20, 29621–1892, 38237–1892 and 22931–1894, Serbian Embassy to k.u.k. Ministry for Foreign Affairs, 24 May 1894.
45. Vienna, HHStA, MdÄ, Adm. Reg., F61, Ktn 20, 36764–1892, k.u.k. Embassy in Konstantinopel to k.u.k. Ministry for Foreign Affairs, 6 September 1892. See also ibid., F57, Ktn 44; Donia, *Islam*, 164.

46. Vienna, HHStA, MdÄ, Adm. Reg., F57, Ktn 44.

47. Vienna, AVA, MdI, Präs. 8, Fasz. 1553, 7814–1917 and 4028–1917.

48. Vienna, HHStA, MdÄ, Adm. Reg., F15, Ktn 10, 467–1916, k.u.k. Ministry of Finance to k.u.k. Ministry of War, 24 May 1916.

49. Ibid.

50. Ibid.

51. Bittiger, *Elite*, 19; Donia, *Islam*, 15; Velikonja, *Religious Separation*, 135; F. Friedman, *The Bosnian Muslims: Denial of a Nation* (Boulder, CO: Westview Press, 1996), 62; Vrankić, *Religion und Politik*, 3.

52. Interview with Kallay in the *Daily Chronicle*, quoted in Velikonja, *Religious Separation*, 120. See also Donia, *Islam*, 14; Heuberger, 'Politische Institutionen', 2,384.

53. Ibid., 2,384; Bittiger, *Elite*, 11, 31; Velikonja, *Religious Separation*, 133; Milojković-Djurić, *The Eastern Question*, 7f., 81f., 120f., 126, 146f.

54. Milojković-Djurić, *The Eastern Question*, 91.

55. Velikonja, *Religious Separation*, 134; Heuberger, 'Politische Institutionen', 2384; Donia, *Islam*, 14.

56. Bittiger, *Elite*, 11, 19; Donia, *Islam*, 14.

57. See P. Stachel, 'Der koloniale Blick auf Bosnien-Herzegowina in der ethnographischen Popularliteratur der Habsburgermonarchie', in J. Feichtinger, U. Prutsch and M. Czáky (eds), *Habsburg postcolonial: Machtstrukturen und kollektives Gedächtnis* (Innsbruck: Studien-Verlag, 2003), 259–75.

58. Donia, *Islam*, 61; Bittiger, *Elite*, 23, 33.

59. Vienna, HHStA, MdÄ, Adm. Reg., F61, Ktn 20, k.u.k. Ministry of Finance to k.u.k. Ministry for Foreign Affairs, 23 October 1891, vertraulicher Bericht zur Lage in Bosnien und der Herzegowina.

60. Circular decree of the Bosnian government, issued 6 October 1879; as quoted in Vrankić, *Religion und Politik*, 647f.

61. Abgeordnetenhaus des österreichischen Reichsrats, *Protokolle* (9th Session, 16 March 1880), 1,892; interpellation of the delegate Richard Clam-Martinic. See also Vrankić, *Religion und Politik*, 648–50.

62. Abgeordnetenhaus des österreichischen Reichsrats, *Protokolle* (9th Session, 10 May 1880), 3,169, 3,171f.

63. Vrankić, *Religion und Politik*, 654f.; Bittiger, *Elite*, 23f.; Donia, *Islam*, 30, 55f.; A. Gottsmann, *Rom und die nationalen Katholizismen in der Donaumonarchie: Römischer Universalismus, habsburgische Reichspolitik und nationale Identitäten 1878–1914* (Vienna: Verlag der Österreichischen Akademie der Wissenschaften, 2010), 78, 81f.

64. Vrankić, *Religion und Politik*, 657f., 666; Bittiger, *Elite*, 24.

65. Vrankić, *Religion und Politik*, 677f. See also Donia, *Islam*, 63f.

66. The figure of 500 is taken from Bittiger, *Elite*, 24. See also Vrankić, *Religion und Politik*, 686f.; Gottsmann, *Rom*, 88f. On the connection between the conversion issue and the emergence of a Muslim movement for autonomy, see Vrankić, *Religion und Politik*, 675; Donia, *Islam*, 129.

67. Donia, *Islam*, 18f.; Vrankić, *Religion und Politik*, 93f., 390f.; A. Keßelring, 'Zwischen Osmanischem Reich und Österreich-Ungarn' in A. Keßelring (ed.), *Wegweiser zur Geschichte: Bosnien-Herzegowina*, 2nd edn (Paderborn: Schöningh, 2007), 30f.; Gottsmann, *Rom*, 78.

68. Vienna, HHStA, MdÄ, Pol. Arch., XXXX., Ktn 210, Frage der Regelung des mohamedanischen Cultus in Bosnien und der Herzegowina, 1879–1885. See also Keßelring, 'Zwischen Osmanischem Reich', 34; Bittiger, *Elite*, 20; Donia, *Islam*, 21f.

69. Donia, *Islam*, 30, 138f., 169, 172f.; Vrankić, *Religion und Politik*, 235f.; Heuberger, 'Politische Institutionen', 2,410; Keßelring, 'Zwischen Osmanischem Reich', 33f.; Bittiger, *Elite*, 21, 26; F. Schmid, *Bosnien und die Herzegovina unter d. Verwaltung Österreich-Ungarns* (Leipzig: Veit, 1914), 669f., 685f.

70. Keßelring, 'Zwischen Osmanischem Reich', 34; Donia, *Islam*, 174.

71. Donia, *Islam*, 141. See also Heuberger, 'Politische Institutionen', 2,383.

72. Donia, *Islam*, 174.

73. Ibid., 181. See also Bittiger, *Elite*, 27; Donia, *Islam*, XIf., 128f., 175; J. Marko, 'Bosnia and Herzegovina: Multi-ethnic or Multinational?', in European Commission for Democracy through Law (ed.), *Societies in Conflict: The Contribution of Law and Democracy to Conflict Resolution* (Strasbourg: Council of Europe Publishing, 2000), 6f.; Veliz, *Politics*, 89f.

74. Donia, *Islam*, 168. See also Heuberger, 'Politische Institutionen', 2,409f.; Velikonja, *Religious Separation*, 134.

75. Schmid, *Bosnien und die Herzegovina*, 643f., 655.

76. Austria, *Provisorisches Wehrgesetz für Bosnien und die Herzegovina und Instruction zur Ausführung desselben* (Vienna, 1881), 7f. On the text of the oath, see Vienna, HHStA, MdÄ, Pol. Arch, XXXX, Ktn 209, Bosnisches Wehrgesetz, 1881–1886.

77. Bernatzik, *Verfassungsgesetze*, 699, 1,037; Austria, *Das Wehrgesetz für Bosnien und die Herzegovina von 1912*, erläutert von Oberst Carl Czapp (Vienna, 1912), 6f. See also Heuberger, 'Politische Institutionen', 2,418; Vrankić, *Religion und Politik*, 31, 47f.

78. Allerhöchstes Handschreiben des Kaisers an die Ministerpräsidenten Österreichs und Ungarns, 5 October 1908. As quoted in Bernatzik, *Verfassungsgesetze*, 1,030.

79. Ibid., 1,037f. See also Heuberger, 'Politische Institutionen', 2,416.

80. Juzbašić, 'Annexion', 260f. On differentiations made at the local level, see Heuberger, 'Politische Institutionen', 2,409f.; Schmid, *Bosnien und die Herzegovina*, 73f.

81. § 5 of the electoral code for Bosnia in: Bernatzik, *Verfassungsgesetze*, 1,050f.; Heuberger, 'Politische Institutionen', 2,417f. Those people who did not belong to one of the religious communities listed, for example the Greek-Catholics or Protestant Christians of the Helvetic confession, could choose an electorate.

82. Velikonja, *Religious Separation*, 137; Vrankić, *Religion und Politik*, 44.

83. Juzbašić, 'Annexion', 283.

84. Heuberger, 'Politische Institutionen', 2,417.

85. Ibid., 2,419, 2,421f.; Donia, *Islam*, 180.

86. London, PRO, FO 45/10227, Colonial Office to Foreign Office, 5 June 1901.

87. L. Hughes, *Moving the Maasai: A Colonial Misadventure* (Basingstoke: Palgrave Macmillan, 2006), 5, 90f.

88. Ibid., 93.

89. Judgement of the High Court in the Case brought by the Maasai Tribe against the Attorney-General of the East Africa Protectorate, 26 May 1913, as quoted in Hughes, *Maasai*, 93. In terms of the law, it is quite interesting that the court distinguished between 'obedience' and 'allegiance', the latter of which 'proper' British subjects owed to the Crown.

90. Judgement of the High Court, 26 May 1913, as quoted in Hughes, *Maasai*, 97f.

91. Ibid., 98.

92. London, PRO, CO 630/1, Regulation No. 7 from 1904, Registration of Births and Deaths. See also ibid., FO 881/8173.

93. London, PRO, RG 36/1–3.
94. London, PRO, HO 144/828/142299.
95. London, PRO, FO 45/10227, Colonial Office to Foreign Office, 5 June 1901.
96. East Africa Legislative Council: London, PRO, CO 544/2 and 6, Minutes of the Legislative Council (22 November 1909), 373.
97. Ibid. (24 May 1917).
98. R.M. Gatheru, *Kenya: From Colonization to Independence, 1888–1970* (Jefferson, NC: McFarland & Co., 2005), 8, 12.
99. R.G. Gregory, *India and East Africa: A History of Race Relations within the British Empire, 1890–1939* (Oxford: Clarendon Press, 1971), 67–70; idem, *South Asians in East Africa: An Economic and Social History, 1890–1980* (Boulder, CO: Westview Press, 1993), 238f.
100. R.D. Wolff, *The Economics of Colonialism: Britain and Kenya, 1870–1930* (New Haven, CT: Yale University Press, 1974), 52f.; Gatheru, *Kenya*, 25, 27; Hughes, *Maasai*, 27f.
101. London, PRO, FO 107/129, Consular Official Cave to Foreign Office, 1 June 1903.
102. Ibid., India Office to Foreign Office, 10 September 1903.
103. Ibid., Colonial Office memorandum on the proposed legislation for excluding undesirables and for expelling them from the new colonies, 1902, p. 3.
104. Ibid., British Consulate in Zanzibar to Foreign Office, 17 March 1904. Impoverished 'Europeans' were most often deported to India because there were no immigration restrictions in place there. See also J. Lonsdale, 'Kenya: Home County and African Frontier', in R. Bickers (ed.), *Settlers and Expatriates: Britons over the Seas* (Oxford: Oxford University Press, 2010), 87.
105. Ibid., Colonial Office and Foreign Office, 11 June 1903.
106. Natal Act of 1897. London, PRO, FO 107/129, Colonial Office memorandum on the proposed legislation for excluding undesirables and for expelling them from the new colonies, 1902.
107. Ibid., Foreign Office to British Consulate in Zanzibar, June 1904.
108. London, PRO, CO 630/2, Regulation No. 17 from 1906. The lower deposit amount for 'Indian' immigrants had to do with the cheaper price of passage to India by ship. London, PRO, FO 107/129, Consulate in Zanzibar to Foreign Office, 17 March 1904.
109. East Africa Executive Council (12 March 1909).
110. East Africa Legislative Council (3 August 1910), 447.
111. London, PRO, CO 630/2, Regulation No. 27 from 1910.
112. East Africa Executive Council (18 September 1915, 4 April 1916, 15 June 1916, 11 January 1917).
113. Ibid. (22 January 1915).
114. Ibid. (24 June 1916, 21 July 1916, 10 May 1917).
115. London, PRO, CO 630/3, Regulation No. 5 from 1918.
116. On the role of the 'white' settlers in German East Africa, see P. Söldenwagner, *Spaces of Negotiation: European Settlement and Settlers in German East Africa, 1900–1914* (Munich: Meidenbauer, 2006); Parsons, *Empires*, 310.
117. London, PRO, CO 544/5, Native Labour Commission, 1912–13, p. 293.
118. Ibid., p. 24f. and 132f.
119. London, PRO, CO 544/5, Native Labour Commission, 1912–13, p. 325.
120. The 'Society to Promote European Immigration' was founded in 1902, and its interests were supported by the governor at the time, Sir Charles Eliot, as well as his successors. Gregory, *India and East Africa*, 71f.

121. These figures are taken from Wolff, *Economics*, 107, which are based on the official statistics. The significant shrinkage of the 'Indian' and 'Arab' population after 1901 was more than likely due to the return of the majority of the railway workers to their home countries after the railway had been completed. There were 3,175 'Europeans' living in East Africa in 1911 (Hughes, *Maasai*, 27), of whom 428 were settlers; the rest worked for the colonial administration or large companies. See also Parsons, *Empires*, 307f.; Lonsdale, 'Kenya'.

122. Wolff, *Economics*, 102f.; Parsons, *Empires*, 313.

123. East Africa Legislative Council (27 November 1912), 41. London, PRO, CO 630/2, Regulation No. 15 from 1915. See also C.O. Abour, *White Highlands No More* (Nairobi: Pan African Researchers, 1970) 21f.; Gatheru, *Kenya*, 9, 25, 30–42; C.W. Hobley, *Kenya from Chartered Company to Crown Colony: 30 Years of Exploration and Administration in British East Africa*, 2nd edn (London: Cass, 1970), 139f.; Wolff, *Economics*, XV, 47, 53, 57; Z. Marsh and G.W. Kingsnorth, *A History of East Africa: An Introductory Survey*, 4th edn (Cambridge: Cambridge University Press, 1972), 112f., 116f.

124. Gregory, *India and East Africa*, 75. See also Gatheru, *Kenya*, 13; Hughes, *Maasai*, 25.

125. On the conflicts between the settlers and the administration, see East Africa Legislative Council, Question Nos. 8, 10 and 16 from 1907. On individual officials who were opposed to these measures and sometimes supported the resistance of 'indigenous' groups, but were not able to bring about changes, see Hughes, *Maasai*, XV, 5.

126. Regulation No. 1 from 1904, Removal of Natives within Special Districts, London, PRO, CO 630/1. Regulation No. 17 from 1908, Provision for the Removal of Natives, and No. 18 from 1909, Removal of Native Political Offenders, ibid., CO 630/2. Regulation No. 33 from 1918, Residence of Native Families on Farms and on Areas not Included in Native Reserves, ibid., CO 630/3. See also Marsh and Kingsnorth, *East Africa*, 133f.; Wolff, *Economics*, 61f.; Hughes, *Maasai*, 5, 23f., 45f.; G.H. Mungeam, *British Rule in Kenya, 1895–1912: The Establishment of Administration in the East Africa Protectorate* (Oxford: Clarendon Press, 1966), 19f.; Hobley, *Kenya*, 125f.

127. Gregory, *India and East Africa*, 76. See also ibid., 82f.

128. East Africa Executive Council (6 November 1908, 29 March 1909). See also London, IOR, L/PO/1/1A, Kenya, restriction of immigration, position of Indians etc.; East Africa Legislative Council (18 January 1915, 23 January 1915). London, PRO, CO 630/3, Regulation No. 12 from 1915. Gregory, *India and East Africa*, 80; Gatheru, *Kenya*, 36; Wolff, *Economics*, 62f.; Hughes, *Maasai*, 26.

129. East Africa Executive Council (8 March 1917).

130. See O.O. Oyelaran and M.O. Adediran, 'Colonialism, Citizenship and Fractured National Identity: The African Case', in T.K. Oommen (ed.), *Citizenship and National Identity: From Colonialism to Globalism* (New Delhi: Sage, 1997), 173–97.

131. East Africa Executive Council (6 November 1908, 7 November 1916, 21 June 1917). See also Wolff, *Economics*, 66f.

132. East Africa Legislative Council (24 February 1919), Governor Northey.

133. Gregory, *India and East Africa*, 93.

134. Ibid., 181.

135. East Africa Executive Council (4 November 1918), 222f. See also Banerjee, *Becoming Imperial Citizens*, 82.

136. Gatheru, *Kenya*, 13; Gregory, *South Asians*, 3, 22; idem, *India and East Africa*, 89; Arbour, *White Highlands*, 22, 341f.

137. London, PRO, CO 630/2, Regulation No. 5 from 1906. See also ibid., CO 630/3, Regulation No. 6 from 1914. East Africa Legislative Council (7 October 1907, 16 November 1908). On the establishment of 'racially' segregated legal codes in neighbouring German East Africa, see D. Nagl, *Grenzfälle: Staatsangehörigkeit, Rassismus und nationale Identität unter deutscher Kolonialherrschaft* (Frankfurt am Main: Lang, 2007).
138. Arbour, *White Highlands*, 345f.; Mungeam, *British Rule*, 184.
139. As quoted in Hughes, *Maasai*, 67.
140. East Africa Legislative Council (31 October 1910), 469f. See also Gatheru, *Kenya*, 9, 29; Arbour, *White Highlands*, 21; Wolff, *Economics*, 99f., 117.
141. East Africa Legislative Council (12 February 1912, 5 March 1912), 6. See also Gatheru, *Kenya*, 29.
142. London, PRO, CO 630/2, Regulation No. 3 from 1905 and No. 9 from 1907, Volunteer Reserve. On the government's complaints about the lack of discipline within these volunteer corps, see East Africa Legislative Council (25 November 1912).
143. Ibid. (23 August 1915). London, PRO, CO 630/3, Regulation No. 29 from 1915.
144. East Africa Legislative Council (2 December 1915), 143. London, PRO, CO 630/3, Regulation No. 31 from 1915.
145. East Africa Legislative Council (2 December 1915).
146. East Africa Executive Council (1 February 1917, 21 March 1917); East Africa Legislative Council (21 May 1917).
147. London, PRO, CO544/10, Report on Native Affairs, 1919, p. 3.
148. East Africa Executive Council (4 November 1918).
149. London, PRO, CO 544/10, Report on Native Affairs, 1919, p. 3.
150. Gatheru, *Kenya*, 39f. On the military service of 'Indians', especially as drivers, see East Africa Executive Council (16 April 1918, 16 May 1918).
151. London, IOR, L/PO/1/1A. See also Gatheru, *Kenya*, 36; Parsons, *Empires*, 315.
152. Gatheru, *Kenya*, 33.
153. East Africa Legislative Council (February 1917).
154. Ibid. (May 1917), 198. London, IOR, L/PJ/6/702, file 2999.
155. East Africa Legislative Council (May 1917).
156. East Africa Legislative Council (20 November 1917). See also Gregory, *India and East Africa*, 182.
157. Ibid., 184.
158. London, IOR, L/PO/1/18, Correspondence between the India and Colonial Offices, 1918–19. See also Gregory, *India and East Africa*, 187f.
159. East Africa Legislative Council (24 February 1919).
160. East Africa Legislative Council (8 April 1919, 9 April 1919). See also Lonsdale, 'Kenya', 95.
161. London, PRO, CO 630/3, Regulation No. 22 from 1919.
162. Gregory, *India and East Africa*, 190; Gatheru, *Kenya*, 36.
163. London, IOR, L/PO/1/1.
164. Ibid.
165. On patterns of inclusive exclusion, see also G. Agamben, *Homo Sacer: Sovereign Power and Bare Life*, transl. by D. Heller-Roazen (Stanford, CA: Stanford University Press, 1998), originally publ. as *Homo Sacer: Il potere sovrano e la nuda vita* (Turin: Einaudi, 1995).
166. Abgeordnetenhaus des österreichischen Reichsrats, *Protokolle*, Ausschussbericht zur Regierungsvorlage bzgl. der Verwaltung Bosniens und der Herzegowina (9th Session,

16 (January 1880), Supplement No. 119, 1f. See also Komlosy, 'Habsburgermonarchie', 25; J. Feichtinger, 'Komplexer k.u.k. Orientalismus: Akteure, Institutionen, Diskurse im 19. und 20. Jahrhundert in Österreich', in R. Born and S. Lemmen (eds), *Orientalismen in Ostmitteleuropa: Diskurse, Akteure und Disziplinen vom 19. Jahrhundert bis zum Zweiten Weltkrieg* (Bielefeld: Transcript 2014), 31–63; Stachel, *Der koloniale Blick*; Kaps and Surman, 'Postcolonial or Post-colonial?', 20.

167. Schmid, *Bosnien*, 30; M. Komjáthy (ed.), *Protokolle des Gemeinsamen Ministerrates der Österreichisch-Ungarischen Monarchie: 1914–1918* (Budapest: Akadémiai Kiadó, 1966), 663; Juzbašić, 'Annexion', 254.

168. S. Ward, 'Imperial Identities Abroad', in S. Stockwell (ed.), *The British Empire: Themes and Perspectives* (Malden, MA: Blackwell, 2008), 230.

169. Heimfelsen refers to the colonists as such in the dedication of his book.

170. Banton, *Racial Theories*, 19f.

171. Ibid., 22.

172. B. Berry and H.L. Tischler, *Race and Ethnic Relations*, 4th edn (Boston, MA: Houghton Mifflin, 1978), 34f.; Banton, *Racial Theories*, 11.

173. Ibid., 45, 68f.

174. Pierson and Chaudhuri, *Nation, Empire, Colony*, 3. See also Banton, *Racial Theories*, 27, 93.

175. Along these lines, Marilyn Lake and Henry Reynolds speak of the 'spread of whiteness as a transnational form of racial identification', in M. Lake and H. Reynolds, *Drawing the Global Colour Line: White Men's Countries and the International Challenge of Racial Equality* (Cambridge: Cambridge University Press, 2008), 3. On the debate over 'whiteness', see also Amesberger and Halbmayr, 'Race'.

176. London, PRO, HO 382/18.

177. B. Hamann, *Hitler's Vienna: A Dictator's Apprenticeship*, transl. by T. Thornton (New York: Oxford University Press, 1999). On the role of racist arguments in the Hungarian context, see M. Turda, 'Race, Politics and Nationalist Darwinism in Hungary, 1880–1918', *Ab Imperio* 1 (2007), 139–64; John, 'National Movements', 89.

178. On the distinction between 'cultural ethnocentrism' and 'physical ethnocentrism (racism)', see U. Pallua, *Eurocentrism, Racism, Colonialism in the Victorian and Edwardian Age: Changing Images of Africa(ns) in Scientific and Literary Texts* (Heidelberg: Winter, 2006) 25f.

179. D. Claussen, *Was heißt Rassismus?* (Darmstadt: Wissenschaftliche Buchgesellschaft, 1994), 16; K. Struve, 'Gentry, Jews, and Peasants: Jews as the Others in the Formation of the Modern Polish Nation in Rural Galicia during the Second Half of the Nineteenth Century', in N.M. Wingfield (ed.), *Creating the Other: Ethnic Conflict and Nationalism in Habsburg Central Europe* (New York: Berghahn Books, 2003), 103–26; W.D. Hund (ed.), *Zigeuner: Geschichte und Struktur einer rassistischen Konstruktion* (Duisburg: Diss, 1996).

180. Vienna, HHStA, MdÄ, Adm. Reg., F61, Ktn 20, 1228/7, Weisung Z 896 I/BH, 18 February 1884. Vienna, HHStA, Konsulatsarchiv Jerusalem, Ktn 140, 43515–1906, Erlass of the k.u.k. Ministry for Foreign Affairs, 18 June 1906.

181. Milojković-Djurić, *The Eastern Question*, 2. See also Kaps and Surman, 'Postcolonial or Post-colonial?', 20. On the interplay of transcontinental and inner-European forms of racism in the United Kingdom, see Young, *English Ethnicity*.

182. East Africa Legislative Council (12 February 1917), 164.

183. Ibid. (24 February 1919), 260, Governor Northey.
184. East Africa Legislative Council (18 February 1918).
185. East Africa Legislative Council (9 December 1918), 243, Hunter.
186. Ibid. (9 December 1918), 244f., Clarke.
187. Governor Eliot in a letter to the Foreign Office in 1904, as quoted in Wolff, *Economics*, 66. On the intellectual background of the paradigm of superiority, especially with respect to the history of science, see Banton, *Racial Theories*, 45, 68f.
188. A speech made by Milner in Johannesburg in May 1903, as quoted in I. Loveland, *By Due Process of Law? Racial Discrimination and the Right to Vote in South Africa, 1855–1960* (Oxford: Hart, 1999), 63.
189. Banton, *Racial Theories*, 92f. See also A. Bashford, *Imperial Hygiene: A Critical History of Colonialism, Nationalism and Public Health* (Basingstoke: Palgrave Macmillan, 2004), 24.
190. Abgeordnetenhaus des österreichischen Reichsrats, *Protokolle*, Ausschussbericht zur Regierungsvorlage bzgl. der Verwaltung Bosniens und der Herzegowina (9th Session, 16 January 1880), Supplement No. 119, 1f. On the civilizing mission in Bosnia, see also Fillafer, 'The "Imperial Idea"', 54; Feichtinger, 'Komplexer Orientalismus'.
191. Pallua, *Eurocentrism*, 25f.; Mungeam, *British Rule*, 154.
192. Kann also distinguishes between extra-European forms of colonialism and intra-European forms in which 'racial' discrimination played a lesser role; see Kann, 'Habsburgermonarchie', 164.

Chapter 4

THE UNITED KINGDOM BETWEEN NATION, STATE AND EMPIRE

In the late nineteenth century, the United Kingdom of Great Britain and Ireland was the heart of a rapidly expanding empire. Yet the purpose and morality of this colonial expansion and its often jingoist or populist accompaniments were hotly contested. Especially as British global dominance threatened to topple at the outset of the twentieth century, the economic question as to whether the mother country ultimately profited from its colonies or whether the imperial project drained the state coffers played a particularly significant role. On the one hand, the tariff reform campaign advocated changing the course from free trade policies to imperialist protectionism, which was supposed to strengthen the cohesion of the empire as well as its domestic markets in order to boost the income from the colonies. But this agenda hit a roadblock of staunch resistance, especially among those who pointed to the huge costs of maintaining British dominance on the high seas. In reality, the British fleet could no longer guarantee the strategic security of the colonies in light of the strength of the German fleet, the naval aspirations of the United States, and the Japanese victory over Russia. These circumstances tipped the scales in the decision to gradually move the dominions, the so-called 'white' settlement colonies, towards self-government. The discussions over the survival or disintegration of the empire were coupled with questions about the unity of the United Kingdom itself, which had been formed by the union of England, Wales and Scotland with Ireland in 1801. Irish demands for Home Rule and national independence in particular fuelled heated political debates and even violent conflicts in England thanks to the presence of Irish immigrants.

When it came to migration, the most significant trends were the influx of Irish workers and other immigrants from the European mainland, as well as emigration to the United States and the dominions. Migration trends were often discussed within the context of social issues such as poverty because migration seemed to facilitate the steady growth of urban slums, but it also offered a potential solution to the problem. The unequal distribution of wealth also led to conflicts between the working class, the middle class and the aristocracy over the reform of the government and rights to political participation. Although the franchise was gradually expanded in the late nineteenth and early twentieth centuries, which contributed to the popularization of political issues in the mass media, some of the aristocratic privileges as well as the monarchist form of state, in which sovereignty rested in the 'Crown in Parliament', remained firmly in place.

Subjecthood and Nationality before 1900

The Defeudalization of the Law

Elements of feudalism shaped the contours of British nationality laws, embodied in the notion of the 'British subject' stemming from the Common Law tradition. This concept bound subjects to the sovereign in a personal reciprocal relationship in which the one side owed allegiance and the other granted protection. The Naturalization Act of 1870, which codified British nationality law comprehensively for the first time, did not affect the core of this legal framework. Yet it did herald modernization in terms of the treatment of emigrants, the avoidance of dual nationality, the shared national status of families and the legal position of foreigners.[1]

The Naturalization Act itself resulted primarily from an agreement that had been made between the United Kingdom and the United States of America in 1868, in which both states promised to treat their respective subjects or citizens who had emigrated and been naturalized in the other state as foreigners.[2] Prior to this point, the number of British subjects who were simultaneously US nationals continually grew thanks to the Common Law principle of 'indelible allegiance' and British statute law that provided for the patrilineal inheritance of British subject status abroad for two generations in keeping with *ius sanguinis*.[3] This led to no end of legal disputes because the Royal Navy pursued the impressment of these individuals to force them to serve aboard its warships while many British Americans sought to avoid the draft into either of the armies of the American Civil War by claiming that they were British subjects.[4] In order to resolve these issues, the law of 1870 allowed for the renunciation and loss of British nationality. Naturalized British subjects who had not given up their original nationality, as well as those individuals born in territories under British rule who had simultaneously acquired a foreign nationality through *ius sanguinis*, were entitled to renounce their British subject status by making a 'declaration of alienage'.[5] Moreover, from 1870 onwards, British nationals ceased to be such once they became naturalized in a foreign country.[6] These regulations effectively did away with the idea of an insoluble bond between sovereign and subject.

The problem of dual nationality also unleashed a fundamental debate about *ius soli* by which a Briton was anyone born on British soil. Over the course of the nineteenth century, several European states had replaced this principle with *ius sanguinis*, which meant that children took on the nationality of their parents regardless of their place of birth.[7] As immigration from these states grew steadily, an increasing number of children were born in the United Kingdom who acquired British nationality by virtue of *ius soli* and, simultaneously, their parents' nationality by virtue of *ius sanguinis*. Consequently, some parliamentarians advocated that children born on British soil to foreign parents should no longer automatically acquire British nationality because the application of *ius soli* 'violated the principle of the Bill, which was that [it] should terminate the double allegiance'.[8] However, this suggestion never achieved the necessary majority in parliament. Rather, the law gave these individuals a choice, but did not force them to choose between their two nationalities. Moreover, the act stipulated that problems that might result from such double allegiances were not to be regulated by any future legal provisions, but rather through 'international accord and treaty'.[9]

Ius soli was primarily supported and justified as a means of integration, as it ensured that the children of immigrants to the UK acquired British nationality.[10] But the fact that *ius soli* simultaneously turned all children born in the British colonies into British subjects was hardly mentioned in the parliamentary debates. Only a member of the Upper House pointed out that the lack of a 'clear and well understood definition of what shall constitute the status of citizenship' would lead to a great deal of ambivalence regarding nationality in the colonial context.[11] Regardless of 'whether the son of an alien shall be considered a British subject ... or ... an alien,' the Earl of Clarendon argued, 'it is clear, when we come to deal with other countries, that as English subjects are of all nations and all tongues, it would be extremely difficult in our Colonies to ascertain who is an Englishman'.[12] The language of this speech itself hints at the ambivalence that already existed in terms of the question as to whether *ius soli* should apply across the entire British Empire. It first refers to British subjects, but then it speaks of English subjects before bringing in the 'Englishman', thereby noting that the ethnic heterogeneity of the colonial context made it virtually impossible to identify true 'Englishmen' among the subjects of the empire.

This confusion of legal and ethnic categories points to the complicated position of 'white' subjects on the periphery of the empire. Their status turned into a particular problem in the Indian princely states at the beginning of the twentieth century. Around this time, the great-grandchildren of immigrant British nationals were in danger of losing their British nationality and becoming subjects of the local ruler instead. As 'Englishmen', however, they were supposed to be kept within the fold of Britishness. On the flip side, the fact that people 'of all nations and all tongues' became subjects by virtue of being born within a British colony was simultaneously considered to be a distorting side effect of *ius soli*. As the debates in 1870 illustrated, it was certainly not the legislature's intention to grant all colonial inhabitants access to British nationality. The ambiguities within British nationality laws thus by no means fostered a hybrid and 'racially' inclusive body of subjects.[13] Rather, the goal was to clearly distinguish between who should legally be considered an 'Englishman' – regardless of *ius soli* – and who should be excluded from this status on the basis of ethnic criteria.

The Dependent Status of Married Women and Children

The tenth section of the Naturalization Act formulated a new principle within British law regarding the 'National status of married women and infant children'. This section made the unity of the family in terms of nationality a legal norm that was designed 'to amend our naturalization law, so as to make it conform more nearly to International law'.[14] Women and minors were supposed to carry the nationality of their husbands or fathers, respectively. Marriage thus came to bear consequences for a woman's nationality. Prior to 1870, a foreign woman who married a Briton acquired British subject status, while a British woman who married a foreigner retained her British nationality.[15] The new law, however, stipulated that the latter lost her British nationality upon marriage.[16] Likewise, the wife of a British national automatically lost her British nationality if her husband was naturalized abroad. Taking up with the demands of the women's rights movement, several parliamentarians argued that special rules should make it easier for these women to regain British nationality upon divorce or the death of their spouse.[17] This request was countered by the argument that a change in nationality would not really affect the 'real rights and privileges' of the women concerned, including their property and inheritance rights. For women, so the reasoning continued, national status was merely 'sentimentally' significant because they did not enjoy any political rights of citizenship in the first place.[18]

The principle that all members of a family should share one nationality also affected minors whose national status followed that of their fathers, even if the latter switched nationalities.[19] However, their legal status was not quite as dependent as that of married women because the children of parents naturalized in a foreign country only lost their British subjects status if they left the UK together with their parent(s).[20] One of the primary reasons for this provision was that 'they may, though under age, be in our Army or Navy', and in this case they should by no means be forced to change their nationality.[21] Moreover, married women as well as children could apply for a 'certificate of re-admission to British nationality'; they were, however, subject to the same naturalization process that had been put in place for other foreigners.[22] Contrary to a nation-state approach, British women who lost their subject status by law were not accorded any privileges when it came to reclaiming their nationality of birth.

The Depoliticization of Real Estate and the Territorialization of Nationality

Another decisive change that the Naturalization Act introduced concerned the property rights of foreigners. While they had previously been barred from acquiring and possessing real estate within the United Kingdom, aliens were now granted the same property rights that subjects enjoyed. Only British ships continued to occupy a special position in that they could only be owned by British subjects.[23] Allowing foreigners to own real estate further dissolved the feudal bond between landed property and political participation, which had already been loosened by the franchise reforms of 1832. As of 1870, nationality replaced property as the central qualification that granted individuals access to political rights. The law explicitly stipulated that property 'shall not qualify an alien for any office or for any municipal, parliamentary or other franchise'.[24] The simultaneous assertion that naturalized aliens were to attain full political rights and were to be completely integrated 'into the British body politic', thus boosted the political value of subject status and naturalization.[25]

However, this deterritorialization of political rights went hand in hand with a reterritorialization of nationality. British nationality lost its character as a 'personal and mutual relationship of protection and allegiance' between monarch and subject, and became more strongly tied to territory instead.[26] This transition was reflected in a gradual modification of Common Law, which had initially declared all those born under the 'dominion and allegiance' of the British Crown to be British subjects. The phrase 'dominion and allegiance' was, however, increasingly replaced by the wording 'dominions and allegiance' in order to more explicitly refer to all territories under British rule. Whereas a person sojourning abroad may well have been under the 'dominion' of the Crown under certain circumstances, she was certainly not located within its 'dominions'.

The act of 1870 thus resulted in the defeudalization and territorialization of nationality, which made British territory the foundation for British subject status. Whoever left this territory could either renounce subjecthood or they would lose it automatically. In reverse, the children of immigrants born within the territory automatically became Britons on the basis of *ius soli*. Therefore, the territorial extension of British rule conferred British nationality to numerous colonial populations, irrespective of ethnic criteria. Interestingly, the fact that imperial expansion turned countless 'non-Europeans' into British nationals was hardly a factor mentioned in the parliamentary debates. Rather, it was repeatedly emphasized that it was necessary to modernize British law in order to bring it up to international standards. The elimination of 'indelible allegiance' and the establishment of nationality as a sine qua non condition for acquiring political rights served this purpose in that both measures effectively pushed out older feudal provisions. Some politicians even went so far as to consider *ius soli* itself as a remnant of bygone times that should be replaced by the allegedly more modern *ius sanguinis*.[27] These advocates of the principle of descent, which had allowed for the unrestricted inheritance of British subject status abroad, as well as those who albeit unsuccessfully advocated the independent nationality of married women, can be seen as early proponents of a nation-state approach to British nationality, which had yet to attain a parliamentary majority in 1870.

The Growing Importance of Ethnic Identities since 1900

Given the equal legal status that was being introduced for naturalized as well as natural-born British subjects, the British parliament debated tightening the qualifications for naturalization in 1870. The draft bill presented by the government proposed that five years of domicile in the UK or five years 'in the service of the Crown' should be required for naturalization.[28] Up to this point, only three years of residence had been necessary. The Lord Chancellor stated the reasons for this change in the House of Lords, citing that Prussia as well as the United States had implemented a five-year term. The Lords, however, countered this point in the draft law, as they voted in favour of keeping the customary three-year term of residence.[29] This change was then reversed by the Lower House, with reference to the extensive political rights that came with naturalization according to the terms of the new act.[30] The Upper House ultimately accepted the five-year requirement, '[c]onsidering that naturalization would confer the full privileges of citizenship'.[31]

In addition to five years of residence, the only other explicit stipulations were that candidates had to prove their intention to remain in residence or continue in the service of the Crown, and to swear an 'oath of allegiance'. That said, however, naturalization itself remained an act of grace on the part of the British sovereign that the Secretary of State for the Home Office granted or refused at his own discretion in the name of the Crown. Even applicants who fulfilled all the stipulated requirements were not entitled to naturalization per se. The authority of the secretary of state was limited, however, because he did not have the right to reverse naturalizations. The reason given for this restriction was that it would re-establish legal inequality between naturalized and natural-born British subjects, and put too much power in the hands of one government minister.[32] At the same time, the law authorized the secretary of state to work out the administrative details for a standard naturalization procedure.[33] As an analysis of naturalization praxis will demonstrate, however, the administration did not always go along with the intention of the law outlined in the parliamentary debates 'to throw the door open wide to foreigners'.[34]

Political, Social and Ethnic Criteria: Naturalization in Praxis

It was rather unusual for more than three hundred naturalizations to take place per year in the United Kingdom before 1890. During the 1890s, however, the number of naturalizations rose, climbing to nine hundred annually at the beginning of the twentieth century. In part, this development can be attributed to the increase in immigration to the UK. But, it also definitely had something to do with the expansion of the political and social rights that British citizenship conferred. Becoming a British national thus became all the more attractive to immigrants. It is difficult to assess how the Home Office made use of its discretionary powers in terms of naturalization, not least because it is impossible to determine how many applications were denied prior to 1903. In addition, only sixty-two denied applications still exist for the entire period between 1870 and 1914. More than half of these remaining applications were from the turn of the century when the British bureaucracy seems to have taken a greater interest in the naturalization process.

The files indicate that the Home Office intensified its inquiries regarding candidates for naturalization during the 1890s. For example, it became common practice to request more detailed police reports.[35] The most frequent reason cited for the denial of a naturalization request was that the applicant had been convicted of a crime or was suspected of having committed one (fourteen cases). Others were denied because the British guarantors who supported their applications did not seem to be trustworthy, or the applicant was suspected of having falsified information (thirteen cases). Republican convictions – as in the case of Karl Marx – as well as moral issues and especially extramarital relations were also grounds for rejection.[36] In other cases, the applicants had not resided long enough in the UK or did not want to settle permanently; some also had debts, were bankrupt or could hardly speak English.

These various reasons cited for the refusal of naturalization applications can be roughly divided between those of a legal/political nature and those with a sociocultural motive. On the one hand, the British authorities wanted to avoid conflicts with other states, which was one reason why it was so important that a naturalized citizen intended to settle permanently in the UK. In 1885, the Home Office noted in the case of John Henry Exshaw, who had been born in Paris, that even if he were to be naturalized (his request was denied), he would not be able to claim the protection of the British state in France if the French government considered him to be a French national.[37] In order to avoid such international complexities, British authorities also denied naturalization to nationals of the Indian princely states because – due to the pseudo-sovereign position of the Indian princes – they were neither supposed to be considered British subjects, nor foreigners.[38] Lastly, it should be noted that some applications were refused on ideological grounds. The Italian national Ernesto Manara, for example, was denied naturalization in 1895 because he had drunkenly yelled out in public in front of the Victoria Hotel on Malta: 'The Maltese people are ill-treated, and are being murdered by the government. ... France for ever! And Russia for ever!'[39]

Whereas legal and political concerns had guided the decisions of the British authorities in naturalization praxis since the 1870s, the 'good character' of applicants did not come into play until the 1890s. From this point on, the Home Office increasingly restricted the access of convicted criminals and other socially deviant individuals to British subject status. Sufficient knowledge of the English language also became necessary after 1900. The general idea was that the proper social integration of naturalized individuals, who had to be in a position to take on the political responsibilities of a British subject, rested on them being able to communicate in English. Noah Cohen, who applied for naturalization in 1901, was the first to be denied on the basis of his poor knowledge of English.[40] Naturalization thus became increasingly restrictive as a result of the new criteria added in the 1890s. The rejection quota calculated by the Home Office itself for the period after 1903 confirms this general impression. In 1903, for example, 4 per cent of the applications were denied; from then on, the rejection quota rose quite steadily to 13.9 per cent in 1908, and then it hovered around 12 per cent thereafter.[41]

It is quite likely that these tightened restrictions primarily affected East European Jews because this practice coincided with parliamentary debates over a more restrictive immigration law that was supposed to put a stop to the immigration of Russian and Polish Jews in particular. Beginning in the late nineteenth century, the Jews who had fled to the UK to escape the pogroms in the Russian Empire attracted a growing amount of public attention. Anti-immigration propaganda depicted the arrival of the East European Jews as an economic and biological danger for the British population in an increasingly xenophobic and racist way.[42] Not least because of such agitation, the more restrictive Aliens Act came into force in 1905.[43]

To a certain extent, the conflicts surrounding Jewish immigration were reflected in the praxis of naturalization. Police reports, for instance, pointed out that an applicant was of a 'Jewish persuasion' or determined that he was 'a Russian Jew'.[44] Some applicants even emphasized their own Jewish descent. Israel Woods, to name one such case, described his parents as Russian nationals and Polish Jews. Due to an anonymous denunciation, however, his application was rejected in 1901 despite a positive police report.[45] Moreover, several 'Jewish' applicants were denied naturalization because of petty crimes or even just suspicions. According to an internal comment on the file in another case, however, the officials of the Home Office actually regretted having to refuse the application of Abraham Leiba-Tarakovsky in 1905 due to his poor English. In fact, they even informed his lawyer that he could resubmit his application once he had improved his English. It is highly likely that the reason the authorities were so cooperative in this case was because Leiba-Tartakovsky was a well-to-do businessman who owned property.[46] In contrast, the application of Morris Prager, a 'journeyman tailor who cannot read or write', was rejected without a second thought.[47]

Additionally, the applications submitted by so-called 'Naturalisation Societies' who often represented 'Jews' were also quite frequently denied (see Illustration 4.1).[48] In exchange for the regular payment of membership fees, these associations advocated the naturalization of their members. As early as the 1880s, the Metropolitan Police criticized the activities of these societies because they made it possible for 'pauper aliens' to submit applications.[49] In the case of Marks Strom, who had bribed his guarantors in 1896, the authorities unsuccessfully tried to implicate the lawyer S. Goldman who was working for the Metropolitan Naturalization Society in this act of fraud. Goldman was then

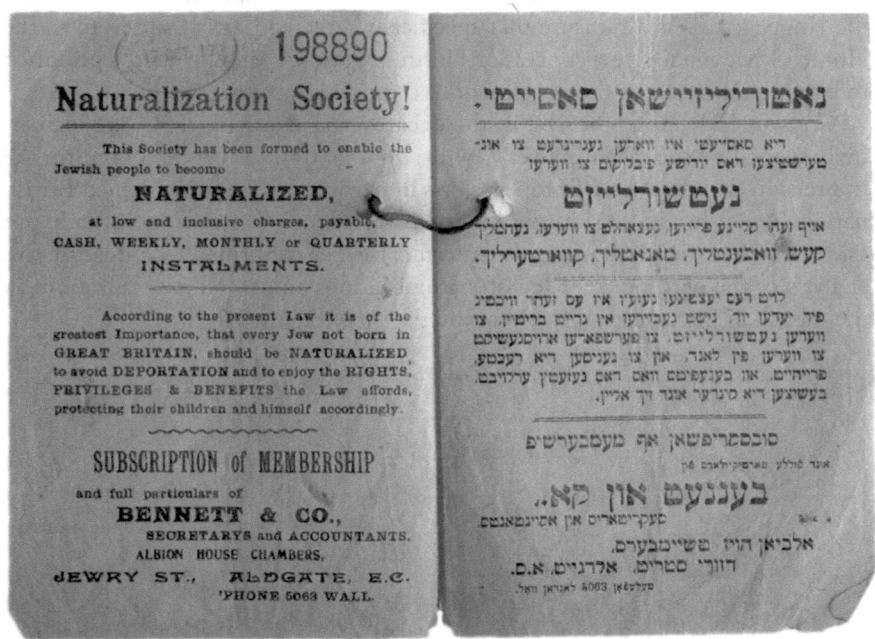

Illustration 4.1. Advertising leaflet from a London naturalization society, 1910. From: London, PRO, HO 144/1102/198890.

informed that if any further irregularities should crop up, he would no longer be entitled to be involved in naturalization cases.[50]

In 1907, the Home Office also accused the lawyer of the Spitalfields Naturalization Society, S.L. Lipshitz, of using dirty methods, and it differentiated between honest and dubious naturalization societies. Within this context, the Home Office decided not to reduce the fee for naturalization, claiming that such a measure would only foster the establishment of even more dubious societies and increase the number of unsuitable applications.[51] In general, however, such explicitly stated reservations coming from the authorities were usually made in reference to the low social status of an applicant as opposed to their ethnic identity.

Several Jewish organizations still claimed, however, that the Home Office consciously aimed to keep poor Jews from becoming British nationals. Since 1892, they had been advocating for a reduction of the fee of five pounds, which was virtually unaffordable for anyone without significant wealth. The Home Office countered their request, initially citing the fact that the fee was supposed to reflect the value of British nationality and prove the ability of the applicant to provide for himself and his family. In 1913, the fee was then reduced to three pounds. The *Jewish Chronicle* described this measure as 'substantial enough to create a feeling of satisfaction in a community which had previously been put off with blunt refusals'.[52] Furthermore, many Jewish representatives deplored the language test as a measure that specifically targeted 'Jewish' applicants. The Home Office made a few concessions in this regard in 1912 in that it promised to be more generous in the assessment of these tests in future.[53]

Consequently, as of the 1890s, the debates over naturalization were increasingly shaped by the disputes over 'Jewish' immigration. A few cases confirm the impression that poor East European Jews in particular were being denied British nationality, although this ethnically exclusive practice was at least partially put aside in 1912–13. Moreover, this pattern is further confirmed by a quantitative analysis of the percentage of Jewish naturalizations among all naturalizations in the month of September at five-year intervals (see Figure 4.1).[54]

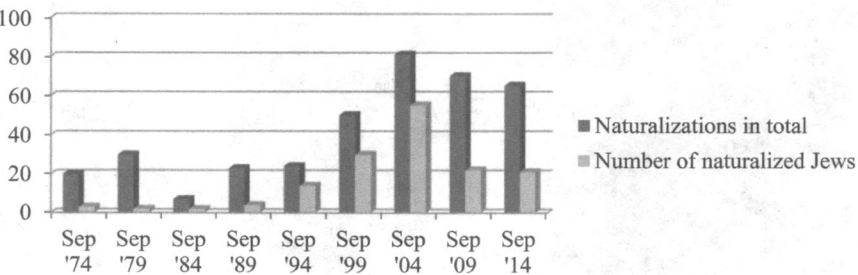

Figure 4.1. Total number of naturalizations in the United Kingdom and the number of naturalized Jews, in absolute figures

As this diagram suggests, the anti-Semitic overtones in the immigration debates led to a significant decrease in the number of naturalizations of Jews between 1904 and 1909, which continued to remain at a comparatively low level even after the British government made some concessions towards the demands of the Jewish organizations in 1912 and 1913.

Generally speaking, immigration policies in the UK were primarily driven by state and political interests at first, but as of the 1890s, social and cultural considerations came to play a larger role.[55] As a result, ethnically exclusive tendencies gained a stronger foothold. The increasing emphasis on cultural criteria, such as language, in administrative praxis contradicted the territorializing intentions of the Naturalization Act of 1870 because it was no longer just the permanent residence of a person within or outside the boundaries of British rule that mattered, but rather his or her cultural identity. Thus, in the early twentieth century, a unique mix of territorial and personal criteria demarcated the boundaries of the community of British nationals, and therefore their access to the rights of citizenship.

Citizenship and Ethnic Exclusion in the United Kingdom

British nationality in and of itself did not, however, bestow the rights of citizenship, because the political and social rights to which British subjects were entitled depended heavily on their place of residence. If a British national transferred his place of residence from Madras to London, for example, he acquired the right to vote for the British parliament if he met the necessary property qualifications. If he then moved on to Mombasa, he lost this right again. Due to this territorial mechanism of inclusion – or rather exclusion – immigration prohibitions could effectively keep certain groups of British subjects from acquiring the rights of citizenship. The dominions followed just such a policy course. They integrated (certain groups of) inhabitants into their body politic by granting them political and social rights, while restrictively regulating access to their territory. Especially in the early twentieth century, this dual strategy was seen by many Britons in the UK as a viable alternative to granting equal rights to all British subjects in a wholesale fashion. In this sense, colonial and peripheral legal developments resulted in significant repercussions in the metropolis.

Accordingly, mechanisms of ethnic differentiation gained a stronger foothold in the UK. Unlike in the dominions, however, the focus was not on those groups who were supposed to be excluded, but rather on those who should be safeguarded against any exclusionary measures because they supposedly deserved privileged treatment. Interestingly, however, the franchise was not marked by such distinctions. Suffrage had been extended to larger portions of the population over the course of the long nineteenth century, culminating in the introduction of universal suffrage for men as well as a limited form of suffrage for women in the Representation of the People Act of 1918. All British subjects residing in the UK, regardless of ethnic identity, thus enjoyed equal rights of suffrage.[56] The Poor Laws were even more inclusive in that they neither differentiated between subjects and 'aliens' nor between different ethnic groups.[57] The Unemployed Workmen Act of 1905 was also similarly inclusive in its wording.[58]

The Old Age Pensions Act of 1908, in contrast, made the difference between nationals and foreigners relevant in terms of social citizenship rights for the first time.[59] According to this act, pensions could only be claimed by an individual who 'for at least twenty years up to the date of the receipt … has been a British subject, and has had his residence … in the United Kingdom'.[60] This stipulation meant that women who lost their status as British subjects upon marriage to a foreigner had no right to pensions, even after divorce or the deaths of their spouses.[61] Both the Old Age Pensions Act as well as the National Insurance Act of 1911, however, outlined exceptions to these rules that resembled a nation-state approach by allowing former British women to claim privileges in terms of social rights, although they were not nationals according to the letter of the law.[62]

That said, however, not only British subject status, but also a long period of residence within the UK was required to claim a pension. These factors prompted a debate in parliament that illustrates quite clearly which groups were supposed to profit from these acts and which were not. On the one side, the argument was made that a Briton who wanted to spend the rest of his days 'with his family in another part of the British Empire' should still be entitled to his pension.[63] On the other side, some representatives questioned whether 'British subjects in India … who were here now' were entitled to a pension, while also expressing apprehension over the fact that 'crowds of foreigners … might come over here in the hope that … they might get a pension'.[64] Despite such fears, the act itself did not institute any kind of explicit inclusion or exclusion on the basis of ethnic criteria. A representative of the government did, however, stress that an ethnically exclusive intent was embedded within the seemingly ethnically neutral nationality and residence requirements. Individuals entitled to pensions, he argued, 'are to be British subjects resident in the United Kingdom for twenty years previously, which, of course, practically makes the provision for British subjects in every sense of the word'.[65]

Whereas British subjects who had immigrated to the UK from other parts of the empire were supposed to be excluded, emigrants who returned to the UK after a long period of absence were by no means supposed to be denied social rights associated with citizenship. To this end, legal commentaries and administrative praxis established the notion of a temporary absence that did not interrupt the official period of residence in the UK. This strategy implied introducing the concept of 'home' into British law.[66] For people who had previously lived in the UK, it was still considered to be their 'home' as long as they did not give up 'the intention of residence', which meant as long as they did not declare their intention never to return.[67] According to this idea, even someone who lived abroad for decades and who did not retain 'rights of property or occupation' that bound him to the place 'to which he looked as a residence upon his return' could claim a pension.[68] As this notion of 'home' emphasized the idea of longing for and finally returning to the mother country, it ultimately imbued emotional ties to British soil with legal relevance.[69]

A comment made by the Lord Chancellor clarifies just who was supposed to profit from this quite vague legal concept in that he spoke of the 'Englishmen, Scotsmen, and Irishmen' who 'had gone out from England to do work and then come back', and were not to be denied a pension.[70] At the same time, such a position contradicted the definition of an old age pension as an 'honourable recognition of services rendered to the State'.[71] Those working and paying taxes abroad did not really serve the British state in any way, which meant that, in the eyes of the Lord Chancellor and others, they were supposed to receive a pension because they were 'Englishmen, Scotsmen, and Irishmen' in what could only be an ethnonational sense. The coupling of subject status and length of residence as the prerequisites for citizenship rights was supposed to exclude non-domestic and 'non-white' Britons, while also imbuing the emotional notion of 'home' with legal relevance in order to include what might be referred to as autochthonous 'white' Britons. Mechanisms of ethnic exclusion and inclusion were thus covered up by the ethnically neutral veneer of the law.[72]

The immigration restrictions outlined in the Aliens Act of 1905, which took effect parallel to the extension of social citizenship rights, more clearly bore the marks of ethnic exclusion. The act introduced immigration controls and permitted the deportation of 'undesirable aliens', which primarily meant the poor, the sick and the convicted.[73] At the same time, the xenophobic and racist character of the agitation against the immigration of 'Jews' contributed significantly to the passing of the law in parliament. This clearly indicates that certain ethnic groups were supposed to be denied entry to the UK.[74] Even the parliamentarians found themselves caught up in contradictions when they tried to protest the anti-Semitic context in which this act emerged. For example, the Liberal MP for Poplar in the East End of London, Sidney Buxton, maintained that his opposition to the immigration of 'Russians' and 'Poles' had nothing to do with the 'question of race', and then concluded directly thereafter that these immigrants were 'neither in race, religion, feeling, language, nor blood ... suitable or advantageous to us'.[75] Prime Minister Arthur Balfour also inconsistently argued that he was only concerned about the 'industrial, social, and intellectual strength of the community', but then went on to forecast a dystopia in which the 'Poles' would push the Britons out of the British Isles. Even if all laws and institutions were to remain the same, Balfour continued, and even if 'the same historical traditions [were still] learned in the elementary schools', even then these 'Polish' Britons would not be 'the nationality we should desire to be our heirs through the ages yet to come'.[76]

Quite similar to the Old Age Pensions Act, the British legislators stood before the problem that the restrictive provisions of the Aliens Act were not supposed to make it more difficult for a 'British born workman returning to visit his family' to enter the UK, even if he had been naturalized in the United States and was therefore, strictly speaking, a foreigner.[77] Unlike other foreigners, these 'native-born' foreigners, as one MP put it, were still supposed to have the right 'to lay their bones in the sacred soil of their own country and in the graves of their forebears'.[78] Along the lines of such statements, only those Britons for whom 'born' meant more than just being born on British soil could make claims to their 'homeland'. These women and men not only came from England, Scotland and Ireland, but they were also emotionally bound to their 'home' in an emphatic way. This bond – it 'might be sentimental, but sentiments' are 'the strongest force in politics' – was more important to many of the MPs than the official nationality of returning emigrants.[79] These legally foreign but ethnically British people were therefore supposed to be exempted from the medical and other examinations that were to be required to enter the country by the Aliens Act. John Henry Whitely, a Liberal MP from Halifax, even went so far as to suggest that the term 'immigrant' should be defined more narrowly for the purposes of the law, along the lines of 'immigrant, if he has not been born in the UK'.[80]

Whitely's recommendation meant nothing less than making birth on UK soil a legal principle all of its own. It destroyed the unity of the 'dominions of the British Crown', at least in the law of the imperial metropolis, and divided all those British subjects who acquired British nationality by virtue of *ius soli* into two groups according to whether or not they were born in the mother country or within another part of the empire. Attorney-General Robert Finlay, who had to deal with this problem in his role as the government's legal advisor, therefore called for an exception for 'all persons born in any part of His Majesty's dominions', and not just those born in the UK, in order to prevent discrimination within the community of British subjects.[81] Despite such objections, the act ultimately read: '[L]eave to land shall not be refused merely on the ground of want of means to any immigrant who ... was born in the United Kingdom, his father being a British subject'.[82] This wording not only stressed that it was the territory of the UK that mattered, but it also made the principle of descent for those born on British soil legally relevant for the first time.[83] By strengthening *ius sanguinis*, the law made it possible for emigrants to retain their legal ties to the homeland, even if they had been naturalized abroad. Consequently, the Aliens Act relativized the ethnically neutral tendency towards territorialization that had come with the Naturalization Act of 1870, and applied elements of a nation-state approach that linked British nationality more closely to the ethnic identity of individual people. The figure of the returning emigrant was essential to this development because it was his or her intended inclusion that paved the way for mechanisms of positive discrimination according to ethnic criteria within the laws of the United Kingdom.

The British Nationality and Status of Aliens Act of 1914

The general trend towards personalization, nationalization and ethnicization continued with the British Nationality and Status of Aliens Act of 1914, which also strengthened the independent national status of married women.[84] In 1901, for example, a government commission refused to grant former British women who had lost their subject status through marriage any kind of legal privileges, and clung to the principle of the legal unity of the family. The commission only recommended introducing special regulations for the sons of these women, which would allow them to enter into the service of the state or the military. Furthermore, the children from the first marriage of widowed British women who had later married foreigners were supposed to remain British nationals. These recommendations were then implemented in the law of 1914.[85] These measures were guided by a stronger nation-state approach and thus tied in with similar regulations found in the Old Age Pensions Act as well as the National Insurance Act of 1911.[86] Some MPs even referred back to the principle of 'indelible allegiance', which was abolished in 1870, to prove that the independent nationality of married women was already firmly anchored in the British legal tradition. In an almost exact reversal of the arguments raised in 1870, the Liberal MP for St Pancras North, Willoughby Dickinson, claimed that '[t]here is no reason why a person should not have two nationalities'.[87]

Yet, these arguments were not able to completely override the objections of the government.[88] In the end, only a few concessions were made towards strengthening the rights of married women in terms of nationality. Women who had lost their British subject status through marriage, for example, could now be renaturalized as widows or divorcees without having to fulfil any residence requirements, and the fee for naturalization was not to exceed five shillings. Moreover, women whose husbands renounced their British nationality after the marriage had taken place could retain their status as British subjects if they made a declaration to this effect.[89] The British Nationality and Status of Aliens Act did not abolish the principle that all members of a family should share one nationality, but it did mitigate its consequences. The women affected by these provisions retained a privileged bond to Britishness, despite officially becoming foreigners by marriage, and were no longer forced to completely sever the legal ties connecting them with their country of origin.

This law also followed a nation-state approach in that it tightened the restrictions on naturalization. It now anchored the language tests, which had often been used before, within the law, thereby adding weight to cultural criteria in the naturalization process. This resulted in a rather interesting problem in that naturalization candidates now had to prove knowledge of a language that a great majority of British subjects did not speak themselves, because as the Liberal MP for Stepney, William Glyn-Jones, put it, '[i]n India we have a population of 300,000,000, all of whom are British subjects and probably none the worse British subjects because most of them have no adequate knowledge of the English language'.[90] The British Nationality and Status of Aliens Act, which regulated naturalization for the entire empire, did allow for language tests in another language, if 'any language is recognised as on an equality with the English language' in the territory in question. But the only languages that were officially equal to English were French in Canada, and Afrikaans in South Africa. None of the countless other non-European languages spoken in the Asian and African parts of the empire had been formally recognized as being on par with English.[91] The importance thus attached to the knowledge of English for the acquisition of British nationality clearly clashed with the multilingual heterogeneity of the empire, and cancelled out older, supra-ethnic concepts of British subjecthood. At the very least, it made a move towards lingual homogenization, which contributed to the 'narrowing of "Britishness" to a white, Christian, Anglo-Saxon identity'.[92]

Additionally, the law provided for the retraction of naturalizations that had already been granted. These provisions granted the government a great deal of leeway, especially in light of the imminent outbreak of war as the law came into force on 7 August 1914. The Secretary of State for the Home Office was supposed to be able to declare that Germans who had been naturalized were now foreigners without much ado, so that they could be treated as 'enemy aliens'. In the years leading up to the war, moreover, German spies had replaced the East European 'Jews' as the object of xenophobic hysteria and the 'other' within the construction of a national British identity.[93] Correspondingly, it was widely believed 'that naturalization does not and cannot change a man heart and soul – least of all an ex-German, in whom there is an inborne love of his Kaiser and his fatherland'.[94]

Alongside these tendencies towards cultural and ethnonational exclusion, the general strengthening of the principle of descent intensified the nationalizing effects of the British Nationality and Status of Aliens Act. The act established the principle of *ius soli* anchored within Common Law for the first time in statute law, and simultaneously reduced the inheritance of British subject status abroad based on *ius sanguinis* to one generation instead of two. But, at the same time, it expanded the territory to which *ius soli* applied for the children of British subjects: 'where by treaty, capitulation, grant, usage, sufferance … His Majesty exercises jurisdiction over British subjects', children who had at least one British parent – the law notably refrained from using gender-specific language – acquired

British nationality upon birth, but not children with non-British parents.[95] This provision applied to all indirectly ruled territories (i.e. protectorates), as well as to all those states in which an extraterritorial British consular jurisdiction was recognized – for example, in the Ottoman and Chinese empires.[96] The law effectively introduced a partial *ius soli* principle in these countries that was also linked to descent in order to allow for British nationality to be passed from one generation to the next ad infinitum. One commentator celebrated these elements of the law as a 'great advance towards a wholesale adoption of the ius sanguinis'.[97]

That said, however, clear ethnically exclusive tendencies cannot be detected in these new regulations because, according to the letter of the law, all subjects profited from the increasing independence of married women in terms of nationality as well as the strengthening of *ius sanguinis*, regardless of their geographic origin or ethnic identity.[98] The India Office pointed out this fact, noting its objections to the expansion of *ius sanguinis* because it would allow the descendants of all British nationals, 'whether they are Asiatics or Europeans', the right to permanently retain their British subject status in the Indian princely states.

However, a proposal put forth by the Conservative MP for the Wirral, Gershom Stewart, that explicitly sought to exclude 'non-white' subjects from becoming British nationals never achieved a majority. Stewart wanted to limit the area within which *ius soli* should apply, and replace the Common Law phrase of 'born within His Majesty's dominions and allegiance' with the wording 'born within His Majesty's dominions specified in the first Schedule of this Act'. As the first schedule of the act listed the dominions, his proposal would have made it impossible for children who were not born in the primarily 'white' portions of the British Empire to become British subjects. This proposal was intended to ensure that the new law 'will not in any way increase our responsibilities as regards our Oriental fellow subjects'.[99] A representative from the Cape Colony expressed this racist idea of exclusion even more clearly in that he demanded that 'Native or non-European peoples' should not be able to become British subjects if they are born in one of the protectorates.[100]

Essentially, these proposals aimed at privileging 'whites' by denying 'non-whites' the right to acquire British nationality. They tried to implement an imperialist approach in all parts of the British Empire that would have contradicted the nation-state tendencies in the Aliens Act and the Old Age Pension Act, which sought to construct a community of nationals tied to the territory of the UK. But such racist ideas met with a lack of support in the British parliament. The governments of the dominions involved in the drafting of the law of 1914, in contrast, were all the more emphatic in their insistence on racist and imperialist notions. Consequently, the British Nationality and Status of Aliens Act was shaped by contradictory influences that ultimately resulted in a strange mix of different approaches to the question of nationality. On the one hand, in keeping with a nation-state idea, it allowed for the exclusion of ex-Germans, and made it easier for Britons who had left the UK to retain their British nationality. On the other hand, the territorial division of the empire into different categories reflected an overarching imperialist push to privilege 'white' male Britons. This discrimination, however, was hidden beneath a veneer of ethnically neutral language that clung to the statist notion of the legal equality of all British subjects in order to at least nominally uphold the unity of British subjecthood.

Intersections of Ethnic, Religious, Social and Gender Differences

The debates over the exclusion of Jewish immigrants, the refusal to grant British subject status to poor naturalization candidates, and the discussions over the independent nationality of married women reveal that the question of ethnic differentiation within the law was tightly linked to other distinctions based on religious, social and gender criteria. This interplay between different axes of what were mostly dichotomous hierarchies has received increasing attention in more recent scholarship under the rubric of 'intersectionality'. In addition to the classic triad of race, class and gender, the following analysis also takes into consideration the religious and confessional differences that played a significant role in the British and Habsburg contexts as well.[101]

The interactions between these axes of discrimination can be approached from three different perspectives. First of all, they can be described as mutually intensifying. In this case, hierarchies based on religious, 'racial', social or gender categories blend into an inseparable, comprehensive matrix of discrimination. Such an amalgamation is clearly reflected in the fact that civilizing missions were not only aimed at the indigenous populations in the colonies, but also the lower classes and women in the metropolis. Furthermore, metaphors that referred to 'the woman' as 'the dark continent' or to the 'effeminate Bengali' expressed such connections as did religious, racist or nationalist arguments supporting the inequality of the sexes.[102] Links like these contrasted a bundle of hegemonic norms – 'white', male, bourgeois, Christian, heterosexual – with a series of subaltern deviations. And the connotations among the latter ensured that each of them remained in a disenfranchised position. Consequently, virulent strains of discrimination based on social and gender criteria were embedded within mechanisms of 'racial' discrimination. In reverse, the breaking of sexist structures also had an anti-racist potential.

Secondly, moments of intersectional interplay could also generate contradictions and incongruence between the different modes of discrimination at work. 'Racial' and social categories, for example, crossed in the guise of indigenous elites or poor 'whites' in the colonial context.[103] The ambivalent position of baptized or Western-educated 'natives' likewise exemplifies the tensions that could result from the simultaneity of different hierarchies. The same holds true for depictions of 'white' women as the bearers of the colonial civilizing mission. This perspective thus points out that focusing on one category of difference alone can never adequately reflect social reality. At the same time, it reveals the instability of the respective hierarchies that were perhaps less clear and inescapable than they appeared at first glance. These hierarchies and categories had to be re-established and continually reinforced, which actually opened the door for reinterpretation and subversion.

Thirdly, intersectionality can also imply that a single form of discrimination took centre stage in a given thematic, regional or historical context, thereby diminishing the relevance of other hegemonies. Along these lines, ethno-national identities reshaped religious-confessional identities and replaced religion as the dominant marker of difference over the course of the long nineteenth century.[104] The same pattern is reflected in the argument that 'racial' difference overshadowed gender difference in the colonial context, which explains why 'white' women were often granted legal equality in the colonies long before they achieved it in the imperial mother countries. The export of social hierarchies from the metropolis to the colonial peripheries where they were translated into racist discrimination points in a similar direction.[105] Other scholars maintain, in contrast, that the emphasis on 'racial' supremacy in the British realm, and ethnonational tensions in the Habsburg context, first and foremost served to distract from the social conflicts between the wealthy and the working classes at home, which actually served to perpetuate the oppression of the latter.[106] These approaches, which could be described using the Marxist vocabulary of main and subordinate contradictions, work from the premise that one form of discrimination was the focal point, although it may have been hiding behind other hierarchies.

Religion

The debates over the legal validity of non-Christian marriages at the end of the nineteenth century in which ethnically neutral arguments clashed with ethnically exclusive agendas clearly illustrate the significance of religion in terms of British nationality. Some sought to deny recognition of non-Christian, potentially polygamous marriages so that the children born abroad to a British subject in such a marriage would be declared illegitimate and therefore excluded from British nationality. On the basis of this argument, the British authorities in Tangier deemed that the children born to Isaac Aaron Abensur were foreigners, despite the fact that their father, a 'Jewish merchant of Moorish nationality' had acquired British nationality in 1896.[107] That this decision not only aimed to exclude subjects living permanently abroad from enjoying the privileges of

British nationality but also discriminated against certain ethnic groups can be clearly seen in the case of Grant from 1888, to which the authorities referred in their discussions over Abensur.[108] Grant had converted to Islam and married a Moroccan woman according to Muslim law. Therefore, his children were considered to be 'non-white' in the eyes of the authorities and were not registered as British subjects by the consulate in Rabat because, according to the official reasoning, they were born into a marriage 'of polygamous character'.[109]

In adopting this perspective, the consular officials maintained an ethnically exclusive standpoint that only recognized the validity of marriages that fulfilled the 'conditio sine qua non of Christian marriage' for purposes of nationality, namely 'that it is the union of a man with a woman to the exclusion of all other unions, to live together to their joint lives' end'.[110] In the eyes of those in favour of exclusion, Jewish and Muslim marriages did not meet this condition. They cited medieval traditions of English law that had refused to recognize 'Jewish' marriages in order to promote the conversion of 'Jewesses' to Christianity. To this effect, women married according to Jewish ritual had been allowed, after converting, to marry Christian men even though their first husbands were still alive. As this reference clearly reveals, the proponents of an ethnically exclusive approach were not as interested in monogamy itself as they were in denying the children of 'non-Christian' parents the right to British nationality. In opposition to this standpoint, the proponents of an ethnically neutral approach not only cited a decision made by the Foreign Office in 1886 that determined that marriages 'between British subjects in Mahommedan countries by ... Jewish Rabbis' were legally valid, but also they emphasized the ramifications associated with such an ethnically exclusive interpretation of the law. 'If it were correct,' they argued, 'it followed that the children of the whole of Her Majesty's Mahometan or Hindoo subjects, if born abroad out of India, were, in contemplation of English law, illegitimate'.[111]

The cases of Abensur and Grant in Morocco were thus tightly linked to the question of whether the descendants of 'Indian' emigrants should still be British subjects. This connection is underscored by the ethnically exclusive intentions behind the emphasis on religious differences and the demands to refrain from recognizing (potentially) polygamous marriages. Ultimately, however, the move to institute more ethnically exclusive policies did not succeed. Rather, the reigning opinion was 'that there is a *ius gentium* in these matters, a comity which treats with tenderness, or at least, with toleration, the usages of a distinct people in this transaction of marriage'.[112] Correspondingly, the law officers in London who were responsible for issuing the government's official legal opinion reinforced the ethnically neutral position, and added that 'for the purpose of inheriting nationality ... a polygamous marriage by a subject of Her Majesty ... must be treated as lawful', especially because '[t]here are many parts of the British Dominions in which polygamous marriages are lawful'.[113] On the basis of this opinion, Abensur's children who were born after his naturalization were ultimately recognized as British subjects.

Even beyond these debates over the significance of non-Christian marriages, there are other indications pointing to the fact that older patterns of religious and/or confessional discrimination were being revived and reinterpreted in racist hierarchies. A civil servant in the India Office pointed out in the discussions over the legal discrimination of 'Indian' subjects that their unequal treatment had nothing to do with their national status and rested merely on their 'race'. This was, he continued, in a way similar to the 'religious disabilities' that had applied to British Catholics alone on the basis of their confessional identity.[114] In the Habsburg Empire, too, the authorities referred back to religious differences when making ethnic distinctions. Yet, for the most part, their intention was to alleviate conflict and not to discriminate. Just as the confessional associations had been granted autonomy in terms of their internal affairs in order to avoid disputes, ethnonational autonomy was supposed to resolve the conflicts between the nationalities in the early twentieth century. This continuity is most clearly reflected in the phrase 'nationales Bekenntnis' (national confession) and in the fact that the registers used to determine ethnonational identities drew on those that were used to delineate confessional groups.

Alongside such transfers, there were a number of other areas in which the production of ethnic differences rested on religious or confessional differences. Catholicism, for example, was an important element of Irish identity in the UK, whereas the Greek Uniate Church was a major identifier within the so-called Ruthenian population.[115] The connection between religious and ethnic difference was particularly strong in Bosnia, where the distinctions between Catholic, Orthodox and Muslim were the basis for the ethnic differentiation between Croats, Serbs and the Muslims, sometimes referred to as Bosniaks. The relationship between religious and ethnic identity was even more complex when it came to the 'Israelites' or 'Jews'. In general, it is often assumed that so-called modern forms of racist anti-Semitism displaced older, Christian-infused anti-Judaism over the course of the nineteenth century. Consequently, the 'Jews' were increasingly seen as a 'racial' group. This factored into the debates of the Aliens Act and the exclusion of 'East European Jews' in British naturalization praxis in the early twentieth century, as well as the anti-Semitic sentiments harboured by some local authorities and consulates in the Habsburg context. The Cisleithanian and the joint Austro-Hungarian government, however, insisted on the confessional character of the Israelite community. On the one hand, they refused to recognize the 'Jews' as a 'Volksstamm' (race) according to the constitution of 1867, but on the other hand, they reinforced the principle of supra-ethnic neutrality in reaction to anti-Semitic discrimination.

Likewise, in India, the production of ethnic difference between Hindus and Muslims was built upon a religious foundation. That said, however, the suffrage system introduced in 1918–19 that recognized ethnic difference highlighted the extent to which religious and 'racial' differences could contradict one another. This is illustrated by the case of the 'Indian Christians' who enjoyed a semi-privileged status as well as an ambivalent intermediary position between 'Europeans' and 'Indian' non-Christians. In a certain sense, adopting Christianity boosted the claims of converts to legal equality vis-à-vis the 'Europeans', but they were still disadvantaged due to 'racial' considerations.[116] The inconsistency between different forms of discrimination highlights the paradoxical nature of the civilizing paradigm that dangled equality like a carrot, only to deny it in the end. But this criss-crossing of sometimes contradictory hierarchies did not emerge in all parts of the British Empire. The franchise in East Africa, for example, rested solely on the 'racial' discrimination between 'Europeans', 'Indians' and 'Africans'. Although there were indeed 'African' and 'Indian' Christians, religious differences did not play a role in this setting.

In general, it can be said that religious differences were more tightly linked to racist hierarchies in the British case as compared to the Habsburg Empire, in which the principles of supra-confessional and supra-ethnic neutrality continued to hold sway.[117] This discrepancy is further underscored by the way in which 'Europeans' who wanted to convert to Islam were handled in each case. Whereas the Habsburg administration reacted rather indifferently when it came to such conversions, the transfer of a 'racially' privileged person to a lesser-privileged religious community threatened the stability of the 'racial'-religious order in the eyes of the British authorities. Not surprisingly, then, the city of Mansura on the Nile delta was abuzz on the morning of 24 June 1882 as the British subject Guiseppe Idonio, most likely from Malta, decided to convert to Islam and made his way to the mosque accompanied by numerous Egyptians. The British consulate promptly asked the Egyptian authorities to put a stop to the impending conversion ceremony, supposedly because the large and anxious crowd presented a threat to public order and not because it wanted to hinder Idonio's conversion to Islam. Despite being detained in the consulate, Idonio still insisted that he wanted to become a Muslim. In response, the British consulate informed the circumcisers that this ritual could lead to death in Idonio's case, because of his age. If he did in fact die, the consulate noted, the circumcisers would be held personally accountable. The file does not indicate whether Idonio ultimately converted or not.[118]

The Habsburg consular authorities, in contrast, were ordered to protect the right of their nationals abroad to freely choose their religion. In 1880, for example, the Imperial and Royal Foreign Ministry in Vienna grappled with the question posed by the consulate in Al-Khartum (now Khartoum in Sudan) as to how to deal with nationals who wanted to convert to Islam. The ministry issued a directive in which it stated that according to Austrian as well as Hungarian law, 'there is no doubt that the conversion of a national of either half of the empire to the Muslim faith by no means entails a loss of nationality'.[119] Rather, it noted, the consulates should defend the privileges of these Muslim Austrians or Hungarians who had successfully converted, vis-à-vis the Turkish authorities. Moreover, they were also supposed to ensure that the conversions were noted in the registers of the respective home municipalities in order to prevent the previous religious communities from making legal demands on the converts. The authorities were also obligated 'to defend the free choice of these nationals'.[120] Judged on the basis of the usual coupling of modernity and secularity, Habsburg administrative praxis was thus clearly more modern than that of the British Empire, in which 'racial' and religious hierarchies were tightly interwoven.

Social Status

Ethnic differences not only overlapped with religious differences, but also social status. Countless examples from the Habsburg Empire demonstrate how hierarchies defined according to status or wealth and those based on ethnonational differences reinforced one another. In Bosnia, for example, Muslim property owners often stood against mostly Croat or Serbian farmers and farmhands, whereas in Galicia, Polish-speaking elites dominated the Ruthenian or Ukrainian-speaking lower classes.[121] These parallels between social and ethnic differences resulted in the legal discrimination of certain ethnonational groups, especially in places where the franchise system offered socially and economically privileged groups broader rights of political participation. In such constellations, social and economic asymmetries fuelled the reproduction of ethnonational differences, and paved the way for indirect discrimination according to ethnicity.

Similarly, social and 'racial' differences were also often conflated in the British Empire, as can clearly be seen in the relationship between 'European' landowners and 'African' farmworkers in East Africa, for instance. A particularly thorough attempt to map social and economic differences onto ethnic distinctions was made in India, where the authorities tried to translate the existing caste system into 'racial categories'. Together with scholars and different local actors, British officials thus wanted to devise a comprehensive hierarchy that was allegedly natural and all-consuming. The fact that it unified several modes of differentiation in a seemingly consistent way lent this hierarchy all the more power.[122]

Such imperialist desires to uncover or establish steadfast hierarchies in the colonial peripheries was tightly linked to the popular utopian notion of an organic and agrarian society in which each person knew his or her place, and accepted it without question. This model corresponded to the social structure of the mother country – at least in the minds of many colonizers – until modernization wreaked its chaos on the traditional order. This nostalgic restoration project was pursued by some members of the British gentry, who tried to cultivate the

life of a lord of the manor in the colonies when they could no longer afford to do so in the UK, or were no longer entitled to such a lifestyle.[123] A particularly poignant example of this export of social hierarchies can be found in the case of the 'European' settler Galbraith Cole in East Africa, a brother-in-law of Lord Delamere, who shot a 'native' he suspected of having stolen a sheep and was acquitted of murder by a 'white' jury. A Liberal daily newspaper in England deplored the outcome of this trial, demanding that 'a class whose deadening domination is only now being lifted from the English countryside' should not be allowed 'to practise a coarser despotism on the natives of Africa'.[124] Even some contemporaries saw this nostalgic project as part of an attempt to hold fast to a disappearing social hierarchy by transplanting it to a colonial context and embedding it within a racist order.

Similar attempts to restore something akin to a strict class hierarchy were also made in the eighteenth and early nineteenth centuries in the territories that later became dominions. By the turn of the century, however, a completely different kind of social utopia had come to shape the developments in Canada, for example. The goal was to achieve as socially homogeneous a society as possible, in which the 'mass of the white population' were to be 'holders of small properties'.[125] But racist discrimination was very much at play here as well. It was generally held to be true in Canada as well as New Zealand and Australia that such an egalitarian utopia could only succeed within an ethnically homogeneous society. Essentially, these notions of social equality thus served to legitimize measures that sought to exclude 'non-whites' and reinforce a racist hierarchy.

As soon as social differences frustrated or disturbed 'racial' discrimination, though, this pattern of inclusion and exclusion was effectively undermined. Despite their 'white' racial identities, poor 'Europeans' had to overcome much greater hurdles in terms of immigration law than wealthy 'Asiatics'.[126] Even the language tests, which were often required for entry into one of the dominions, were primarily intended to filter out uneducated lower-class immigrants as opposed to 'Asiatic' elites. In 1911, British officials criticized this practice because it could not guarantee the exclusion of all 'Indians' regardless of their social status.[127] The desire to erode the special treatment afforded wealthy and highly regarded 'non-white' immigrants is illustrated by the fact that the Canadian Immigration Act of 1911 replaced 'class' with 'race' as a criterion for exclusion.[128] The tightening of the immigration restrictions meant that controls and entry prohibitions had a greater chance of affecting every 'Indian subject of His Majesty, however high, cultured or influential he may be'.[129] As a result, racist discrimination gained the upper hand while social differences became less relevant. This lumping together of all 'Indians' regardless of their social status into a 'racial' category corresponded to a certain extent with the attempt made by the Indian nationalist movement to integrate the members of different social classes into a solidified nation that could defended itself against the discrimination of its well-to-do members, as well as against the exploitation of its indentured labourers.[130]

Comparable processes of integration involving different social groups within an ethnonational community also took place in Austria-Hungary. Czech business-men, workers and employees, for example, increasingly began to identify with the same nationalist ideas. In reverse, common economic interests could also integrate a social group across ethnonational lines. The Austrian social democratic movement in particular represented this kind of a supra-ethnic union in that it claimed to represent the interests of Czech, German, Polish, Italian, Slovenian, and other workers equally.[131] Moreover, the Cisleithanian authorities, as demonstrated in the new regulations on the right of domicile in 1896, insisted upon a strict adherence to supra-ethnic neutrality, especially within the context of social citizenship rights, which – at least theoretically – meant that all poor citizens, regardless of nationality, were supposed to benefit equally from welfare measures. Along similar lines, the introduction of universal male suffrage in 1907 was supposed to banish the 'phantom of nationalist thought' from the realm of politics by channelling public attention towards supra-ethnic social and economic interests.[132] Contrary to these hopes, however, the advocacy of the interests of a given social class often intensified ethnonational differences. This was exactly what happened with the Moravian Compromise of 1905 that effectively guaranteed the social group of large landowners a permanent privileged status by dividing the general population into two ethnonational electorates. Whereas social and ethnonational differences were thus continually competing for dominance in Cisleithania, a much clearer trend can be discerned within the British case, in which racist discrimination increasingly pushed class distinctions out of the way.

Gender

A similar picture emerges from a comparison of the interplay of gender and ethnic differences in the Habsburg and British contexts. The Cisleithanian women's associations, much like the Austrian social democrats, found themselves faced by the question of whether they should focus on the discrimination encountered by all women, regardless of their ethnonational identities, or whether they should push for the equality of German, Czech, Polish, Italian and other mothers and wives within a nationalist framework.[133] At the heart of the matter was the sexual discrimination mechanisms embedded within the franchise, which women's rights advocates fought against until the end of the dual monarchy in 1918 with a seemingly contradictory mix of supra-ethnic and nationalistic strategies.[134] Women's suffrage was first introduced on a large scale in the states that grew out of the collapsed empire, and primarily enveloped ethnically exclusive nations such as the German-Austrian Republic.[135] Accordingly, a pattern ultimately triumphed that linked the erosion of gender hierarchies to the emergence of a nation-state that imagined itself as ethnically homogeneous.

This constellation in which the emancipatory inclusion of women was coupled with ethnic exclusion also appeared in the British realm. It was particularly pervasive in East Africa, where the suffrage regulations of 1919 excluded the 'Indian' and 'African' populations while simultaneously enfranchising 'European' women. Especially within a colonial context, the elimination of gender asymmetries often strengthened 'racial' discrimination. Accordingly, many women's rights advocates based the claims of 'white' women to equality on their 'racial' superiority and their special role in the reproduction of the 'white race' and the civilizing of the 'natives'.[136] Women in Canada and the UK were also granted political rights of citizenship after the end of the First World War, which many saw as recognition of their contribution to the British war effort.[137] But in both cases, the inclusion of women also went hand in hand with the implementation of ethnically exclusive immigration policies.

In nationality law, gender and ethnic discrimination were interwoven in a rather contradictory way. The patriarchal emphasis on the unity of the family brought disadvantages for married women in that they had to share the nationality of their husbands and had no right to an independent nationality of their own. In the case of 'non-white' women married to 'Europeans', this principle did in fact keep them from being discriminated against according to 'racial' criteria because they shared the privileged legal status of their husbands. Thus, the emancipatory impetus to demand an independent national status for married women had ethnically exclusive ramifications for such 'non-white' wives, and eased their exclusion. Along these lines, the Canadian Immigration Act of 1911 stipulated, especially with regard to any 'Asiatic' married woman, that she 'shall not be held to have acquired Canadian citizenship by virtue of her husband being a Canadian citizen'.[138]

Whereas the advent of gender equality in terms of nationality law could thus intensify mechanisms of 'racial' exclusion, gender hierarchy and ethnic discrimination were often conflated in the legal regulation of sexual relations in the colonies. In this context, male 'Europeans' enjoyed a privileged status above that of 'white' women as well as 'non-white' men, while 'non-white' women were firmly entrenched at the bottom of the sexual hierarchy where gender and ethnic subalternity overlapped. On the one hand, the colonial order in general perpetuated the sexual exploitation of women by men. An East African ordinance from 1907, for instance, circumvented the abolishment of slavery by explicitly permitting concubinage.[139] A little over a decade later, the British colonial administration also determined 'that no steps to abolish the practice of circumcising girls should be taken'.[140] On the other hand, colonial law tolerated sexual relations between 'white' men and 'non-white' women, although it simultaneously sought to discourage sexual contact between 'European' women and 'non-European' men. Given the idea that the supposedly dominant sexual partner belonged to the reputedly superior 'race' in the first scenario, the second constellation threatened to disrupt established gender and 'racial' hierarchies.[141] Consequently, East African courts could sentence 'any white woman who voluntarily permits any native to have unlawful carnal connection with her' to up to five years in prison.[142] Simultaneously, the authorities kept a very close eye on the sexual behaviour of 'European' women. In 1912, for example, the East African government requested a detailed police report on a 'Swedish woman cohabiting with Indians in Nairobi'. Presumably due to this case, it became easier to deport 'undesirable white women' before the year was out.[143] Male 'natives' who had or tried to have sex with 'white' women also had to reckon with harsh consequences.[144] The East African Legislative council wanted to punish 'African' as well as 'Indian' men with five years' imprisonment for engaging in sexual contact with female 'Europeans'. Correspondingly, it suggested that 'rape by a native on a white woman' should be punished by death.[145] The Colonial Office opposed these measures, but it was nonetheless still possible for suspicions of prohibited sexual activity to be fatal for 'non-whites'. As a point in case, the 'European' settler Grogan murdered a 'Rikshaboy' in 1908 after his sister complained about the way the man had looked at her. The court only sentenced Grogan to two months of hard labour for the crime.[146] Thus, while the erosion of male privileges was coupled with intensified ethnic exclusion in terms of suffrage and nationality, sexist and racist discrimination were tightly interwoven within the colonial control of sexual relations.

In general, ethnic, religious, social and sexual distinctions were interlaced in a variety of ways. Sometimes they collided with each other, but sometimes they were mutually reinforcing or one criterion came to replace another in determining the dominant hierarchy. In both the Habsburg and British empires, ethnonational and 'racial' differences gained a stronger foothold around the turn of the century. But whereas social differences sometimes mitigated the relevance of ethnic identities or infiltrated them in Austria-Hungary, racist discrimination came to dominate over all other forms of asymmetry in the British Empire. In those places where different categories had once contradicted each other, as in the case of the 'non-European' wives of 'Europeans' or wealthy 'non-whites', at the dawn of the twentieth century it was 'racial' identity alone that afforded privileges or entailed discrimination. An ethnicization of the law was thus well on its way.

Notes

1. On this interpretation, see especially Dummett and Nicol, *Subjects*.
2. On the Bancroft treaties between the US and the German states, which resembled this agreement, see Fahrmeir, *Citizens and Aliens*, 50; Grawert, *Staat und Staatsangehörigkeit*, 233.

3. In 1870 alone, approximately 153,000 Britons emigrated to the US; see B.R. Mitchell, *British Historical Statistics* (Cambridge: Cambridge University Press, 1988), 81f. On the connections between sinking transportation costs, rising emigration figures and the new nationality law, see UK Parliament, *Commons and Lords: The Parliamentary Debates, House of Commons, House of Lords*, vol. 199 (London), c. 1122, 1128.

4. UK Parliament, *Commons and Lords*, vol. 199, c. 1122f.; V. Bevan, *The Development of British Immigration Law* (London: Croom Helm, 1986), 108; Grawert, *Staat und Staatsangehörigkeit*, 50f., 233. Conflicts over naval impressment had already been sparked by the British–American War of 1812. On the problem of dual nationality in the Civil War, see UK Parliament, *Lords*, vol. 199 (10 March 1870), c. 1604f.

5. UK Acts, 33 Vict. ch. 14, sec. 3 and 4.

6. UK Acts, 33 Vict. ch. 14, sec. 6.

7. UK Parliament, *Lords*, vol. 199 (3 March 1870) c. 1119, Lord Chancellor.

8. UK Parliament, *Commons*, vol. 200 (28 April 1870), c. 2020, Vernon Harcourt. See also UK Parliament, *Lords*, vol. 199 (10 March 1870), c. 1608, Lord Westbury. The advocates of such reforms pointed to the limited *ius soli* that applied in France as a model; see Brubaker, *Citizenship*, 93.

9. UK Parliament, *Lords*, vol. 199 (3 March 1870), c. 1122, Lord Chancellor.

10. UK Parliament, *Commons*, vol. 200 (28 April 1870), c. 2021f., Sir Roundell Palmer.

11. UK Parliament, *Lords*, vol. 199 (3 March 1870), c. 1127, Lord Chancellor.

12. Ibid. (3 March 1870), c. 1133, Earl of Clarendon.

13. In contrast, Karatani, *British Citizenship*, interprets this legal ambiguity in a positive way, suggesting that it was a situation that opened up possibilities for the development of multifarious and intermediate identity positions.

14. UK Parliament, *Commons*, vol. 200 (25 April 1870), c. 1741, Mr Jessel.

15. Fahrmeir, *Citizens and Aliens*, 46.

16. M.P. Baldwin, 'Subject to Empire: Married Women and the British Nationality and Status of Aliens Act', *Journal of British Studies* 40(4) (2001), 526.

17. UK Parliament, *Commons*, vol. 200 (25 April 1870), c. 1740, Mr Kinnaird.

18. Ibid., (25 April 1870), c. 1741, Solicitor General, Sir Roundell Palmer and Mr Jessel.

19. In the case of a widowed mother with underage children, the nationality of the mother determined the nationality of the children. UK Acts, 33 Vict. ch. 14, sec. 10.3.

20. UK Acts, 33 Vict. ch. 14, sec. 10.5.

21. UK Parliament, vol. 199, c. 1124; UK Parliament, *Commons*, vol. 200 (25 April 1870), c. 1741, Sir Roundell Palmer.

22. UK Parliament, *Lords*, vol. 199 (3 March 1870), c. 1127, Lord Chancellor.

23. The Naturalization Act also did away with the right of foreigners to a 'jury de medietate linguae', half of whose members were to be subjects and half foreigners. UK Acts, 33 Vict. ch. 14, sec. 5.

24. UK Acts, 33 Vict. ch. 14, sec. 2. See also UK Parliament, *Commons*, vol. 200 (25 April 1870), c. 1735, Solicitor General.

25. Ibid. (25 April 1870), c. 1739, Solicitor General. See also UK Acts, 33 Vict. ch. 14, sec. 7.

26. Grawert, *Staat und Staatsangehörigkeit*, 52.

27. United Kingdom, *Report of the Inter-departmental Committee*, 6. On *ius sanguinis* as an element of the modernization of the law in the nineteenth century, see also Gosewinkel, *Einbürgern und Ausschließen*, 423.

28. UK Acts, 33 Vict. ch. 14, sec. 7.
29. UK Parliament, *Lords*, vol. 199, c. 1616.
30. UK Parliament, *Commons*, vol. 200, c. 1739.
31. UK Parliament, *Lords*, vol. 201 (9 May 1870), c. 390, Lord Chancellor.
32. UK Parliament, *Lords*, vol. 199, c. 1616f.
33. UK Parliament, *Lords*, vol. 199, c. 1616.
34. UK Parliament, *Lords*, vol. 199 (10 March 1870), c. 1618, Lord Penzance.
35. Fahrmeir, *Citizens and Aliens*, 93. See also L. Tabili, *Global Migrants, Local Culture: Natives and Newcomers in Provincial England, 1841–1939* (Basingstoke: Palgrave Macmillan, 2011), 140–42.
36. London, PRO, HO45/9366/36228. The police report from August 1874 determined that this 'man has not been loyal to his own King and Country'.
37. London, PRO, HO 45/9580/85527A.
38. London, PRO, HO 144/316/B7560. The application of Kuman B. Narayan from Kuch Behar was refused without reason in 1889, in agreement with the India Office.
39. The police report also notes: 'At these expressions he was so excited that he knocked over two beer glasses'. London, PRO, HO 144/383/B19917.
40. London, PRO, HO 144/625/B36331.
41. London, PRO, HO 45/10537/154320/45, 11 September 1909; PRO, HO 45/14736/11, September 1930. See also Baldwin, *Making*.
42. S. Terwey, *Moderner Antisemitismus in Großbritannien, 1899–1919: Über die Funktion von Vorurteilen sowie Einwanderung und nationale Identität* (Würzburg: Königshausen & Neumann, 2006), 61f., mentions the increasing critique directed against the naturalization of Jews during this period. At the same time, demands for the introduction of *ius sanguinis* reappeared in order to prevent the children of immigrants from becoming British subjects; see Baldwin, *Making*, 65.
43. C. Holmes, 'Die Einwanderung nach Großbritannien in Vergangenheit und Gegenwart', in K. Schönwälder and I. Sturm-Martin (eds), *Die britische Gesellschaft zwischen Offenheit und Abgrenzung: Einwanderung und Integration vom 18. bis zum 20. Jahrhundert* (Berlin: Philo, 2001), 17–31; Cesarani, 'The Changing Character', 61f. For a detailed analysis of the British policies controlling migration in the early twentieth century, see C. Reinecke, *Grenzen der Freizügigkeit: Migrationskontrolle in Großbritannien und Deutschland, 1880–1930* (Munich: Oldenbourg, 2010).
44. London, PRO, HO 144/354/B14881, Zelig Perelman, 1893. London, PRO, HO 144/467/V31725, Jacob Richman, 1900. Both applications were denied.
45. London, PRO, HO 144/625/B36384.
46. London, PRO, HO 144/805/134516.
47. London, PRO, HO 144/853/151616, 1907.
48. London, PRO, HO 144/625/B36331. Noah Cohen's application was submitted in 1901 by the Metropolitan Naturalization Society; Israel Rabbinowitz' application was put forth by the Spitalfields Naturalization Society. London, PRO, HO 144/807/13 5184, 1905.
49. London, PRO, HO 45/9482/1749A.
50. London, PRO, HO 144/403/B23051.
51. London, PRO, HO 45/12183, Memorandum on the Naturalization Societies in Manchester, Leeds and London, 1907. Within the context of the discussions over the naturalization fees in 1880, Baldwin makes reference to an anti-Semitic note written by a

Home Office official who had spoken out in favour of raising the fee in order to discourage undesirable Jewish applicants; see Baldwin, *Making*, 72f.

52. London, PRO, HO 45/12183, Naturalisation Fee, 1892–1913, Excerpt from the *Jewish Chronicle* dated 28 February 1913. On the debate over the naturalization fee, see also Baldwin, *Making*, 87f.

53. London, PRO, HO 45/10687/226279.

54. London, PRO, HO 45. This assessment of the naturalization lists is primarily based on whether or not the applicants, their parents and their children bore typically Jewish names – such as Moses, Chaim, Deborah and Sarah. Such a criterion is admittedly rather imprecise, but it at least allowed for a count of the cases in which the officials of the Home Office could assume the Jewish identity of the applicant based solely on the application itself.

55. Baldwin, *Making*, II, in a similar vein distinguishes between political and national criteria in naturalization praxis. However, Baldwin stresses the predominance of ethnically neutral, political interests throughout (ibid., 62, 92), whereas the analysis presented here concludes that British naturalization policies increasingly came to rely cultural and ethnically exclusive criteria as well.

56. J. Hostettler and B.P. Block, *Voting in Britain: A History of the Parliamentary Franchise* (Chichester: Barry Rose, 2001), 354. The reductions in the period of residence required to be listed on the voter registers even accelerated the process by which British immigrants could acquire political citizenship rights. C. Seymour, *Electoral Reform in England and Wales: The Development and Operation of the Parliamentary Franchise, 1832–1885* (New Haven, CT: Yale University Press, 1915), 271; H.L. Morris, *Parliamentary Franchise Reform in England from 1885 to 1918* (New York: Columbia University, 1921), 87.

57. Fahrmeir, *Citizens and Aliens*, 171; H. Davey, *Poor Law Settlement and Removal* (London: Stevens and Sons, 1908), 3f.

58. UK Acts, 5 Edw. 7 ch. 18.

59. UK Acts, 8 Edw. 7 ch. 40 and 1&2 Geo. 5 ch. 55. The distinction between subjects and foreigners became legally relevant in both cases in the clauses outlining potential financial claims on the national coffers.

60. UK Acts, 8 Edw. 7 ch. 40, sec. 2(2).

61. H.J. Hoare, *Old Age Pensions: Their Actual Working and Ascertained Results in the United Kingdom* (London: P.S. King, 1915), 34.

62. UK Acts, 1&2 Geo. 5 ch. 55, I.45.3. and 1&2 Geo. 5 ch. 16, 3.1 See also Hoare, *Pensions*, 192.

63. UK Parliament, *Commons*, vol. 190 (23 June 1908), c. 1567f., Mr Austen Chamberlain.

64. Ibid., vol. 191 (6 July 1908), c. 1359f., Mr Kinnaird. The term 'foreigners' here also included 'Indian' subjects of the British Crown.

65. UK Parliament, *Lords*, vol. 192 (20 July 1908), c. 1339, Viscount Wolverhampton.

66. A strict definition of 'residence' as 'uninterrupted … actual presence' was thereby eroded. D.O. Evans, *The Old Age Pensions Act, 1908. With Notes* (London: Sweet & Maxwell, 1908), 95. See also UK Parliament, *Lords*, vol. 193 (28 July 1908), c. 1106, Lord Lansdowne. On the notion of 'home', see Bickers, 8 Harper/Constantine, 308, 338.

67. Evans, *Old Age Pensions*, 32.

68. Hoare, *Pensions*, 37.

69. On court judgements regarding lapsed intentions to return, see ibid., 38f.

70. UK Parliament, *Lords*, vol. 193 (28 July 1908), c. 1107, Viscount Wolverhampton.

71. Evans, *Old Age Pensions*, 2.

72. In particular, positive mechanisms of inclusion based on ethnic criteria have been largely overlooked in scholarship; they contradict the notion that the ethnicization of the law in the UK first took place after the First World War. Baldwin, *Making*, 61; Terwey, *Antisemitismus*.

73. UK Acts, 5 Edw. 7 ch. 13, sec. 3.1.

74. C. Holmes, *Anti-Semitism in British Society: 1867–1939* (London: Arnold, 1979), 26f., 70f., 89–91. See also Cesarani, 'The Changing Character', 61.

75. UK Parliament, *Commons*, vol. 145 (2 May 1905), c. 761. On the clearly anti-Semitic elements of the debates, see ibid., c. 716, Major Evans Gordon and c. 787, Mr Forde Ridley.

76. Ibid. (2 May 1905), c. 804, 796. On the argument regarding the inability to assimilate, and references to the restrictive immigration policies in the dominions in this context, see also ibid. (2 May 1905), c. 724f., Mr Herbert Samuel.

77. UK Parliament, *Commons*, vol. 148 (27 June 1905), c. 305, Mr Kinnaird.

78. Ibid. (27 June 1905), c. 405f., Mr Flynn.

79. Ibid. (11 July 1905), c. 356.

80. UK Parliament, *Commons*, vol. 148 (27 June 1905), c. 306.

81. Ibid., vol. 149 (11 July 1905), c. 348.

82. UK Acts, 5 Edw. 7 ch. 13, sec. 1.3.

83. Therefore, Dummett and Nicol are incorrect in their assertion that ancestry was legally irrelevant 'for persons born on "English soil"' until 1981; see Dummett and Nicol, *Subjects*, 22.

84. See Baldwin, 'Subject to Empire', 528.

85. United Kingdom, *Report of the Inter-departmental Committee*, 16f. UK Acts, 4&5 Geo. 5 ch. 17, sec. II.5.2 and III.12.

86. UK Parliament, *Commons*, vol. 65, c. 1462, 1470f., 1492 and passim.

87. Ibid., vol. 62 (13 May 1914), c. 1468f.

88. Ibid., vol. 65 (29 July 1914), c. 1466, Mr Harcourt.

89. UK Acts, 4&5 Geo. 5 ch. 17, sec. II.2.5, III.10 and III.19.1(j).

90. UK Parliament, *Commons*, vol. 65 (29 July 1914), c. 1475f.

91. UK Acts, 4&5 Geo. 5 ch. 17, sec. II.8.1.

92. Cesarani, 'The Changing Character', 63.

93. Terwey, *Antisemitismus*, 83–86; T. Boghardt, *Spies of the Kaiser: German Covert Operations in Great Britain during the First World War Era* (Basingstoke: Palgrave Macmillan, 2004).

94. W.B. Odgers, *Nationality and Naturalization* (London: Jordan, 1916), 1. See also C. Holmes, *John Bull's Island: Immigration and British Society, 1871–1971* (Basingstoke: Macmillan, 1988), 97f.

95. UK Acts, 4&5 Geo. 5 ch. 17, sec. I.1.1.

96. These stipulations resulted from a suggestion made by the Foreign Office, who wanted to ensure a privileged legal status for the descendants of British subjects in the Ottoman Empire. London, IOR, L/PJ/6/702, file 2977, Foreign Office to Home Office, 10 November 1904.

97. Odgers, *Nationality*, 7. Baldwin claims, in contrast, that 'arguments for descent-based nationality laws ... never developed into concrete legal proposals'; Baldwin, *Making*, 69. See also Terwey, *Antisemitismus*, 201f.

98. London, IOR, L/PJ/6/731, file 2469, Indian Government to India Office, 27 July 1905.

99. UK Parliament, *Commons*, vol. 65 (29 July 1914), c. 1472.

100. London, IOR, L/PJ/6/679, file 1155, Report of the Attorney General of the Cape Colony, 7 December 1903.

101. See S. Bhattacharya, 'Reflections on Intersectionality: Bell Hooks', *Indian Journal of Dalit and Tribal Social Work* 1(1) (2012), 61–90; Ballhatchet, *Race*; H. Fischer-Tiné and S. Gehrmann (eds), *Empires and Boundaries: Rethinking Race, Class, and Gender in Colonial Settings* (New York: Routledge, 2009); Juneja and Pernau, 'Einleitung'; J. Nagel, 'Ethnic Troubles: Gender, Sexuality and the Construction of National Identity', in H. Kriesi and K. Armingeon, *Nation and National Identity: The European Experience in Perspective* (Chur: Rüegger, 1999); Pierson and Chaudhuri, *Nation, Empire, Colony*; Sinha, *Colonial Masculinity*; Wildenthal, 'Race, Gender, and Citizenship'; A.L. Stoler (ed.), *Haunted by Empire: Geographies of Intimacy in North American History* (Durham, NC: Duke University Press, 2006).

102. Sinha, *Colonial Masculinity*; R. Runge-Beneke, *Indien in britischen Augen: Über den Zusammenhang von Frauenbildern, Indienprojektionen, Herrschaftsphantasien und Männlichkeitsvorstellungen* (Göttingen: Muster-Schmidt, 1996); Juneja and Pernau, 'Einleitung', 32–37; Nagel, 'Ethnic Troubles', 89f., 101; G.L. Mosse, *The Image of Man: The Creation of Modern Masculinity* (New York: Oxford University Press, 1996). On the mixing of the categories of the so-called caste system with religious, social and 'racial' categories, see Bayly, *Caste*, 18, 119f. On the characterization of specific groups within the population as 'male' or 'female', see G. Rand, '"Martial Races" and "Imperial Subjects": Violence and Governance in Colonial India, 1857–1914', *European Review of History* 13(1) (2006), 1–20.

103. H. Fischer-Tiné, *Low and Licentious Europeans: Race, Class and 'White Subalternity' in Colonial India* (New Delhi: Orient Blackswan, 2009); Cannadine, *Ornamentalism*. See also Sinha, *Colonial Masculinity*, 1; McGranahan and Stoler, 'Introduction', 10; Mann, 'Torchbearers', 24; T.G. Ashplant, 'Dis/Connecting Whiteness: Biographical Perspectives on Race, Class, Masculinity and Sexuality in Britain c.1850–1930', *L'Homme* 16(2) (2005), 68.

104. Wieland developed this thesis in his comparison of Bosnia and India; see Wieland, *Nationalstaat*. See also P. Werth, 'Imperiology and Religion: Some Thoughts on a Research Agenda', in K. Matsuzato (ed.), *Imperiology: From Empirical Knowledge to Discussing the Russian Empire* (Sapporo: Slavic Research Center, Hokkaido University, 1997), 51, 54f.; O. Turij, '"Der ruthenische Glaube" und die "treuen Ruthenen": Die habsburgische Politik bezüglich der griechisch-katholischen Kirche', in H.-C. Maner (ed.), *Grenzregionen der Habsburgermonarchie im 18. und 19. Jahrhundert: Ihre Bedeutung und Funktion aus der Perspektive Wiens* (Münster: Lit, 2005), 123–32; Burbank, 'Imperial Rights', 400. Juneja and Pernau refute the assertion that religion as the premodern constructor of identity was replaced by the nation; Juneja and Pernau, 'Einleitung', 27f. See also Gottsmann, *Rom*, 28.

105. See, among others, R. Terborg-Penn, 'Enfranchising Women of Color: Women Suffragists as Agents of Imperialism', in R.R. Pierson and N. Chaudhuri (eds), *Nation, Empire, Colony: Historicizing Gender and Race* (Bloomington, IN: Indian University Press, 1998), 41–56; Wildenthal, 'Race, Gender, and Citizenship'; Cannadine, *Ornamentalism*; K. McKenzie, 'Social Mobilities at the Cape of Good Hope: Lady Anne Barnard, Samuel Hudson, and the Opportunities of Empire, c.1797–1824', in T. Ballantyne and A. Burton, *Moving Subjects: Gender, Mobility, and Intimacy in an Age of Global Empire* (Urbana, IL: University of Illinois Press, 2009), 274–95.

106. M. Csáky, 'Die Vielfalt der Habsburgermonarchie und die nationale Frage', in U. Altermatt (ed.), *Nation, Ethnizität und Staat in Mitteleuropa* (Vienna: Böhlau, 1996), 45; Komlosy, 'Habsburgermonarchie', 20.

107. London, PRO, FO 881/6944, Registration as British Subjects at Her Majesty's Consulate at Tangier of the Infant Children of Isaac Aaron Abensur, and on the Legitimacy of Children of Burmese Marriages contracted by 'lex loci' in Siam, 1897.

108. Baldwin, *Making*, 66f.

109. London, PRO, FO 881/6944.

110. Ibid. In particular, the jurist Davidson put forth these ethnically exclusive arguments in the Foreign Office. On the importance of monogamy as an imperialistic standard, see also T. Loos, *Subject Siam: Family, Law, and Colonial Modernity in Thailand* (Ithaca, NY: Cornell University Press, 2006), 100–29.

111. Ibid. This quote is taken from a memo that summarized the positions voiced by the legal experts of the Foreign Office and the India Office in their joint deliberations.

112. Ibid., Dr Tristram in a memo quoting Lord Stowell, 9 February 1877.

113. Ibid., Law Officers Opinion, May 1897.

114. London, IOR, L/PJ/6/500, file 101, Draft of a letter to the Indian government, October 1898.

115. Gottsmann, *Rom*, 225–28.

116. H.M. Carey, *God's Empire: Religion and Colonialism in the British World, c.1801–1908* (Cambridge: Cambridge University Press, 2011), 26.

117. Steinmetz, 'Return to Empire', 346, traces the dichotomy between 'white' and 'black' back to Christian roots. J. Gascoigne, 'Introduction: Religion and Empire, an Historiographical Perspective', *Journal of Religious History* 32(2) (2008), 160, speaks of a general 'link between empires and Christianity'.

118. London, PRO, FO 926/17, Consulate in Mansura to British Vice Consulate in Cairo, 24 June 1882, 25 June 1882, 26 June 1882.

119. Vienna, HHStA, Konsulat Jerusalem, Ktn. 141, Weisung des k.u.k. Außenministeriums, 3 May 1880.

120. Ibid.

121. In order to keep the Muslim elites on its side, the Habsburg administration repeatedly dismissed demands for agricultural reforms, and thereby perpetuated this congruence of social and ethno-religious differences. See Koller, 'Bosnien', 212.

122. Bayly, *Caste*. On the coupling of religious and social boundaries, see Juneja and Pernau, 'Einleitung', 36–43.

123. Cannadine, *Ornamentalism*; McKenzie, 'Social Mobilities'.

124. *Manchester Daily Guardian*, as quoted in Hughes, *Maasai*, 69. Cf. Cannadine, *Ornamentalism*, 39.

125. London, IOR, L/PJ/6/888, file 3168, report by Mackenzie King, March 1908.

126. A Canadian regulation introduced in 1910 exempted immigrants 'of Asiatic origin' from the restrictions if they had $200 with them. London, IOR, L/PJ/6/864, file 1371, Indian Emigration into Canada, 1908–1910. In a similar way, the Aliens Act of 1905 in the UK differentiated between 'steerage' passengers and 'cabin' passengers, the latter being permitted to enter the country without restriction.

127. London, IOR, L/PJ/5/462. See also M. Lake, 'From Mississippi to Melbourne via Natal: The Invention of the Literacy Test as a Technology of Racial Exclusion', in A. Curthoys

and M. Lake (eds), *Connected Worlds: History in Transnational Perspective* (Canberra: ANU E Press, 2005), 209–29.

128. London, IOR, L/PJ/6/864, file 1371, Indian Emigration into Canada, 1908–1910.

129. Indian Legislative Council, Proceedings of the Council, vol. 48 (25 February 1910), 282, Raja of Dighapatia. See also London, IOR, L/PO/1/1A, Kenya, restriction of immigration, position of Indians.

130. Galanter, *Competing Equalities*, 24.

131. On this as well as the formation of an ethnonational wing within social democracy, see H. Mommsen, *Die Sozialdemokratie und die Nationalitätenfrage im habsburgischen Vielvölkerstaat* (Vienna: Europa-Verlag, 1963); King, *Budweisers*, 81f.; M. Cattaruzza, *Sozialisten an der Adria: Plurinationale Arbeiterbewegung in der Habsburgermonarchie*, trans. K. Krieg (Berlin: Duncker & Humblot, 2011); Ruthner, '"k.(u.) k. postcolonial"?'.

132. Adler, *Wahlrecht*, 48. See also Strakosch-Graßmann, *Wahlrecht*, 21.

133. H. Zettelbauer, *'Die Liebe sei Euer Heldentum': Geschlecht und Nation in völkischen Vereinen der Habsburgermonarchie* (Frankfurt am Main: Campus, 2005), 15; Healy, 'Becoming Austrian', 3; A. Leszczawski-Schwerk, 'Juden und Jüdinnen als postkoloniale Subjekte im Spannungsfeld frauenemanzipatorischer Bestrebungen (1890–1914) im Österreichischen Galizien', *Historyka: Studia Metodologiczne* 42 (2012), 217f., 228; Bader-Zaar, 'Gaining the Vote', 197.

134. On the link between nationality, masculinity and military service in Austria, see C. Hämmerle, 'Back to the Monarchy's Glorified Past? Military Discourses on Male Citizenship and Universal Conscription in the Austrian Empire, 1868–1914', in S. Dudink, K. Hagemann and A. Clark (eds), *Representing Masculinity: Male Citizenship in Modern Western Culture* (New York: Palgrave Macmillan, 2007), 151–68. On the step-by-step abolishment of some existing women's suffrage rights in the second half of the nineteenth century, see Bader-Zaar, 'Gaining the Vote', 192.

135. Hirschhausen, 'Von imperialer Inklusion'. On the proposal to introduce a separate, gender-based electorate only for women, see Bader-Zaar, 'Gaining the Vote', 198.

136. Terborg, 'Women of Color', 44.

137. C. Andrew, 'Women as Citizens in Canada', in P. Boyer, L. Cardinal and D. Headon (eds), *From Subjects to Citizens: A Hundred Years of Citizenship in Australia and Canada* (Ottawa: University of Ottawa Press, 2004), 95–106. See also Baldwin, 'Subject to Empire', 529, 535.

138. London, IOR, L/PJ/6/864, file 1371, Indian Emigration into Canada.

139. London, PRO, CO 630/2, Regulation No. 7 from 1907, for the abolition of the Legal Status of Slavery.

140. East Africa Executive Council (31 October 1918). Female circumcision continues to persist to this day, despite international outrage over this practice.

141. On the role of sexuality in colonial power imbalances, see Ballhatchet, *Race*, 1; Baldwin, 'Subject to Empire', 538f.

142. London, PRO, CO 630/3, Regulation No. 7 from 1913, to amend the Criminal Laws in relation to Rape and other Sexual Offences.

143. East Africa Executive Council (10 June 1912, 28 October 1912).

144. London, PRO, CO 630/3, Regulation No. 7 from 1913, to amend the Criminal Laws in relation to Rape and other Sexual Offences.

145. East Africa Legislative Council (27 March 1913, 31 March 1913).

146. Abour, *White Highlands*, 345.

Chapter 5

EMPIRES AND ETHNIC HETEROGENEITY

While the previous chapters have dealt with the legal and administrative handling of ethnic diversity in specific territories within the Habsburg and British empires, this chapter compares both empires as a whole. In addition to exploring the influence of varying legal traditions, it focuses on the way in which British, Austrian and Hungarian nationals were dealt with abroad because empires tended to act as single political units vis-à-vis foreign states in such cases. Moreover, it examines British attempts to standardize laws across the empire, touching on the structural differences that contributed to a lack of interest in this kind of an endeavour in the Habsburg Empire. Thanks to the dualist nature of the Habsburg Empire, the governments in Cisleithania and Transleithania primarily dealt with nationality issues independent of one another. The British Empire, in contrast, had a hierarchical structure, which meant that the government in London retained a great deal of influence over the nationality policies in its colonies as well as in the self-governing dominions, because all subjects were bound to the British Crown.

Ethnic Neutrality in the Late Nineteenth Century

In the last third of the nineteenth century, the principle of ethnic neutrality guided the way both empires dealt with ethnic differences within their borders, at least in terms of legislature. The Austrian authorities, clearly influenced by statist principles, followed a course of supra-ethnic equality. Likewise, the government in Bosnia and Herzegovina sought to establish neutral policies defined by statist interests. Hungarian law, in contrast, drew on a nation-state perspective in which an ethnically inclusive notion of the nation prevailed. Imperialist ten-

Notes for this chapter begin on page 234.

dencies only played a significant role on the cross-imperial level, where the legal status of Hungarians and Austrians was superior to that of Bosnians.

The British Empire was marked by a similar mix of different strains of thought. Whereas the principle of ethnic neutrality was well established in the UK, Canada initially aimed at ethnic inclusion within a nation-state framework, while a stance that ambivalently combined statist and imperialist perspectives emerged in India. This constellation resulted in a variety of conflicts between the defenders of ethnic neutrality and the advocates of an ethnically exclusive politics of 'racial' discrimination that erupted over issues such as the Indian Code of Criminal Procedure. Paradoxically, the promise of equality made in 1858 was followed by 'racially' exclusive measures in the dominions that sparked intensive debates over the status of 'Indian' subjects. Faced with these tensions, the government in London tried to cling to its principle of ethnic neutrality – at least officially – but this became all the more difficult as time went on. Consequently, by the late nineteenth century, imperialist mechanisms of discrimination gained a strong foothold in British law, hidden beneath a veil of ethnic neutrality.

'Subjects', 'Citizens' and Different Legal Traditions

The legal nature of the term 'subject' itself opened the door for subcutaneous discrimination in the British context. In contrast to Roman law and the revolutionary concepts of the Napoleonic Code, British jurists stressed that the idea of a 'citizen' (i.e. *civis*, *citoyen* or *Staatsbürger*) was foreign to Common Law, which clung to its feudal roots by using the term 'subject'. British law thus spoke of 'allegiance' as a personal relationship between the protective sovereign and the obedient subject, rather than 'citizenship', which defined the relationship between a state and its members who were guaranteed rights in exchange for the fulfilment of certain duties. Unlike the 'citizen', therefore, the 'subject' could only claim protection and not rights.[1] At first glance, the so-called 'rights of Englishmen' dating back to at least the seventeenth century, which promised citizens protection against the interference of the state and entitled them to government by consent, seem to contradict this narrow understanding of subjecthood. But upon closer inspection, even the use of 'Englishmen' and not 'British subjects' in the wording of this phrase indicates that these rights were not bestowed upon all British subjects in equal measure. Thus, it was possible to cite the venerable right of an Englishman to be tried by one's peers in the debates over the Indian Ilbert Bill in order to justify discriminating between 'European British Subjects' and 'natives', who were also subjects of the Crown.[2]

Whereas British subject status did not confer equality or any rights beyond that of protection, Austrian law used the term *Staatsbürger* ('citizen'), which was explicitly tied to notions of equality.[3] In this respect, the ABGB of 1811 clearly resembled the Roman tradition it referred to, as well as its Napoleonic counter-part. As part of the Josephine reforms, it sought to dismantle the hierarchical tradition of the estates by introducing the notion of legal equality for all citizens. In a similar vein, the *Staatsgrundgesetze* (fundamental or constitutional laws) of 1867 adopted a model that was 'republican' in origin to map out the framework for a constitutional monarchy that followed statist principles and was not influenced by the idea of the nation-state. These laws guaranteed all Austrian citizens the same rights, which corresponded with the military draft instituted just a year later and that applied equally – at least in theory – to all citizens. During the constitutional era, Hungarian law was also influenced by this approach, reflected, for example, in the opinion that the status of Bosnian nationals as 'less-privileged imperial citizens' or 'second-class citizens' was a problematic deviation from the principle of equality that needed to be remedied.[4] In the Habsburg context, the adherence to the legal equality of all citizens put a damper on discrimination. Such a notion of equality, however, was not nearly as well anchored within British law. This difference played a fundamental role in steering these two empires along different paths of law in the early twentieth century.

Ethnic Neutrality and Habsburg Nationals Abroad

Did administrative praxis actually live up to theory when it came to equality in the Habsburg Empire? An analysis of the way in which the Imperial and Royal consulates dealt with the Austrian citizens and Hungarian nationals living abroad sheds light on this question. In Hungary, law and politics were imbued with a stronger sense of nation, which meant that they enabled emigrants to retain their Hungarian nationality abroad. In Austria, by contrast, efforts were made to achieve congruency between the community of nationals and the resident population – in keeping with statist aspirations – which meant that the Cisleithanian government did not have a vested interest in those who left the country for good. However, both the Austrian and joint governments did devote a great deal of attention to emigrants who had not yet fulfilled their military service obligations. This statist interest in military conscription guided the administrative praxis of the Imperial and Royal consulates, which were responsible for calling up draftees, examining candidates and other issues related to conscription.[5] The example of Berthold Hanl from Bohemia illustrates just how insistent the authorities were in tracking down draftees at the end of the nineteenth century. Hanl was travelling with the music band of a Mr Hirsch in South and South East Asia, which meant that the Imperial and Royal consulates in Bombay, Rangoon, Calcutta and Singapore all became involved in sorting out his military service obligations.[6]

With regard to conscription, the Imperial and Royal authorities adopted a principle of neutrality in that they treated all male nationals equally, regardless of ethnic identity, and forced them to serve in the army. In the late nineteenth century, the authorities more or less followed this principle of ethnic neutrality when it came to protecting nationals abroad as well. 'Jewish' Austrians and Hungarians, in particular, enjoyed the protection of the Imperial and Royal government when resident in foreign countries. Although the 'Jews' often faced discrimination at home in Austria-Hungary, and some political parties even demanded their legal exclusion, the Habsburg consulates generally treated Jews as equal citizens. This was especially apparent in the Ottoman Empire, which had passed a law in 1869 in which it claimed sovereignty over most of the Austrian–Hungarian nationals living within its boundaries. A number of Jews were part of this group that was supposed to lose some of the legal privileges associated with Habsburg protection at the will of the sultan. The Imperial and Royal government firmly opposed these efforts and stood up for the interests of its 'Jewish' and other denizens or protected persons (*Schutzgenossen*).[7]

This protected status initially developed out of certain prerogatives that the Turkish government had granted to the major European powers within its territory. Correspondingly, non-Muslim individuals who were deemed to be nationals by these European governments enjoyed a number of privileges, including tax exemptions. However, not all the individuals who fell under the protection of the Habsburg authorities were in fact Austrian or Hungarian nationals. Given these circumstances, the Turkish authorities requested that the consulate in Rustchuk (now Ruse in Bulgaria) provide a register of the 'Imperial and Royal nationals and de facto subjects residing in the Vilayet' in 1871, in order to review the legality of all claims to Habsburg protection.[8] The consulate refused because it feared ramifications for those under its protection. At the same time, the consul made it clear that the Turkish authorities were not authorized to decide whether individuals with consular passports had a right to these privileges or not. In particular, he wanted to make sure that Austrian subjects were 'de facto relieved of the difficult and onerous burden of proving their descent from Austrian parentage'. The Imperial and Royal Foreign Ministry also defended the legality of consular protection that had been obtained prior to the Turkish law of 1869 in its correspondence with the Turkish government. In all other cases, it asserted, the Turkish authorities had to provide proof for their claims to sovereignty over anyone who had been issued a passport by the Imperial and Royal authorities.[9] This position basically guaranteed all those under Habsburg protection the retention of their privileges. Simultaneously, by insisting on the rights of its protégés, the Imperial and Royal government also demonstrated its international prestige vis-à-vis Constantinople and the other powers.

Similarly, the Austrian government also defended the interests of its citizens in other foreign states in order to uphold its international prestige as well as its humanitarian interest in the welfare of its denizens. In the winter of 1876/77, a number of Austrian 'Jews' were driven out of their villages in a series of anti-Semitic pogroms in Romania. Their 'misery and distress' immediately motivated

Cisleithanian politicians to demand a Habsburg intervention on behalf of those affected in the interest of the 'monarchy's position of power'.[10] The 'ill-treatment' of Galician workers in Romania led to similar appeals.[11] None of these situations prompted the Habsburg authorities to assert a general political position on the issue of nationality law in which it promised to increase the protection afforded emigrants abroad. Yet these examples illustrate that the Imperial and Royal authorities guaranteed emigrants protection, irrespective of ethnic identity.

Especially in cases of so-called white slavery, the Habsburg authorities made a concerted effort to protect nationals abroad. At the beginning of the 1890s, for example, the sixteen-year-old Sara Friedmann left the house of her parents in Galicia and never returned. In 1895, her father received a letter from Constantinople in which she described how she had been abducted and sold 'to the brothel owner Menasche Gottmann'. She bid her father to 'take the steps necessary to ensure for her release from the hands of the procurer with the appropriate authorities'. She also complained about having been mistreated, and accused some of the lower officials of the Imperial and Royal Consulate in Constantinople of working with the brothel owners. Especially because of these accusations, the authorities searched diligently for Sara Friedmann and ultimately located her in the 'public brothel of Moische Gottmann'. Surprisingly, however, she told the consular officials that she 'was completely satisfied with her situation'. After she had left her parents, she explained, she had met Josef Goldstaub, who took her to Constantinople for 100 marks and found her a place in a brothel. According to her account, Josef Goldstaub had then sent the letter to Galicia in her name, without her knowledge. Sara Friedmann resisted being sent home by the authorities as part of their efforts to repatriate prostitutes, employing a trick within nationality law: 'In order to circumvent the jurisdiction of the Imperial and Royal consulate, she claimed to have obtained Ottoman nationality'. The consular authorities, however, were not deterred by her statement. They argued that Sara Friedmann, as a minor, was not legally entitled to change her nationality without the consent of her parents. Ultimately, she was 'transported' back to Galicia under escort and against her will.[12]

Unlike Sara Friedmann, Anna Königsberg, who was also from Galicia, did not refuse the protection of the consulate in a similar case. Despite the fact that Königsberg had officially lost her Austrian citizenship by marrying the Russian national Aaron Daniel in Cape Town in 1899, the Imperial and Royal consulate nonetheless came to her aid. Her husband had brought her to Buenos Aires, where he lived off the 'earnings of his wife for seven months in a women's house run by Lisa Feldmann'. After Königsberg had escaped from the brothel, the consulate assisted her in attaining a divorce and returning to Austria.[13] If there was any suspicion of white slavery, the Imperial and Royal authorities even stepped in to protect 'Jewish' Austrian women, regardless of whether it was against their will or doubtful as to whether they were still nationals in a legal sense.

The Ethnic Heterogeneity of Individuals Registered with the Imperial and Royal Consulates

The question as to the verifiability or proof of Austrian and Hungarian national-ity abroad points to the significance of the consular registries, which were the administrative foundation for any such claims. Especially since Habsburg pro-tection afforded certain privileges in the Ottoman Empire, the consular records from here are particularly telling. In the consular district of Beirut, with its subsidiary offices in Aleppo, Damascus, Cyprus, Haifa, Tripoli and Jaffa, a 'register of subjects' from 1866 lists 125 people, all of whom were of the Jewish faith. The lists for Tunis and Tripoli for the same year counted twenty Catholic, one Protestant, one Greek Orthodox and forty-five Israelite families, most of the latter, based on their names, seemed to come from the Italian-speaking parts of the empire.[14] Another register from Morocco, that was put together in 1915 after France and Spain had established protectorates in the territory, still exists. It includes all those in the service of the Imperial and Royal consulates as well as employees of Austrian and Hungarian companies. The list also contains the names of Muslims who were neither Austrian nor Hungarian nationals.[15] This administrative praxis of registering nationals or denizens illustrates that the Habsburg consulates granted individuals of different religions or ethnic identities equal diplomatic protection.

Registers that have survived from the Imperial and Royal consulate in Jerusalem indicate that 205 Austrian and Hungarian nationals were registered in 1896. This number shrank to 98 in 1905 and 73 in 1911 before climbing up to 148 in 1914. Approximately 80 to 90 per cent of those listed were 'Jews'.[16] The lower numbers around the turn of the century might have resulted from a waning interest on behalf of the authorities and/or the emigrants themselves in registration; they might also have been an expression of scepticism towards Zionist emigration within diplomatic circles. The jump in registrations in 1914 was clearly linked to the outbreak of the First World War. The consulate in Jerusalem alone processed the military induction of twenty-two Hungarians and fifteen Austrians during the war (see Illustration 5.1).[17] Almost all of these draftees were young men of the Jewish faith. In this sense, the Habsburg consular authorities made sure they treated all nationals equally, not only in terms of rights and privileges, but also in terms of duties.

Imperial and Royal Diplomatic Protection in Bulgaria, and the Exclusion of 'Jews'

In some places, however, anti-Semitic prejudices definitely influenced Habsburg administrative praxis. Especially with respect to military service, rumours

Illustration 5.1. Photographs of Austrian and Hungarian conscripts in Jerusalem, 1914–1916. From: Vienna, HHStA, Konsulat Jerusalem, Ktn. 146.

circulated that the 'Israelites' tried to avoid conscription more so than other Austrians and Hungarians. In 1884, the Imperial and Royal consulate in Rustchuk responded to complaints made by the Bulgarian government that resident 'Jews' who were presumably Bosnian nationals illegally evaded military conscription by claiming Austrian diplomatic protection. A consular official even referred to the 'well-known aversion among East European Jews against the fulfilment of military service obligations'.[18] The authorities then confiscated the passports of the people in question, thereby depriving them of their former privileges as Imperial and Royal protected persons.[19] Whereas the consular authorities protected their protégés in most cases from being conscripted in Bulgaria, they denied 'Jewish' Bosnians this protection, thereby discriminating along ethnic lines.[20] Similar prejudices surfaced elsewhere as well. In 1891 the police arrested a Galician 'Jew' for failing to fulfil his military service obligations. As the man had been naturalized in the United States of America, this action violated bilateral treaties. The authorities justified this move on the basis of accusations 'that Israelites from Galicia in particular often sought to evade military conscription by emigration'.[21] Moreover, when 'Jewish' Hungarians resident in Jerusalem complained in 1910 that the Imperial and Royal consulate had refused to issue them new passports, the response of the Imperial and Royal government insinuated that the new, stricter passport regulations were in part designed to force 'Jewish' emigrants in particular to fulfil their military service obligations.[22]

However, such anti-Semitic prejudices by no means guided the policies adopted by all the consular administrations. When Imperial and Royal diplomatic protection was eliminated in Bulgaria in 1911 because it had repeatedly sparked conflicts between Sofia and Vienna, all protégés who were neither Austrian nor Hungarian nationals automatically lost their privileges as protected persons. In order to improve the situation of those affected by this change, the embassy in Sofia, with the support of the Imperial and Royal Foreign Ministry, tried to foster their naturalization in Cisleithania. Among the forty-one families and individuals recommended for naturalization, there were a number of people of the Jewish faith or Jewish descent.[23] The Imperial-Royal Ministry of the Interior, however, was not very amenable to this idea, so these former protected persons lost their claims to Habsburg protection.[24] Yet, the consulate officials still tried to help them. In 1918, however, it was concluded that the conflict with the Bulgarian authorities was no longer worth the risk, given the lack of prospects, and that it would be better to get rid of 'such elements' voluntarily before it was too late.[25]

British Protected Persons: The Inclusive Exclusion of 'Non-Whites'

Whereas the Imperial and Royal consular authorities primarily adhered to a principle of ethnic neutrality and sought to support all nationals and protected persons equally, apart from a few instances in which anti-Semitism came into play, British diplomatic officials approached the issue of protected persons from a different direction. Akin to the Imperial and Royal Schutzgenossen, British protected persons also owed their special legal status to privileges that non-Muslims and the European powers enjoyed in the Ottoman Empire. The institution of protected persons dissolved slowly along with the Ottoman Empire in the Habsburg case, but the figure of the British protected person survived. It was reinterpreted around the turn of the century as a less-privileged national status enjoyed by the populations of British protectorates. The line drawn between this status and that of a British subject, which afforded certain legal advantages, often ran along ethnic lines.

The Foreign Jurisdiction Act of 1890 declared all individuals who enjoyed the protection of the British Crown abroad to be British protected persons. This definition did not rest on ethnic distinctions and therefore reflected the older legal tradition of ethnic neutrality. In the 1890s, a memorandum issued by the British Foreign Office still referred to 'Persons under British protection, styled, "British-protected persons"' in this sense. It emphasized that these individuals were 'not entitled to British nationality' and were therefore not British subjects.[26] At the same time, the memorandum underscored the international scope of this legal status, noting that it only afforded diplomatic protection abroad. Especially in Morocco, Egypt and Turkey, this protected status caused problems. The British consular authorities – unlike their Habsburg counterparts – had already made concessions to the sultan's government regarding sovereignty over the protégés of the European powers in the 1890s. A memorandum from the Foreign Office noted that too many people had been granted protection in the past, and that their number should be reduced by changing the registration praxis. It also stressed that the claim to protection could not be inherited, and recommended that the names of all family members should be removed from the registers upon the death of a protected person. The consular authorities were supposed to insist on the protection afforded to those already registered in order to uphold British prestige, but the Foreign Office instructed them, as a rule, to relinquish the protection of those for whom the Turkish authorities had raised reasonable doubts as to the legitimacy of claims to protection. Ultimately, only those currently employed in the service of the British government were supposed to enjoy full diplomatic protection.[27]

Simultaneously, the memorandum also outlined an understanding of the term 'protected person' that was going to supplant that of the old international law tradition in due course. It spoke of British protected persons as 'natives of States or places under British protection, such as the British spheres of influence in Africa'. Yet it also noted that the legal status of these people had only been a theoretical problem up until then.[28] The memorandum was not completely accurate in this assumption because there had been discussions over the legal status of individuals born in British protectorates towards the end of the nineteenth century. Paradoxically, this question had arisen within the United Kingdom itself over twenty years before it sparked legal disputes in places such as East Africa. In 1889, a 23-year-old physician, Kuman B. Narayan from Kuch Behar, a protected or princely state in India, applied for naturalization in London. His case raised the issue of whether he was a foreigner or a subject; if the latter was true, then naturalization made absolutely no sense. As the British authorities were well aware of the far-reaching consequences of this nationality issue, they skirted around the problem by denying Narayan's application without citing any reasons. This move effectively carved out a grey area between subjecthood and alienness, 'between two stools', for nationals of the protectorates.[29]

When this problem arose again in a similar case in 1901, a memo from the Home Office clearly stated that 'Birth in a British Protectorate is not equivalent as regards nationality to Birth in British Dominions'.[30] This legal position was contested by an opinion from 1906 on British nationality law that put forth the diametrically opposed notion that a 'person, though not born in a place over which the King of England exercises direct sovereignty, if he is born in the dominions of a prince subject and doing homage to the King of England, is born within the King's allegiance, and therefore a natural-born subject and no alien; ... such is ... the condition of the subjects of the feudatory princes of India'.[31] In the end, though, this argument did not prevail, and the idea that individuals born in the protectorates were not entitled to British subject status emerged triumphant. Legal experts in the India Office along with the Home Office shared the opinion that birth in these territories bestowed 'claims to protection under the Foreign Jurisdiction Act', but not British subjecthood.[32] Those affected thus became foreigners who enjoyed the protection of the British state abroad. In 1901, an official in the Home Office suggested legally granting these individuals British protected person status, with reference to an identical suggestion made by the viceroy of India. The term 'protected person' in this sense, however, did not make its way into British nationality law until after 1945. Nonetheless, the debates over the issue illustrate how this concept was extracted from the Ottoman context around the turn of the century and turned into a category used to describe the less-privileged nationals of the British protectorates.

An opinion written by the Law Officers in 1901 clearly exemplifies the fact that this reinterpretation aimed to exclude 'natives' from British subject status in that it determined that those born in East Africa and the other protectorates were not British subjects because '[i]t has not yet been thought expedient to confer [this] status ... upon the natives of Protectorates'.[33] Strictly speaking, however, this policy affected not only 'natives', but also 'Europeans' born in the protectorates. Therefore, it is not surprising that legal regulations and administrative practices were put into place around the same time that made it possible for 'white' British subjects and their descendants to retain British nationality and thus their legal privileges in the protectorates. This move was clearly reflected in the birth registers in East Africa. The establishment of the less-privileged British protected person status therefore had a racist dimension in that it assigned the great majority of the 'non-white' population of the British Empire an inferior position in terms of nationality.[34]

What was so perfidious about this protected status was that it excluded those individuals from subjecthood, but not entirely from British nationality per se. This 'inclusive exclusion' thus banished protected persons to a grey area between nationals and non-nationals that was located outside the boundaries of the usual categories of international law.[35] On the one hand, they were subject to British sovereignty as illustrated in the enforcement of military conscription in East Africa. At the same time, however, they could hardly assert any kind of legal claims on the British government because they were not subjects. Through this inclusive exclusion, they had to bear all the duties of a subject, but they were denied the rights of a citizen.

The Protection of Nationals: Ethnic Neutrality in the British Context

Despite such discriminatory tendencies with regard to the 'non-white' population within the empire, the British government defended the interests of its subjects and dependants in foreign countries, regardless of ethnic identity. At least until the end of the nineteenth century, the British consular authorities acted in an ethnically neutral manner when it came to diplomatic protection. They supported all subjects in the same way, even 'non-Europeans'. In doing so, they not only emphasized their role as benevolent protectors along orientalist lines, but also they exposed the despotic nature of the non-European states in which they had to protect their denizens against brutal officials. With reference to its extra-territorial jurisdiction, in 1878 the British consulate in Amoy (now Xiamen in China) demanded that the local authorities release an imprisoned British subject of Chinese descent: 'After some hours of expostulation [the consul] returned to the consulate, and almost as he entered it a chair was set down at the door containing the corpse of the man he had endeavoured to save. He had been beaten to death in the Yamen'.[36]

Sometimes British officials risked conflicts with other European colonial powers in order to protect the interests of their 'non-white' subjects. In the 1890s, the British consul in the French colony of Réunion, Mr Bennett, repeatedly tried to protect the rights of the indentured labourers from India working on the local sugar cane plantations. Bennett protested against arbitrary arrests and intervened in the case of two women who were forced to work against their will.[37] In general, he tried to insist upon the implementation of the French Nationality Act of 1889, which granted French nationality to the children of immigrants born in Réunion, and therefore proscribed their legal equality with French citizens. But the French colonial authorities as well as the plantation owners almost always sought to circumvent the law in practice. Neither the India Office nor the Foreign Office supported Bennett's efforts in this regard, and the 'Europeans' in Réunion were openly hostile to the idea. Nevertheless, Bennett stubbornly but unsuccessfully continued to advocate the rights of Indian immigrants, because, as he put it, 'justice cares for none of these things'.[38]

The efforts of consular officials to defend the interests of 'non-European' subjects or protégés were more likely to succeed when the international prestige of the British Crown was at stake. When the government of Siam (now Thailand) raised doubts as to the rights of some 'Shan headmen' to British protection, the consular authorities were able to insist on the privileges of these headmen who were considered to be allies of the British Empire. In this case, the British authorities opposed the demands of the Siamese government in order to uphold '[t]he value and prestige of British nationality'.[39]

As these examples illustrate, the British authorities, like their Habsburg counterparts, largely pursued a course of ethnic neutrality when it came to asserting diplomatic protection until the beginning of the twentieth century. What mattered most was not the ethnic identity of those involved, but rather their legal status as subjects or protected persons. Correspondingly, international law and bilateral treaties were of paramount importance. For the most part, the consular authorities relied on a traditional understanding of diplomacy and sovereignty as well as protection that could be termed 'old European'. After the turn of the century, however, this tradition lost ground as ethnic differences became all the more relevant.

The Ethnicization of the Law in the Early Twentieth Century

The analysis of the development of law and administrative praxis in Canada and Hungary, India and Austria, and East Africa and Bosnia, as well as in the United Kingdom, has shown that, around 1900, ethnic differences became increasingly significant in all these territories when it came to nationality and migration regulations, as well as access to the rights of citizenship. This process resulted in the establishment of mechanisms that either recognized differences or discriminated along ethnic lines. But what effect did these ethnicizing trends have at the overarching imperial level? Looking at how imperial authorities dealt with their own nationals abroad can shed light on this issue. Moreover, the treatment of 'non-European' migrants within the empire and the debates over an empire-wide nationality act offer additional insights in the British context.

Ethnic Difference and British Consular Praxis

First of all, there is the fundamental question regarding whether the administrative handling of certain groups made it more or less possible for them to retain British nationality abroad. Children born abroad to a British father could only claim subjecthood – *qua iure sanguinis* – if they could provide documents proving their descent from a British national. Effectively, this meant that their names had to be found within official consular birth registers. A closer look at the registers in those districts in which British subjects of different origin and ethnicity were permanently resident reveals whether ethnic criteria came into play in administrative praxis. One such place was the French colony of Réunion in the Indian Ocean. It was home to many indentured labourers from India as well as some immigrants from the UK and the British colonies on the Arabian Peninsula. Similarly, the West Coast of the United States was populated by immigrants from the mother country as well as some from Hong Kong and India. In Siam, businessmen and engineers from the UK also lived alongside British immigrants from India, Singapore, modern-day Malaysia, and Hong Kong. Moreover, these three examples reflect the differences in international law when it came to different types of foreign territories. Whereas Réunion was the colony of another European power, and the United States was a sovereign foreign country, Siam was a semi-colonial state whose policies were greatly influenced by the British and French governments, and which granted the European powers extraterritorial jurisdiction over their own nationals.

Since the consular birth registers did not record the language, religion or geographic origin of the parents of a child, the following analysis is based on the names of the family members provided. Although this is not always a clear-cut criterion, it nonetheless allows for a relatively reliable identification of 'Indian' and 'Chinese' migrants who made up the majority of the British subjects in the Indian and Pacific ocean regions, alongside 'European' immigrants. Table 5.1 illustrates the percentage of 'non-white' subjects among the total number of registered births.[40]

The very small number of registered births in Réunion makes a quantitative analysis difficult. That said, however, it is surprising that the British authorities did not record the births of the children of Indian immigrants, despite the efforts made by Consul Bennett on behalf of their rights. Two of the three registered 'non-European' births between 1911 and 1915 – Hosmar I. Cassim and Hassan I. Cassim – were born to 'Arabian' immigrants as opposed to 'Indian' parents. Since the consulate did not record the births of the children of 'Indian'

Table 5.1. Number of 'non-Europeans' among the total number of registered births of British subjects from the lists of the consulates in Réunion, on the US West Coast, and in Siam, in absolute figures

Consular Districts	Reunion	US West Coast	Siam
Years			
1871–75	0 of 1	0 of 14	0 of 11
1881–85	0 of 3	0 of 24	0 of 28
1891–95	0 of 0	0 of 37	0 of 27
1901–05	0 of 2	0 of 26	4 of 58
1911–15	3 of 4	0 of 30	2 of 61
Total	**3 of 10**	**0 of 131**	**6 of 185**

subjects, it was ultimately impossible for these children to prove their British subject status, which effectively excluded them from the community of British nationals.

The consulates on the US West Coast registered a much greater number of births, but given the much larger number of immigrants, these figures surely reflected only a small portion of the children born to British subjects in this region. Without a doubt, the figure of 131 births registered by the consulates was far too low to be representative in any way. Generally, the lack of registered births was connected to the fact that British subject status bore very few material or legal advantages in the United States. Consequently, British parents did not make an effort to register the births of their children, especially if they intended to become naturalized Americans. The complete absence of children born to British immigrants from Asia in these registers can either be attributed to waning interest on the part of the immigrants themselves or to 'racially' discriminatory administrative practices. Regardless of the reasons behind this absence, these 'non-European' children born on the US West Coast were effectively denied British subject status.

The situation in Siam, by contrast, was all the more telling. Although the total number of British subjects in Siam was likely to have been much lower than on the US West Coast, the consulate registered more births. Unlike in the United States, important privileges were attached to British nationality in Siam. British nationals not only fell under British consular jurisdiction, but they were also released from Siamese tax and military service obligations.[41] As a result, 'non-European' subjects also sought to register the births of their children in Siam, and they were sometimes successful as the few entries from the early twentieth century indicate. Since all British subjects in Siam had a vested interest in the registration of births, the question remains as to why there were so few children of 'Asiatic' parents recorded on the lists. Did the consular officials pursue a course of ethnic exclusion by enabling only 'whites' to prove British nationality?

The Consular Register of British Subjects in Siam, and the Exclusion of 'Asiatics'

Thankfully, numerous other documents apart from the consular birth registers themselves shed light on the British registration praxis in Siam. By and large, the debates surrounding this issue were less focused on birth records than on the lists kept by the consulates of locally resident British subjects. The certificates documenting that a person had been registered on these lists protected those in question against claims made by the Siamese government, and in particular its attempts to force all 'non-European' inhabitants of Siam to pay taxes and serve in the military, regardless of whether they were British nationals or not. Consequently, the Siamese authorities sought to prevent the consular registration of 'non-white' subjects, while these subjects themselves were particularly keen to see their names on the consular lists. This conflict forced the British authorities to delve into the details of the matter and decide which subjects should be protected and therefore officially registered.

The whole situation was further complicated by a tricky constellation within international law. Burma, which bordered Siam, officially became part of the British Empire in 1886 and thereby lost its independence. The nationality of those individuals who emigrated from Burma to Siam prior to 1886 was thus highly contested. Were these migrants, who made up the largest group of 'Asiatic' Britons in Siam, British subjects or not? Initially, the India Office in particular was willing to make concessions to the Siamese government. In 1896, for instance, it spoke out in favour of refusing to register those in question as British subjects, because 'the extension of our lists of protected British (Asiatic) subjects is not to be desired'.[42] A year later, however, the Law Officers of the British government issued a contrary opinion that insisted that all Burmese subjects had acquired British nationality through the annexation of Burma, including those who had already been living in Siam prior to 1886. Yet although their reading of the law seemed to be quite inclusive at first glance, it was nevertheless possible to interpret their opinion in different ways. As of 1886, there was no Burmese law on nationality that clearly defined who was to be considered a Burmese national. This effectively made the claims of Burmese emigrants to British nationality contestable. Likewise, the Law Officers failed to address the question of whether those who had become British subjects through the annexation of Burma could bestow this status to their children born in Siam by virtue of *ius sanguinis*. For all intents and purposes, these legal experts recommended that each case be dealt with on an individual basis and in agreement with the Siamese authorities.[43]

The British and Siamese governments then came to an agreement in 1899 that 'natives of Burmah or the British Shan States, who became domiciled in Siam before the 1st January, 1886', should not be registered as British nationals.

This privilege was thus only reserved for such 'persons of Asiatic descent' who had been born 'in the Queen's dominions'.[44] Furthermore, through this agreement, the British government implicitly prevented the registration of children born to 'non-white' subjects in Burma prior to 1886, and in Siam, because – strictly speaking – they were born outside the realm of the British Crown. The British–Siamese agreement of 1899 made it impossible for those affected to prove their British nationality, despite the fact that they were actually British subjects according to the letter of the law. This applied in particular to children born to 'Asiatic' subjects in Siam.

However, regardless of the terms of this agreement, the British government still insisted that it alone had the right to determine who was to enjoy the protection of the Crown.[45] The consulates took advantage of this prerogative in cases involving individuals who had not been registered properly within the time frame dictated by the Registration Ordinance, or British subjects who had travelled to Siam without a passport.[46] In addition to 'European' Britons, two groups mainly profited from this praxis: the 'Shan headmen' and Burmese who had been raised according to English standards and worked for British companies in Siam.[47] As the deprivation of British subjecthood in these cases might have led to the 'loss of British prestige and indignation among British subjects',[48] the Foreign Office in London insisted on diplomatic protection for the 'Shan headmen', who were to be considered British subjects – despite the 1899 agreement – 'till they die out'.[49]

When 'Asiatics' who belonged to neither the educated middle class nor the traditional elite tried to claim British nationality, the consulates almost always refrained from asserting their rights, and willingly left the decision up to the Siamese government. Due to the lack of interest in protecting such run-of-the-mill 'Asiatics', the British government did not even protest when the Siamese authorities simply ignored the registration certificates that were actually supposed to entitle their holders to the protection of the British Crown. Since falsified certificates were quite common and the counterfeit business was in full swing, a memorandum issued by the Foreign Office noted that one could not demand that the Siamese authorities recognize these certificates as valid documents. Especially when 'Asiatics' tried to use such certificates to claim British protection, the memo continued, it was only natural to doubt the authenticity of their claims.[50] Subsequently, British officials almost never objected when Siamese officials confiscated registration certificates. In 1907, for instance, 'Payatoga U, a shan' and 'Puetory Novta, or Suty, a resident of Hbun Yuon' lost their certificates this way, and the consulate hardly bothered to support their claims to entitlement to the protection of the British state.[51]

Siamese enforced recruitment in 1914 once again raised the question of whether 'non-white' British subjects were to be protected against the claims of the local authorities. Whereas one official advocated that all 'Asiatic British subjects' should be protected against recruitment through the issuance of certificates, superior officials insisted that such documents were not worth the paper they were written on.[52] According to their logic, it would not make sense to delude the Siamese authorities into thinking 'that by issuing a Certificate we actually, in some semi-magical way, convert a person, who otherwise would be a Siamese subject, into a British subject'.[53] Theoretically, the British authorities thus insisted upon the privileges of all British subjects, regardless of whether they were in the possession of a registration certificate or not. In practice, however, the consular officials were directed only to issue such documents in exceptional cases, and to be very restrictive, in particular when it came to claims to protection voiced by 'Asiatics'.[54] The authorities therefore discriminated against 'non-white' British subjects, and effectively denied them the privileges to which they were legally entitled.

Migration within the Empire and the Dynamics of Equality and Discrimination

The ethnicization of British subject status and the establishment of racist practices not only appeared in the case of British nationals abroad but also within the empire itself, and especially in the treatment of immigrants from India in the dominions. Migration within the British Empire thus repeatedly sparked clashes between mechanisms of racist discrimination introduced within the dominions and the demands of the Indian nationalist movement for equality. As the Canadian example has shown, discrimination directed against 'non-white' subjects in the self-governing colonies emerged at least in part out of the assumption that equal citizenship could only exist within an ethnically homogeneous population. In the early twentieth century, this idea not only fed into an ethnically exclusive, nation-state approach in Canada, but also it led to the introduction of political and social rights of citizenship coupled with 'racially' exclusive migration regulations in places like New Zealand.[55] The dominions thus followed a model of 'colonial nationalism', as put forth by Richard Jebb, that aimed at the 'promotion and protection of nation-states' through the ethnic homogenization of certain parts of the empire.[56] This exclusive, nation-state perspective that denied 'non-whites' membership in the body politic while welcoming 'whites' inevitably led to discrimination within the community of British subjects according to ethnic criteria.

The Indian nationalist movement protested against these exclusionary measures by demanding that all British nationals, regardless of origin and 'racial' identity, should be entitled to the same rights, in keeping with an ethnically neutral statist standpoint. In 1910, Gopal Krishna Gokhale, a representative from the moderate wing of the nationalist movement in Pune, outlined before the Indian Legislative Assembly the 'galling and degrading indignities and humiliations' endured by 'His Majesty's Indian subjects' in other parts of the British Empire: the pseudo-slavery of the indenture system, mistreatment by employers, the raising of special taxes, the denial of suffrage, limits on the right to acquire property, the allocation of special areas of residence, prohibitions against entry to territories and even the violent expulsion from some territories.[57] Along with other members of the Indian National Congress, Gokhale also emphasized 'the depth and intensity of public feeling' that these injustices had 'aroused in this country in all quarters'.[58]

These words reflected the danger that the exclusionary and discriminatory policies in the dominions might have added fuel to the fires of protest against British rule in India. An example from Canada exemplifies this connection. In March 1908, the Canadian authorities ordered the deportation of a group of 'Indian' immigrants who had come to British Columbia aboard the *Monteagle*. Numerous 'Indians' in Vancouver protested this move, and one of their representatives telegraphed the following to London (verbatim): 'mass meeting natives of india protest deportation exclusion from canada british subjects claim government protection throughout empire if our interest overlooked brothers in india must necess resent your governments neglect'.[59] The India Office and the Indian government responded with the assurance that they would push for an improvement in the legal position of 'Indian' subjects in the dominions. Akin to the way in which the British government advocated the interests of its nationals abroad vis-à-vis foreign states in the name of its international prestige, the government in Delhi also sought to uphold its prestige within the empire

Illustration 5.2. Entry denied: Indian passengers on board the *Komagata Maru* in Vancouver, BC, James L. Quiney, 1914. From: City of Vancouver Archives, CVA 7–125.

by insisting on the 'status and privileges of Indian emigrants as subjects of the British Empire'.[60]

Whereas this phrasing alluded to the non-egalitarian tradition of the term 'subject', the representatives of the Indian nationalist movement argued almost excessively with the words 'citizen' and 'citizenship'.[61] They demanded equal rights for all British subjects, regardless of 'racial' identity, within the framework of a statist and supra-ethnic concept of equality, thereby explicitly touching upon the difference between the egalitarian notion of 'citizenship' as opposed to the subservient concept of 'allegiance'. Sachchidananda Sinha, a member of the Legislative Council in Bihar, cited Lord Curzon in this context, who had pointed to 'equal citizenship [as] the only basis upon which you will expect the loyalty of an Asiatic population to an alien rule to be permanently developed or maintained'. These were, Sinha continued, 'wise words [that] lay down the only sound and healthy ideal of citizenship on which the great British Empire can exist as a real political unit. Set aside this ideal and the Empire will be reduced to a mere agglomeration of States and the nominal allegiance to the Crown will not be sufficient to stop its disintegration'.[62]

To a certain extent, the imperial metropolis tried to mediate between these two poles, namely the discriminatory intentions of the dominions and the demands for equality within the Indian nationalist movement. In doing so, however, it neither upheld the promise of equality given in the Queen's Proclamation of 1858 nor mitigated the discrimination against 'Indian' subjects.[63] Rather, the government in London advocated hiding such unequal treatment beneath a veneer of ethnically neutral wording in order to avoid an all too apparent collision with the Indian nationalist movement's demands for equality. A memorandum that the India Office and the Colonial Office had prepared for the Imperial Conference of 1911, for example, requested that the governments of the dominions refrain from explicitly discriminating against 'Indian' subjects on the basis of 'racial' criteria. A handwritten comment by an official on the memo noted that it would be completely useless 'to attempt to veil the fact that the policy of building up new nations of European blood within the Empire is absolutely incompatible with the idea that every British subject, whatever his race, shall have free right of ingress to any part of the Empire'.[64] This comment was written by Sir Herbert Risley who, having spent most of his time while part of the Indian Civil Service attempting to classify the Indian population into racist categories by means of anthropometric measurements, had recently been appointed to the post of permanent secretary in the India Office. Risley's words not only summarized the idea of 'colonial nationalism' in a nutshell, but also they indicated that many high-ranking members of the government in London sympathized with this political course. Nonetheless, the imperial metropolis insisted on an ethnically neutral facade for such racist policies of exclusion in order to prevent their centrifugal potential from tearing apart the empire-wide community of British subjects.

The literacy test required in Natal, for example, was particularly well suited to this purpose. Although it officially coupled permission to enter the country with written knowledge of a European language (see Illustration 5.3 for a literacy test required of a naturalization candidate in the UK), this test made it possible, as

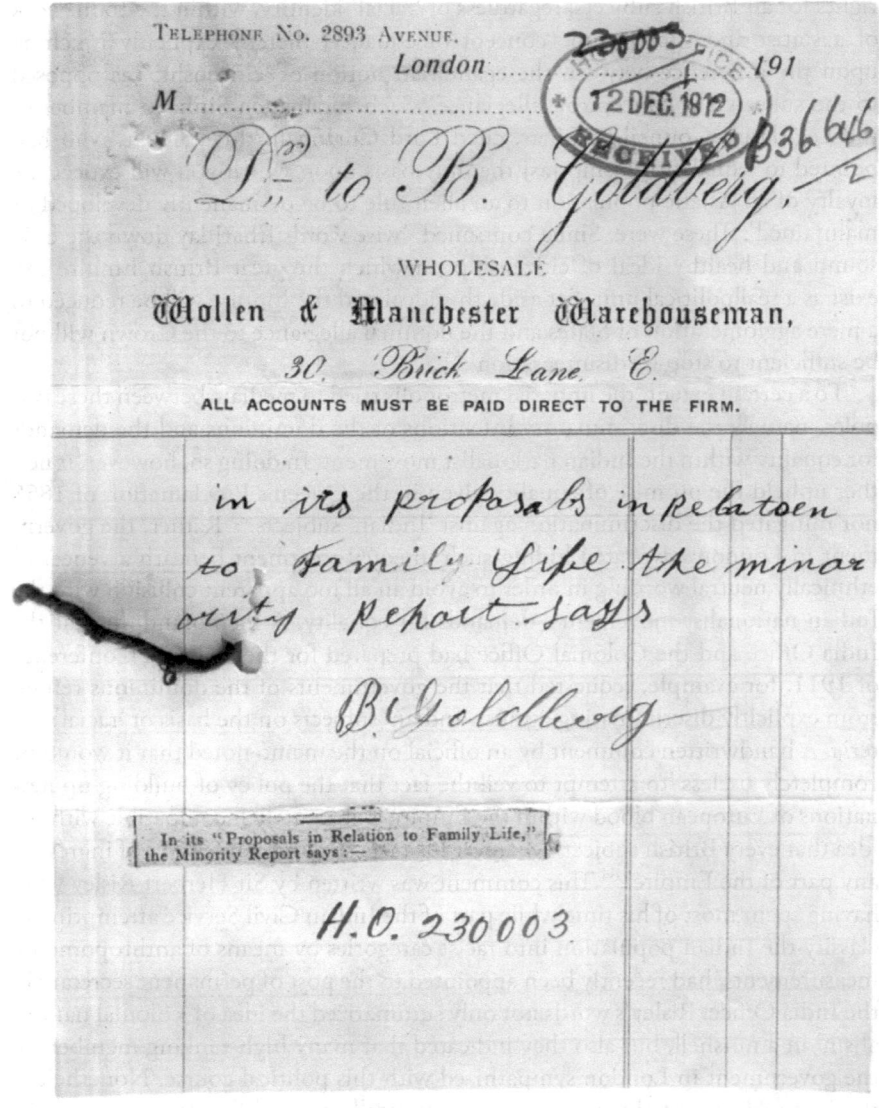

Illustration 5.3. Family life and minority report: Writing test of the naturalization candidate Benjamin Goldberg, 1912. From: London, PRO, HO 144/971/B36646.

Risley explained, 'in its application to individual cases, … to exclude Indians on racial grounds'.[65] Yet, it was also quite clear to him that educated 'Indians' could potentially overcome this hurdle, which meant that the 'racially' exclusive intentions of this policy would become quite apparent over time:

> And as soon as the test is worked so as to exclude an educated Indian, Mr Ghandi will get his innings. He will say 'Here is Mr. Chose, B.A., B.L., Barrister-at-Law, an accomplished scholar and a learned lawyer who wishes to practise his profession in the Orange Free State. He knows Sanskrit, English, French and German, and all the languages of a liberal education. He was asked to write 50 words in Swedish! How many Englishmen know Swedish?' And so on, the various strings of agitation being skilfully pulled in India and England.[66]

Risley therefore suggested following the Canadian example and denying entry to immigrants on the basis of whether they came from a certain longitudinal spectrum. In order to make sure that this regulation did not detract from the freedom of mobility of 'European' migrants, an 'Immigration Officer' was supposed to 'determine questions of domicile' on a case-by-case basis.[67] The efficacy of this measure as well as other exclusionary practices rested on the ad hoc decisions made by officials who had been granted a great deal of discretion and leeway. They almost always judged the matter on the basis of the appearance of the person in question. Such administrative tricks that privileged 'whites' and excluded 'non-whites' without having to explicitly formulate this racist discrimination in the wording of the law contributed greatly to the spread of imperialist tactics of discrimination at the imperial level.

Ethnic Difference in the British Nationality Act of 1914

The British Nationality and Status of Aliens Act bore discriminatory elements in a very similar way. First and foremost, this new nationality law from 1914 was supposed to standardize the rules for naturalization across the empire. Naturalized Britons were therefore supposed to be considered British subjects throughout the empire, regardless of where they had been naturalized. Prior to this point, naturalizations had only been valid within individual territories. People who had acquired British subject status in the UK, for example, were still considered to be foreigners in Canada.[68] Through the establishment of standard regulations, the British Nationality and Status of Aliens Act was intended to implement the idea that 'a British subject anywhere is a British subject everywhere' and strengthen the cohesion of the British Empire. Not only the Home Office, the India Office and the Colonial Office were involved in the deliberations over the new law, but also the governments of the dominions and India.

The talks soon devolved into a disagreement that resembled the one regarding the status of 'Indian' migrants in the empire. The dominions, on the one side, demanded 'racially' exclusive provisions. One representative from the Cape Colony suggested that 'a distinction should be drawn between applicants of European descent and those of non-European descent'.[69] One from Transvaal argued that only the naturalizations of 'Europeans' should be valid throughout the empire.[70] The Indian government, in contrast, criticized these racist suggestions and noted that it was not 'advisable to grant the privileges of universal citizenship to foreign Europeans and deny them to foreign Asiatics'.[71] At the same time, it also feared that 'difficulties would arise from the grant to foreign Asiatics of certificates of naturalization to have effect beyond British India'.[72] Delhi naturally assumed that the dominions were 'determined not to admit Chinese and other Asiatics to the privilege of citizen-ship' and would deny naturalized 'Asiatics' the rights to which they were entitled.[73] At the core of its objections, the Indian government suspected that a standardized naturalization procedure for the whole empire might make the discrimination against 'non-European' subjects quite apparent and, in turn, fuel the fires of the protests of the Indian nationalist movement against the exclusionary policies in the dominions, and against British rule as a whole.

The reasons provided by the India Office in its dismissal of the objections coming from Delhi were indicative of the fact that the government in London would ultimately side with the dominions. In a handwritten note, an official described the term 'citizen-ship' that had been brought up by the Indian government as 'an ambiguous phrase that has probably given rise to a confusion of thought'.[74] In contrast to citizens, the argument went, subjects did not have any claims to equal rights. From this perspective, legal equality for all British subjects was really a moot point, and in the end, it was this position that informed the wording of the law. The government in London continued to reject explicit 'racial' discrimination, but it by no means insisted upon the principle of ethnic neutrality. Rather, the British home secretary, Herbert Gladstone, reacted to the racist demands put forth by some dominions in 1907 by noting that the UK had naturalized 'extremely few persons of non-European descent' up to that point and suggesting that the immigration laws in the dominions should continue to deny entry to 'non-white' subjects. According to Gladstone, it was not necessary to treat all British subjects as equals, regardless of ethnic identity.[75] Winston Churchill made this even clearer, as home secretary in 1911, when he maintained: 'Nothing now proposed would affect the validity and effectiveness of local laws regulating immigration or the like, or differentiating between classes of British subjects'.[76]

Although the government officials in London wanted to avoid protests in India and therefore explicit 'racial' discrimination, they did not fundamentally object to privileges for 'white' subjects or disadvantages for 'non-white' subjects.

Correspondingly, one of the most significant provisions of the British Nationality and Status of Aliens Act of 1914 is buried in its last section: 'Nothing in this Act shall take away or abridge any power vested in, or exercisable by, the Legislature or Government of any British Possession ..., or prevent any such Legislature or Government from treating differently different classes of British subjects'.[77] Thus, at the outset of the twentieth century, not only the administrative praxis of the British consulates and the immigration policies of the dominions, but also British nationality law, followed an imperialist course of racist discrimination.

The Imperial and Royal Consulates: Austrian Statism versus Hungarian Nationalism

The development of nationality laws in the Habsburg Empire took a completely different direction. To start with, there was no nationality law that applied for the whole empire because this would have necessitated a compromise between both halves of the empire. Whereas the nationals of the British Empire all shared a single subject status, the Habsburg Empire was composed of Austrian citizens alongside Hungarian nationals and Bosnians. Moreover, the legal treatment of migrants from within the empire also differed significantly. Although there were large migration movements within the Danube monarchy, the attempts to regulate these movements in order to establish ethnically homogeneous territories did not play nearly as prominent a role as in the British Empire. The imperial authorities, for instance, quickly and firmly squashed the efforts of the Viennese magistrate to prevent the immigration of 'Czechs' and 'Jews'.

Unlike in the dominions, where it was assumed that political and social rights could only be extended within an ethnically homogeneous population, experts in Austria did not necessarily see a contradiction between ethnic heterogeneity and equal citizenship. The establishment of national electorates in the early twentieth century in Moravia, Galicia, Bukovina and Bosnia, as well as the introduction of universal male suffrage in Austria, attest to the hope at the imperial level that loyalty to the Emperor or – from a Marxist perspective – class conflict would banish the 'phantom of national thought' from the political stage.[78] But a link between legal and ethnic homogenization could be detected in Hungarian magyarization policies. Moreover, this connection informed the idea of instituting a federal system within the dual monarchy in which the borders of the individual states were supposed to coincide with the national settlement areas.[79] Such territory-based approaches, however, never displaced the prevailing tactic of recognizing difference at the level of individual people with the creation of ethnonational communities within an ethnically heterogeneous space.[80] Ultimately, the development of Habsburg nationality and citizenship laws was influenced by the coexistence of different approaches. Whereas a statist policy of recognition was put in place in Austria and a nation-state perspective dominated in Hungary, the joint government largely upheld the statist principle of ethnic neutrality.

The friction between these different ways of dealing with ethnic heterogeneity also affected the Imperial and Royal consulates. In particular, varying attitudes towards emigration played a decisive role in their administrative praxis.[81] The Austrian government as well as the joint imperial government continued to focus on the ethnically neutral, military and economic interests of the state, and therefore wanted to restrict the emigration of young men more tightly. Moreover, they were not very keen on fostering national bonds between emigrants and the homeland because they feared the financial burdens for the state that might ensue. The Hungarian government, in contrast, had a vested interest in caring for emigrants and promoting remigration within its nation-state framework.

Not the least because of such concerns, the number of consulates and their respective budgets continued to grow, especially in North and South America. In 1907, the consular authorities in the United States spent 5,750 Kronen on legal aid work, advocating the interests of Austrian and Hungarian nationals before US courts. In the words of the Habsburg officials, the main goal was to protect 'our fellow nationals from exploitive elements'.[82] The sum spent on this purpose increased in later years to 24,000 Kronen in 1909, 30,000 in 1911 and then 47,500 in 1912.[83] Additionally, the consulates provided funds to support emigrants in extreme cases, or financed their return home.[84] The Imperial-Royal Ministry of Trade and the Royal Hungarian Ministry of the Interior also helped to finance homes for emigrants in New York run by Austrian and Hungarian aid agencies. In 1910, for example, the Austrian government provided 10,000 Kronen, while the Hungarian government sent 12,500 Kronen.[85] Generally the government in Budapest made a greater effort to assist emigrants, demonstrated in part by its willingness to guarantee a loan of 160,000 Kronen for the Hungarian aid agency in New York.[86]

The Cisleithanian Ministry of Trade also requested additional funds and personnel for Argentina due to 'the constant and significant expansion of the agenda of our consular authorities as a result of emigration and the lively nature of our commercial and other economic relations'.[87] It noted that a growing number of workers in dire need were appealing to the local consulates 'for support, be it through money or hospital care or the like'.[88] The example of the 'Romanian seasonal workers' from Bukovina, whose repatriation was mandated by the consulate in Buenos Aires in March 1912 'to avoid further scandals', hints at the principles adopted by the Austrian authorities in dealing with such cases.[89]

This group 'of 270 – mostly young – people in rural attire, who had travelled to Argentina under the "management" of three first-class passengers' was mentioned in the reports of the Imperial and Royal Consul Hoenning. Major Gruber, Mr Negrusz and the Secretary of the Raiffeisen Bank in Bukovina, Dr Stratyjczuk, were the supervisors accompanying these labour migrants who were supposed to help to take in the harvest in Argentina.[90] The provincial board (*Landesausschuss*) in Czernowitz (now in Ukraine) had initiated this enterprise in the hope that the wages earned by these seasonal migrants could help to alleviate the poverty of their families at home. The three supervisors were supposed to ensure that these migrants returned to the 'fatherland' after their work had been done.[91] As Consul Hoenning noted, however, these three men had their own ideas. They wanted to retain a portion of the workers' wages for themselves, and they had even told some of their fellow passengers during their Atlantic crossing that they were thinking about buying land in Argentina and renting it out to the farmers they had brought with them.[92] These functionaries, who were joined by Mr Lukasiewicz in Buenos Aires, thus wanted to establish on foreign soil a copy of their estates at home, and preside over them as large landowners. Their plans, as well as the entire project of transcontinental labour migration, fell apart in the end.

A number of factors contributed to the failure of their efforts. First of all, the Argentinian authorities mistrusted the four supervisors as well as the enterprise as a whole because it made use of funds and infrastructure that were supposed to be used to attract immigrants willing to settle permanently in Argentina, and not to sponsor seasonal migration. Secondly, the supervisors insisted that the group remain together, which made it difficult to put them to work and even delayed their arrival at the farms until several weeks after the harvest had begun. Thirdly, the Argentinian farmers complained that the migrant workers from Bukovina either purposely or inadvertently damaged the machinery. And lastly, the migrant workers themselves did not behave as the sponsors of the project had initially hoped. Rather than saving money for their return or to send to their families, they immediately spent some of their wages on drink. Moreover, they often quite cleverly played their employers, their 'official travel guides' and the Argentinian authorities against one another. It was said that 'they walk away from their work at the slightest complaint', repeatedly citing the promises that had been made to them in Bukovina. The workers complained about the food and that they often had to work on Sundays or more than the maximum of ten hours a day. According to a consular report, they did not like the food 'because instead of the coffee promised to them in Europe, they got bitter Mate, instead of polenta just mutton, instead of bread only hard crackers (the unleavened local wheat bread known as "galetta")'.[93]

Consular official Fuchs put the failure of the project down to the workers from Bukovina and demanded that 'only the best, sober, reasonably intelligent material should be sent' for such projects in the future.[94] Consul Hoenning, in contrast, accused the organizers of the project of harbouring exploitive intentions. The migrants, according to his calculations, would have had to use five months' wages just to pay back the money that had been advanced to them to cover their travel costs, especially given that the supervisors retained about one-third of their wages. In a certain sense, this model resembled that of the British system of indentured labour. The consul described the whole thing as a poor business for the 'hard-working farmers – and only their well-being can be of interest to us'.[95] Ultimately, this endeavour sparked a protracted disagreement between the Imperial and Royal Foreign Ministry, the Imperial-Royal ministries of the Interior and of Trade, as well as the Bukovina provincial board, over who was supposed to pay for the return trip of the now some 160 unemployed Austrian citizens who could not remain in Argentina because the local authorities were refusing to ensure their welfare. In the end, the employment agency of the Bukovina provincial board took over the costs of repatriation. The Ministry of Trade summed up the matter, noting that it was not planned to repeat such an enterprise.[96]

Three different constellations of interests with respect to migration can be detected within this example. On the one hand, the authorities feared that the emigration of young men in particular might weaken the state militarily. At the same time, however, they wanted to turn a profit by putting the human 'material' of Austria to work abroad. And lastly, the consular authorities stressed the duty of the state to ensure the welfare of its emigrants from the lower social classes and protect them against exploitation. Read along statist lines, all three arguments either served to promote the interests of the state or equal citizenship; ethnic or national differences were not part of the picture. As early as 1904, the Imperial-Royal Ministry of the Interior had determined – with reference to these three strains of thought – that the Cisleithanian emigration policies, unlike their Transleithanian counterparts, were intended to 'restrict emigration in the interest of the military power of the state, with respect to the economic disadvantages associated with regular large-scale emigration, as well as in light of the fact that emigration had spelt ruin for many emigrants personally'.[97]

Hungarian Emigration Policies and Ethnic Discrimination

In the early twentieth century, Hungary's emigration policies were definitely more strongly influenced by nation-state concerns. The Transleithanian government had a vested interest in maintaining the bonds between its nationals abroad and the nation at home. Consequently, it generally made more of an effort than the Austrian government to ensure the welfare of its emigrants by providing informational brochures, homes, teachers and pastoral care. As one Reichstag deputy put it, these 'patriotic teachings' were supposed to heal the 'sick souls' of emigrant workers in particular, and imbue their children with the 'Hungarian spirit'.[98] The Hungarian government therefore demanded that the Imperial and Royal consulates should employ more Hungarian-speaking officials and do their utmost to ensure the well-being of emigrants rather than just intervening in military conscription matters. In keeping with this promise, the Hungarian Ministry of the Interior stressed that 'the government cannot shy the task of rescuing citizens in foreign lands, whenever possible, from utter ruin,' and that the consulates should 'give these emigrants in their unfortunate situations any support possible'; and 'if their situation cannot be made bearable in any other way, a report should be sent as to their transport home, including the costs that result thereof'.[99]

The Hungarian government was clearly more willing to take over the costs of such measures than its Austrian counterpart, and it even set up a fund in 1903 to finance such services for emigrants. While the Imperial and Royal consulates therefore readily supported Hungarian nationals, they were less eager to help Austrian citizens. They only did so after the consular officials had determined which domestic municipality would bear the requisite costs. Needy Austrians thus had to produce evidence – like passports, work books or certificates – that documented their place of domicile in Cisleithania.[100] For emigrants who spoke Magyar, in contrast, merely 'knowledge of this language' was enough to 'legitimize those in question as nationals' and ensure that they would receive consular aid.[101]

The fact that these regulations privileged Hungarian-speaking nationals over Hungarians who spoke Slovenian, Romanian, German, Serbian or Croatian points to the ethnicization of Hungarian emigration policies in the early twentieth century. In addition, an article from 1909 about the opening of a Hungarian home for emigrants in New York also reflects this trend in that it refers to the institution as a 'home for Arpad's sons' (see Illustration 5.4).[102] Unlike the figure of Stephan, who was associated with the establishment of a multi-ethnic realm in the eleventh century, the name 'Árpád', and with it the memory of the Magyar conquest in the ninth century, stood for an ethnically exclusive notion of the Hungarian nation.[103] The metaphoric reference to 'Arpad' also points towards the increasingly ethnically exclusive intentions of Hungarian emigration policies.

Complaints submitted over discrimination against Croatian-speaking emigrants by the consular authorities sought to counter the privileging of a certain ethnic group. Newspaper commentaries in 1904, for example, accused that Croatian-speakers were neglected in favour of Germans and Magyars, and that they had to speak English or German in order to deal with officials at the consulate. Moreover, it was charged that 'when they sought support, they were turned away with the comment that a consulate was not a poor house, while there was no shortage of financial support for Germans and Hungarians'.[104] In the same year, a parliamentarian from the Croatian People's Party in the Austrian Reichsrat, Juraj Biankini, voiced objections to the discrimination against Dalmatian emigrants.[105] Similar accusations were made against a Hungarian immigrants' home in New York in 1910.[106] Although the Hungarian government largely ignored these accusations, the Austrian government tried to pacify them by promising to appoint additional Croatian-speaking consular officials.[107] The Imperial and Royal general consul in New York denied these charges in the name of the

Heim für Arpad's Söhne

Das neue ungarische Einwandererheim gestern unter großer Festlichkeit seiner Bestimmung übergeben.

In Gegenwart distinguirter Ehrengäste wurde gestern Nachmittag die Einweihung des Ungarischen Einwanderungsheimes vollzogen und das Institut seiner Bestimmung übergeben. Wie vorauszusehen war, gestaltete sich dieser Akt zu einer eindrucksvollen Festlichkeit, die durch wichtige Momente noch eine besondere Bedeutung erhielt. Baron Hengelmueller von Hengervar, der österreichisch-ungarische Botschafter in Washington, wie auch Baron Ambroszhi, der Kanzler der Botschaft, und Alexander Nuber von Pereked, der hiesige österreichisch-ungarische General-Konsul, hatten mit Freuden der Einladung der

Der Monarch ist im ungarischen Krönungsornat dargestellt, in der einen Hand hält er das Reichsschwert, während er die andere auf den Tisch gestützt hat, auf welchem die Krone Ungarns liegt. Auf der anderen Seite des Zimmers hängt das Bild des Präsidenten Taft und gleich neben der Thür befindet sich eine Gedenktafel aus rothem Marmor mit den Namen der Protektoren des Heims und der Beamten der Ungarischen Hilfsgesellschaft.

Der Fest-Akt.

Das Zimmer, in welchem der festliche Akt vollzogen wurde, erwies sich als viel zu klein, um alle Besucher zu fassen; viele mußten wieder umkehren, ohne überhaupt Eintritt erlangt zu haben.

Das neue Ungarische Einwanderer-Heim, Ecke Pearl und Moore Str.

Illustration 5.4. Ethnicization of the Hungarian nation abroad: Article entitled 'Heim für Arpad's Söhne', with a drawing of the Hungarian emigrants' home in New York, in *New Yorker Revue*, Sunday, 21 November 1909. From: Vienna, HHStA, MdÄ, Admin. Reg., F 15, *Auswanderung*, Ktn. 31.

joint government, stating that the consulate guaranteed '*every* immigrant from Hungary, without respect to nationality, advice, protection, aid and support; [n]either the privileging of Magyar immigrants nor discrimination against the Slavs, Croats, Germans or Romanians of Hungarian nationality has been taking place'.[108] The varying responses of the governments were informed by different approaches to handling ethnic heterogeneity. With the appointment of additional consular personnel, the Austrian government sought to ensure that all ethnonational groups were treated equally while still recognizing the validity of national differences. The joint government, in contrast, insisted upon a course of supra-ethnic neutrality, while the Hungarian government pursued an ethnically exclusive stance informed by their notion of a nation-state.

Ethnic Difference in the Administrative Praxis of the Imperial and Royal Consulates

Not least because of these impulses to recognize and/or discriminate on the basis of ethnicity, ethnic differences became more significant for the Imperial and Royal authorities in their dealings with 'nationals of the Austro-Hungarian monarchy' living abroad. In 1901, a census in the United States counted 65,000 'German-Austrians', 400,000 'Czechs', 350,000 'Poles and Galician Jews', 150,000 'Ruthenians', 55,000 'Slovenes', 15,000 'Austrian Croats and Dalmatians', 5,000 'Italians', 200,000 'Magyars and German Hungarians', and 60,000 'Hungarian Croats'.[109] A good ten years later, the statistics were broken down according to the categories 'Germans, Bohemians, Slovakians, Poles, Ruthenians, Serbo-Croats and Slovenes, Italians, Romanians, Magyars, Jews and others'.[110] This categorization illustrates that ethnonational, and in particular linguistically defined identities, were increasingly superimposed upon nationality, for example by conflating Austrian and Hungarian Croats into a single category. The Imperial and Royal consulates carefully registered such ethnicization and nationalization tendencies. In part, they supported these developments because they made it possible for emigrants to uphold their ethno-confessional traditions. For instance, in 1901, the Imperial and Royal Foreign Ministry pointed out that there was a lack of Catholic schools for emigrants from the Habsburg Empire in Canada, and that 'the Greek-Catholic Ruthenian immigrants often fall prey to Orthodox and Presbyterian propaganda due to the lack of clergymen'.[111] In a way, the government thus exported the Cisleithanian politics of recognition that aimed to foster the retention of ethnic identities.

Yet, the consulates themselves were mostly sceptical about the growing importance of ethnic differences. It was easier for 'nationally homogeneous states', according to one such argument, to enforce the military conscription of nationals abroad than it was for the ethnically heterogeneous Habsburg Empire.

Moreover, along this line of thought, 'national associations' may contribute to the 'temporary preservation of the national character of our emigrants', but they were not suited to be 'breeding grounds' within which a sense 'for the duties of citizenship' that emigrants 'owed to the homeland' could flourish. They thus ultimately counteracted the military interests of the monarchy.[112] As the official representatives of the monarchy, the Imperial and Royal diplomats themselves also maintained a kind of Habsburg identity they hovered, so to speak, above the different ethnicities within the empire. From this vantage point, they thought very little of emigrants who mentally brought the ethnonational conflicts of the homeland with them as they crossed the Atlantic.

This type of attitude surfaced quite clearly in the conflicts over the appointment of Dr Wolff as vice consul in Córdoba, Argentina in 1912. Objections were raised against this well-to-do doctor by one of the 'German professors at the university in Córdoba, named Dr Harperath ... by means of petitions that he had a number of workers sign'. The habitus of Wolff's opponents raises suspicions that anti-Semitic sentiments played a role in the competition over this prestigious post. According to the report of one of the consular officials, approximately eighty Czech-speaking workers, under the leadership of Harperath, 'had come together in a mutual aid association,' the sole purpose of which was 'to hold drinking sessions'.[113] On the basis of this fraternity-like sociability, it can be presumed that Wolff's opponents were nationalist in their outlook, which makes the alliance between these Czech workers and the German professor even more surprising. Quite possibly it was their shared anti-Semitism that made it possible for them to overcome the German–Czech animosity abroad to combat a mutual enemy who was probably of Jewish heritage.

However, Wolff's ethnic identity remained relatively unclear. The consular report about him only described him as a landowner and art expert who was loyal to Austria-Hungary, and who obviously identified so greatly with the ethnically heterogeneous monarchy that his own ethnic identity was considered irrelevant. The ethnonational background of his opponents, on the other hand, was explicitly mentioned in the report. Moreover, the official who wrote the report seemed to dislike Harperath in that he described the professor as 'certainly incapable of carrying out the office of an Imperial and Royal Vice Consul'.[114] The fact that the consular authorities so clearly sided with Wolff, whose ethnic identity was irrelevant to them, while showing contempt for his nationalistic opponent, clearly illustrates how deeply the principle of supra-ethnic neutrality continued to shape the attitudes of diplomats and consular officials in the early twentieth century.

Coming from this perspective, the Imperial and Royal authorities viewed ethnic discrimination as a praxis that was foreign to them but might very well influence the migration policies of other states. They took careful note of the racist exclusions implemented by countries of immigration in order to be able to adapt their own emigration policies accordingly. When the president of the

Canadian waterways corporation, Magrath, announced in 1916 'that after the war, the Germans and the Austrians will be welcomed as immigrants, but the Italians and the Balkan peoples should be excluded', the Habsburg officials paid attention.[115] A year later, they also took notice of the fact that the reverse trend seemed to be appearing in the United States. Habsburg officials remarked that 'Slavic immigrants' had previously been considered the 'deteriorators of the American racial mix' and were, 'with the exception of the Czechs', regarded as 'culturally inferior to the average of the other white immigrants, who do not come from Eastern Europe'. Through the First World War, however, 'the Union has discovered its sympathy for the "oppressed small nations"', Habsburg officials commented in 1917, pointing out that 'Slavic' immigrants were of late facing less discrimination.[116]

Within the Imperial and Royal consulates themselves, however, racist arguments or sentiments only played a marginal role at best. Anti-Semitic prejudices about 'the well-known tendency of the Eastern European Jews to neglect their military service obligations' may have justified some measures that disadvantaged 'Jewish' Austrians or Hungarians.[117] Consular officials also tended to be mistrusting of 'Slavic nationalities' because 'their members are far too often turned against the fatherland ... by extremely keen pan-Slavic agitation'.[118] But, even as these two examples indicate, it was primarily the supra-ethnic military and political interests of the monarchy that shaped the administrative praxis of the Imperial and Royal consular authorities who, for the most part, adhered to the statist principle of ethnic neutrality until the collapse of the Habsburg monarchy.

Biopower and Ethnicization: Splitting the Population or Splitting the Power

The joint Habsburg government, therefore, did not follow the broad trend towards ethnicization that emerged in the early twentieth century in different places across the globe. While the Hungarian government increasingly adopted an ethnically exclusive nation-state approach, ethnic differences became more prominent in Austria within the framework of a politics of recognition. In contrast, the 'racially' exclusive policies of the dominions and the racist discrimination in colonies such as East Africa gained a strong foothold in the British Empire. Thus, the process of ethnicization led in quite different directions in both of these imperial formations. Whereas discrimination according to 'racial' criteria was ultimately codified in law for the entire empire with the British Nationality and Status of Aliens Act of 1914, the ethnic neutrality of the joint imperial government coexisted alongside exclusive policies adopted in Hungary and the strategies of recognition employed by the Austrian government in a kind of contradictory simultaneity.

Alongside divergent legal traditions, the respective political structures of the two empires were primarily responsible for the different trajectories of ethnicization. The dualism of the Habsburg Empire and the existence of separate Austrian and Hungarian nationalities allowed for competing approaches within the imperial framework. From this perspective, it was rather coincidental that the statist, supra-ethnic policies of Austria and the ethnically inclusive, nation-state ideas in Hungary at the end of the nineteenth century rested on similar principles of ethnic neutrality. This shared foundation crumbled with the turn of the century – not the least through the annexation of Bosnia – leaving behind a field of conflict in which different ways of dealing with ethnic heterogeneity competed for supremacy. In the British case, by contrast, the generally hierarchical structure of the empire, with the government of the UK at the top and the shared status of British subjects throughout the empire, paved the way for the dominance of imperialist discrimination within the law and administrative praxis.

British Liberalism versus Habsburg Authoritarianism?

This finding contradicts the conventional characterization of the British Empire as the prime example of liberalism, and the Habsburg Empire as the 'prison of nations' (*Völkerkerker*) and a hotbed of authoritarian rule. Yet, it would still be quite misleading to simply turn this around and depict the British Empire as a hierarchical imperialist structure while praising Austria-Hungary as a peaceful precursor of modern multiculturalism. Rather, the goal is to criticize the very distinction between authoritarian and liberal forms of government, which is tightly linked to the classic East–West dichotomy. Therefore it is essential to replace it with a more nuanced analytical terminology.[119]

The concept of biopower can be used as a foundation for such an endeavour if it is understood as a form of government that is primarily concerned with life and the optimization of the life of the individual.[120] From this perspective, the 'biopolitical paradigm of modernity' is not the concentration camp, as some authors argue, but rather apparatuses such as systems of health insurance and pensions.[121] These structures of power aiming to promote, foster and preserve life largely arose in the nineteenth century alongside older mechanisms of rule that rested on sovereignty and the power over life and death. From then on, the trinity of sovereignty, death and the law was accompanied by the triad of biopower, life and norm that viewed the individual as a living being rather than a subject of the law.[122] Biopower thus focuses on the population in two distinct ways: as a totality of living beings in a biological sense and as body politic in a political sense. Biopower sought to track and steer the population's migration as well as its reproduction and mortality rates, in addition to opinion-building processes, through new methods of knowledge production such as demography, public opinion research, statistics and prognostics.[123]

Consequently, biopower was firmly connected to specific forms of governmentality that were based on the assumption of natural facts and spontaneous processes. Biopolitical government relied upon and used these circumstances and forces that it sought to manage indirectly. Simultaneously, this type of governance was also limited by the naturalness of these facts and dynamics because it could only act with them and not against them.[124] The distinction between biopolitical or governmental power structures characterized as laissez-faire, incentive and promotive, and older sovereign forms of rule resting on prohibitions, discipline and domination is particularly useful in examining nationality and citizenship.[125] Along these lines, the following section differentiates between mechanisms of power that promote and those that prohibit.

A look at the political debates over migration in the Habsburg context reveals that the Habsburg administration was well-versed in promotive ideas. The governments saw migration movements in particular as natural, economically induced phenomena that could only be fostered and managed but not suppressed. In the debates over the Emigration Act of 1908, for example, a member of the Hungarian parliament stressed that emigration could not be hindered through a law because it was a natural consequence of the international 'disparity of wages'. Therefore, as he argued, emigration prohibitions could not stop the economically fatal loss of human capital. From this perspective, only promotive economic policies that did not violate the right to mobility and a close cooperation between civil society and government could help to alleviate this problem.[126]

A draft of the Austrian Emigration Act put forth by the Imperial-Royal Ministry of Trade in 1913 illustrates the significance of promotive governance even more clearly. 'Movements that arise out of the life of peoples and the construction of states', it read, 'will not be created or eliminated through laws'. Rather, it continued, they must 'be taken as facts brought about by the course of the world and determined by the march of time'.[127] The 'wave of emigrants' was thus seen as a natural power that could not be prohibited, but could very well 'be properly steered', which was primarily dependent on maintaining the 'bond' between emigrants and the homeland.[128] It was hoped, therefore, that emigration could be harnessed to make it more useful for the monarchy and to ensure that the Habsburg economy would profit from a boom in Austrian shipping, from an increase in the export of goods to North America, and from emigrants sending money to their families back home.[129]

However, the appearance of such promotive techniques of government in the early twentieth century by no means made older forms of prohibitive rule obsolete. The standpoint maintained by the Imperial and Royal Ministry of War confirms this point as it criticized the draft of the Ministry of Trade for unduly protecting 'the free mobility of the person' and serving the interests of migrant workers first and foremost. The 'war administration', it claimed, had to work to limit emigration in the interests of 'military strength', which was quite clearly intended to be prohibitive.[130] In its final form, the law combined this restrictive element with a promotive dimension by barring foreign agencies from recruiting emigrants, but making an exception for those European countries in which the governments guaranteed Austrian emigrants 'legal security' as well as the preservation of their nationality and confession.[131] Thus, it not only reflected the prohibitive agenda of the Ministry of War, but also the intention of the Ministry of Trade to protect and support emigrants abroad.

Thus, older prohibitions were not simply replaced by modern promotive measures. It would also be misleading to interpret the increase in liberal-governmental techniques as a victory for freedom writ large.[132] On the contrary, these practices intensified and perfected the exercise of power, making a utopian future free of power evermore inconceivable; in addition, prohibitive modes of rule continued to exist alongside such promotive strategies of governance.[133] This coexistence of promotive and prohibitive structures can also be found in Canadian migration politics. Along biopolitical-governmental lines it was argued that 'Government policy may to a small extent quicken or direct the flow, but great economic laws rather than Government policy are responsible for the rise of the tide'.[134] Convinced of this fact, the Canadian government thus fostered the immigration of Britons and other 'Europeans' in particular, while also seeking to steer this 'flow into productive tasks'.[135] Simultaneously, it reacted to the influx of 'Asiatic' immigrants with prohibitions and restrictions, as seen in the deportation of the 'Indian' immigrants who came to British Columbia aboard the *Monteagle* in 1908.

Promotive and Prohibitive Measures, and the Role of Ethnic Differences

The Canadian example exemplifies how tightly the distinction between promotive and prohibitive techniques of governance could be linked to ethnic differences, because it was 'whites' who mostly benefited from support while 'non-whites' were primarily confronted with prohibitions. In general, this constellation left a deep imprint on migration policies in the British Empire. On the one hand, a variety of attempts were made to attract 'white' immigrants to Canada, East Africa and other parts of the empire.[136] Moreover, as the British authorities made a concentrated effort to advocate the legal privileges of 'white' subjects in the semi-colonial context, such as in Siam, they also sponsored the mobility of this population in other states. On the other hand, this protection was denied to most 'non-white' migrants, which made matters even more precarious for them. The prohibitions and exclusions directed at 'non-white' immigrants to the dominions took these measures to the next level. Similarly, the system of indentured labour was subject to strict and rigid control, despite the fact that, at least initially, it fostered the mobility of 'Indian' labourers in particular.[137] In East Africa, the 'non-white' population also suffered under prohibitive measures, especially in the form of resettlement policies.

In the British case, such racist discrimination ensured that 'whites' profited from promotive measures while 'non-whites' were subjected to prohibitions.[138] In terms of governmental techniques, these policies drew a clear line between those whose lives were supposed to be preserved and improved in a biopolitical sense, and those who were still supposed to be subjected to sovereign rule, including its fatal effects. Racism, therefore, defines 'the break between what must live and what must die'.[139] In a less exaggerated way, it can be said that racist arguments justified exclusion in a biopolitical context and determined who was to benefit from promotive measures and who was to suffer under prohibitions.

By contrast, prohibitive and promotive techniques of governance were not divided along ethnic lines in the Habsburg Empire. Such a constellation only appeared when the ethnically exclusive nation-state policies of the Hungarian government led to discrimination against Croatian-speaking emigrants within the Imperial and Royal consulates. Apart from this example, neither prohibitions nor promotive policies specifically targeted a certain ethnonational group. From the restrictive standpoint of the Ministry of War, ethnicity was completely insignificant. In an ethnically neutral way, it wanted to ensure that all nationals fulfilled their military service obligations. As this was easier to enforce when conscripts lived in the country, the Ministry of War was thus in favour of restrictive emigration policies.

Likewise, the promotive emigration policies put forth by the Austrian Ministry of Trade did not aim to privilege or discriminate against specific ethnic groups. Rather, the ministry wanted to make it possible for emigrants abroad to preserve their respective nationalities and confessions.[140] Essentially, this meant that the Habsburg authorities wanted to ensure that each ethnic group had an equal right to 'cultivate its nationality and language', even when abroad. This export of a politics of recognition vis-à-vis ethnonational differences ultimately sought to permanently bind emigrants and their descendants to the homeland in order to boost their economic usefulness for the monarchy.

At the same time, this support of identity-building processes can also be interpreted as a reaction to a naturally occurring need for ethnonational identification. From a biopolitical-governmental perspective, it was thought that such processes could not be prohibited, but merely steered to correspond with the interests of the state. Such considerations point to yet another link between promotive techniques of governance and ethnic difference that was diametrically opposed to the racist variant that prevailed in the British case.[141] In Bosnia, for example, the distinction between prohibitive and promotive measures was clearly detectable within the context of identity politics. At first, the government had tried to generate a supra-confessional, Bosnian national identity by suppressing the emergence of separate ethno-religious identities among Muslims, Catholics and Orthodox Christians. After the turn of the century, however, it moved towards a politics of recognition that promoted the construction of different ethnic identities and ultimately fed into the establishment of ethnically distinct electorates.

In this case, the dark side of the biopolitical-governmental exercise of power was not the exclusion of certain ethnic groups from benefits, but rather that individuals were forced to choose a specific, permanent ethnic identity This disciplining aspect could be seen in the countless policies regulating schooling, language and suffrage, such as those in Moravia and Bukovina, that made it virtually impossible for people to switch between different ethnonational identities.[142] Interestingly, these promotive policies of recognition primarily affected the political rights of citizenship in Cisleithania, which meant that they addressed the population as the body politic.[143] However, in terms of social rights and poor relief, which dealt with the population as a totality of living beings in a biological sense, the authorities strongly adhered to the principle of ethnic neutrality.[144] The Austrian government, for example, crushed the attempts of local authorities to discriminate against certain ethnic groups by denying them public support, as in the case of the Viennese magistrate. The Cisleithanian administration thus enforced the equal treatment of all citizens, regardless of ethnicity.

The reverse was true in the United Kingdom. The link between promotive techniques of governance and racist exclusion was especially pronounced in the Old Age Pensions Act and the National Insurance Act – in other words, regulations that pertained to social citizenship rights.[145] Suffrage laws, by contrast, ensured the political participation of all male subjects resident in the United Kingdom who met the corresponding property qualifications in an ethnically neutral way. Consequently, it was possible for someone like Dadabhai Naoroji, who was originally from Bombay, to be elected to the House of Commons as the Liberal MP for Finsbury Central in 1892.[146] In other parts of the British Empire in which residents enjoyed more extensive rights, such as in the dominions, however, 'non-whites' were mostly excluded from the social as well as the political rights of citizenship.

Splitting the Population versus Splitting the Power: A British–Habsburg Comparison

A complex picture has emerged in the Habsburg context as to the connection between ethnic differences and prohibitive or promotive measures in terms of migration policies, as well as political and social rights of citizenship. Sometimes prohibitions were tied to ethnic neutrality, as in the standpoint maintained by the Ministry of War; but promotive measures, such as access to social rights of citizenship, could also rest on ethnic equality. Simultaneously promotive policies regarding migration and suffrage supported the construction and maintenance of ethnic differences and identities in keeping with a politics of recognition that was linked to biopolitical-governemental arguments. The disagreement between the Ministry of War and the Ministry of Trade demonstrates the extent to which prohibitive and promotive strategies coexisted and competed in the Habsburg Empire.

Thus, for Austria-Hungary, power was split, in that advocates of different techniques of government struggled for supremacy.[147] This competition resulted in a kind of balance between ethnic neutrality and the recognition of difference. The government, in turn, treated the population as a single totality and as an ethnically heterogeneous union of equal nationalities. As a result of this constellation, racist discrimination was never able to gain the upper hand in the Habsburg Empire. Moreover, conflicts with advocates of prohibitive power structures hindered the further advancement of promotive measures, especially those related to social citizenship rights. In many British territories, on the other hand, the social welfare system was clearly more comprehensive than in Cisleithania. New Zealand, in particular, was seen as the global frontrunner in terms of sociopolitical benefits.[148] In the dominions as well as in the UK, however, this promotive power structure was tightly linked with racist mechanisms of exclusion; the more privileges enjoyed by 'white' subjects, the more radical the exclusion of 'non-whites'.[149] Racist discrimination infiltrated migration policies and regulated access to the political and social rights of citizenship. Whereas power was split in the Habsburg Empire, it was the population that was split in the British case.

This contrast becomes all the more poignant in terms of military conscription. As the United Kingdom, New Zealand and Canada did not introduce conscription until the third or fourth year of the First World War, it was rather clear that there was a great deal of scepticism towards such coercive measures that were, in a sense, a classic element of the sovereign-prohibitive exercise of power. Moreover, the governmental-promotive emphasis on voluntary participation allowed conscientious objectors to evade military service. A similar policy would have been unthinkable in Austria-Hungary. In the Habsburg context, the enforcement of military service obligations formed the core of the prohibitive exercise of power.[150] Yet, at least theoretically, the Habsburg authorities conscripted all citizens in the same way, regardless of ethnonational identity. In the British case, however, the option to refuse to serve was only available to 'white' subjects. As the example of East Africa shows, 'non-whites' who tried to evade conscription met with a harsh fate; the attempt by some Maasai to avoid being forced into the army was countered with a punitive expedition sent by the government in 1918 that cost the lives of many 'natives'.

Thus, due to the specific mixture of competing promotive and prohibitive strategies of governance, ethnic neutrality as well as the recognition of difference shaped the way in which the Habsburg authorities dealt with ethnic heterogeneity. In the British context, on the other hand, the greater significance of promotive structures of power intensified the development of a racist discrimination that allowed 'whites' to profit from privileges while 'non-whites' were subjected to prohibitions.

Notes

1. J.W. Salmond, 'Citizenship and Allegiance', *Law Quarterly Review* 18(69) (1902), 49–63; H.S.Q. Henriques, *The Law of Aliens and Naturalization: Including the Text of the Aliens Act 1905* (London: Butterworth, 1906); E.L. de Hart, 'The English Law of Nationality and Naturalisation', *Journal of the Society of Comparative Legislation* 2(1) (1900), 11–26. See also Cesarani, 'The Changing Character', 58f.; C. Harzig, 'From State Constructions to Individual Opportunities: The Historical Development of Citizenship in Europe', in D. Hoerder, C. Harzig and A. Shubert (eds), *The Historical Practice of Diversity: Transcultural Interactions from the Early Modern Mediterranean to the Postcolonial World* (New York: Berghahn Books, 2003), 210; R. Hansen, *Citizenship and Immigration in Post-war Britain: The Institutional Origins of a Multicultural Nation* (Oxford: Oxford University Press, 2000), 38; Gorman, *Imperial Citizenship*, 19f.; Banerjee, *Becoming Imperial Citizens*, 2, 25; Parsons, *Empires*, 8f., 14; Galanter, *Competing Equalities*, 19; M.P. Schennach, 'Der "Österreicher" als Rechtskonstrukt? Zur Formierung einer österreichischen Staatsbürgerschaft in der ersten Hälfte des 19. Jahrhunderts', *Zeitschrift für Neuere Rechtsgeschichte* 33(3–4) (2011), 152–76.
2. Indian Legislative Council, Proceedings of the Council, vol. 23 (7 January 1884), 45, Thomas. See also Banerjee, *Becoming Imperial Citizens*, 18; Young, *English Ethnicity*, 20.
3. Burger, 'Passwesen und Staatsbürgerschaft'; Komlosy, 'Habsburgermonarchie', 25.
4. F. Schmid, *Bosnien*, 30; for the formulation used by Finance Minister Burián in the session of the common government on 27 September 1918, see Komjáthy, *Protokolle*, 663.
5. Vienna, HHStA, Konsulat Jerusalem, Ktn. 146. See also ibid., MdÄ, Adm. Reg., F 8, Ktn. 140 and 141.
6. Vienna, HHStA, MdÄ, Adm. Reg., F 8, Ktn. 204, 46707–1899.
7. Vienna, HHStA, MdÄ, Adm. Reg., F 57, Ktn. 9.
8. Vienna, HHStA, MdÄ, Adm. Reg., F 57, Ktn. 9. The vilayet was an administrative unit within the Ottoman Empire.
9. Ibid., k.u.k. Consulate in Rustschuk to k.u.k. Embassy in Konstantinopel, 3 May 1871, and k.u.k. Ministry for Foreign Affairs to Sublime Porte, 6 September 1869.
10. Abgeordnetenhaus des österreichischen Reichsrats, *Protokolle* (20 January 1877), 8147f., Interpellation Dr Promber.
11. Vienna, AVA, MdI, Allg., 8/1, Ktn. 357, 31594–1893 and 4068–1894, Report of the Statthalterei in Lemberg, 1893, and of the k.u.k. Ambassador in Romania, 1894.

12. Ibid., 35850–1895, 6864–1896 and 9765–1896.
13. Ibid., Ktn. 206, 40741–1902.
14. Vienna, HHStA, MdÄ, Adm. Reg., F 57, Ktn. 5, Untertanenverzeichnisse 1861–1870, Türkei.
15. Ibid., Ktn. 42, 47751–1914, 3786–1916 and 5810–1917.
16. Ibid., Ktn. 140 and 141. First and last names were used to judge whether those listed on the registers were of the Jewish faith.
17. Ibid., Ktn. 146.
18. Vienna, HHStA, MdÄ, Adm. Reg., F 61, Ktn 20, 2730–1884, k.u.k. Embassy in Sofia to k.u.k. Ministry for Foreign Affairs, 24 January 1884.
19. Ibid., 2730–1884 and 4295–1884, k.u.k. Embassy in Sofia to k.u.k. Ministry for Foreign Affairs, 24 January 1884, k.u.k. Ministry of Finance, Department for Bosnia and Hercegovina, to k.u.k. Ministry for Foreign Affairs, 18 February 1884.
20. Ibid., 1228–1882, k.u.k. Ambassador in Sofia to k.u.k. Ministry for Foreign Affairs, 1 January 1882. See also ibid., 16190–1882.
21. Vienna, AVA, MdI, Allg., 8/1, Ktn. 357, 12786–1891 and 16676–1891, k.k. Ministry of Justice to k.k. Ministry of the Interior, 18 June 1891, report of the Statthalterei Lemberg, 5 August 1891.
22. Vienna, HHStA, MdÄ, Adm. Reg., F 8, Ktn. 140, Report of the k.u.k. Consul in Jerusalem, 25 July 1910, and the reply from the k.u.k. Ministry for Foreign Affairs, 7 December 1910.
23. Vienna, HHStA, MdÄ, Adm. Reg., F 57, Ktn. 42, 44405–1911. The Habsburg officials also sought to help their Armenian protected persons in Bulgaria in a similar way; see ibid., Embassy in Sofia to k.u.k. Ministry for Foreign Affairs, 16 March 1918.
24. Ibid., 60789–1911, k.k. Ministry of the Interior to k.u.k. Ministry for Foreign Affairs, 19 September 1911.
25. Ibid., Attachment to Report No. 1182/A, k.u.k. Embassy in Konstantinopel, 16 March 1918.
26. London, PRO, FO 881/6882, Memo on Nationality and Protection, Sir H. Bergne, 14. October 1892, revised in accordance with latest enactments, Mr E.C. Hertslet, 30 October 1896, printed for the use of the Foreign Office, April 1897.
27. Ibid.; see also Berchtold, *Recht und Gerechtigkeit*, 225–30.
28. London, PRO, FO 881/6882, Memo on Nationality and Protection.
29. London, IOR, L/PJ/6/269, file 160, Commentary on the Naturalization Application of Kumar Bhabendra Narayan.
30. London, PRO, HO 144/462/B32357, Memo on Naturalisation from K.S. Ranjitsinghi, Mr Longley, 26 July 1901.
31. Henriques, *Law of Aliens*, 31. Interestingly, Henriques compares the status of the nationals of the Indian princely states with the former legal status of the Walesians 'until the time when their whole country was annexed in the reign of Edward I'.
32. London, PRO, HO 144/462/B32357, Memo by the Lords of the Judicial Committee of the Council of the Secretary of State for India, 27 January 1899 and Memo from Mr Longley, 26 July 1901.
33. London, PRO, HO45/10227/B36600, Law Officers to Foreign Office, Report by R.B. Finlay and Edward Carson, 5 June 1901, p. 3.
34. On the ethnically exclusive effects of British protected person status in the Nationality Act of 1948, see Dummett and Nicol, *Subjects*; Cesarani, 'The Changing Character';

K. Paul, *Whitewashing Britain: Race and Citizenship in the Postwar Era* (Ithaca, NY: Cornell University Press, 1997).

35. See Agamben, *Homo Sacer*, 8. This ambivalent grey area between 'inside' and 'outside' was tightly linked to the ambiguity that crept into the European concept of sovereignty in the colonial context. See A. Pagden, 'Fellow Citizens and Imperial Subjects: Conquest and Sovereignty in Europe's Overseas Empires', *History and Theory* 44(4) (2005), 28–46. Berchtold, *Recht und Gerechtigkeit*, 225, speaks of a 'grey zone' in this context.

36. London, PRO, FO 228/2156, Correspondence resp. British Protection to Anglo-Chinese in China, 1878–86.

37. London, IOR, L/PJ/6/387B, file 2118, Consul Bennett to Foreign and India Office, November 1894, and to the Governor of Reunion, August 1894.

38. London, IOR, L/PJ/6/387B, file 2118, Consul Bennett to the Governor of Reunion, 11 September 1894. On the debate over the indentured labourers in the French colonies, see also Daviron, 'Mobilizing Labour', 485; Sturman, 'Indian Indentured Labor', 1458f.

39. London, PRO, FO 881/8295, Report of the Consulate in Chiang Mai, November 1900, and Foreign Office to the Embassy in Bangkok, 11 December 1901.

40. London, PRO, GRO, F 615–617, F 620–622, F 626–628, F 634–638 and F 642–644, Consular Birth Indices from Réunion, San Francisco, Portland, Bangkok and Chiang Mai. On the consular registers from the Ottoman Empire, see Berchtold, *Recht und Gerechtigkeit*, 77f.

41. On extraterritorial jurisdiction in semi-colonial Thailand, see Loos, *Subject Siam*, 40–46.

42. London, PRO, FO 881/7550, Registration in Siam (1896–1900), India Office to Foreign Office, 7 September 1896.

43. London, PRO, FO 881/6944, Registration in Siam (1892–1897).

44. London, PRO, FO 881/8295, Registration of British Subjects in Siam, 1901.

45. Ibid., Foreign Office and Embassy in Bangkok, 11 December 1901. On the leeway afforded consulate officials, see also Berchthold, *Recht und Gerechtigkeit*, 225.

46. London, PRO, FO 881/8295, Embassy in Bangkok to Foreign Office, 19 July 1901.

47. Ibid., Consulate in Chiang Mai to Embassy in Bangkok, 20 December 1900 and 23 July 1901.

48. Ibid., Consulate in Chiang Mai to Embassy in Bangkok, 23 July 1901.

49. Ibid., Memo of the Foreign Office official W. Maycock, 14 October 1901.

50. London, PRO, FO 881/7550, Registration in Siam (1896–1900), p. 31.

51. London, PRO, FO 821/80, Consulate Officer Crosby from Muarg Juim to Vice Consul Stringer in Chiang Mai, 4 January 1907. See also Berchthold, *Recht und Gerechtigkeit*, 230.

52. London, PRO, FO 821/80, Consulate Officer Le May to Vice Consul Wood in Chiang Mai, 21 March 1914.

53. Ibid., Vice Consul Wood in Chiang Mai to Consulate Officer Le May, 26 March 1914.

54. Ibid.

55. Lusk, *Social Welfare*. See also J. Stapleton, 'Citizenship versus Patriotism in Twentieth-Century England', *Historical Journal* 48(1) (2005), 152.

56. Jebb, 'The Imperial Problem of Asiatic Immigration', 594f.

57. Indian Legislative Council, Proceedings of the Council (25 February 1910).
58. Ibid. (31 January 1908). See also Sturman, 'Indian Indentured Labor', 1462f.
59. London, IOR, L/PJ/6/864, file 1371, Mr Mdayram to India Office, 23 March 1908. A parliamentary inquiry in the House of Commons resulted out of the context of the 'Monteagle Incident' on 25 March 1908. On the similar case of the *Komagata Maru* from 1914 (see Illustration 8), see H. Johnston, *The Voyage of the Komagata Maru: The Sikh Challenge to Canada's Colour Barrier* (Delhi: Oxford University Press, 1979); Day, *Multiculturalism*, 140; Harper and Constantine, *Migration*, 175.
60. Indian Legislative Council, Proceedings of the Council (31 January 1908), Mr Finlay.
61. Indian Legislative Council, Proceedings of the Council (25 February 1910). These terms were used thirteen times by members of the Indian Legislative Council in the debates on this day alone.
62. Indian Legislative Council, Proceedings of the Council (25 February 1910).
63. The notion that London insisted upon upholding the principle of ethnic neutrality vis-à-vis the dominions, however, is still quite widespread within scholarship. See, for example, Gorman, *Imperial Citizenship*, 159.
64. London, IOR, L/PJ/5/462, Memo, 1911.
65. Ibid.; see also Lake, 'From Mississippi to Melbourne'.
66. Ibid., confidential letter from Risley to Malcolm Seton, 11 May 1911.
67. Ibid.
68. See London, IOR, L/PJ/6/343, file 692.
69. Colonial Conference 1907, Command Paper No. 3524, House of Commons (London), 794–99, Report of Victor Sampson, 6/7 April 1904.
70. Ibid., p. 536, General Botha.
71. London, IOR, L/PJ/6/714, file 923, Indian Government to India Office, 16 May 1905.
72. Ibid.
73. London, IOR, L/PJ/6/500, file 101, Indian Government to India Office, 1 September 1898.
74. Ibid.
75. Colonial Conference 1907, Command Paper, 181, 538f.
76. M. Ollivier (ed.), *The Colonial and Imperial Conferences from 1887 to 1937*, vol. 2, *Imperial Conferences* (Ottawa: Cloutier, 1954), 86f.
77. UK Acts, 4&5 Geo. 5 ch. 17, sec. III.26.1.
78. Adler, *Wahlrecht*, 48.
79. Popovici, *Die Vereinigten Staaten*; A. Fischhof, *Oesterreich und die Bürgschaften seines Bestandes: Politische Studie* (Vienna: Wallishausser, 1869).
80. Springer, *Kampf*; Bauer, *Nationalitätenfrage*.
81. On migration in the later years of the Habsburg monarchy, see A. Steidl, 'Ein ewiges Hin und Her: Kontinentale, transatlantische und lokale Migrationsrouten in der Spätphase der Habsburgermonarchie', *Österreichische Zeitschrift für Geschichtswissenschaften* 19(1) (2008), 15–42.
82. Vienna, HHStA, MdÄ, Adm. Reg., F8, Ktn. 268, Protokoll der Konsulatskonferenz in Washington, 1911.
83. Ibid., Ktn. 267, 36668–1907, 38148–1909, 36023–1911, 73977–1912. The monarchy had consulates in the United States in New York, Pittsburgh, Cleveland, Chicago, Philadelphia and San Francisco. In 1912, the consulates in Canada – in Winnipeg and Montreal – were given 12,000 Kronen for legal aid work for the first time. See also ibid.,

Ktn. 268, 66336–1912, k.u.k. Embassy in Washington to k.u.k. Ministry for Foreign Affairs, 2 September 1912.

84. Vienna, HHStA, MdÄ, Adm. Reg., F 15, Ktn. 7, Memorandum über Auswanderungsfragen, May 1901.

85. Ibid., 56090–1910, Ausweise über die österreichischen Auswandererheime, 30 August 1910.

86. Ibid., Ktn. 31, 75166–1910, k.u.k. Ministry of the Interior to k.u.k. Ministry for Foreign Affairs, 14 September 1910.

87. Vienna, HHStA, MdÄ, Adm. Reg., F 8, Ktn 261, 23425–1912, k.k. Ministry of Commerce to k.u.k. Ministry for Foreign Affairs, 22 April 1912.

88. Ibid., 3321–1912, Bericht über die Dienstreise des Konsular-Attachés Fuchs nach Córdoba, Santa Fé, Paraná, Chaco und Corrientes.

89. Ibid., F 15, Ktn. 36, k.u.k Consulate in Buenos Aires to k.u.k. Ministry for Foreign Affairs, 7 March 1912. On seasonal transatlantic labour migration, see also Steidl, 'Ein ewiges Hin und Her'.

90. Vienna, HHStA, MdÄ, Adm. Reg., F 15, Ktn. 36, Report of Consul Hoenning from Buenos Aires, 20 February 1912.

91. Ibid., Report of the Consular Official Fuchs, 8 February 1912.

92. Ibid., Comments by Consul Hoenning on the Report by Consular Official Fuchs.

93. Ibid., Report of the k.u.k. Consular Official Fuchs, 8 February 1912.

94. Ibid.

95. Ibid., Comments by Consul Hoenning on the Report by Consular Official Fuchs.

96. Ibid., Landesausschuss of Bukowina to Landeshauptmann von Hormuzaki, 6 March 1912, Memo regarding phone conversation between k.u.k. Ministry for Foreign Affairs and k.k. Ministry of Commerce, 7 March 1912, k.u.k. Consulate in Buenos Aires to k.u.k. Ministry for Foreign Affairs, 10 March 1912, k.u.k. Ministry for Foreign Affairs to k.k. Ministry of Commerce, 13 March 1912, and Einsichtsakt of the Ministry of Commerce.

97. Vienna, HHStA, MdÄ, Adm. Reg., F 15, Ktn 8, 34607–1904, k.k. Ministry of the Interior to k.u.k. Ministry for Foreign Affairs, 9 May 1904.

98. *Pester Lloyd*, 14 November 1908, 4, Madaráß in the debate on the emigration bill.

99. Vienna, HHStA, MdÄ, Adm. Reg., F 15, Ktn. 31, 106399–1900, k.u.k. Ministry of the Interior to k.u.k. Ministry for Foreign Affairs, 15 November 1900.

100. Vienna, HHStA, MdÄ, Adm. Reg., F 8, Ktn. 140, 51980–1908, Zirkularschreiben of the k.u.k. Ministry for Foreign Affairs to the Vertretungsbehörden, 3 September 1908. See also ibid., 17823–1914, Zirkularschreiben of the k.u.k. Ministry for Foreign Affairs to the Vertretungsbehörden, 14 April 1914.

101. Ibid., 34813–1905, Zirkularschreiben Ministry for Foreign Affairs to the Vertretungsbehörden, 1 May 1905.

102. *New Yorker Revue*, Sunday, 21 November 1909. See Vienna, HHStA, MdÄ, Admin. Reg., F 15, Ktn. 31.

103. To a certain extent, this resembles the distinction between Alfred and Arthur in the English context. See Young, *English Ethnicity*, 15f.

104. Vienna, HHStA, MdÄ, Adm. Reg., F 8, Ktn 267, 74360–1904.

105. Ibid. Dalmatia was the name for what is today the Adriatic coast of Croatia. While this region belonged to Cisleithania, the rest of contemporary Croatia constituted a part of Transleithania.

106. Ibid., F 15, Ktn. 31, 68229–1910.
107. Ibid., F 8, Ktn. 267, 74360–1904.
108. Ibid., F 15, Ktn. 31, 68229–1910. Emphasis in the original.
109. Ibid., Ktn. 7, Memorandum über Auswanderungsfragen, May 1901.
110. Ibid., Ktn. 31, 75669–1913, k.k. Ministry of the Interior to k.u.k. Ministry for Foreign Affairs, 20 November 1913.
111. Vienna, HHStA, MdÄ, Adm. Reg., F 15, Ktn. 7, Memorandum über Auswanderungsfragen, May 1901.
112. Ibid., F 8, Ktn. 268, Protokoll der Konferenz der k.u.k. Konsuln in den USA, 1911.
113. Ibid., Ktn. 261, 3321–1912, Bericht über die Dienstreise des Konsular-Attachés Fuchs nach Córdoba, Santa Fé, Paraná, Chaco und Corrientes.
114. Ibid.
115. Vienna, HHStA, MdÄ, Adm. Reg., F 15, Ktn. 10, 66530–1916, österreichisch-ungarische Kolonialgesellschaft to k.u.k. Ministry for Foreign Affairs, 15 March 1916.
116. Ibid., österreichisch-ungarische Kolonialgesellschaft to k.u.k. Ministry for Foreign Affairs, 31 August 1917.
117. Vienna, HHStA, MdÄ, Adm. Reg., F 61, Ktn 20, 2730–1884, k.u.k. Embassy in Sofia to k.u.k. Ministry for Foreign Affairs, 24 January 1884.
118. Vienna, HHStA, MdÄ, Adm. Reg., F 15, Ktn. 7, Memorandum über Auswanderungsfragen, May 1901.
119. Burbank, 'Imperial Rights', 399; Geulen, *Wahlverwandte*, 37f.
120. Argast discusses this approach in the context of nationality and citizenship; see Argast, *Staatsbürgerschaft*, 16, 46–60; Foucault, *Security, Territory, Population*.
121. On the concentration camp as a biopolitical paradigm, see Agamben, *Homo Sacer*, 117. Agamben distinguishes between 'bios' and 'zoe' in this context, and not like Foucault between 'bios' and 'thanatos'. For a critique of Agamben's concept, see also P. Sarasin, 'Zweierlei Rassismus? Die Selektion der Fremden als Problem in Michel Foucaults Verbindung von Biopolitik und Rassismus', in M. Stingelin (ed.), *Biopolitik und Rassismus* (Frankfurt am Main: Suhrkamp, 2003), 55–79; P. Purtschert, K. Meyer and Y. Winter, 'Einleitung', in P. Purtschert, K. Meyer and Y. Winter (eds), *Gouvernementalität und Sicherheit: Zeitdiagnostische Beiträge im Anschluss an Foucault* (Bielefeld: Transcript, 2008), 11; M. Foucault, '*Society Must Be Defended*': Lectures at the Collège de France, 1975–1976, ed. M. Bertani and A. Fontana, trans. D. Macey (London: Penguin Books, 2004), 296; Lemke, 'Analytik der Biopolitik', 84f.
122. Foucault, *Histoire de la sexualité I*; Lemke, 'Analytik der Biopolitik', 80.
123. Foucault, *Security, Territory, Population*, idem, *The Birth of Biopolitics*, 21f. See also Lemke, 'Analytik der Biopolitik', 80f., 83; Schmidt, *Statistik und Staatlichkeit*; Purtschert, Meyer and Winter, 'Einleitung', 12.
124. Foucault, *Security, Territory, Population*; idem, *The Birth of Biopolitics*, 16f.
125. Lemke, 'Analytik der Biopolitik', 80. See also Argast, *Staatsbürgerschaft*, 20, 324f., 332.
126. *Pester Lloyd*, Friday, 13 November 1908, 4, Beck. See also the speech by Representative Bernáth.
127. Vienna, HHStA, MdÄ, Adm. Reg., F 15, Ktn. 10, 75669–1913, allgemeine Erläuterungen, p. 29.
128. Ibid., p. 51.

129. Vienna, HHStA, MdÄ, Adm. Reg., F 15, Ktn. 7, Memorandum über Auswande-rungsfragen, May 1901.
130. Vienna, HHStA, MdÄ, Adm. Reg., F 15, Ktn. 10, 18118–1913, k.u.k. Ministry of War to k.u.k. Ministry for Foreign Affairs, 11 March 1913. See also C. Hämmerle, 'Ein gescheitertes Experiment? Die Allgemeine Wehrpflicht in der multieth-nischen Armee der Habsburgermonarchie', *Journal of Modern European History* 5(2) (2007), 237.
131. Vienna, HHStA, MdÄ, Adm. Reg., F 15, Ktn. 10, 75669–1913, Entwurf eines öster-reichischen Auswanderungsgesetzes von 1913. See also Bader-Zaar, 'Foreigners', 149.
132. Foucault, *The Birth of Biopolitics*, 62f. See also Purtschert, Meyer and Winter, 'Einleitung', 13f.
133. Lemke, 'Analytik der Biopolitik', 82. On this coexistence, see also S. Opitz, 'Zwischen Sicherheitdispositiven und Securitization: Zur Analytik illiberaler Gouvernementalität', in P. Purtschert, K. Meyer and Y. Winter (eds), *Gouverne-mentalität und Sicherheit: Zeitdiagnostische Beiträge im Anschluss an Foucault* (Bielefeld: Transcript, 2008), 216.
134. J.S. Woodsworth, *Strangers within Our Gates, or, Coming Canadians* (Toronto: University of Toronto Press 1972 [orig. published 1909]), 29, as quoted in Day, *Multiculturalism*, 133.
135. Ibid., 130.
136. See Fedorowich, 'The British Empire', 88f.; Harper and Constantine, *Migration*, 6, 17f.; R. Bickers, 'Introduction: Britains and Britons over the Seas', in R. Bickers (ed.) *Settlers and Expatriates: Britons over the Seas* (Oxford: Oxford University Press, 2010), 9; S. Swain and M. Hillel, *Child, Nation, Race and Empire: Child Rescue Discourse, England, Canada and Australia, 1850–1915* (Manchester: Manchester University Press, 2010), 120.
137. See Harper and Constantine, *Migration*, 5; Daviron, 'Mobilizing Labour', 487–92.
138. According to Argast, a similar distinction – albeit along lines of gender difference as opposed to ethnicity – shaped Swiss citizenship laws that privileged men and disadvan-taged women; see Argast, *Staatsbürgerschaft*, 20, 332. In the context of current political debates on migration, see also K. Meyer and P. Purtschert, 'Migrationsmanagement und die Sicherheit der Bevölkerung', in P. Purtschert, K. Meyer and Y. Winter (eds), *Gouvernementalität und Sicherheit: Zeitdiagnostische Beiträge im Anschluss an Foucault* (Bielefeld: Transcript, 2008), 163–65.
139. Foucault, 'Society Must Be Defended', 254. See also Sarasin, 'Zweierlei Rassismus?'; E. Gutiérrez Rodríguez, 'Gouvernementalität und die Ethnisierung des Sozialen: Migration, Arbeit und Biopolitik', in M. Pieper and E. Gutiérrez Rodríguez (eds), *Gouvernementalität: Ein sozialwissenschaftliches Konzept in Anschluss an Foucault* (Frankfurt am Main: Campus 2003), 161–78; Lemke, 'Analytik der Biopolitik', 84.
140. Vienna, HHStA, MdÄ, Adm. Reg., F 15, Ktn. 10, 75669–1913.
141. See Foucault, *Security, Territory, Population*; idem, *The Birth of Biopolitics*, 242f.
142. See Day, *Multiculturalism*, 4.
143. On the connection between democracy, the public and 'the mediation of ethnic con-flict', see Lieven, 'Dilemmas of Empire', 189f.
144. The distinction between the population as a totality of living beings and as the body politic corresponds to a certain extent with Karl Renner's suggestion to organize the population in two ways, one following economic-statist criteria, and the other ethnic-national ones. Springer, *Grundlagen*, 208.

145. On the sometimes close connection between social rights of citizenship and nationalist or racist discourses in the British context, see also V. Crossman, *Politics, Pauperism and Power in Late Nineteenth-Century Ireland* (Manchester: Manchester University Press), 2006.

146. See Regan-Lefebvre, *Cosmopolitan Nationalism*, 143.

147. On similar conflicts between promotive and prohibitive approaches in the Swiss context, see Argast, *Staatsbürgerschaft*, 324f.

148. Lusk, *Social Welfare*.

149. See F. Dikötter, 'The Racialization of the Globe: An Interactive Interpretation', *Ethnic and Racial Studies* 31(8) (2008), 1486f.; Bashford, *Imperial Hygiene*, 137.

150. See Hämmerle, 'Back to the Monarchy's Glorified Past?', 156, 160; eadem, 'Ein gescheitertes Experiment?'.

Conclusion

At the turn of the century, an ethnicization process had begun to unfurl in both the Habsburg and British empires. It not only shaped developments at the imperial level, but also in different parts of each empire. Canada and Hungary, for example, adopted more and more ethnically exclusive policies after 1900. Simultaneously, changes in the franchise system in the Austrian lands and the Indian provinces accelerated the establishment of ethnic identities and made them all the more relevant. Meanwhile, the political significance of ethno-confessional differences increased in Bosnia at the same time that racist discrimination was stepped up in East Africa. Likewise, ethnically exclusive mechanisms came into play in the United Kingdom with the Aliens Act of 1905 and the social welfare measures introduced in 1908 and 1911.

These ethnicization processes emerged within both empires, regardless of whether nationality laws were based on *ius soli*, as in the British context, or *ius sanguinis*, as in the Habsburg Empire. By and large, British law construed ethnic differences along territorial lines. Birth within a certain part of the British Empire or access to a given territory determined who was entitled to material rights. However, the actual wording of the respective laws and regulations refrained from explicitly mentioning any ethnically exclusive or racist intentions. Instead, the British government relied on the idea that ethnic identities were visible, which theoretically made it possible for local officials to decide who was to receive preferential treatment based on looks. Consequently, the territorial dimension of British nationality law actually enabled the introduction of racist practices beneath a veil of ethnic neutrality. In the Habsburg context, by contrast, ethnicization took place at the level of the individual person. Complex mechanisms were developed in Austria to cat-

---

Notes for this chapter begin on page 259.

egorize citizens according to ethnonational identities. Although these methods primarily rested on the subjective identification of individuals with certain groups as well as shared languages, descent also came to play a greater role as time went on.

Thus, when all is said and done, this comparison of empires has demonstrated that *ius soli* and *ius sanguinis* were relatively insignificant when it came to these ethnicization processes. In light of the general trend towards ethnicization, moreover, it has proven that it is misleading to differentiate between ethnically exclusive and politically inclusive versions of nationality and citizenship law within historical analysis. What mattered was not whether ethnic differences were incorporated into laws, but rather the way in which this occurred. It is thus more astute to investigate the particular effects of the ethnicization processes that emerged in almost all European states and empires at the outset of the twentieth century.[1] In which ways did ethnic identities and differences gain a foothold in the Habsburg and British contexts specifically? As this study has shown, the manifest conflict between ethnically neutral and racially discriminatory tendencies in the British Empire resulted in the triumph of an imperialist approach that granted privileges and imposed disadvantages along ethnic lines. In the Habsburg Empire, however, a nation-state approach coexisted with a statist perspective. In addition to ethnically exclusive and ethnically neutral constellations, the principle of recognition also made it possible to deal with ethnic heterogeneity by distinguishing between different ethnic identities without discriminating against certain groups.

The Ethnicization of the Law around 1900 as a Cross-European Phenomenon

Yet the question still remains as to why the construction of ethnic identities and differences accelerated around 1900, gaining evermore legal significance as time went on. Four major processes that resounded well beyond the boundaries of the British and Habsburg empires contributed to this development, namely the mobilization of populations, the democratization of political structures, the establishment of promotive techniques of governance, especially in terms of social welfare, and the increasing legal regulation of social relationships.

The different chapters have outlined how migration – such as the Croatian-speaking Hungarian emigrants who went to the United States, Indian workers who went to East Africa, and English subjects of the British Crown who migrated overseas – and the mobility of populations in general contributed significantly to the establishment of legal mechanisms of inclusion and exclusion defined according to ethnic criteria. Thus, the ethnicization of the law went hand in hand with the first wave of modern globalization around the turn of the century. Economic dynamics and technical innovations not only spurred a surge in the number of migrants around the world at this time, but they also allowed people to travel even greater distances. This resulted in first-time encounters between members of various ethnic groups that had never had contact before, making the question of how to deal with ethnic differences all the more pressing. Simultaneously, this mobility contributed on an abstract level to the dissolution of local and familial social structures, which meant that new bonds had to be created to anchor these otherwise 'untethered' individuals. Sometimes, different notions of solidarity resting on national identity or class consciousness collided within such identity-building processes. When viewed from this perspective, the emphasis on ethnic differences also appears to be part of a strategy designed to distract from growing class conflicts. Lastly, accelerated forms of communication intensified the global transfer of nationalist and racist ideas that, in turn, simultaneously sparked ethnicization processes in different parts of the world.[2]

In addition to migration, democratization was another major factor in these ethnicization processes. The gradual expansion of suffrage rights steadily increased the number of people and groups who had to be integrated into the political sphere. The Hungarian example in particular – and that of Canada to a degree – demonstrates that it was thought that ethnically exclusive concepts of the nation would ensure more cohesion than older, multi-ethnic notions. Generally speaking, the relevance of ethnic differences often increased within the context of suffrage reforms, as in Moravia, Bosnia and India. In the UK, for example, ethnocultural criteria came to play a greater role in naturalization praxis as more political rights were bestowed on the basis of British subject status. At the same time, this widening of the political sphere weakened the hold of elitist understandings of politics with their emphasis on customs of international law and the preservation of national prestige that had dominated well into the late nineteenth century. Such perspectives generally ignored the popular side of political culture that was developing around 1900 within the context of domestic struggles for recognition that often resulted in the establishment of hierarchies between different ethnic groups. The case of East Africa aptly illustrates this transition. Whereas the local administration largely pursued an ethnically neutral course under the aegis of the Foreign Office until about 1905, the Colonial Office began to consult more heavily with the non-official 'European' residents of the protectorate when making its decisions, gradually putting imperialist policies of discrimination in place. This does not imply that political participation and ethnic neutrality were mutually exclusive, but at least for the period around 1900, a close link between democratization and ethnicization became evident.[3]

The introduction of promotive techniques of governance also contributed to the increased significance of ethnic differences. However, this link was much stronger in the British Empire than in its Habsburg counterpart. In Austria-Hungary, only faint lines can be traced between ethnicizing trends and the government's attempts to ensure the well-being of its population. One such link appeared in the financial aid privileges enjoyed by Magyar-speaking Hungarian emigrants who approached the Imperial and Royal consulates, as well as in the migration policies pursued by the Austrian Ministry of Trade that tried to assist emigrants in maintaining their ethnic identities abroad. By contrast, the promotive focus on the lives of individuals led to the broader establishment of social citizenship rights in the dominions and the UK itself. However, the question as to who should profit from these rights was almost always framed in an ethnically exclusive way, such as in the wording of the Old Age Pensions Act of 1908. In Canada, sociopolitical intentions and social welfare measures were even more clearly attached to mechanisms of racial discrimination because it was assumed that an equal socio-economic distribution of income, wealth and opportunity could only be achieved within an ethnically homogeneous society. From this perspective, the exclusion and discrimination directed at the 'non-white' population was deemed essential for the successful establishment of promotive techniques of governance.

Ultimately, the general trend towards the legal regulation of the social realm and its relationships played a decisive role in increasing the significance of ethnic differences within laws. The tendency to clearly define all socially relevant distinctions in a legal way and to translate these into unambiguous categories that could hold up in court was tightly linked to bureaucratization processes. It fostered the establishment of administrative praxes such as separate national registers for Czech- and German-speaking voters in Moravia. Simultaneously, efforts to achieve the most precise assessment of ethnic differences led to the introduction of legal terms such as 'home' in the British Old Age Pensions Act, and the 'European British subject' in the Indian Code of Criminal Procedure, which were supposed to ensure that 'whites' benefited from the privileges associated with racist discrimination directed at 'natives'. Although these legal definitions and attempts at clarification usually crumbled in the face of the complexity of ethnic identification, boundary crossings and the ambivalence of real-life situations, they nonetheless attest to the importance of the law in dealing with ethnic heterogeneity. This finding contradicts the popular assumption that discrimination and the rule of law were always incompatible because the law was supposed to serve as a bulwark against racism.[4] But rather than merely pointing out this contradiction, it is important to pose more probing questions: How was it possible for the law to become an element of racist politics? How did codification and ethnicization become mutually reinforcing processes?[5]

The Different Effects of Ethnicization in the British and Habsburg Empires

The general increase in the significance attached to ethnic differences in law and administrative practices manifested itself in highly divergent ways in both imperial constellations. The specific answers that emerged in response to the question of how to maintain imperial cohesion in light of the growing relevance of ethnic identities determined the path of ethnicization in each empire. In the British Empire, the integration of 'white' subjects within a so-called 'imperial nation', as well as discrimination directed against 'non-whites', lit the way forward. In the Habsburg Empire, the joint government continued to adhere to its principle of ethnic neutrality while Austria adopted policies of recognition and Hungary pursued a course of assimilation and exclusion. A look at the dynamics of expansion, patterns of migration, legal traditions and the political structures characteristic of the two empires helps to explain why they adopted different approaches when it came to dealing with ethnic heterogeneity.

The triumph of imperialist discrimination in the British case was tightly linked to the rapid expansion of the empire around the turn of the century and the corresponding migration of 'European' settlers to the colonies as well as 'Indian' subjects to the dominions. As a result, people who used to live far away from one another suddenly came into close contact, which decisively influenced perceptions of ethnic difference. These encounters seemed to confirm the assumption that ethnic identities were apparent and visible, and they fostered the dominance of bipolar or tripolar constellations of difference (i.e. between 'whites' and 'non-whites', or between 'Europeans', 'Asiatics' and 'Africans').[6] Both of these developments made it easier for racist mechanisms of discrimination to take hold in the British Empire.

In the Habsburg context, by contrast, migration within the empire itself did not generate comparable effects. Moreover, even taking the annexation of Bosnia into account, Austria-Hungary expanded to a much lesser degree. Unlike Britain's global empire, the Danube monarchy had grown through a gradual process of incorporation within a geographically continuous space. By the eighteenth century at the latest, it had also developed a tradition of accommodating different language communities within multipolar constellations where multilingualism was rather common. Due to this complex matrix of difference, it was difficult to clearly delineate ethnic identities. As a result, the list of distinctions, especially in Cisleithania, was far more varied than the black-and-white categories that racist discrimination relied upon. Thus, the population of the British Empire was not more heterogeneous than that of the Habsburg Empire, but the game of identity politics between familiarity and alterity followed significantly different rules in each case.

Additionally, divergent legal traditions also played a decisive role: whereas discriminatory distinctions were fostered by the feudal concept incorporated in the 'British subject', the egalitarian notion of citizenship in the Habsburg Empire stood in their way. Consequently, within the Habsburg monarchy, the disadvantaged status of Bosnian nationals was seen as a constitutional problem in violation of the principle of equality that had come to characterize the dualistic relationship between the governments in Budapest and Vienna. The joint Imperial and Royal government and the monarch may have presided alongside, or rather above, this dualistic constellation, but the Habsburg imperial metropolis was comparatively weak. Likewise, the partial autonomy of the Cisleithanian Crown Lands kept the influence of the government in Vienna in check. This relatively flat political hierarchy resting on negotiation and compromise corresponded more or less with the legal emphasis on equal citizenship stemming from the tradition of enlightened absolutism. Combined with the administrative focus on the economic and military interests of the state, this inclination towards equality contributed significantly to the establishment of a statist way of dealing with ethnic heterogeneity that initially manifested itself in a neutral stance and then later in policies of recognition.

In the British case, a comparable appreciation of equality within a utilitarian framework only informed the promises of equality made to Indian subjects, which – as the debates over the Ilbert Bill show – never bore fruit. Rather, the emphasis on an often rigid hierarchy between 'whites' and 'non-whites' resting upon the right of conquest effectively split the population along biopolitical lines into a group that was supposed to profit from promotive measures and one that was supposed to be subjected to prohibitions. This hierarchy was also reflected in the imperialist and asymmetrical distribution of power between the peripheral colonial portions of the empire and the imperial metropolis. Furthermore, the transition from informal methods of control to formal colonial rule in the early twentieth century strengthened the hierarchical nature of this relationship. At the same time, the elevation of the governments of the dominions to more or less equal partners of the government in London did little to weaken these hierarchies.

All told, this distinction between a clearly hierarchical political structure in the British context and a barely hierarchical political constellation in the Habsburg Empire proved to be highly significant. First of all, it meant that imperial entanglements played a much greater role in the British Empire than in the Danube monarchy. Whereas different approaches to ethnic heterogeneity could coexist in the Habsburg Empire, simply because there were separate nationality rights in different parts of Austria-Hungary, an imperialist form of discrimination established its dominance throughout the British Empire after 1900. The fact that the imperial metropolis, the dominions and the 'European' settlers largely shared the same intentions in this respect also accelerated this process within the British realm.[7] Secondly, the different political structures influenced the demands voiced by the respective nationalist movements on the imperial periphery in distinct ways. Whereas the call for supra-ethnic equality was the core aim of the Indian nationalist movement, the nationalist parties in Cisleithania were most interested in acquiring more autonomy because similar demands for equality made little sense in the absence of an asymmetrical colonial imbalance of power. Thirdly, the imperialistic hierarchy in the British Empire essentially blocked any moves towards ethnically neutral legal equality because such impulses contradicted the basic inequality of the empire's political structure, which was tightly linked to racist notions of superiority and inferiority.

Imperial Formations beyond the East–West Dichotomy

One might ask whether this comparison of the British and Habsburg empires has merely demonstrated, rather unsurprisingly, that the two empires dealt with ethnic heterogeneity differently, due to their more or less hierarchical structures (with the British and the Habsburg cases marking opposite ends of the spectrum). Such a simple conclusion, however, does not do justice to the complexity of the empirical findings of this study. For one, it ignores the fact that law and administrative praxis in both empires in the late nineteenth century were equally informed by the statist principle of ethnic neutrality. Likewise, it glosses over the discrepancies that emerged within different parts of each empire. Therefore, a two-dimensional typology that only differentiates between a more or less asymmetrical relationship between the metropolis and the periphery, and maps this distinction onto a spectrum of discrimination and recognition in dealing with ethnic heterogeneity, cannot begin to describe the multivalent reality of imperial formations. The same applies to models that categorize empires into those characterized by integration and those marked by processes of differentiation. While the latter highlighted legal inequality, the former relied on legal equalization that would ultimately and hypothetically turn the imperial structure into a homogenous nation-state – for example, the French colonial empire in North Africa in the second half of the twentieth century.[8]

These dimensions are undoubtedly relevant, but they are by no means sufficient for a thorough analysis. Above all, as this study has pointed out, they fail to take into account the vital distinction between recognition and discrimination as well as the spectrum between processes of homogenization and equalization associated either with nation-state approaches or with statist perspectives. Accordingly, by taking into account the imperialist, statist and nation-state approaches to dealing with ethnic heterogeneity outlined in this book, a typology of imperial formations emerges that spans five paradigms. First of all, empires could adopt an ethnically neutral principle of equality that was valid for each subject or national. This statist notion of equality informed the perspectives of the joint government in the Habsburg context and the Indian nationalist movement in the British case. By contrast, the second statist paradigm, that of recognition, emphasized the equality of different ethnonational groups, as in Cisleithania. In diametrical opposition to this standpoint, the third paradigm was based on the granting of privileges or the imposition of disadvantages for specific ethnic groups; such imperialist discrimination was enforced in East Africa. Discriminatory mechanisms located on the outer borders of a national community delineate the fourth paradigm, which was the exclusionary version of the nation-state approach. It was employed after 1900 in Canada, where the goal was to achieve ethnic homogeneity within the borders of the country. The fifth paradigm prevailed when the national project of integration was applied to multi-ethnic nations, as was the case in Hungary before the turn of the century. In such constellations, the nation-state approach went hand in hand with either the recognition of difference or the principle of supra-ethnic neutrality.

Other empires and (post-)imperial territories can also be situated along the spectrum defined by these five paradigms. The Soviet Union, for example, exhibited elements of a multi-ethnic nation-state, as did post-colonial India with its 'unity in diversity'. The French Empire, in contrast, wavered between homogenizing nation-state tendencies and imperialist measures of discrimination aimed at specific populations such as the Algerian 'Muslims' or the 'Indian' immigrants of Réunion.[9] Strains of a politics of recognition appeared in the Millet system in the Ottoman Empire as well as in the legal pluralism of the Russian Empire.[10] Similar to the Russian case, where recognition coexisted with a class-based system of discrimination as well as integration processes typical of a nation-state, the German colonial empire also featured a mix of discriminatory hierarchies paired with integrative homogenizing trends and a statist tradition that aimed to achieve supra-ethnic equality.[11]

As in the British and Habsburg contexts, the respective political structures of these imperial formations, combined with their specific legal traditions, patterns of migration and dynamics of expansion, shaped the way they reacted to the challenge of ethnic heterogeneity. These factors by and large determined the location of each empire or part thereof within the fivefold spectrum outlined above. This typology allows for a more precise description of different imperial constellations than the classic twofold distinction between maritime and continental empires, especially since the latter rests on the normatively loaded opposition between modern colonial empires in Western Europe and backward traditional empires in Eastern Europe.[12] Such a bipolar contrast glosses over the major similarities between so-called 'Western' and 'Eastern' imperial formations, and neglects the significant variance within these two categories. Moreover, the simplified reliance on just two types of imperial formations, namely a Western-colonial and an Eastern-continental variant, ignores the diversity within these respective empires, as some parts of the same empire developed different ways of dealing with ethnic heterogeneity. For example, the developments in Canada resembled those in Hungary while the situation in India mirrored that of Austria, despite the fact that both empires generally adopted a very different approach in the early twentieth century.

Empires, States, Nation-States and the Three Approaches

The strength of the conceptual framework developed in this book that differentiates between imperialist, statist and nation-state approaches in dealing with ethnic heterogeneity is that it allows for a more nuanced interpretation than any of the existing, rather oversimplified dichotomies. Furthermore, its empirical insights have generated a more complete profile for these three main approaches. As the Bosnian case exemplified, imperialist discrimination could not only be based on racist hierarchies, but also on differences in national status. Bosnian nationals were disadvantaged in the Habsburg Empire regardless of their ethnic identity. East African policies, by contrast, privileged all 'Europeans' and disadvantaged all 'non-Europeans', without respect to whether or not they were British subjects. Furthermore, the crucial phenomenon of inclusive exclusion has often been overlooked within the context of imperialist discrimination. It produced ambivalent grey zones between belonging and not-belonging in places such as Bosnia and East Africa that made it possible for the authorities to burden certain groups with obligations without having to grant them any rights in return.

Moreover, the analysis of statist policies in Austria has demonstrated that the desire to transform the resident population into a legally homogeneous citizenry – which was at the theoretical core of the statist approach – played only a minimal role in praxis. The overriding factors in the Cisleithanian as well as the Indian context were the economic and military interests of the state, the power of the largely autocratic bureaucracy and the desire to integrate different ethnonational groups into a common political framework. Statist policies of recognition can therefore be seen as a sidestepping strategy that partly accommodated the demands of nationalist movements by granting them rights of autonomy and political participation within the overarching imperial structure, without having to sacrifice the cohesion of the empire.

Finally, this book has pointed out that a nation-state approach could rest on the idea of an ethnically homogeneous nation as well as on a multi-ethnic one. It has illustrated that ethnically exclusive immigration restrictions were not the only means by which the external border of the national community could be reined in. Regulations that fostered the inclusion of particular groups, such as the 'Englishmen and Scotchmen and Irishmen' who returned to the UK after losing their status as British subjects, could serve the same purpose. Above all, however, the analysis presented here has illustrated that a nation-state approach could gain a foothold within imperial formations, especially in sub-metropolitan and semi-peripheral territories such as Canada and Hungary. Consequently, it can be said that a nation-state approach was not necessarily dependent on the existence of an independent nation-state.

These insights revise the rather narrow-sighted focus on nation-states and the nation-state approach within scholarship on citizenship and nationality.[13] Studies in this field have all too often ignored the imperialist and discriminatory dimensions of the law, potentially skewing the perspectives on countries such as the United Kingdom, which has often been falsely depicted as a paradigmatically liberal and inclusive example.[14] Research also tends to overlook the significance of statist approaches, or to dismiss them as relics left over from the eighteenth century. Statist notions of neutrality and recognition, however, were very much alive and well in the twentieth century. Although the nation-state model began to make heavy inroads, statist thought was by no means irrelevant, as seen in the affirmative action legislation passed in the United States, beginning in the 1960s. Moreover, such policies demonstrate just how much statist notions of recognition and the multi-ethnicity of nation-states were interwoven. In late nineteenth-century Hungary, an ethnically inclusive nation-state approach indeed overlapped with a statist emphasis on supra-ethnic neutrality, thereby exhibiting a combination between nation and neutrality that has hardly been discussed by earlier studies.

On the whole, this book has shown that the three approaches to dealing with ethnic heterogeneity almost never appeared in a pure form, as they were almost always bound up in a more or less tenuous mix of competing notions. In India, for example, imperialistic and statist perspectives collided, while all three models coexisted in the United Kingdom. Thus, in terms of these three approaches, nuanced differences can be detected between empires, states and nation-states, but categorical distinctions make little sense. It is certainly not the case that imperialist notions only prevailed within empires or that all nation-states would exclusively rely on a nation-state approach. To this extent, widening the perspective to include imperialist and statist aspects questions the existing scholarly focus on nation-state ideals of political and ethnic homogeneity, even outside the realm of citizenship and nationality. Although the nation-state as a form of unity became the dominant model in the twentieth century, most nation-state formations were marked by ambivalence and heterogeneity, not to mention the existence of neo-imperial structures such as in the Soviet Union and multinational states as in Yugoslavia.[15] This is not surprising, given that almost all nation-states are post-imperial political entities, although they may have tried (unsuccessfully) to dismiss their imperial heritage.

The fact that there were never any 'pure' nation-states also challenges older scholarship that has all too often described the relationship between empires and nationalist movements as a battle between imperial-centripetal and nationalist-centrifugal forces. In contrast, this study has proved – in keeping with more recent scholarship – that imperial structures and national ambitions could not only coexist, but also be mutually reinforcing.[16] The far from continually confrontational relationship between the Indian nationalist movement and the imperial metropolis is just one case in point, as are the nation-state tendencies within the dominions and the United Kingdom itself. The less hierarchical structure of the Habsburg Empire, on the other hand, prevented a similar nationalization of the metropolis.[17] Rather, Austria-Hungary was shaped by cooperative nationalisms that played out in (semi-)peripheral spaces such as Hungary, Moravia and Croatia. Ultimately, such non-confrontational aspects of nationalist movements stabilized the imperial framework from which they in turn profited.[18] Empires, as it were, contributed to the establishment of nationalist movements, and these nationalist movements reinforced the empires in reverse.

The First World War as a Decisive Turning Point?

These symbiotic entanglements could turn into antagonistic disentanglements under certain circumstances. For the Habsburg Empire, the First World War was indeed one of these constellations. Not surprisingly, the outbreak of war made the enforcement of military service requirements for all citizens and nationals a key concern for the imperial government. Consequently, the war heightened the importance of the statist commitment to ethnic neutrality that rested upon the foundation of an autocratic administration favoured by the Imperial and Royal Ministry of War. Accordingly, promotive measures and the recognition of difference with respect to suffrage and the constitutional structure of the monarchy were relegated to the sidelines. Likewise, the far-reaching repeal of parliamentary and judicial checks and balances, only some of which were reinstituted as the war dragged on, effectively undermined democratic rights of participation as well as cultural autonomy.[19] However, the centralizing effects of the war and the accompanying propaganda strategies did strengthen imperial loyalty and a sense of belonging.[20] But, at the same time, the excesses of violence sometimes aimed at specific ethnic groups as well as the radicalization of centrifugal nationalist movements fuelled by the enemy counteracted these centripetal tendencies.[21] It thus became all the more difficult to maintain a sense of multi-ethnic unity within the empire.

It was this unravelling of unity that, together with defeat on the battlefield, led to the collapse of Habsburg rule. The nationality and citizenship laws of the national successor states that emerged in its wake did not draw on the Habsburg tradition of ethnic neutrality or the Cisleithanian emphasis on recognition, but rather adopted the Hungarian model of an ethnically exclusive nation-state. Over the course of time, racist overtones often sharpened the exclusionary tenor of these policies. The German-Austrian republic thus denied Jews participation in the newly constituted national community.[22] As most of the successor states adopted similar anti-Semitic policies of exclusion, the now stateless Habsburg 'Jews' found themselves in a very precarious situation in the interwar years that, in retrospect, was surely a harbinger of what was to come with the Nazi ascension to power.[23]

In light of the catastrophic outcome, it almost seems trivial to try to trace the beginnings of this exclusion and discrimination directed against Jews. Yet important insights can still be gained by questioning to what extent this marginalization was triggered by the First World War or whether it rested on earlier developments. Regardless of the undeniable prevalence of anti-Semitic attitudes and practices in the pre-war history of Austria-Hungary, this question hints at some problematic dimensions of the nation-state and statist approaches that influenced the way in which the late Habsburg monarchy dealt with ethnic heterogeneity. On the one hand, the comparably rapid establishment of exclusive and discriminatory measures after 1918 demonstrated that the prior dominance of policies of neutrality or recognition did not necessarily correspond with the convictions of most of the population. Rather, these statist policies stemmed from the powerful influence of a rather small administrative elite, which relatively easily switched its course – at least to some extent – after the war.  On the other hand, links can be detected between the recognition of difference in Habsburg Cisleithania and the exclusionary discrimination later put in place in the successor states, as both these approaches necessitated the clearest demarcation of ethnic identities possible.[24] If this 'dark side' of recognition is taken into account, then the First World War no longer appears to be the decisive turning point that caused the harmonious unity of the multi-ethnic empire to dissolve suddenly into a merciless battle between different nations and 'races'. Rather, the war can be more aptly described as a kind of catalyst that accelerated the ethnicization processes that had already begun around 1900, and steered them in a certain direction.[25]

Approached from this perspective, the new political and social order that emerged in Central, Southern and Eastern Europe after 1918 did away with the specific circumstances that had allowed for the coexistence of different approaches relying on recognition, exclusion or discrimination in the Habsburg Empire. Within this new constellation, moreover, a statist form of recognition made little sense. The governments of almost all the newly created states sought to integrate and bind their populations within a nation-state framework that aimed at homogenization.[26] Simultaneously, the United States' insistence on the right of national self-determination magnified these developments. Given these circumstances, the implementation of measures of recognition that went against the grain would have been quite risky for any individual successor state. Thus, it can be said that the war accelerated the ethnicization of the law that had already set in around the turn of the century, while also whittling this process down to its ethnically exclusive elements within the framework of a nation-state.

With respect to the British Empire, even more evidence supports the idea that the fin-de-siècle was a more decisive turning point than the First World War. In the case of East Africa, the war intensified the discrimination directed at the 'African' population, especially with mandatory military service requirements for the men; after 1918, however, only the 'Europeans' profited from the introduction of political participation rights. The situation in Canada was quite similar. On the one hand, measures aimed at internal homogenization along nation-state lines continued. In 1917, moreover, suffrage was granted to war nurses and women whose men, sons, brothers or fathers were soldiers; universal women's suffrage followed in 1918.[27] On the other hand, 'non-enfranchised Indians' did not benefit from this wave of emancipation. Despite the fact that they were required to fulfil mandatory military service in 1916–17, they were still denied full Canadian citizenship after the war.[28] Exclusionary immigration laws and practices were also tightened and increasingly directed against newcomers from Southern and Eastern Europe in addition to 'Asiatic' immigrants in the 1920s.[29]

Comparably, although the Indian government did not introduce compulsory military service – not the least because officials feared anti-colonial revolts by armed 'natives' – India nonetheless contributed significant financial and personnel resources to the British war effort.[30] But, put mildly, the legal improvements that had been promised in return for these contributions never lived up to the expectations of the Indian nationalist movement. During the war, the government actually intensified its control over the population and its efforts to subdue undesirable opinions, especially nationalist ideas. Likewise, although the Montagu–Chelmsford reforms extended political participation rights in 1918–19, they also reinforced the imperialist privileges enjoyed by 'Europeans'. Concessions with regard to the demands for 'Home Rule' or the elimination of racist discrimination were by no means on the horizon.[31] Even at the imperial level, the British Empire made no move towards supra-ethnic equality. The Imperial War Conference may have promised 'Indian' subjects emancipation in 1917, but it supported the retention of discriminatory immigration policies in the dominions just a year later, in 1918.[32]

In the United Kingdom itself, the war did not heighten exclusion and discrimination aimed at 'non-white' Britons initially. A regulation passed in 1917 extended the provisions that had been established in the Aliens Restriction Act of 1914 for enemy foreigners to include 'Asiatic' nationals of allied states. In order to hide the fact 'that Asiatics are aimed at', the decree named particular nationalities – specifically, 'Chinese, Japanese, Siamese, Persians, Egyptians'.[33] Indian subjects of the British Crown, however, were still not affected by these restrictions. It was not until the 1920s that a regulation was introduced that required the registration of 'coloured seamen', which also applied to 'non-white'

subjects of the British Crown.[34] After the Second World War, the UK ampli-
fied its discriminatory immigration policies by denying entry to 'non-white'
British subjects.[35] These racist restrictions were part of the disastrous afterglow
of imperial problems and traditions within a dissolving empire. This process was
also reflected in the separation of Pakistan and India, which built upon existing
franchise distinctions between Muslims and Hindus, and in the expulsion of the
'Indian' population from Uganda in 1972.

Modernization and the Survival or Collapse of Empires

The turn of the century marked a major shift in the history of nationality and citizenship laws. Processes of ethnicization were set in motion at this time that were
further intensified and modified during the First World War, but whose core
effects could still be felt well into the late twentieth century. That said, however,
some critics might still question whether the war was nonetheless a very decisive
factor because it led to the dissolution of the Habsburg Empire and the expansion of the British Empire. In fact, some might even claim that the war revealed
that the British way of dealing with ethnic heterogeneity was ultimately more
capable of coping with the challenges of modernity than the Habsburg approach.

But, there are four main points that refute such an argument. First of all,
the war not only marked the beginning of the disintegration of the Danube
monarchy, but also that of the British Empire. With the loss of Ireland, the
British Empire also lost part of its own metropolis; simultaneously, the dominions insisted evermore emphatically on their autonomy.[36] When seen from this
perspective, the break-up of both imperial formations set in at the same time.
The Habsburg Empire, however, collapsed with catastrophic resonance while the
British Empire broke apart more gradually.

Secondly, the implicit assumption that the disintegration of the Habsburg
Empire was inevitable given the tensions between imperial centripetal forces
and their nationalist centrifugal counterparts needs to be critically questioned.
According to this line of thought, the war was more or less just an arbitrary
catalyst – the random spark that set off a powder keg bursting at the seams.[37]
However, the counterfactual argument that Austria-Hungary would not have
collapsed in 1918 had it not been embroiled in the war and suffered defeat raises
some doubts. As this study has made clear, the relationship between imperial
formations and nationalist movements prior to 1914 was by no means so antagonistic that the resulting conflicts would have inevitably led to the disintegration
of the empire. On the contrary, nationalizing tendencies and imperial structures
could work cooperatively in a mutually reinforcing way. But, for far too long,
scholars have neglected these cohesive elements because they have clung to the
assumption that the downfall of the Habsburg monarchy was unavoidable.[38] Yet

with a more objective gaze, it becomes clear that most contemporaries did not see the end of the Habsburg Empire coming. The problematic contradictions that might have hindered the success of the Austrian emphasis on recognition over the long term, for example, only appear in retrospect. On the one hand, this approach ensured the cohesion of the empire by allowing for pacts such as the Moravian Compromise and guaranteeing the equality of different nationalities. In order to achieve this goal, however, these policies of recognition essentially had to make political actors out of the different ethnonational groups. Thus, in a way, they actually laid the foundations for the dissolution of the imperial formation that they actually sought to uphold.[39] But in the end, it was not these contradictions but the lost war that proved to be decisive for the collapse of the empire in 1918.

Thirdly, it can be argued that the British Empire did not survive 1918 largely intact because its internal affairs were in better order and the majority of its subjects were more loyal than in the Habsburg Empire; rather, the conflicts between imperial cohesion, national autonomy and demands for supra-ethnic equality were just as difficult to resolve in the British Empire after 1918 as they were in the Habsburg Empire before 1914. Therefore, it was not that the British Empire adopted a more just or balanced way of dealing with ethnic heterogeneity that accounts for why the empire did not crumble until a few decades after the war while Austria-Hungary collapsed in its wake. Rather, the most important factor was that the British Empire emerged as the triumphant military power. Structural factors also contributed to the survival of the empire that were linked to its hierarchical organization and the emphasis on inequality in British law. These asymmetries tended to result in a comparably small group of privileged subjects who were loyal supporters of the imperial structure from which they personally profited. The much larger group of disadvantaged and dissatisfied subjects hardly factored into imperial politics because their political participation was quite limited. A political awakening within this group began to occur in the early twentieth century, but it was not until the 1940s that the balance of power had shifted enough so that parts of the empire seceded from the imperial union.[40] Up to this point, the correspondence between political hierarchy and legal discrimination had ensured the relative stability of the British Empire.

By contrast, the manoeuvring between different contradictory approaches for dealing with the complexity of ethnic heterogeneity in the Habsburg context actually destabilized the empire. Furthermore, the coexistence of divergent policies and the weak hierarchical structure of the empire stood in the way of the emergence of a clearly delineated, privileged and nationalized metropolis.[41] Consequently, the position of the German-speaking population of Cisleithania differed greatly from that of 'whites' from the United Kingdom who moved throughout the global British Empire. Rather than privileging an ethnonational group, the joint Austro-Hungarian government upheld the same standards for all 'nationalities' in keeping with its premise of supra-ethnic neutrality. Quite obviously, though, the Habsburg approach could not permanently resolve the conflicts between nationalization and democratization on the one hand and imperial heterogeneity on the other. The more consistent adherence to discriminatory measures in the British Empire, by contrast, was at least partly able to alleviate these tensions or funnel them into a paradoxical concordance. But, given this background, is it really appropriate to describe the British solution as modern and the Habsburg variant as backward?

This question brings us to the fourth objection that can be raised against the thesis that the British Empire was better able to cope with the challenges of modernity than the Habsburg Empire. It touches on the more fundamental issue of the implicit normativity of the distinction between modernity as a positive step forward and backwardness as a deplorable state.[42] After all, although the imperialist discrimination of the British Empire was initially able to ensure the survival of the empire, it by no means meshes with the general assumption that all things modern merit acclaim and imitation. As the analysis of the British case has exemplified, this understanding of modernity is oversimplified; at best, modernization was an ambivalent process with many advantages but also fraught with disadvantages. Approached from such a perspective, modernity in the British Empire seems to have been more strongly Janus-faced than in the Habsburg context. On the one hand, it was marked by a comparably more intensive implementation of governmental and promotive mechanisms of power, which produced social ramifications beyond the boundaries of the law that benefited not only the 'whites' but also portions of the 'non-white' population over the long term. On the other hand, these newly created forms of agency were underpinned by ever stronger measures of exclusion and discrimination. Consequently, the British example illustrates that racism was by no means an aberration, but rather an inherent part of modernization processes.[43]

In reverse, however, the strict adherence to so-called backward structures of sovereign or prohibitive power accounts for the lesser role of racist discrimination in the Habsburg Empire. To a certain extent, the backwardness of the Imperial and Royal government served as a bulwark against the implementation of an excessive form of biopolitical racism. That said, however, Habsburg policies were not solely guided by the prohibitive insistence on the principle of supra-ethnic neutrality; rather, they also exhibited elements of recognition and promotive governance, for example in terms of the franchise or emigration.[44] Accordingly, the Austro-Hungarian model could best be described as one of defensive modernization that – in keeping with enlightened-absolutist Josephinism – combined repressive and emancipatory elements.[45]

At the same time, it seems to make little sense to contrast the supposedly admirable example of progressive British modernity with the supposedly deplorable backwardness of the Habsburg Empire. The diametric opposition between political inclusion in the West and ethnic exclusion in the East, as this book has clearly illustrated, does not hold up within imperial contexts.[46] Whereas racist exclusion and discrimination shaped the law and administrative praxis in the British Empire, supra-ethnic notions of equality and the recognition of difference guided the way the Habsburg Empire sought to deal with ethnic heterogeneity. But, it would be just as misleading to simply turn this normatively loaded opposition on its head by insisting that the Austro-Hungarian approach was more modern than the British strategy that exhibited a reactionary form of racism. The real insight to be gleaned from this comparison of the British and Habsburg empires is that the assumption of a fundamental opposition between modern and liberal empires in the West and traditional and authoritarian empires in the East very much falls short of the mark.

The critique of the idea that Britain was well ahead of the backward Habsburg Empire when it came to modernity rests primarily on the realization that this East–West dichotomy is normative and ahistoric, and therefore an analytical tool riddled with weaknesses. The examples presented in this book have clearly demonstrated that such an oversimplified and static picture cannot do justice to the complexities of the matter at hand, nor does it allow for a dynamic analysis of changes over time. In Hungary, for example, a supra-ethnic understanding of the nation was replaced by an ethnically exclusive notion; in Canada, the inclusion of 'European' immigrants corresponded to the exclusion of 'Asiatic' immigrants; in Austria, the nationalities were increasingly defined as ethnically exclusive collectives; and in the British Empire, the idea of ethnic neutrality was gradually pushed out by an imperialist model of discrimination. The multivalent simultaneity of different dynamics suggests that neither of these empires can be clearly placed along a uniform spectrum of modernity, but rather that there were different forms of modernity, each of which had its own possibilities and problems. Whereas the defensive modernization process within the Habsburg context bound prohibitive restrictions together with legal equality and the recognition of differences, the more intensive implementation of promotive mechanisms of power in the British case went hand in hand with racist discrimination.

Without a doubt, even present-day conflicts over how to deal with ethnic heterogeneity are still informed and influenced by these very same approaches.[47] For instance, political conflicts over immigration – and not only in Austria or the UK – have often led to the coupling of questions about political participation and the preservation of welfare measures with xenophobic or racists demands for the exclusion of certain groups. Likewise, only prohibitive anti-discrimination laws or the establishment of human rights norms have been able to guarantee the implementation of supra-ethnic equality by counteracting discriminative practices.[48] Indeed, the recognition of difference, which was such a vital aspect of the Habsburg solution to the question of ethnic heterogeneity, still guides the way in which multicultural immigration societies such as Canada approach the issue of ethnic diversity.[49] But even in these present-day examples, the recognition of differences always runs the risk of establishing rigid categories that can all too easily result in discrimination. Thus, from a contemporary perspective, historical constellations such as that of Cisleithania, in which governments sought to reconcile the recognition of differences with an awareness of the instability of ethnic identities and the adherence to a principle of supra-ethnic equality, are particularly interesting. Not the least, these historical examples instil hope that it may be possible to achieve legal equality within ethnically heterogeneous societies in the future.

Notes

1. The significance of the turn of the century as a watershed is also emphasized by Geulen, *Wahlverwandte*, 28f., and Schennach, 'Der "Österreicher" als Rechtskonstrukt?', 153, for the US and Germany; for France, see G. Noiriel, *Le creuset français: Histoire de l'immigration XIXe–XXe siècle*, (Paris: Editions du Seuil, 2006); for Romania and Serbia, see Müller, *Staatsbürger auf Widerruf*; and for Switzerland, see Argast, *Staatsbürgerschaft*.
2. J. Osterhammel and N.P. Petersson, *Geschichte der Globalisierung: Dimensionen, Prozesse, Epochen* (Munich: Beck, 2003). On the construction of ethnic identities as the result of modernization processes, see Esser, 'Ethnische Differenzierung', 244, and R.L. Rudolph, 'Nationalism and Empire in Historical Perspective', in R.L. Rudolph and D.F. Good (eds), *Nationalism and Empire: The Habsburg Empire and the Soviet Union* (New York: St. Martin's Press, 1992), 3–12; Berger and Miller, 'Nation-Building', 317.
3. On the connection between democracy and ethnicization, see M. Mann, *The Dark Side of Democracy: Explaining Ethnic Cleansing* (Cambridge: Cambridge University Press, 2005); King, *Budweisers*, 48f., 80f.; Cooper, 'Empire Multiplied', 270. Lake and Reynolds, *Drawing the Global Colour Line*, 9, describe this relationship in the colonial context: 'In the figure of the white man, the imperialist became a democrat and the democrat an imperialist'.
4. On the idea of racist politics implemented outside of the rule of law, see F. Neumann, *Behemoth: The Structure and Practice of National Socialism, 1933–1944*, 2nd edn (New York: Oxford University Press, 1944). On the link between the constitutional order and racist politics in the context of National Socialism, see also Gosewinkel, *Einbürgern und Ausschließen*, 369–420.
5. Cf. Kolsky, *Colonial Justice*.
6. Along these lines, Cooper speaks of '"otherness" carried to an extreme' in 'Empire Multiplied', 268; Steinmetz refers to the 'overarching binarism' of modern empires in contrast to the multi-ethnicity of – in his words – traditional empires, in 'Return to Empire', 245.
7. Lieven, 'Dilemmas of Empire', 183, speaks of 'a common and thoroughly racialist pride in "Britishness"' as being a major factor that ensured the cohesion of the empire.
8. Tilly, 'How Empires End'; Komlosy, 'Habsburgermonarchie'; McGranahan and Stoler, 'Introduction'; Lieven, 'Dilemmas of Empire'; Cooper, 'Empire Multiplied'; idem, 'From Imperial Inclusion'.

9. Saada, *Les enfants de la colonie*; Weil, *Qu'est-ce qu'un Français?*; Cooper, 'Empire Multiplied', 269.

10. On the Ottoman Empire, see Komlosy, 'Habsburgermonarchie'; Lieven, 'Dilemmas of Empire', 192–96; Werth, 'Imperiology and Religion', 53. On the Russian context, see Kirmse, 'Law and Empire'; Werth, 'Imperiology and Religion'; Burbank, 'Imperial Rights', 400–3, 429; Lieven, 'Dilemmas of Empire', 180f. On the nationalization of the Russian metropolis, see Berger and Miller, 'Nation-Building', 318–20. Burbank criticizes this thesis; see 'Imperial Rights', 404–6.

11. Gosewinkel, *Einbürgern und Ausschließen*; Wildenthal, 'Race, Gender, and Citizenship'.

12. For another argument against this dichotomy between modern and traditional empires, see Miller, 'The Value and Limits', 21. On approaches to empires that seek to overcome this dichotomy, see Komlosy, 'Habsburgermonarchie'; Berger and Miller, 'Nation-Building'.

13. Brubaker, *Citizenship*; Argast, *Staatsbürgerschaft*; Gosewinkel, 'Citizenship'.

14. Dummett and Nicol, *Subjects*; Baldwin, *Making*; Fahrmeir, *Citizens and Aliens*.

15. Burbank, 'Imperial Rights', 397, refers to the 'nation-state' as 'a short-lived phenomenon but a long-lived construct'. For a critique of the focus on the nation-state model, see also Banerjee, *Becoming Imperial Citizens*. On the transitions between nation-state and imperial formations, see Hirschhausen and Leonhard, 'Beyond Rise', 31.

16. Berger and Miller, 'Nation-Building', 317; Cole and Unowsky, *The Limits of Loyalty*; Judson, *Guardians*.

17. Lieven, 'Dilemmas of Empire', 188; Berger and Miller, 'Nation-Building', 318f., 321. For an opposing standpoint, see Hoerder, 'Monocultural Nation-State Paradigm', 5.

18. The distinction between cooperation and confrontation is tightly linked to the more common differentiation between moderate and radical forms of nationalism; Komlosy, 'Habsburgermonarchie', 40. On the dismissal of this separation in its strict form, see Cole and Unowsky, *The Limits of Loyalty*; Canny, 'Foreword'; Judson, *Guardians*; Zahra, *Kidnapped Souls*.

19. Cf. Lieven, 'Dilemmas of Empire', 196; Moll, *Kein Burgfrieden*.

20. Deák, 'The Fall'; Healy, 'Becoming Austrian', 34f.

21. See M. Rauchensteiner, *Der Tod des Doppeladlers: Österreich-Ungarn und der Erste Weltkrieg* (Graz: Styria-Verlag, 1993), 178f.; Jászi, *Dissolution*, 16; A. Holzer, *Das Lächeln der Henker: Der unbekannte Krieg gegen die Zivilbevölkerung, 1914–1918* (Darmstadt: Primus, 2008); M. v. Hagen, *War in a European Borderland: Occupations and Occupation Plans in Galicia and Ukraine, 1914–1918* (Seattle, WA: Herbert J. Ellison Center for Russian, East European, and Central Asian Studies, University of Washington, 2007); Miller, 'The Value and Limits', 31; Burger, *Heimatrecht und Staatsbürgerschaft*, 120f.

22. Hirschhausen, 'Von imperialer Inklusion', 17f.; Stourzh, 'Ethnic Attribution'; Burger, *Heimatrecht und Staatsbürgerschaft*, 134–40.

23. See Burger, *Heimatrecht und Staatsbürgerschaft*, 132f.; C. Fink, *Defending the Rights of Others: The Great Powers, the Jews, and International Minority Protection, 1878–1938* (Cambridge: Cambridge University Press, 2004).

24. Stourzh, 'Ethnic Attribution'. King has argued, however, that '[i]n becoming a legal category, nationhood had to lose some of its ethnic essence'; see King, *Budweisers*, 15.

25. In a similar way, Bernhard Struck, 'Grenzziehungen nach dem Ersten Weltkrieg als Problem von Periodisierung und Territorialisierung in einer transnationalen Geschichte

Ostmitteleuropas', *Comparativ: Zeitschrift für Globalgeschichte und vergleichende Gesellschaftsforschung* 20(1–2) (2010): 81–99, 92f., has argued that the turn of the century was a more important caesura than the First World War.

26. Cf. Wingfield, *Flag Wars*; Bader-Zaar, 'Women's Suffrage', 198.

27. Andrew, 'Women as Citizens', 96.

28. Nichols, *Indians*, 254–56. Pearson puts forth a different claim; see Pearson, 'Theorizing Citizenship', 993.

29. Knowles, *Forging our Legacy*. On the intensification of ethnically exclusive policies in Canada within the context of the First World War, see also Day, *Multiculturalism*, 139; P.E. Roy, *The Oriental Question: Consolidating a White Man's Province, 1914–41* (Vancouver: University of British Columbia Press, 2003).

30. See T.R. Metcalf, *Imperial Connections: India in the Indian Ocean Arena, 1860–1920* (Berkeley, CA: University of California Press, 2007), 68–135.

31. *The Montagu-Chelmsford Reform Proposals*, 133f.; Besant, *India's Hour*, 1f.

32. Gregory, *India and East Africa*, 181f.

33. London, PRO, HO 45/10836/330000.

34. London, PRO, HO 213/777, The Origins of HO Documents of Identity (for Aliens). See also D. Cesarani, 'Anti-Alienism in England after the First World War', *Immigrants and Minorities* 6(1) (1987), 5–29; Dummett and Nicol, *Subjects*, 145f., 160f.

35. On the ethnicization of British law after 1945, see Paul, *Whitewashing Britain*; Dummett and Nicol, *Subjects*; Cesarani, 'The Changing Character'; Harper and Constantine, *Migration*, 6.

36. See R. Hyam, *Britain's Declining Empire: The Road to Decolonisation, 1918–1968* (Cambridge: Cambridge University Press, 2006); Biagini, *British Democracy*. Interestingly, Hart, *The I.R.A. at War*, interprets the conflicts in Ireland as an ethnic power struggle, while F. Keisinger, *Unzivilisierte Kriege im zivilisierten Europa? Die Balkankriege und die öffentliche Meinung in Deutschland, England und Irland 1876–1913* (Paderborn: Schöningh, 2008), 141f., compares the situation in Ireland to the violence that occurred in South Eastern Europe at the same time.

37. Komlosy describes the nationalization processes as an endogenous 'motor' and the war as the exogenous 'catalyst' for the disintegration of the Habsburg Empire; see 'Habsburgermonarchie', 13, 22, 36. See also Lieven, 'Dilemmas of Empire', 190, 199.

38. D.L. Unowsky, *The Pomp and Politics of Patriotism: Imperial Celebrations in Habsburg Austria, 1848–1916* (West Lafayette, IN: Purdue University Press, 2005), 184; G.B. Cohen, 'Neither Absolutism nor Anarchy: New Narratives on Society and Government in Late Imperial Austria', *Austrian History Yearbook* 29(1) (1998), 37–61; Veliz, *Politics*, 65; Fillafer, 'The "Imperial Idea"'.

39. See Lieven, 'Dilemmas of Empire', 190f.

40. On the issue of whether this disintegration process can actually be described as peaceful, see S. Stockwell, 'Ends of Empire', in S. Stockwell (ed.), *The British Empire: Themes and Perspectives* (Malden, MA: Blackwell, 2008), 270.

41. Cooper, 'Empire Multiplied', 270; Berger and Miller, 'Nation-Building', 321.

42. See, for example, D. Hüchtker, 'Rückständigkeit als Strategie oder Galizien als Zentrum europäischer Frauenpolitik: Beitrag zum Themenschwerpunkt "Europäische Geschichte – Geschlechtergeschichte"', *Themenportal Europäische Geschichte* (2009), retrieved 22 February 2017 from http://www.europa.clio-online.de/essay/id/artikel-3549.

43. See Geulen, *Wahlverwandte*, 42.

44. On the growing significance of civil society structures in the Habsburg context, see Unowsky, *The Pomp and Politics*; Lieven, 'Dilemmas of Empire', 190; Cohen, 'Nationalist Politics', 244.

45. See H. Reinalter (ed.), *Josephinismus als aufgeklärter Absolutismus* (Vienna: Böhlau, 2008).

46. Reifowitz speaks of an inclusive 'civic nationalism' in the Cisleithanian context; see I. Reifowitz, *Imagining an Austrian Nation: Joseph Samuel Bloch and the Search for a Multiethnic Austrian Identity, 1846–1919* (Boulder, CO: East European Monographs, 2003), 9.

47. S. Benhabib, *The Claims of Culture: Equality and Diversity in the Global Era* (Princeton, NJ: Princeton University Press, 2002); Banerjee, *Becoming Imperial Citizens*.

48. K. Henrard and R. Dunbar (eds), *Synergies in Minority Protection: European and International Law Perspectives* (Cambridge: Cambridge University Press, 2008).

49. Day, *Multiculturalism*; Winter, 'Neither "America" nor "Québec"'. On the present-day implications of ethnic heterogeneity in Austria, see Lieven, 'Dilemmas of Empire', 188f.

BIBLIOGRAPHY

Archives

London
Public Records Office (PRO)
Colonial Office (CO)
    Foreign Office (FO)
    Home Office (HO)
    Registrar General (RG)
    General Registrar's Office (GRO)

India Office Records (IOR)
    Public and Judicial (L/PJ)
    Private Office Papers (L/PO)
    Official Publications (V)
    European Manuscripts (Mss. Eur.)

Vienna, Austrian State Archives
    Haus-, Hof- und Staatsarchiv (HHStA)
        Ministerium des Äußern (MdÄ), Administrative Registratur (Adm. Reg.)
            F 8: Konsulate
            F 15: Auswanderung
            F 57: Untertanen, Staatsangehörigkeit
            F 61: Bosnien und Herzegowina
        Ministerium des Äußern (MdÄ), Politisches Archiv (Pol. Arch.)
            XXXX.: Interna 1848–1918
            Konsulatsarchiv Jerusalem
    Allgemeines Verwaltungsarchiv (AVA)
        Ministerium des Innern (MdI), Allgemeine Reihe (Allg.)
            8: Staatsbürgerschaft
            11: Heimatrecht
        Ministerium des Innern (MdI), Präsidiale Reihe (Präs.)
            8: Staatsbürgerschaft
            31: Landtage

Legislation

Canada
The Indian Act, 1876.

An Act to Amend the Acts Relating to Naturalization and Aliens, 1903.
Immigration Act, 1910.

India
Act 25 of 1861 (Code of Criminal Procedure)
Act 3 of 1864 (Foreigners)
Act 6 of 1869 (Emigration)
Act 22 of 1870 (European British Subjects)
Act 7 of 1871 (Indian Emigration)
Act 10 of 1871
Act 10 of 1872
Act 3 of 1884 (Code of Criminal Procedure)
Act 5 of 1898
Act 14 of 1910 (Emigration)
Act 3 of 1915 (Foreigners Amendment)

Austria
Allgemeines Bürgerliches Gesetzbuch (ABGB)
RGBl. 1871, Nr. 74 (Bancroft-Treaty)
RGBl. 1879, Nr. 43 (Bosnia)
RGBl. 1896, Nr. 105 (Legal Residence, *Heimatrecht*)

Hungary
GA L from 1879 (Nationality)
GA IV from 1886 (Renaturalization)
GA IV from 1903 (Emigration)
GA II from 1909 (Emigration)

United Kingdom
33 Vict. ch. 14   Naturalization (1870)
53&54 Vict. c. 7   Foreign Jurisdiction Act (1890)
5 Edw. 7 ch. 18   Unemployed Workmen (1905)
5 Edw. 7 ch. 13   Aliens (1905)
8 Edw. 7 ch. 40   Old Age Pensions (1908)
1&2 Geo. 5 ch. 55   National Insurance (1911)
4&5 Geo. 5 ch. 17   British Nationality and Status of Aliens (1914)

Government Publications

Canada
Annual Report of the Department of Indian Affairs, Ottawa, 1885.
Annual Report of the Department of Indian Affairs, Ottawa, 1890.

East Africa
East Africa Legislative Council: London, PRO, CO 544/2 and 6, Minutes of the Legislative
    Council.
East Africa Executive Council: London, PRO, CO 544/3 and 14, Minutes of the Executive
    Council.

India

Indian Legislative Council: (Abstract of the) Proceedings of the Council of the Governor General of India, assembled for the purpose of making laws and regulations, Calcutta.

General Rules and Orders made under Enactments in force in British India, Calcutta, 1915.

General Rules and Orders made under Enactments in force in British India, Calcutta, 1907.

Austria

Abgeordnetenhaus des österreichischen Reichsrats: Stenographische Protokolle der Sitzungen des Abgeordnetenhauses des Reichsrats, Wien.

Das Wehrgesetz für Bosnien und die Herzegovina von 1912. Erläutert von Oberst Carl Czapp, Wien 1912.

Provisorisches Wehrgesetz für Bosnien und die Herzegovina und Instruction zur Ausführung desselben, Wien 1881.

United Kingdom

UK Parliament, *Commons and Lords: The Parliamentary Debates*, House of Commons, House of Lords, London.

Colonial Conference 1907, Command Paper No. 3524, House of Commons, London.

Report of the Inter-departmental Committee Appointed to Consider the Doubts and Difficulties which Have Arisen in Connexion with the Interpretation and Administration of the Acts Relating to Naturalization, London, 1901.

Periodicals

Pester Lloyd, Budapest.

Arbeiterinnen-Zeitung, Vienna.

Der Bund, Vienna.

Zeitschrift für Frauenstimmrecht, Vienna.

Monographs

Adler, V. *Das allgemeine, gleiche und direkte Wahlrecht und das Wahlunrecht in Oesterreich.* Vienna: Bretschneider, 1893.

Balogh, P. 'Die Wahlbezirke und die Nationalitäten'. *Pester Lloyd*, 8 November 1908.

Bauer, O. *Die Nationalitätenfrage und die Sozialdemokratie.* Vienna: Brand, 1907.

Berényi, S. *Der Erwerb und der Verlust der ungarischen Staatsbürgerschaft*, trans. I. Schwartz. Leipzig: Duncker & Humblot, 1906.

Bernatzik, E. *Über nationale Matriken: Inaugurationsrede.* Vienna: Manz, 1910.

——— (ed.). *Die österreichischen Verfassungsgesetze: Mit Erläuterungen*, 2nd edn. Vienna: Manz, 1911.

Besant, A. *India's Hour of Destiny: Being the Address of the Chairman of the Reception Committee of the Special Madras Provincial Conference, Aug 3 1918.* Adyar: Commonweal Office, 1918.

Caro, L. *Auswanderung und Auswanderungspolitik in Österreich.* Leipzig: Duncker & Humblot, 1909.

Davey, H. *Poor Law Settlement and Removal.* London: Stevens and Sons, 1908.

Dicey, A.V. 'A Common Citizenship for the English Race'. *Contemporary Review* 71 (April 1897), 457–76.

Evans, D.O. *The Old Age Pensions Act, 1908: With Notes.* London: Sweet & Maxwell, 1908.

Fischhof, A. *Oesterreich und die Bürgschaften seines Bestandes: Politische Studie.* Vienna: Wallishausser, 1869.

Freisler, W. 'Der mährische Ausgleich'. *Deutschradikales Jahrbuch mit Zeitweiser für 1913* 1 (1912), 206–11.

Fürth, E. von. 'Die Teilnovelle zum allgemeinen bürgerlichen Gesetzbuche'. *Der Bund* 9(9) (1914), 1–5.

Gaertner, F. *Der Ausbau der Sozialversicherung in Oesterreich.* Tübingen: Laupp Jr., 1909.

Groedel, A. *Die Ersitzung der Staatsangehörigkeit.* Greifswald: J. Abel, 1894.

Gumplowicz, L. *Das Recht der Nationalitäten und Sprachen in Oesterreich-Ungarn.* Innsbruck: Wagner, 1879.

Harrasowsky, P.H. Ritter von. *Geschichte der Codification des österreichischen Civilrechtes.* Vienna: Manz, 1868.

Hart, E.L. de. 'The English Law of Nationality and Naturalisation'. *Journal of the Society of Comparative Legislation* 2(1) (1900), 11–26.

Heimfelsen, J.K. *Die deutschen Kolonien in Bosnien.* Vienna: Gerold & Co., 1911.

Henriques, H.S.Q. *The Law of Aliens and Naturalization: Including the Text of the Aliens Act 1905.* London: Butterworth, 1906.

Herrnritt, R.H. von. *Nationalität und Recht dargestellt nach der österreichischen und ausländischen Gesetzgebung.* Vienna: Manz, 1899.

———. 'Die Ausgestaltung des österreichischen Nationalitätenrechts durch den Ausgleich in Mähren und in der Bukowina'. *Österreichische Zeitschrift für öffentliches Recht* 1(5–6) (1914), 583–95.

Herzfelder, H. 'Die Stellungnahme der Frauen zum Reformentwurf des bürgerlichen Gesetzbuches'. *Der Bund* 8(4) (1913), 13–14.

——— (H. H.). 'Die Novelle zum allg[emeinen] bürgerl[ichen] Gesetzbuche'. *Zeitschrift für Frauenstimmrecht* 4(8) (1914), 2.

Hoare, H.J. *Old Age Pensions: Their Actual Working and Ascertained Results in the United Kingdom.* London: P.S. King, 1915.

Hobley, C.W. *Kenya from Chartered Company to Crown Colony: 30 Years of Exploration and Administration in British East Africa,* 2nd edn. London: Cass, 1970.

Howell, A. *Naturalization and Nationality in Canada: Expatriation and Repatriation of British Subjects; Aliens their Disabilities and their Privileges in Canada.* Toronto: Carswell & Co., 1884.

Jebb, R. *Studies in Colonial Nationalism.* London: E. Arnold, 1905.

———. 'The Imperial Problem of Asiatic Immigration'. *Journal of the Royal Society of Arts* 56(2892) (1908), 585–603.

Kaan, J. 'Die Arbeiter-Unfallversicherung in Oesterreich', in Special-Comité für Socialökonomie, Hygiene und öffentliches Hilfswesen (ed.), *Sociale Verwaltung in Österreich am Ende des 19. Jahrhunderts.* Vol. 1, *Socialökonomie* (Vienna: Franz Deuticke, 1900), 1–24.

Karminski, F. *Zur Codification des österreichischen Staatsbürgerschaftsrechtes: Eine staatsrechtliche Studie.* Vienna: Manz, 1887.

Lusk, H.H. *Social Welfare in New Zealand: The Result of Twenty Years of Progressive Social Legislation and its Significance for the United States and Other Countries.* London: Heinemann, 1913.

Meinecke, F. *Weltbürgertum und Nationalstaat: Studien zur Genesis des deutschen Nationalstaates.* Munich: Oldenbourg, 1908.

Milner, E. *Die österreichische Staatsbürgerschaft und der Gesetzesartikel L:1879 über den Erwerb und Verlust der ungarischen Staatsbürgerschaft.* Tübingen: F. Fues, 1880.

The Montagu-Chelmsford Reform Proposals: With a Foreword by Annie Besant. Madras: Sons of India, n.d. (ca. 1918).

Morris, H.L. *Parliamentary Franchise Reform in England from 1885 to 1918*. New York: Columbia University, 1921.

Neo-Fabian Society. *Problems of Reform in the Government of India*. Madras: Neo-Fabian Society, 1919.

Odgers, W.B. *Nationality and Naturalization*. London: Jordan, 1916.

Parker, E.W. *Outlines of Constitutional Law—India: Containing a Summary of the Statutes of Parliament Relating to the Government of India, Including the Indian Councils Acts, 1861–1909, and the Regulations made thereunder*. Allahabad: Pioneer Press, 1910.

Polner, E. von. 'Das Staatsrecht des Königreichs Ungarn und seiner Mitländer', in A. von Berzeviczy (ed.), *Ungarn: Land und Volk, Geschichte, Staatsrecht, Verwaltung und Rechtspflege, Landwirtschaft, Industrie und Handel, Schulwesen, wissenschaftliches Leben, Literatur, bildende Künste* (Budapest: Verlag des Franklin-Vereines, 1917), 214–67.

Popovici, A.C. *Die Vereinigten Staaten von Groß-Österreich: Politische Studien zur Lösung der nationalen Fragen und staatsrechtlichen Krisen in Österreich-Ungarn*. Leipzig: Elischer, 1906.

Reeves, W.P. *Das politische Wahlrecht der Frauen in Australien*, trans. R. Grazer. Leipzig: Dietrich, 1904.

'Die Reform des Allgemeinen Bürgerlichen Gesetzbuches'. *Der Bund* 3(1) (1908), 1–3.

Russ, V. *Der Sprachenstreit in Oesterreich: Ein Beitrag zur sprachlichen Ordnung in der Verwaltung*. Vienna: Konegen, 1884.

Salmond, J.W. 'Citizenship and Allegiance'. *Law Quarterly Review* 18(69) (1902), 49–63.

Sanyal, R.G. (ed.). *The Record of Criminal Cases: As between Europeans and Natives for the Last Hundred Years*, 2nd edn. Calcutta: Sanyal & Co., 1896.

A Scheme for Reforms: Passed by the National Congress on Dec 29 1916, and by the All-India Muslim League on Dec 31 1916. Adyar: Commonweal Office, 1917.

Schmid, F. *Bosnien und die Herzegovina unter d. Verwaltung Österreich-Ungarns*. Leipzig: Veit, 1914.

Schubert, A. *Das Deutschtum im Wirtschaftshaushalte Österreichs*. Vol. 2, *Die Abgabenleistungen d. Deutschen in Österr. an den Staat*. Reichenberg: R. Gerzabek & Co., 1906.

Scott, D.C. 'Indian Affairs, 1867–1912', in A. Shortt and A.G. Doughty (eds), *Canada and its Provinces: A History of the Canadian People and their Institutions by One Hundred Associates*. Vol. 7, *The Dominion: Political Evolution* (Toronto: Glasgow, Brook & Company, 1914), 593–626.

Scott, W.D. 'Immigration and Population', in A. Shortt and A.G. Doughty (eds), *Canada and its Provinces: A History of the Canadian People and their Institutions by One Hundred Associates*. Vol. 7, *The Dominion: Political Evolution* (Toronto: Glasgow, Brook & Company, 1914), 517–90.

Seeley, J.R. *The Expansion of England: Two Courses of Lectures*, rev. edn. Leipzig: Tauchnitz, 1884.

Seymour, C. *Electoral Reform in England and Wales: The Development and Operation of the Parliamentary Franchise, 1832–1885*. New Haven, CT: Yale University Press, 1915.

Shaw, A. 'An American View of Home Rule and Federation'. *Contemporary Review* 62 (September 1892), 305–18.

Skene, A. Freiherr von. *Der nationale Ausgleich in Mähren 1905.* Vienna: Konegen, 1910.

Special-Comité für Socialökonomie, Hygiene und öffentliches Hilfswesen (ed.). *Sociale Verwaltung in Oesterreich am Ende des 19. Jahrhunderts: Aus Anlass der Weltausstellung Paris 1900*, 2 vols. Vienna: Deuticke, 1900.

Spitzer, M. 'Zur Reform des bürgerlichen Gesetzbuches'. Pts. 1 and 2. *Der Bund* 3(2) (1908), 4–5; and 4(8) (1909), 1–3.

Springer, R. [K. Renner]. *Der Kampf der österreichischen Nationen um den Staat: Theil 1: Das nationale Problem als Verfassungs- und Verwaltungsfrage.* Leipzig: Deuticke, 1902.

———. *Grundlagen und Entwicklungsziele der Österreichisch-Ungarischen Monarchie.* Vienna: Deuticke, 1906.

'Die Stellung der Frau im Rechte der Kulturstaaten', *Arbeiterinnen-Zeitung* 21(25) (1912), 2–3.

Strakosch-Graßmann, G. *Das allgemeine Wahlrecht in Österreich seit 1848.* Leipzig: Deuticke, 1906.

Thon, J. *Die Juden in Oesterreich.* Berlin: Lamm, 1908.

Ulbrich, J. *Das Staatsrecht der österreichisch-ungarischen Monarchie.* Freiburg im Breisgau: Mohr, 1884.

Winter, F. 'Die Reform des bürgerlichen Rechtes'. Pts. 1 to 4, *Arbeiterinnen-Zeitung* 17(7–10) (1908).

Source Collections

Bolognese-Leuchtenmüller, B. *Wirtschafts- und Sozialstatistik Österreich-Ungarns.* Vol. 1, *Bevölkerungsentwicklung und Berufsstruktur, Gesundheits- und Fürsorgewesen in Österreich 1750–1918.* Vienna: Verlag für Geschichte und Politik, 1978.

Dodd, W.F. (ed.). *Modern Constitutions: A Collection of the Fundamental Laws of Twenty-Two of the Most Important Countries of the World, With Historical and Bibliographical Notes.* Chicago, IL: The University of Chicago Press, 1909.

Keith, A.B. (ed.). *Speeches & Documents on Indian Policy 1750–1921.* Vol. 1. London: Milford, 1922.

Komjáthy, M. (ed.). *Protokolle des Gemeinsamen Ministerrates der Österreichisch-Ungarischen Monarchie: 1914–1918.* Budapest: Akadémiai Kiadó, 1966.

Ollivier, M. (ed.). *The Colonial and Imperial Conferences from 1887 to 1937.* Vol. 2, *Imperial Conferences.* Ottawa: Cloutier, 1954.

Slattery, B., and L. Charlton (eds). *Canadian Native Law Cases.* Vol. 2, *1870–1890.* Saskatoon: University of Saskatchewan, Native Law Centre, 1981.

Smith, D.G. (ed.). *Canadian Indians and the Law: Selected Documents, 1663–1972.* Toronto: McClelland, 1975.

Secondary Literature

Abour, C.O. *White Highlands No More.* Nairobi: Pan African Researchers, 1970.

Agamben, G. *Homo Sacer: Sovereign Power and Bare Life*, trans. D. Heller-Roazen. Stanford, CA: Stanford University Press, 1998. Originally Published as *Homo Sacer: Il potere sovrano e la nuda vita* (Turin: Einaudi, 1995).

Alderman, G. (ed.). *Governments, Ethnic Groups and Political Representation.* Aldershot: Dartmouth, 1993.

Amesberger, H., and B. Halbmayr. 'Race/"Rasse" und Whiteness: Adäquate Begriffe zur Analyse gesellschaftlicher Ungleichheit?' *L'Homme* 16(2) (2005), 135–43.

Andrew, C. 'Women as Citizens in Canada', in P. Boyer, L. Cardinal and D. Headon (eds), *From Subjects to Citizens: A Hundred Years of Citizenship in Australia and Canada* (Ottawa: University of Ottawa Press, 2004), 95–106.

Argast, R. *Staatsbürgerschaft und Nation: Ausschließung und Integration in der Schweiz 1848–1933*. Göttingen: Vandenhoeck & Ruprecht, 2007.

Ashplant, T.G. 'Dis/Connecting Whiteness: Biographical Perspectives on Race, Class, Masculinity and Sexuality in Britain c.1850–1930'. *L'Homme* 16(2) (2005), 68–85 (doi: 10.7767/lhomme.2005.16.2.68).

Babejová, E. *Fin-de-Siècle Pressburg: Conflict & Cultural Coexistence in Bratislava 1897–1914*. New York: Columbia University Press, 2003.

Bader-Zaar, B. 'Foreigners and the Law in Nineteenth-Century Austria: Juridical Concepts and Legal Rights in the Light of the Development of Citizenship', in A. Fahrmeir, O. Faron and P. Weil (eds), *Migration Control in the North Atlantic World: The Evolution of State Practices in Europe and the United States from the French Revolution to the Inter-War Period* (New York: Berghahn Books, 2003), 138–52.

———. 'Women's Suffrage and War: World War I and Political Reform in a Comparative Perspective', in I. Sulkunen, S. Nevala-Nurmi and P. Markkola (eds), *Suffrage, Gender and Citizenship: International Perspectives on Parliamentary Reforms* (Newcastle: Cambridge Scholars Publishing, 2009), 193–218.

———. 'Gaining the Vote in a World of Transition: Female Suffrage in Austria', in B. Rodríguez-Ruiz and R. Rubio-Marín (eds), *The Struggle for Female Suffrage in Europe: Voting to Become Citizens* (Leiden: Brill, 2012), 191–206.

Baier, D. *Sprache und Recht im alten Österreich: Art. 19 des Staatsgrundgesetzes vom 21. Dezember 1867, seine Stellung im System der Grundrechte und seine Ausgestaltung durch die oberstgerichtliche Rechtsprechung*. Munich: Oldenbourg, 1983.

Baldwin, M.P. 'Subject to Empire: Married Women and the British Nationality and Status of Aliens Act'. *Journal of British Studies* 40(4) (2001), 522–56.

———. 'Making British Subjects: The Development of British Nationality Law, 1870–1939'. Ph.D. dissertation. University of London, 2003.

Ballhatchet, K. *Race, Sex and Class under the Raj: Imperial Attitudes and Policies and their Critics, 1793–1905*. London: Weidenfeld and Nicolson, 1980.

Banerjee, S. *Becoming Imperial Citizens: Indians in the Late-Victorian Empire*. Durham, NC: Duke University Press, 2010.

Banton, M. *Racial Theories*, 2nd edn. Cambridge: Cambridge University Press, 1998.

Barkey, K. 'Thinking about Consequences of Empire', in K. Barkey and M. von Hagen (eds), *After Empire: Multiethnic Societies and Nation-Building* (Boulder, CO: Westview Press, 1997), 99–114.

Barkey, K., and M. von Hagen. Conclusion to *After Empire: Multiethnic Societies and Nation-Building* (Boulder, CO: Westview Press, 1997), 181–89.

Barth, F. (ed.). *Ethnic Groups and Boundaries: The Social Organization of Culture Difference*. Boston, MA: Little, Brown & Company, 1969.

Bashford, A. *Imperial Hygiene: A Critical History of Colonialism, Nationalism and Public Health*. Basingstoke: Palgrave Macmillan, 2004.

Bauböck, R., A. Heller and A.R. Zolberg (eds). *The Challenge of Diversity: Integration and Pluralism in Societies of Immigration*. Aldershot: Avebury, 1996.

Bayly, S. *Caste, Society and Politics in India from the Eighteenth Century to the Modern Age*. Cambridge: Cambridge University Press, 1999.

Belich, J. *Replenishing the Earth: The Settler Revolution and the Rise of the Anglo-World, 1783–1939.* Oxford: Oxford University Press, 2009.

Belmessous, S. *Assimilation and Empire: Uniformity in French and British Colonies, 1541–1954.* Oxford: Oxford University Press, 2013.

Bendix, R. 'Ethnology, Cultural Reification, and the Dynamics of Difference in the Kronprinzenwerk', in N.M. Wingfield (ed.), *Creating the Other: Ethnic Conflict and Nationalism in Habsburg Central Europe* (New York: Berghahn Books, 2003), 149–66.

Benhabib, S. *The Claims of Culture: Equality and Diversity in the Global Era.* Princeton, NJ: Princeton University Press, 2002.

Benton, L. *A Search for Sovereignty: Law and Geography in European Empires, 1400–1900.* Cambridge: Cambridge University Press, 2010.

Berchtold, J. *Recht und Gerechtigkeit in der Konsulargerichtsbarkeit: Britische Exterritorialität im Osmanischen Reich 1825–1914.* Munich: Oldenbourg, 2009.

Berger, S., and A. Miller. 'Nation-Building and Regional Integration, c. 1800–1914: The Role of Empires'. *European Review of History* 15(3) (2008), 317–30 (doi: 10.1080/13507480802082649).

Berry, B., and H.L. Tischler. *Race and Ethnic Relations*, 4th edn. Boston, MA: Houghton Mifflin, 1978.

Bevan, V. *The Development of British Immigration Law.* London: Croom Helm, 1986.

Bhaba, H.K. *The Location of Culture*, reprint. London: Routledge, 1994.

Bhattacharya, S. 'Reflections on Intersectionality: Bell Hooks'. *Indian Journal of Dalit and Tribal Social Work* 1(1) (2012), 61–90.

Biagini, E.F. *British Democracy and Irish Nationalism 1876–1906.* Cambridge: Cambridge University Press, 2007.

Bickers, R. 'Introduction: Britains and Britons over the Seas', in R. Bickers (ed.), *Settlers and Expatriates: Britons over the Seas* (Oxford: Oxford University Press, 2010), 1–17.

Bittiger, T. *An Elite in Transition: The Muslims of Bosnia and Hercegovina under Austro-Hungarian Rule, 1878–1914.* Berlin: Osteuropa-Institut der Freien Universität Berlin, 2001.

Boghardt, T. *Spies of the Kaiser: German Covert Operations in Great Britain during the First World War Era.* Basingstoke: Palgrave Macmillan, 2004.

Bose, N.S. *Racism, Struggle for Equality and Indian Nationalism.* Calcutta: KLM, 1981.

Bose, S., and A. Jalal. *Modern South Asia: History, Culture, Political Economy.* Delhi: Oxford University Press, 1997.

Boyer, J.W. *Karl Lueger (1844–1910): Christlichsoziale Politik als Beruf*, trans. O. Binder. Vienna: Böhlau, 2010.

Britz, G. *Kulturelle Rechte und Verfassung: Über den rechtlichen Umgang mit kultureller Differenz.* Tübingen: Mohr Siebeck, 2000.

Brix, E. *Die Umgangssprachen in Altösterreich zwischen Agitation und Assimilation: Die Sprachenstatistik in den zisleithanischen Volkszählungen 1880–1910.* Vienna: Böhlau, 1982.

Brownlie, R.J. '"A Better Citizen than Lots of White Men": First Nations Enfranchisement – An Ontario Case Study, 1918–1940'. *Canadian Historical Review* 87(1) (2006), 29–52.

Brubaker, R. *Citizenship and Nationhood in France and Germany.* Cambridge, MA: Harvard University Press, 1992.

———. *Ethnicity without Groups.* Cambridge: Harvard University Press, 2004.

Brubaker, R., and F. Cooper. 'Beyond "Identity"'. *Theory and Society* 29(1) (2000), 1–47 (doi: 10.1023/A:1007068714468).

Burbank, J. 'An Imperial Rights Regime: Law and Citizenship in the Russian Empire'. *Kritika* 7(3) (2006), 397–431 (doi: 10.1353/kri.2006.0031).

Burbank, J., and F. Cooper. *Empires in World History: Power and the Politics of Difference*. Prineton, NJ: Princeton University Press, 2010.

Burger, H. *Sprachenrecht und Sprachengerechtigkeit im österreichischen Unterrichtswesen: 1867– 1918*. Vienna: Verlag der Österreichischen Akademie der Wissenschaften, 1995.

———. 'Passwesen und Staatsbürgerschaft', in W. Heindl and E. Saurer (eds), *Grenze und Staat: Paßwesen, Staatsbürgerschaft, Heimatrecht und Fremdengesetzgebung in der öster- reichischen Monarchie 1750–1867* (Vienna: Böhlau, 2000), 1–173.

———. *Heimatrecht und Staatsbürgerschaft österreichischer Juden: Vom Ende des 18. Jahrhunderts bis in die Gegenwart*. Vienna: Böhlau, 2014.

Burton, A. (ed.). *After the Imperial Turn: Thinking with and through the Nation*. Durham, NC: Duke University Press, 2003.

Cannadine, D. *Ornamentalism: How the British Saw their Empire*. Oxford: Oxford University Press, 2001.

Canny, N. 'Foreword' to *Ireland and the British Empire*, edited by Kevin Kenny (Oxford: Oxford University Press, 2005), ix–xix.

Caplan, J., and J. Torpey (eds). *Documenting Individual Identity: The Development of State Practices in the Modern World*. Princeton, NJ: Princeton University Press, 2001.

Carey, H.M. *God's Empire: Religion and Colonialism in the British World, c.1801–1908*. Cambridge: Cambridge University Press, 2011.

Carter, S. *Aboriginal People and Colonizers of Western Canada to 1900*. Toronto: University of Toronto Press, 1999.

Cattaruzza, M. *Sozialisten an der Adria: Plurinationale Arbeiterbewegung in der Habsburg- ermonarchie*, trans. Karin Krieg. Berlin: Duncker & Humblot, 2011.

Cesarani, D. 'Anti-Alienism in England after the First World War'. *Immigrants and Minorities* 6(1) (1987), 5–29 (doi: 10.1080/02619288.1987.9974645).

———. 'The Changing Character of Citizenship and Nationality in Britain', in D. Cesarani and M. Fulbrook (eds), *Citizenship, Nationality and Migration in Europe* (London: Routledge, 1996), 57–73.

Claussen, D. *Was heißt Rassismus?* Darmstadt: Wissenschaftliche Buchgesellschaft, 1994.

Cohen, A.P. (ed.). *Signifying Identities: Anthropological Perspectives on Boundaries and Contested Values*. London: Routledge, 2000.

Cohen, D., and M. O'Connor (eds). *Comparison and History: Europe in Cross-National Perspective*. New York: Routledge, 2004.

Cohen, G.B. 'Neither Absolutism nor Anarchy: New Narratives on Society and Government in Late Imperial Austria'. *Austrian History Yearbook* 29(1) (1998), 37–61 (doi: 10.1017/ S006723780001479X).

———. 'Nationalist Politics and the Dynamics of State and Civil Society in the Habsburg Monarchy, 1867–1914'. *Central European History* 40(2) (2007), 241–78 (doi: 10.1017/ S0008938907000532).

Cohn, B.S. *The Census, Social Structure and Objectification in South Asia*, reprint. Copenhagen: Soertryk, 1984.

———. *India: The Social Anthropology of a Civilization*. New Delhi: Oxford University Press, 2000.

Cole, L., and D.L. Unowsky (eds). *The Limits of Loyalty: Imperial Symbolism, Popular Allegiances, and State Patriotism in the Late Habsburg Monarchy*. New York: Berghahn Books, 2007.

Colley, L. *Captives: Britain, Empire and the World, 1600–1850*. London: Jonathan Cape, 2002.

Collingham, E.M. *Imperial Bodies: The Physical Experience of the Raj, c. 1800–1947*. Cambridge: Polity, 2001.

Conrad, C., and J. Kocka. 'Einführung', in C. Conrad and J. Kocka (eds), *Staatsbürgerschaft in Europa: Historische Erfahrungen und aktuelle Debatten* (Hamburg: Ed. Körber-Stiftung, 2001), 9–28.

Conrad, S. 'Doppelte Marginalisierung: Plädoyer für eine transnationale Perspektive auf die deutsche Geschichte'. *Geschichte und Gesellschaft* 28(1) (2002), 145–69.

Conze, W. 'Rasse', in O. Brunner, W. Conze and R. Koselleck (eds), *Geschichtliche Grundbegriffe*. Vol. 5, *Pro–Soz*, reprint (Stuttgart: Klett-Cotta, 1994), 135–78.

Cooper, F. 'Empire Multiplied: A Review Essay'. *Comparative Studies in Society and History* 46(2) (2004), 247–72 (doi: 10.1017/S0010417504000131).

———. 'From Imperial Inclusion to Republican Exclusion? France's Ambiguous Postwar Trajectory', in C. Tshimanga, D. Gondola and P.J. Bloom (eds), *Frenchness and the Africa Diaspora: Identity and Uprising in Contemporary France* (Bloomington, IN: Indiana University Press, 2009), 91–119.

———. *Citizenship between Empire and Nation: Remaking France and French Africa, 1945–1960*. Princeton, NJ: Princeton University Press, 2014.

Crossman, V. *Politics, Pauperism and Power in Late Nineteenth-Century Ireland*. Manchester: Manchester University Press, 2006.

Csáky, M. 'Die Vielfalt der Habsburgermonarchie und die nationale Frage', in U. Altermatt (ed.), *Nation, Ethnizität und Staat in Mitteleuropa* (Vienna: Böhlau, 1996), 44–64.

Csizmadia, A. 'Die Entwicklung des ungarischen Staatsbürgerschaftsrechts', in H. Lentze and P. Putzer (eds), *Festschrift für Ernst Carl Hellbling* (Salzburg: Fink, 1971), 93–126.

Darwin, J. 'Imperial Twilight, or When Did the Empire End?', in Phillip Buckner (ed.), *Canada and the End of Empire* (Vancouver: UBC Press, 2005), 15–24.

———. 'Britain's Empires', in S. Stockwell (ed.), *The British Empire: Themes and Perspectives* (Malden, MA: Blackwell, 2008), 1–20.

Daviron, B. 'Mobilizing Labour in African Agriculture: The Role of the International Colonial Institute in the Elaboration of a Standard of Colonial Administration, 1895–1930'. *Journal of Global History* 5(3) (2010), 479–501 (doi: 10.1017/S1740022810000239).

Day, R.J.F. *Multiculturalism and the History of Canadian Diversity*. Toronto: University of Toronto Press, 2000.

Deák, I. *Beyond Nationalism: A Social and Political History of the Habsburg Officer Corps 1848–1918*. New York: Oxford University Press, 1990.

———. 'The Fall of Austria-Hungary: Peace, Stability, and Legitimacy', in Geir Lundestad (ed.), *The Fall of Great Powers: Peace, Stability, and Legitimacy* (Oslo: Scandinavian University Press, 1994), 81–102.

Deak, J. *Forging a Multinational State: State Making in Imperial Austria from the Enlightenment to the First World War*. Stanford, CA: Stanford University Press, 2015.

Dikötter, F. 'The Racialization of the Globe: An Interactive Interpretation'. *Ethnic and Racial Studies* 31(8) (2008), 1478–96 (doi: 10.1080/01419870802208388).

Donia, R.J. *Islam under the Double Eagle: The Muslims of Bosnia and Hercegovina, 1878–1914*. New York: East European Quarterly, 1981.

Dudink, S., K. Hagemann and A. Clark (eds). *Representing Masculinity: Male Citizenship in Modern Western Culture*. New York: Palgrave Macmillan, 2007.

Dummett, A. *Citizenship and Nationality*. London: Battley, 1976.

Dummett, A., and A. Nicol. *Subjects, Citizens, Aliens and Others: Nationality and Immigration Law*. London: Weidenfeld and Nicolson, 1990.

Eisenstadt, S.N. *The Political Systems of Empires*. New York: Free Press, 1969.

——— (ed.). *Multiple Modernities*. New Brunswick, NJ: Transaction Publishers, 2002.

Emerson, R. *From Empire to Nation: The Rise to Self-Assertion of Asian and African People*. Cambridge, MA: Harvard University Press, 1967.

Erikson, T.H. *Ethnicity and Nationalism: Anthropological Perspectives*. London: Pluto Press, 1993.

Esser, H. 'Ethnische Differenzierung und moderne Gesellschaft'. *Zeitschrift für Soziologie* 17(4) (1988), 235–48 (doi: 10.1515/zfsoz-1988-0401).

Evans, R.J.W. *Austria, Hungary, and the Habsburgs: Essays on Central Europe c. 1683–1867*. Oxford: Oxford University Press, 2006.

Fahrmeir, A.K. 'Nineteenth-Century German Citizenships: A Reconsideration'. *Historical Journal* 40(3) (1997), 721–52.

———. *Citizens and Aliens: Foreigners and the Law in Britain and the German States, 1789–1870*. New York: Berghahn Books, 2000.

Fanon, F. *Black Skin, White Masks*, trans. C.L. Markmann. New York: Grove Press, 1967.

Fedorowich, K. 'The British Empire on the Move, 1760–1914', in Sarah Stockwell (ed.), *The British Empire: Themes and Perspectives* (Malden: Blackwell, 2008), 63–100.

Feichtinger, J. 'Komplexer k.u.k. Orientalismus: Akteure, Institutionen, Diskurse im 19. und 20. Jahrhundert in Österreich', in R. Born and S. Lemmen (eds), *Orientalismen in Ostmitteleuropa: Diskurse, Akteure und Disziplinen vom 19. Jahrhundert bis zum Zweiten Weltkrieg* (Bielefeld: Transcript, 2014), 31–63.

Feichtinger, J., U. Prutsch and M. Csáky (eds). *Habsburg postcolonial: Machtstrukturen und kollektives Gedächtnis*. Innsbruck: Studien-Verlag, 2003.

Ferguson, N. *Empire: The Rise and Demise of the British World Order and the Lessons for Global Power*. New York: Basic Books, 2002.

Fillafer, F.L. 'The "Imperial Idea" and Civilising Missions'. *Historyka: Studia Metodologiczne* 42 (2012), 37–60.

Fink, C. *Defending the Rights of Others: The Great Powers, the Jews, and International Minority Protection, 1878–1938*. Cambridge: Cambridge University Press, 2004.

Fischer, H., and K. Gündisch. *Eine kleine Geschichte Ungarns*. Frankfurt am Main: Suhrkamp, 1999.

Fischer-Tiné, H. 'National Education, Pulp Fiction and the Contradictions of Colonialism: Perceptions of an Educational Experiment in Early Twentieth-Century India', in H. Fischer-Tiné and M. Mann (eds), *Colonialism as Civilizing Mission: Cultural Ideology in British India* (London: Anthem, 2004), 229–47.

———. *Low and Licentious Europeans: Race, Class and 'White Subalternity' in Colonial India*. New Delhi: Orient Blackswan, 2009.

Fischer-Tiné, H, and S. Gehrmann (eds). *Empires and Boundaries: Rethinking Race, Class, and Gender in Colonial Settings*. New York: Routledge, 2009.

Fletcher, I.C., L.E. Nym Mayhall and P. Levine (eds). *Women's Suffrage in the British Empire: Citizenship, Nation and Race*. London: Routledge, 2000.

Flynn, G.Q. *Conscription and Democracy: The Draft in France, Great Britain, and the United States*. Westport, CT: Greenwood Press, 2002.

Foucault, M. *Histoire de la sexualité*. Vol. 1, *La volonté de savoir*. Paris: Gallimard, 1976.

———. *'Society Must Be Defended': Lectures at the Collège de France, 1975–1976*, ed. M. Bertani and A. Fontana, trans. D. Macey. London: Penguin Books, 2004.

———. *Security, Territory, Population: Lectures at the Collège de France, 1978–79*, ed. M. Senellart, trans. G. Burchell. Basingstoke: Palgrave Macmillan, 2007.

———. *The Birth of Biopolitics: Lectures at the Collège de France, 1978–79*, ed. M. Senellart, trans. G. Burchell. Basingstoke: Palgrave Macmillan, 2008.

Fransman, L. *Fransman's British Nationality Law*, 3rd edn. London: Bloomsbury Professional, 2011.

Freifeld, A. *Nationalism and the Crowd in Liberal Hungary, 1848–1914*. Washington, DC: Woodrow Wilson Center Press, 2000.

Friedman, F. *The Bosnian Muslims: Denial of a Nation*. Boulder, CO: Westview Press, 1996.

Galanter, M. *Competing Equalities: Law and the Backward Classes in India*. Berkeley, CA: University of California Press, 1984.

Gammerl, B. 'Der Vergleich von Reich zu Reich: Überlegungen zum Imperienvergleich anhand des britisch-habsburgischen Beispiels', in A. Arndt, J.C. Häberlen and C. Reinecke (eds), *Vergleichen, Verflechten, Verwirren? Europäische Geschichtsschreibung zwischen Theorie und Praxis* (Göttingen: Vandenhoeck & Ruprecht, 2011), 221–42.

Gascoigne, J. 'Introduction: Religion and Empire: An Historiographical Perspective'. *Journal of Religious History* 32(2) (2008), 159–78 (doi: 10.1111/j.1467-9809.2008.00712.x).

Gatheru, R.M. *Kenya: From Colonization to Independence, 1888–1970*. Jefferson, NC: McFarland & Co., 2005.

Gerö, A. *The Hungarian Parliament (1867–1918): A Mirage of Power*, trans. J. Patterson and E. Koncz. New York: Columbia University Press, 1997.

Getty, I.A.L., and A.S. Lussier (eds). *As Long as the Sun Shines and Water Flows: A Reader in Canadian Native Studies*. Vancouver: University of British Columbia Press, 1983.

Geulen, C. *Wahlverwandte: Rassendiskurs und Nationalismus im späten 19. Jahrhundert*. Hamburg: Hamburger Edition, 2004.

Giordano, C. 'Ethnizität und das Motiv des mono-ethnischen Raumes in Zentral- und Osteuropa', in U. Altermatt (ed.), *Nation, Ethnizität und Staat in Mitteleuropa* (Vienna: Böhlau, 1996), 22–33.

Glassheim, E. 'Between Empire and Nation: The Bohemian Nobility, 1880–1918', in P.M. Judson and M.L. Rozenblit (eds), *Constructing Nationalities in East Central Europe* (New York: Berghahn Books, 2005), 61–88.

Glassl, H. *Nationale Autonomie im Vielvölkerstaat: Der Mährische Ausgleich*. Munich: Sudetendeutsche Stiftung, 1977.

Gledhill, J. 'The Power of Ethnic Nationalism: Foucault's Bio-power and the Development of Ethnic Nationalism in Eastern Europe'. *National Identities* 7(4) (2005), 347–68 (doi: 10.1080/14608940500334432).

Gogolák, L. 'Ungarns Nationalitätengesetze und das Problem des magyarischen National- und Zentralstaates', in A. Wandruszka and P. Urbanitsch (eds), *Die Habsburgermonarchie 1848–1918*, Vol. 3, *Die Völker des Reiches*, Part 2 (Vienna: Verlag der Österreichischen Akademie der Wissenschaften, 1980), 1207–303.

Gorman, D. *Imperial Citizenship: Empire and the Question of Belonging*. Manchester: Manchester University Press, 2006.

Gosewinkel, D. 'Citizenship, Subjecthood, Nationality: Concepts of Belonging in the Age of Modern Nation States', in K. Eder and B. Giesen (eds), *European Citizenship between National Legacies and Postnational Projects* (Oxford: Oxford University Press, 2001), 17–35.

———. *Einbürgern und Ausschließen: Die Nationalisierung der Staatsangehörigkeit vom Deutschen Bund bis zur Bundesrepublik Deutschland.* Göttingen: Vandenhoeck & Ruprecht, 2001.

———. 'Staatsangehörigkeit und Nationszugehörigkeit in Europa während des 19. und 20. Jahrhunderts', in A. Gestrich and L. Raphael (eds), *Inklusion/Exklusion: Studien zu Fremdheit und Armut von der Antike bis zur Gegenwart* (Frankfurt am Main: Peter Lang, 2004), 207–27.

———. *Schutz und Freiheit? Staatsbürgerschaft in Europa im 20. und 21. Jahrhundert.* Berlin: Suhrkamp, 2016.

Gottsmann, A. *Rom und die nationalen Katholizismen in der Donaumonarchie: Römischer Universalismus, habsburgische Reichspolitik und nationale Identitäten 1878–1914.* Vienna: Verlag der Österreichischen Akademie der Wissenschaften, 2010.

Grant, K., P. Levine and F. Trentmann (eds). *Beyond Sovereignty: Britain, Empire and Transnationalism, c. 1880–1950.* Basingstoke: Palgrave Macmillan, 2007.

Grawert, R. *Staat und Staatsangehörigkeit: Verfassungsgeschichtliche Untersuchung zur Entstehung der Staatsangehörigkeit.* Berlin: Duncker & Humblot, 1973.

Gregory, R.G. *India and East Africa: A History of Race Relations within the British Empire, 1890–1939.* Oxford: Clarendon Press, 1971.

———. *South Asians in East Africa: An Economic and Social History, 1890–1980.* Boulder, CO: Westview Press, 1993.

Guibernau, M., and J. Rex (eds). *The Ethnicity Reader: Nationalism, Multiculturalism and Migration.* Cambridge: Polity Press, 1997.

Gutiérrez Rodriguez, E. 'Gouvernementalität und die Ethnisierung des Sozialen: Migration, Arbeit und Biopolitik', in M. Pieper and E. Gutiérrez Rodriguez (eds), *Gouvernementalität: Ein sozialwissenschaftliches Konzept in Anschluss an Foucault* (Frankfurt am Main: Campus, 2003), 161–78.

Haber, P. *Die Anfänge des Zionismus in Ungarn (1897–1904).* Cologne: Böhlau, 2001.

Hagen, M. von. *War in a European Borderland: Occupations and Occupation Plans in Galicia and Ukraine, 1914–1918.* Seattle, WA: Herbert J. Ellison Center for Russian, East European, and Central Asian Studies, University of Washington, 2007.

Hahn, S. 'Inclusion and Exclusion of Migrants in the Multicultural Realm of the Habsburg "State of Many Peoples"'. *Histoire Sociale / Social History* 33(66) (2000), 307–24.

Hall, D.J. 'Clifford Stifton and Canadian Indian Administration 1896–1905', in I.A.L. Getty and A.S. Lussier (eds), *As Long as the Sun Shines and Water Flows: A Reader in Canadian Native Studies* (Vancouver: University of British Columbia Press, 1983), 120–44.

Hamann, B. *Hitler's Vienna: A Dictator's Apprenticeship*, trans. Thomas Thornton. New York: Oxford University Press, 1999.

Hämmerle, C. 'Back to the Monarchy's Glorified Past? Military Discourses on Male Citizenship and Universal Conscription in the Austrian Empire, 1868–1914', in S. Dudink, K. Hagemann and A. Clark (eds), *Representing Masculinity: Male Citizenship in Modern Western Culture* (New York: Palgrave Macmillan, 2007), 151–68.

———. 'Ein gescheitertes Experiment? Die Allgemeine Wehrpflicht in der multiethnischen Armee der Habsburgermonarchie'. *Journal of Modern European History* 5(2) (2007), 222–43 (doi: 10.17104/1611-8944_2007_2_222).

Hansen, R. *Citizenship and Immigration in Post-war Britain: The Institutional Origins of a Multicultural Nation*. Oxford: Oxford University Press, 2000.

Harper, M., and S. Constantine. *Migration and Empire*. Oxford: Oxford University Press, 2010.

Harring, S.L. *White Man's Law: Native People in Nineteenth-Century Canadian Jurisprudence*. Toronto: University of Toronto Press, 1998.

Hart, P. *The IRA at War: 1916–1923*. Oxford: Oxford University Press, 2003.

Harzig, C. 'From State Constructions to Individual Opportunities: The Historical Development of Citizenship in Europe', in D. Hoerder, C. Harzig and A. Shubert (eds), *The Historical Practice of Diversity: Transcultural Interactions from the Early Modern Mediterranean to the Postcolonial World* (New York: Berghahn Books, 2003), 203–20.

Haslinger, P. 'Staatsrecht oder Staatsgebiet? Böhmisches Staatsrecht, territoriales Denken und tschechisches Emanzipationsbestreben 1890–1914', in D. Willoweit and H. Lemberg (eds), *Reiche und Territorien in Ostmitteleuropa: Historische Beziehungen und politische Herrschaftslegitimation* (Munich: Oldenbourg, 2006), 345–58.

Haupt, H.-G., and J. Kocka. 'Historischer Vergleich: Methoden, Aufgaben, Probleme: Eine Einleitung', in H.-G. Haupt and J. Kocka (eds), *Geschichte und Vergleich: Ansätze und Ergebnisse international vergleichender Geschichtsschreibung* (Frankfurt am Main: Campus, 1996), 9–45.

Healy, M. 'Becoming Austrian: Women, the State, and Citizenship in World War I'. *Central European History* 35(1) (2002), 1–35.

Hein-Kircher, H. 'Jewish Participation in the Lemberg Local Self-Government: The Provisions of the Lemberg Statute of 1870'. *Simon-Dubnow-Institute Yearbook* 10 (2011), 237–54.

Henrard, K., and R. Dunbar (eds). *Synergies in Minority Protection: European and International Law Perspectives*. Cambridge: Cambridge University Press, 2008.

Heuberger, V. 'Politische Institutionen und Verwaltung in Bosnien und der Hercegovina 1878 bis 1918', in Helmut Rumpler (ed.), *Die Habsburgermonarchie 1848–1918*. Vol. 7, *Verfassung und Parlamentarismus*. Part 2, *Die Regionalen Repräsentativkörperschaften* (Vienna: Verlag der Österreichischen Akademie der Wissenschaften, 2000), 2383–425.

Himka, J.-P. 'Nationality Problems in the Habsburg Monarchy and the Soviet Union: The Perspective of History', in R.L. Rudolph and D.F. Good (eds), *Nationalism and Empire: The Habsburg Empire and the Soviet Union* (New York: St. Martin's Press, 1992), 79–93.

Hippler, T. *Citizens, Soldiers and National Armies: Military Service in France and Germany, 1789–1830*. London: Routledge, 2008.

Hirschhausen, U. von. 'Von imperialer Inklusion zur nationalen Exklusion: Staatsbürgerschaft in Österreich-Ungarn 1867–1923'. WZB Discussion Paper (SP IV 2007–403) (2007). Retrieved 22 February 2017 from http://hdl.handle.net/10419/49610.

Hirschhausen, U. von, and J. Leonhard. 'Beyond Rise, Decline and Fall: Comparing Multi-ethnic Empires in the Long Nineteenth Century', in J. Leonhard and U. von Hirschhausen (eds), *Comparing Empires: Encounters and Transfers in the Long Nineteenth Century* (Göttingen: Vandenhoeck & Ruprecht, 2011), 9–34.

Hirschmann, E. '*White Mutiny*': The Ilbert Bill Crisis in India and Genesis of the Indian National Congress. New Delhi: Heritage, 1980.

Hobsbawm, E.J. *Nations and Nationalism since 1780: Programme, Myth, Reality*. Cambridge: Cambridge University Press, 1991.

————. 'The End of Empires', in K. Barkey and M. von Hagen (eds), *After Empire: Multiethnic Societies and Nation-Building* (Boulder, CO: Westview Press, 1997), 12–16.

Hoerder, D. 'Revising the Monocultural Nation-State Paradigm: An Introduction to Transcultural Perspectives', in D. Hoerder, C. Harzig and A. Shubert (eds), *The Historical Practice of Diversity: Transcultural Interactions from the Early Modern Mediterranean to the Postcolonial World* (New York: Berghahn Books, 2003), 1–12.

Hofmeister, H. 'Landesbericht Österreich', in P.A. Köhler and H.F. Zacher (eds), *Ein Jahrhundert Sozialversicherung in der Bundesrepublik Deutschland, Frankreich, Großbritannien, Österreich und der Schweiz* (Berlin: Duncker & Humblot, 1981), 445–729.

Holmes, C. *Anti-Semitism in British Society: 1867–1939*. London: Arnold, 1979.

————. *John Bull's Island: Immigration and British Society, 1871–1971*. Basingstoke: Macmillan, 1988.

————. 'Die Einwanderung nach Großbritannien in Vergangenheit und Gegenwart', in K. Schönwälder and I. Sturm-Martin (eds), *Die britische Gesellschaft zwischen Offenheit und Abgrenzung: Einwanderung und Integration vom 18. bis zum 20. Jahrhundert* (Berlin: Philo, 2001), 17–31.

Holzer, A. *Das Lächeln der Henker: Der unbekannte Krieg gegen die Zivilbevölkerung, 1914–1918*. Darmstadt: Primus, 2008.

Horvath, T., and G. Neyer (eds). *Auswanderungen aus Österreich: Von der Mitte des 19. Jahrhunderts bis zur Gegenwart*. Vienna: Böhlau, 1996.

Hostettler, J., and B.P. Block. *Voting in Britain: A History of the Parliamentary Franchise*. Chichester: Barry Rose, 2001.

Hroch, M. *Social Preconditions of National Revival in Europe: A Comparative Analysis of the Social Composition of Patriotic Groups among the Smaller European Nations*, trans. B. Fowkes. Cambridge: Cambridge University Press, 1985.

————. *European Nations: Explaining their Formation*, trans. K. Graham. London: Verso, 2015.

Hüchtker, D. 'Rückständigkeit als Strategie oder Galizien als Zentrum europäischer Frauenpolitik: Beitrag zum Themenschwerpunkt "Europäische Geschichte – Geschlechtergeschichte"'. *Themenportal Europäische Geschichte* (2009). Retrieved 22 February 2017 from http://www.europa.clio-online.de/essay/id/artikel-3549.

Hughes, L. *Moving the Maasai: A Colonial Misadventure*. Basingstoke: Palgrave Macmillan, 2006.

Hund, W.D. (ed.). *Zigeuner: Geschichte und Struktur einer rassistischen Konstruktion*. Duisburg: Diss, 1996.

Hutchinson, J., and A.D. Smith (eds). *Ethnicity*. Oxford: Oxford University Press, 1996.

Hyam, R. *Britain's Declining Empire: The Road to Decolonisation, 1918–1968*. Cambridge: Cambridge University Press, 2006.

Janos, A.C. *The Politics of Backwardness in Hungary, 1825–1945*. Princeton, NJ: Princeton University Press, 1982.

Jászi, O. *The Dissolution of the Habsburg Monarchy*. Chicago, IL: University of Chicago Press, 1929.

Jenkins, R. *Rethinking Ethnicity: Arguments and Explorations*. London: Sage, 1997.

John, M. 'National Movements and Imperial Ethnic Hegemonies in Austria, 1867–1918', in D. Hoerder, C. Harzig and A. Shubert (eds), *The Historical Practice of Diversity: Transcultural Interactions from the Early Modern Mediterranean to the Postcolonial World* (New York: Berghahn Books, 2003), 87–105.

Johnston, H. *The Voyage of the Komagata Maru: The Sikh Challenge to Canada's Colour Barrier.* Delhi: Oxford University Press, 1979.

Judson, P.M. 'Constructing Nationalities in East Central Europe: Introduction', in P.M. Judson and M.L. Rozenblit (eds), *Constructing Nationalities in East Central Europe* (New York: Berghahn Books, 2005), 1–18.

———. *Guardians of the Nation: Activists on the Language Frontiers of Imperial Austria.* Cambridge, MA: Harvard University Press, 2006.

Juneja, M., and M. Pernau. 'Einleitung', in M. Juneja and M. Pernau (eds), *Religion und Grenzen in Indien und Deutschland: Auf dem Weg zu einer transnationalen Historiographie* (Göttingen: V&R unipress, 2008), 9–51.

Juzbašić, D. 'Die Annexion von BosnienHerzegowina und die Probleme bei der Erlassung des Landesstatutes'. *SüdostForschungen* 68 (2009), 247–97.

Kaelble, H. 'Die interdisziplinären Debatten über Vergleich und Transfer', in H. Kaelble and J. Schriewer (eds), *Vergleich und Transfer: Komparatistik in den Sozial-, Geschichts- und Kulturwissenschaften* (Frankfurt am Main: Campus, 2003), 469–93.

Kann, R.A. 'Zur Problematik der Nationalitätenfrage in der Habsburgermonarchie 1848–1918', in A. Wandruszka and P. Urbanitsch (eds), *Die Habsburgermonarchie 1848–1918.* Vol. 3, *Die Völker des Reiches*, Part 2 (Vienna: Verlag der Österreichischen Akademie der Wissenschaften, 1980), 1304–38.

Kaplan, W. (ed.). *Belonging: The Meaning and Future of Canadian Citizenship.* Montreal: McGill-Queen's University Press, 1993.

Kaps, K., and J. Surman. 'Postcolonial or Post-colonial? Post(-)colonial Perspectives on Habsburg Galicia'. *Historyka: Studia Metodologiczne* 42 (2012), 7–35.

Karády, V. 'Egyenlötlen elmagyarosodás, avagy hogyan vált Magyarország magyar nyelvü országgá: Történelmi-szociológiai vázlat'. *Századvég* 6(2) (1990), 5–37.

Karatani, R. *Defining British Citizenship: Empire, Commonwealth, and Modern Britain.* London: Frank Cass, 2003.

Kelly, T.M. *Without Remorse: Czech National Socialism in Late-Habsburg Austria.* Boulder, CO: East European Monographs, 2006.

Keßelring, A. 'Zwischen Osmanischem Reich und Österreich-Ungarn', in A. Keßelring (ed.), *Wegweiser zur Geschichte: Bosnien-Herzegowina*, 2nd edn (Paderborn: Schöningh, 2007), 29–42.

King, J. *Budweisers into Czechs and Germans: A Local History of Bohemian Politics, 1848–1948.* Princeton, NJ: Princeton University Press, 2002.

Kirmse, S.B. 'Law and Empire in Late Tsarist Russia: Muslim Tatars Go to Court'. *Slavic Review* 72(4) (2013), 778–801 (doi: 10.5612/slavicreview.72.4.0778).

Knowles, V. *Forging our Legacy: Canadian Citizenship and Immigration, 1900–1977.* Ottawa: Citizenship and Immigration Canada, 2000.

Kohn, H. *Nationalism: Its Meaning and History.* Princeton, NJ: Van Nostrand, 1955.

Koller, M. 'Bosnien und die Herzegowina im Spannungsfeld von "Europa" und "Außereuropa": Der Aufstand in der Herzegowina, Südbosnien und Süddalmatien (1881–1882)', in H.-C. Maner (ed.), *Grenzregionen der Habsburgermonarchie im 18. und 19. Jahrhundert: Ihre Bedeutung und Funktion aus der Perspektive Wiens* (Münster: Lit, 2005), 197–216.

Kolm, E. *Die Ambitionen Österreich-Ungarns im Zeitalter des Hochimperialismus.* Frankfurt am Main: Lang, 2001.

Kolsky, E. *Colonial Justice in British India: White Violence and the Rule of Law.* Cambridge: Cambridge University Press, 2010.

Komlosy, A. 'Habsburgermonarchie, Osmanisches Reich und Britisches Empire: Erweiterung, Zusammenhalt und Zerfall im Vergleich'. *Zeitschrift für Weltgeschichte* 9(2) (2008), 9–62 (doi: 10.3726/84526_9).

Konrad, H. (ed.). *'Daß unsre Greise nicht mehr betteln gehn!': Sozialdemokratie und Sozialpolitik im deutschen Reich und in Österreich-Ungarn 1880 bis 1914.* Vienna: Europaverlag, 1991.

Kontler, L. *Millennium in Central Europe: A History of Hungary.* Budapest: Atlantisz Publishing House, 1999.

Kořalka, J. *Tschechen im Habsburgerreich und in Europa 1815–1914: Sozialgeschichtliche Zusammenhänge der neuzeitlichen Nationsbildung und der Nationalitätenfrage in den böhmischen Ländern.* Vienna: Verlag für Geschichte und Politik, 1991.

Koselleck, R. 'Volk, Nation, Nationalismus, Masse', in O. Brunner, W. Conze and R. Koselleck (eds), *Geschichtliche Grundbegriffe: Historisches Lexikon zur politisch-sozialen Sprache in Deutschland.* Vol. 7, *Verw–Z* (Stuttgart: Klett-Cotta, 1992), 141–431.

Kövér, G. 'Inactive Transformation: Social History of Hungary from the Reform Era to World War I', in G. Gyáni, G. Kövér and T. Valuch (eds), *Social History of Hungary from the Reform Era to the End of the Twentieth Century* (Boulder, CO: Social Science Monographs, 2004), 1–267.

Kriesi, H., and K. Armingeon (eds). *Nation and National Identity: The European Experience in Perspective.* Chur: Rüegger, 1999.

Kusber, J. 'Grenzregionen, Randprovinzen, Vielfalt der Peripherie im Habsburgerreich: Zusammenfassende Anmerkungen und Ausblick', in H.-C. Maner (ed.), *Grenzregionen der Habsburgermonarchie im 18. und 19. Jahrhundert: Ihre Bedeutung und Funktion aus der Perspektive Wiens* (Münster: Lit, 2005), 235–43.

Kwan, J. 'The Austrian State Idea and Bohemian State Rights: Contrasting Traditions in the Habsburg Monarchy, 1848–1914', in L. Eriksonas and L. Müller (eds), *Statehood before and beyond Ethnicity: Minor States in Northern and Eastern Europe, 1600–2000* (Brussels: P.I.E. Lang, 2005), 243–73.

Lake, M. 'From Mississippi to Melbourne via Natal: The Invention of the Literacy Test as a Technology of Racial Exclusion', in A. Curthoys and M. Lake (eds), *Connected Worlds: History in Transnational Perspective* (Canberra: ANU E Press, 2005), 209–29.

Lake, M., and H. Reynolds. *Drawing the Global Colour Line: White Men's Countries and the International Challenge of Racial Equality.* Cambridge: Cambridge University Press, 2008.

Layne, C., and B.A. Thayer. *American Empire: A Debate.* New York: Routledge, 2007.

Leighton, D. 'A Victorian Civil Servant at Work: Lawrence Vankoughnet and the Canadian Indian Department, 1874–1893', in I.A.L. Getty and A.S. Lussier (eds), *As Long as the Sun Shines and Water Flows: A Reader in Canadian Native Studies* (Vancouver: University of British Columbia Press, 1983), 104–19.

Lemke, T. 'Eine Analytik der Biopolitik: Überlegungen zu Geschichte und Gegenwart eines umstrittenen Begriffs'. *Behemoth – A Journal on Civilisation* 1(1) (2008), 72–89 (doi: 10.1524/behe.2008.0009).

Leonhard, J., and U. von Hirschhausen. '"New Imperialism" oder "Liberal Empire"? Niall Fergusons Empire-Apologetik im Zeichen der "Anglobalization"'. *Zeithistorische Forschungen* 3(1) (2006), 121–28. Retrieved 23 February 2017 from http://www.zeithistorische-forschungen.de/1-2006/id=4525.

———. 'Does the Empire Strike Back? The Model of the Nation in Arms as a Challenge for Multi-ethnic Empires in the Nineteenth and Early Twentieth Century'. *Journal of Modern European History* 5(2) (2007), 196–223 (doi: 10.17104/1611-8944_2007_2_194).

Leser, N. 'Die Arbeiterbewegung: Solidarität der Sozialisten?', in F. Seibt (ed.), *Die Chance der Verständigung: Absichten und Ansätze zu übernationaler Zusammenarbeit in den böhmischen Ländern 1848–1918* (Munich: Oldenbourg, 1987), 101–15.

Leszczawski-Schwerk, A. 'Juden und Jüdinnen als postkoloniale Subjekte im Spannungsfeld frauenemanzipatorischer Bestrebungen (1890–1914) im Österreichischen Galizien'. *Historyka: Studia Metodologiczne* 42 (2012), 213–29.

Li, P.S. 'Chinese Diaspora in Occidental Societies: Canada and Europe', in D. Hoerder, C. Harzig and A. Shubert (eds), *The Historical Practice of Diversity: Transcultural Interactions from the Early Modern Mediterranean to the Postcolonial World* (New York: Berghahn Books, 2003), 134–51.

Lieven, D. 'Dilemmas of Empire 1850–1918: Power, Territory, Identity'. *Journal of Contemporary History* 34(2) (1999), 163–200.

Lindström, F. *Empire and Identity: Biographies of the Austrian State Problem in the Late Habsburg Empire*. West Lafayette, IN: Purdue University Press, 2008.

Lonsdale, J. 'Kenya: Home County and African Frontier', in R. Bickers (ed.), *Settlers and Expatriates: Britons over the Seas* (Oxford: Oxford University Press, 2010), 74–111.

Loos, T. *Subject Siam: Family, Law, and Colonial Modernity in Thailand*. Ithaca, NY: Cornell University Press, 2006.

Lorenz, C. 'Comparative Historiography: Problems and Perspectives'. *History and Theory* 38(1) (1998), 25–39.

Loveland, I. *By Due Process of Law? Racial Discrimination and the Right to Vote in South Africa, 1855–1960*. Oxford: Hart, 1999.

Luft, R. 'Die Mittelpartei des mährischen Großgrundbesitzes 1879 bis 1918: Zur Problematik des Ausgleichs in Mähren und Böhmen', in Ferdinand Seibt (ed.), *Die Chance der Verständigung: Absichten und Ansätze zu übernationaler Zusammenarbeit in den böhmischen Ländern 1848–1918* (Munich: Oldenbourg, 1987), 187–243.

———. 'Politischer Pluralismus und Nationalismus: Zu Parteienwesen und politischer Kultur in der tschechischen Nation vor dem Ersten Weltkrieg'. *Österreichische Zeitschrift für Geschichtswissenschaften* 2(3) (1991), 72–87.

Macklem, P. *Indigenous Difference and the Constitution of Canada*. Toronto: University of Toronto Press, 2001.

Mahase, R. '"Plenty a Dem Run Away": Resistance by Indian Indentured Labourers in Trinidad, 1870–1920'. *Labor History* 49(4) (2008), 465–80.

Malíř, J. 'Der mährische Landtag', in H. Rumpler (ed.), *Die Habsburgermonarchie 1848–1918*. Vol. 7, *Verfassung und Parlamentarismus*. Part 2, *Die Regionalen Repräsentativkörperschaften* (Vienna: Verlag der Österreichischen Akademie der Wissenschaften, 2000), 2057–103.

Maner, H.-C. (ed.). *Grenzregionen der Habsburgermonarchie im 18. und 19. Jahrhundert: Ihre Bedeutung und Funktion aus der Perspektive Wiens*. Münster: Lit, 2005.

Mann, M. '"Torchbearers upon the Path of Progress": Britain's Ideology of a "Moral and Material Progress" in India. An Introductory Essay', in H. Fischer-Tiné and M. Mann (eds), *Colonialism as Civilizing Mission: Cultural Ideology in British India* (London: Anthem, 2004), 1–26.

———. *The Dark Side of Democracy: Explaining Ethnic Cleansing*. Cambridge: Cambridge University Press, 2005.

Marko, J. 'Bosnia and Herzegovina: Multi-ethnic or Multinational?', in European Commission for Democracy through Law (ed.), *Societies in Conflict: The Contribution of Law and*

Democracy to Conflict Resolution (Strasbourg: Council of Europe Publishing, 2000), 92–118.

Marsh, Z., and G.W. Kingsnorth. *A History of East Africa: An Introductory Survey*, 4th edn. Cambridge: Cambridge University Press, 1972.

Marshall, T.H., and T. Bottomore. *Citizenship and Social Class*. London: Pluto Press, 1992.

Matthes, J. 'The Operation Called "Vergleichen"', in J. Matthes (ed.), *Zwischen den Kulturen?: Die Sozialwissenschaften vor dem Problem des Kulturvergleichs* (Göttingen: Schwartz, 1992), 75–99.

Maxwell, A. *Choosing Slovakia: Slavic Hungary, the Czechoslovak Language and Accidental Nationalism*. London: I.B. Tauris, 2009.

McGranahan, C., and A.L. Stoler. 'Introduction: Refiguring Imperial Terrains', in A.L. Stoler, C. McGranahan and P.C. Perdue (eds), *Imperial Formations* (Santa Fe, NM: School for Advanced Research Press, 2007), 3–42.

———. Preface to *Imperial Formations*, edited by A.L. Stoler, C. McGranahan and P.C. Perdue (Santa Fe, NM: School for Advanced Research Press, 2007), ix–xii.

McKenzie, K. 'Social Mobilities at the Cape of Good Hope: Lady Anne Barnard, Samuel Hudson, and the Opportunities of Empire, c.1797–1824', in T. Ballantyne and A. Burton (eds), *Moving Subjects: Gender, Mobility, and Intimacy in an Age of Global Empire* (Urbana: University of Illinois Press, 2009), 274–95.

Menon, V.P. *Montagu-Chelmsford Reforms*. Bombay: Bharatiya Vidya Bhavan, 1965.

Metcalf, T.R. *The New Cambridge History of India*. Vol. 3.4, *Ideologies of the Raj*. Cambridge: Cambridge University Press, 1994.

———. *Imperial Connections: India in the Indian Ocean Arena, 1860–1920*. Berkeley, CA: University of California Press, 2007.

Meyer, K., and P. Purtschert. 'Migrationsmanagement und die Sicherheit der Bevöl-kerung', in P. Purtschert, K. Meyer and Y. Winter (eds), *Gouvernementalität und Sicherheit: Zeitdiagnostische Beiträge im Anschluss an Foucault* (Bielefeld: Transcript, 2008), 149–72.

Middell, M. 'Kulturtransfer und historische Komparatistik: Thesen zu ihrem Verhältnis', in M. Middell (ed.), *Kulturtransfer und Vergleich* (Leipzig: Leipziger Universitäts-Verlag, 2000), 7–41.

Miller, A. 'The Value and the Limits of a Comparative Approach to the History of Contiguous Empires on the European Periphery', in K. Matsuzato (ed.), *Imperiology: From Empirical Knowledge to Discussing the Russian Empire* (Sapporo: Slavic Research Center, Hokkaido University, 1997), 19–32.

Miller, J.R. 'Petitioning the Great White Mother: First Nations' Organizations and Lobbying in London', in *Reflections on Native–Newcomer Relations: Selected Essays* (Toronto: University of Toronto Press, 2004), 217–41.

Milojković-Djurić, J. *The Eastern Question and the Voices of Reason: Austria-Hungary, Russia, and the Balkan States 1875–1908*. New York: Columbia University Press, 2002.

Mitchell, B.R. *British Historical Statistics*. Cambridge: Cambridge University Press, 1988.

Moll, M. *Kein Burgfrieden: Der deutsch-slowenische Nationalitätenkonflikt in der Steiermark 1900–1918*. Innsbruck: StudienVerlag, 2007.

Mommsen, H. *Die Sozialdemokratie und die Nationalitätenfrage im habsburgischen Vielvölkerstaat*. Vienna: Europa-Verlag, 1963.

Morrison, A.S. *Russian Rule in Samarkand 1868–1910: A Comparison with British India*. Oxford: Oxford University Press, 2008.

Morton, D. 'Divided Loyalities? Divided Country?', in William Kaplan (ed.), *Belonging: The Meaning and Future of Canadian Citizenship* (Montreal: McGill-Queen's University Press, 1993), 50–63.

Mosse, G.L. *The Image of Man: The Creation of Modern Masculinity.* New York: Oxford University Press, 1996.

Motyl, A.J. 'From Imperial Decay to Imperial Collapse: The Fall of the Soviet Empire in Comparative Perspective', in R.L. Rudolph and D.F. Good (eds), *Nationalism and Empire: The Habsburg Empire and the Soviet Union* (New York: St. Martin's Press, 1992), 15–43.

Müller, D. *Staatsbürger auf Widerruf: Juden und Muslime als Alteritätspartner im rumänischen und serbischen Nationscode: Ethnonationale Staatsbürgerschaftskonzepte 1878–1941.* Wiesbaden: Harrassowitz, 2005.

Mungeam, G.H. *British Rule in Kenya, 1895–1912: The Establishment of Administration in the East Africa Protectorate.* Oxford: Clarendon Press, 1966.

Münkler, H. *Reich, Nation, Europa: Modelle politischer Ordnung.* Weinheim: Beltz, Athenäum, 1996.

———. *Imperien: Die Logik der Weltherrschaft: Vom Alten Rom bis zu den Vereinigten Staaten,* 2nd edn. Berlin: Rowohlt, 2005.

Nagel, J. 'Ethnic Troubles: Gender, Sexuality and the Construction of National Identity', in H. Kriesi and K. Armingeon (eds), *Nation and National Identity: The European Experience in Perspective* (Chur: Rüegger, 1999), 85–107.

Nagl, D. *Grenzfälle: Staatsangehörigkeit, Rassismus und nationale Identität unter deutscher Kolonialherrschaft.* Frankfurt am Main: Lang, 2007.

Nash, M. *The Cauldron of Ethnicity in the Modern World.* Chicago, IL: University of Chicago Press, 1989.

Nathans, E. *The Politics of Citizenship in Germany: Ethnicity, Utility and Nationalism.* Oxford: Berg, 2004.

Neumann, F. *Behemoth: The Structure and Practice of National Socialism, 1933–1944,* 2nd edn. New York: Oxford University Press, 1944.

Nichols, R.L. *Indians in the United States and Canada: A Comparative History.* Lincoln, NE: University of Nebraska Press, 1998.

Noiriel, G. *Etat, nation et immigration: Vers une histoire du pouvoir.* Paris: Gallimard, 2001.

———. *Le creuset français: Histoire de l'immigration XIXe–XXe siècle.* Paris: Editions du Seuil, 2006.

Nolte, H.-H. (ed.). *Imperien: Eine vergleichende Studie.* Schwalbach: Wochenschau-Verlag, 2008.

Northrup, D. *Indentured Labor in the Age of Imperialism, 1834–1922.* Cambridge: Cambridge University Press, 1995.

Oommen, T.K. (ed.). *Citizenship and National Identity: From Colonialism to Globalism.* New Delhi: Sage, 1997.

Opitz, S. 'Zwischen Sicherheitdispositiven und Securitization: Zur Analytik illiberaler Gouvernementalität', in P. Purtschert, K. Meyer and Y. Winter (eds), *Gouvernementalität und Sicherheit: Zeitdiagnostische Beiträge im Anschluss an Foucault* (Bielefeld: Transcript, 2008), 201–28.

Osterhammel, J. 'Imperien im 20. Jahrhundert: Eine Einführung'. *Zeithistorische* Forschungen 3(1) (2006), 4–13. Retrieved 23 February 2017 from http://www.zeithistorische-forschungen.de/1-2006/id=4627.

Osterhammel, J., and N.P. Petersson. *Geschichte der Globalisierung: Dimensionen, Prozesse, Epochen.* Munich: Beck, 2003.

Owen, N. *The British Left and India: Metropolitan Anti-Imperialism, 1885–1947.* Oxford: Oxford University Press, 2007.

Oyelaran, O.O., and M.O. Adediran. 'Colonialism, Citizenship and Fractured National Identity: The African Case', in T.K. Oommen (ed.), *Citizenship and National Identity: From Colonialism to Globalism* (New Delhi: Sage, 1997), 173–97.

Pagden, A. 'Fellow Citizens and Imperial Subjects: Conquest and Sovereignty in Europe's Overseas Empires'. *History and Theory* 44(4) (2005), 28–46.

Pallua, U. *Eurocentrism, Racism, Colonialism in the Victorian and Edwardian Age: Changing Images of Africa(ns) in Scientific and Literary Texts.* Heidelberg: Winter, 2006.

Parsons, T.H. *The Rule of Empires: Those Who Built Them, Those Who Endured Them, and Why They Always Fall.* Oxford: Oxford University Press, 2010.

Paul, K. *Whitewashing Britain: Race and Citizenship in the Postwar Era.* Ithaca, NY: Cornell University Press, 1997.

Pearson, D. 'Theorizing Citizenship in British Settler Societies'. *Ethnic and Racial Studies* 25(6) (2002), 989–1012 (doi: 10.1080/0141987022000009403).

Pernau, M. *Ashraf into Middle Classes: Muslims in Nineteenth-Century Delhi.* New Delhi: Oxford University Press, 2013.

Péter, L. *Hungary's Long Nineteenth Century: Constitutional and Democratic Traditions in European Perspective.* Collected Studies, edited by M. Lojkó. Leiden: Brill, 2012.

Pierson, C. *The Modern State.* London: Routledge, 1996.

Pierson, R.R., and N. Chaudhuri (eds). *Nation, Empire, Colony: Historicizing Gender and Race.* Bloomington, IN: Indiana University Press, 1998.

Piper, N. *Racism, Nationalism and Citizenship: Ethnic Minorities in Britain and Germany.* Aldershot: Ashgate, 1998.

Pircher, W. 'Von der Population zum Volk: Biopolitik und Volkszählung in Österreich', in M. Stingelin (ed.), *Biopolitik und Rassismus* (Frankfurt am Main: Suhrkamp, 2003), 80–111.

Prokopovych, M. *Habsburg Lemberg: Architecture, Public Space, and Politics in the Galician Capital, 1772–1914.* West Lafayette, IN: Purdue University Press, 2009.

Purtschert, P., K. Meyer and Y. Winter. 'Einleitung', in P. Purtschert, K. Meyer and Y. Winter (eds), *Gouvernementalität und Sicherheit: Zeitdiagnostische Beiträge im Anschluss an Foucault* (Bielefeld: Transcript, 2008), 7–18.

Puttkammer, J. von. *Schulalltag und nationale Integration in Ungarn: Slowaken, Rumänen und Siebenbürger Sachsen in der Auseinandersetzung mit der ungarischen Staatsidee 1867–1914.* Munich: Oldenbourg, 2003.

Ra'anan, U. 'Nation and State: Order out of Chaos', in U. Ra'anan, M. Mesner, K. Armes, and K. Martin (eds), *State and Nation in Multi-ethnic Societies: The Breakup of Multinational States* (Manchester: Manchester University Press, 1991), 3–32.

Rahden, T. van. *Jews and Other Germans: Civil Society, Religious Diversity, and Urban Politics in Breslau, 1860–1925*, trans. Marcus Brainard. Madison, WI: University of Wisconsin Press, 2008.

Raman, K.K. 'Utilitarianism and the Criminal Law in Colonial India: A Study of the Practical Limits of Utilitarian Jurisprudence'. *Modern Asian Studies* 28(4) (1994), 739–91.

Rand, G. '"Martial Races" and "Imperial Subjects": Violence and Governance in Colonial India, 1857–1914'. *European Review of History* 13(1) (2006), 1–20 (doi: 10.1080/13507480600586726).

Rauchensteiner, M. *Der Tod des Doppeladlers: Österreich-Ungarn und der Erste Weltkrieg.* Graz: Styria-Verlag, 1993.

Regan-Lefebvre, J. *Cosmopolitan Nationalism in the Victorian Empire: Ireland, India and the Politics of Alfred Webb.* Basingstoke: Palgrave Macmillan, 2009.

Reifowitz, I. *Imagining an Austrian Nation: Joseph Samuel Bloch and the Search for a Multiethnic Austrian Identity, 1846–1919.* Boulder, CO: East European Monographs, 2003.

Reinalter, H. (ed.). *Josephinismus als aufgeklärter Absolutismus.* Vienna: Böhlau, 2008.

Reinecke, C. *Grenzen der Freizügigkeit: Migrationskontrolle in Großbritannien und Deutschland, 1880–1930.* Munich: Oldenbourg, 2010.

Robb, P.G. *The Government of India and Reform: Policies towards Politics and the Constitution, 1916–1921.* Oxford: Oxford University Press, 1976.

Robinson, F. 'Municipal Government and Muslim Separatism in the United Provinces, 1883 to 1916', in J. Gallagher, G. Johnson and A. Seal (eds), *Locality, Province and Nation: Essays on Indian Politics, 1870 to 1940* (Cambridge: Cambridge University Press, 1973), 69–121.

———. *Separatism among Indian Muslims: The Politics of the United Provinces' Muslims 1860–1923.* Delhi: Oxford University Press, 1993.

Roy, A. *Gendered Citizenship: Historical and Conceptual Explorations.* New Delhi: Orient Longman, 2005.

Roy, P.E. *A White Man's Province: British Columbia Politicians and Chinese and Japanese Immigrants, 1858–1914.* Vancouver: University of British Columbia Press, 1989.

———. *The Oriental Question: Consolidating a White Man's Province, 1914–41.* Vancouver: University of British Columbia Press, 2003

Rudolph, R.L. 'Nationalism and Empire in Historical Perspective', in R.L. Rudolph and D.F. Good (eds), *Nationalism and Empire: The Habsburg Empire and the Soviet Union* (New York: St. Martin's Press, 1992), 3–12.

Rudolph, R.L., and D.F. Good. *Nationalism and Empire: The Habsburg Empire and the Soviet Union.* New York: St. Martin's Press, 1992.

Runge-Beneke, R. *Indien in britischen Augen: Über den Zusammenhang von Frauenbildern, Indienprojektionen, Herrschaftsphantasien und Männlichkeitsvorstellungen.* Göttingen: Muster-Schmidt, 1996.

Rürup, M. 'Lives in Limbo: Statelessness after Two World Wars'. *Bulletin of the German Historical Institute* 49 (Fall 2011), 113–34.

Rusinow, D. 'Ethnic Politics in the Habsburg Monarchy and its Successor States: Three "Answers" to the National Question', in R.L. Rudolph and D.F. Good (eds), *Nationalism and Empire: The Habsburg Empire and the Soviet Union* (New York: St. Martin's Press, 1992), 243–67.

Ruthner, C. '"k.(u.) k. postcolonial"? Für eine neue Lesart der österreichischen (und benachbarter) Literatur/en', in W. Müller-Funk, P. Plener and C. Ruthner (eds), *Kakanien revisited: Das Eigene und das Fremde (in) der österreichisch-ungarischen Monarchie* (Tübingen: Francke, 2002), 93–103. Retrieved 23 February 2017 from http://www.kakanien.ac.at/beitr/theorie/CRuthner1.pdf.

Saada, E. *Les Enfants de la colonie: Les métis de l'Empire français entre sujétion et citoyenneté.* Paris: La Découverte, 2007.

Sarasin, P. 'Zweierlei Rassismus? Die Selektion der Fremden als Problem in Michel Foucaults Verbindung von Biopolitik und Rassismus', in Martin Stingelin (ed.), *Biopolitik und Rassismus* (Frankfurt am Main: Suhrkamp, 2003), 55–79.

Schennach, M.P. 'Der "Österreicher" als Rechtskonstrukt? Zur Formierung einer öster-reichischen Staatsbürgerschaft in der ersten Hälfte des 19. Jahrhunderts'. *Zeitschrift für Neuere Rechtsgeschichte* 33(3–4) (2011), 152–76.

Schieder, T. 'Typologie und Erscheinungsform des Nationalstaats in Europa'. *Historische Zeitschrift* 202(1) (1966), 58–81.

Schmid, J. *Kampf um das Deutschtum: Radikaler Nationalismus in Österreich und dem Deutschen Reich 1890–1914*. Frankfurt am Main: Campus, 2009.

Schmidt, D. *Statistik und Staatlichkeit*. Wiesbaden: Verlag für Sozialwissenschaften, 2005.

Schoedl, G. *Alldeutscher Verband und deutsche Minderheitenpolitik in Ungarn 1890–1914: Zur Geschichte des deutschen 'extremen Nationalismus'*. Frankfurt am Main: Lang, 1978.

Schönwälder, K., and I. Sturm-Martin (eds). *Die britische Gesellschaft zwischen Offenheit und Abgrenzung: Einwanderung und Integration vom 18. bis zum 20. Jahrhundert*. Berlin: Philo, 2001.

Schöpflin, G. 'Jewish Assimilation in Hungary: A Moot Point', in B. Vago (ed.), *Jewish Assimilation in Modern Times* (Boulder, CO: Westview Press, 1981), 75–88.

Seeler, H.-J. *Das Staatsangehörigkeitsrecht Österreichs*, 2nd edn. Frankfurt am Main: Metzner, 1966.

Sinha, A.N. *Law of Citizenship and Aliens in India*. London: Asia Publishing House, 1962.

Sinha, M. *Colonial Masculinity: The 'Manly Englishman' and the 'Effeminate Bengali' in the Late Nineteenth Century*. Manchester: Manchester University Press, 1995.

Sippel, H. 'Die Klassifizierung "des Afrikaners" und "des Europäers" im Rahmen der dualen Kolonialrechtsordnung am Beispiel von Deutsch-Südwestafrika', in A. Eckert and J. Müller (eds), *Transformationen der europäischen Expansion vom 16. bis zum 20. Jahrhundert* (Rehburg-Loccum: Evangelische Akademie Loccum, Protokollstelle, 1997), 154–70.

Smith, A.D. *The Ethnic Origins of Nations*. Oxford: Blackwell, 1986.

Smith, M.M. *How Race Is Made: Slavery, Segregation, and the Senses*. Chapel Hill, NC: University of North Carolina Press, 2006.

Söldenwagner, P. *Spaces of Negotiation: European Settlement and Settlers in German East Africa, 1900–1914*. Munich: Meidenbauer, 2006.

Soysal, Y.N. *Limits of Citizenship: Migrants and Postnational Membership in Europe*. Chicago, IL: University of Chicago Press, 1994.

Spinner, J. *The Boundaries of Citizenship: Race, Ethnicity, and Nationality in the Liberal State*. Baltimore, MD: Johns Hopkins University Press, 1994.

St. Germain, J. *Indian Treaty-Making Policy in the United States and Canada, 1867–1877*. Lincoln, NE: University of Nebraska Press, 2001.

Stachel, P. 'Der koloniale Blick auf Bosnien-Herzegowina in der ethnographischen Popularliteratur der Habsburgermonarchie', in J. Feichtinger, U. Prutsch and M. Czáky (eds), *Habsburg postcolonial: Machtstrukturen und kollektives Gedächtnis* (Innsbruck: Studien-Verlag, 2003), 259–75.

Štaif, J. 'The Image of the Other in the Nineteenth Century: Historical Scholarship in the Bohemian Lands', in N.M. Wingfield (ed.), *Creating the Other: Ethnic Conflict and Nationalism in Habsburg Central Europe* (New York: Berghahn Books, 2003), 81–100.

Stanley, G.F.G. 'As Long as the Sun Shines and Water Flows: An Historical Comment', in I.A.L. Getty and A.S. Lussier (eds), *As Long as the Sun Shines and Water Flows: A Reader in Canadian Native Studies* (Vancouver: University of British Columbia Press, 1983), 1–26.

Stapleton, J. 'Citizenship versus Patriotism in Twentieth-Century England'. *Historical Journal* 48(1) (2005), 151–78 (doi: 10.1017/S0018246X0400425X).

Steidl, A. 'Ein ewiges Hin und Her: Kontinentale, transatlantische und lokale Migrationsrouten in der Spätphase der Habsburgermonarchie'. *Österreichische Zeitschrift für Geschichtswissenschaften* 19(1) (2008), 15–42.

Steinmetz, G. 'Return to Empire: The New U.S. Imperialism in Comparative Historical Perspective'. *Sociological Theory* 23(4) (2005), 339–67 (doi: 10.1111/j.0735-2751.2005.00258.x).

Stiller, M. *Eine Völkerrechtsgeschichte der Staatenlosigkeit: Dargestellt anhand ausgewählter Beispiele aus Europa, Russland und den USA.* Vienna: Springer, 2011.

Stockwell, S. 'Ends of Empire', in S. Stockwell (ed.), *The British Empire: Themes and Perspectives* (Malden, MA: Blackwell, 2008), 269–93.

Stoler, A.L. (ed.). *Haunted by Empire: Geographies of Intimacy in North American History.* Durham, NC: Duke University Press, 2006.

Stoler, A.L., C. McGranahan and P.C. Perdue (eds). *Imperial Formations.* Santa Fe, NM: School for Advanced Research Press, 2007.

Stourzh, G. *Die Gleichberechtigung der Nationalitäten in der Verfassung und Verwaltung Österreichs 1848–1918.* Vienna: Verlag der Österreichischen Akademie der Wissenschaften, 1985.

———. 'The Multinational Empire Revisited: Reflections on Late Imperial Austria'. *Austrian History Yearbook* 23 (January 1992), 1–22 (doi: 10.1017/S006723780000285X).

———. 'Ethnic Attribution in Late Imperial Austria: Good Intentions, Evil Consequences', in R. Robertson and E. Timms (eds), *The Habsburg Legacy: National Identity in Historical Perspective* (Edinburgh: Edinburgh University Press, 1994), 67–83.

Struck, B. 'Grenzziehungen nach dem Ersten Weltkrieg als Problem von Periodisierung und Territorialisierung in einer transnationalen Geschichte Ostmitteleuropas'. *Comparativ: Zeitschrift für Globalgeschichte und vergleichende Gesellschaftsforschung* 20(1–2) (2010), 81–99.

Struve, K. 'Gentry, Jews, and Peasants: Jews as the Others in the Formation of the Modern Polish Nation in Rural Galicia during the Second Half of the Nineteenth Century', in N.M. Wingfield (ed.), *Creating the Other: Ethnic Conflict and Nationalism in Habsburg Central Europe* (New York: Berghahn Books, 2003), 103–26.

Stuchtey, B. *Die europäische Expansion und ihre Feinde: Kolonialismuskritik vom 18. bis in das 20. Jahrhundert.* Munich: Oldenbourg, 2010.

Sturman, R. 'Indian Indentured Labor and the History of International Rights Regimes'. *American Historical Review* 119(5) (2014), 1439–65.

Swain, S., and M. Hillel. *Child, Nation, Race and Empire: Child Rescue Discourse, England, Canada and Australia, 1850–1915.* Manchester: Manchester University Press, 2010.

Szász, Z. 'Die Ziele und Möglichkeiten der ungarischen Regierungen in der Nationalitätenpolitik im 19. Jahrhundert', in F. Glatz and R. Melville (eds), *Gesellschaft, Politik und Verwaltung in der Habsburgermonarchie* (Stuttgart: Steiner, 1987), 325–41.

———. 'Inter-Ethnic Relations in the Hungarian Half of the Austro-Hungarian Empire'. *Nationalities Papers* 24(3) (1996), 391–408 (doi: 10.1080/00905999608408455).

Tabili, L. *Global Migrants, Local Culture: Natives and Newcomers in Provincial England, 1841–1939.* Basingstoke: Palgrave Macmillan, 2011.

Taylor, C. 'The Politics of Recognition', in C. Taylor, *Multiculturalism and 'the Politics of Recognition': An Essay*, edited by A. Gutman (Princeton, NJ: Princeton University Press, 1992), 25–74.

————. *Reconciling the Solitudes: Essays on Canadian Federalism and Nationalism*, ed. G. Laforest. Montreal: McGill-Queen's University Press, 1993.

Terborg-Penn, R. 'Enfranchising Women of Color: Women Suffragists as Agents of Imperialism', in R.R. Pierson and N. Chaudhuri (eds), *Nation, Empire, Colony: Historicizing Gender and Race* (Bloomington, IN: Indiana University Press, 1998), 41–56.

Terwey, S. *Moderner Antisemitismus in Großbritannien, 1899–1919: Über die Funktion von Vorurteilen sowie Einwanderung und nationale Identität*. Würzburg: Königshausen & Neumann, 2006.

Ther, P. *In der Mitte der Gesellschaft: Opperntheater in Zentraleuropa 1815–1914*. Vienna: Oldenbourg, 2006.

Thompson, A. *The Empire Strikes Back?: The Impact of Imperialism on Britain from the Mid-Nineteenth Century*. Harlow: Pearson Longman, 2005.

Tilly, C. 'How Empires End', in K. Barkey and M. von Hagen (eds), *After Empire: Multiethnic Societies and Nation-Building* (Boulder, CO: Westview Press, 1997), 1–11.

Tönsmeyer, T. 'Der böhmische Adel zwischen Revolution und Reform, 1848–1918/21: Ein Forschungsbericht'. *Geschichte und Gesellschaft* 32(3) (2006), 364–84.

Torpey, J. *The Invention of the Passport: Surveillance, Citizenship and the State*. Cambridge: Cambridge University Press, 2000.

Trevisiol, O. *Die Einbürgerungspraxis im Deutschen Reich 1871–1945*. Göttingen: V&R unipress, 2006.

Turda, M. 'Race, Politics and Nationalist Darwinism in Hungary, 1880–1918'. *Ab Imperio* (1) (2007), 139–64.

Turij, O. '"Der ruthenische Glaube" und die "treuen Ruthenen": Die habsburgische Politik bezüglich der griechisch-katholischen Kirche', in H.-C. Maner (ed.), *Grenzregionen der Habsburgermonarchie im 18. und 19. Jahrhundert: Ihre Bedeutung und Funktion aus der Perspektive Wiens* (Münster: Lit, 2005), 123–32.

Ucakar, K. *Demokratie und Wahlrecht in Österreich: Zur Entwicklung von politischer Partizipation und staatlicher Legitimationspolitik*. Vienna: Verlag für Gesellschaftskritik, 1985.

Ungvári, T. *The 'Jewish Question' in Europe: The Case of Hungary*. Boulder, CO: Social Science Monographs, 2000.

Unowsky, D.L. *The Pomp and Politics of Patriotism: Imperial Celebrations in Habsburg Austria, 1848–1916*. West Lafayette, IN: Purdue University Press, 2005.

————. 'Peasant Political Mobilization and the 1898 Anti-Jewish Riots in Western Galicia'. *European History Quarterly* 40(3) (2010), 412–35 (doi: 10.1177/0265691410370098).

Velikonja, M. *Religious Separation and Political Intolerance in Bosnia-Herzegovina*. College Station: Texas A&M University Press, 2003.

Veliz, F. *The Politics of Croatia-Slavonia 1903–1918: Nationalism, State Allegiance and the Changing International Order*. Wiesbaden: Harrassowitz, 2012.

Vrankić, P. *Religion und Politik in Bosnien und der Herzegowina (1878–1918)*. Paderborn: Schöningh, 1998.

Wagner, J. *A History of Migration from Germany to Canada, 1850–1939*. Vancouver, BC: UBC Press, 2006.

Waligora, M. 'What Is Your "Caste"? The Classification of Indian Society as Part of the British Civilizing Mission', in H. Fischer-Tiné and M. Mann (eds), *Colonialism as Civilizing Mission: Cultural Ideology in British India* (London: Anthem, 2004), 141–62.

Walz, S. *Staat, Nationalität und jüdische Identität in Österreich vom 18. Jahrhundert bis 1914*. Frankfurt am Main: Lang, 1996.

Wandruszka, A., and P. Urbanitsch (eds). *Die Habsburgermonarchie 1848–1918*. Vol. 2, *Verwaltung und Rechtswesen*. Vienna: Verlag der Österreichischen Akademie der Wissenschaften, 1975.

Wank, S. 'The Habsburg Empire', in K. Barkey and M. von Hagen (eds), *After Empire: Multiethnic Societies and Nation-Building* (Boulder, CO: Westview Press, 1997), 45–57.

Ward, S. 'Imperial Identities Abroad', in Sarah Stockwell (ed.), *The British Empire: Themes and Perspectives* (Malden, MA: Blackwell, 2008), 219–43.

Wassertheurer, P. 'Deutscher und tschechischer Nationalismus im österreichischen Kaiserreich', in H. Timmermann, E. Voráček and R. Kipke (eds), *Die Beneš-Dekrete: Nachkriegsordnung oder ethnische Säuberung: Kann Europa eine Antwort geben?* (Münster: Lit, 2005), 41–53.

Weber, M. *Wirtschaft und Gesellschaft: Die Wirtschaft und die gesellschaftlichen Ordnungen und Mächte: Nachlaß*. Vol. 2, *Religiöse Gemeinschaften*, ed. H.G. Kippenberg, P. Schilm and J. Niemeier. Tübingen: Mohr, 2001.

Weeks, T.R. 'Nationality, Empire, and Politics in the Russian Empire and USSR: An Overview of Recent Publications'. *H-Soz-u-Kult* (29 October 2012). Retrieved 24 February 2017 from http://hsozkult.geschichte.hu-berlin.de/forum/2012-10-001.

Weil, P. *Qu'est-ce qu'un Français? Histoire de la nationalité française depuis la Révolution*. Paris: Grasset, 2002.

Welskopp, T. 'Stolpersteine auf dem Königsweg: Methodenkritische Anmerkungen zum internationalen Vergleich in der Gesellschaftsgeschichte'. *Archiv für Sozialgeschichte* 35 (1995), 339–67.

Werner, M., and B. Zimmermann. 'Vergleich, Transfer, Verflechtung: Der Ansatz der Histoire croisée und die Herausforderung des Transnationalen'. *Geschichte und Gesellschaft* 28(4) (2002), 607–36.

Werth, P. 'Imperiology and Religion: Some Thoughts on a Research Agenda', in K. Matsuzato (ed.), *Imperiology: From Empirical Knowledge to Discussing the Russian Empire* (Sapporo: Slavic Research Center, Hokkaido University, 1997), 51–67.

Wieland, C. *Nationalstaat wider Willen: Politisierung von Ethnien und Ethnisierung der Politik: Bosnien, Indien, Pakistan*. Frankfurt am Main: Campus, 2000.

Wieviorka, M. *Kulturelle Differenz und kollektive Identitäten*, trans. R. Voullié. Hamburg: Hamburger Edition, 2003.

Wildenthal, L. 'Race, Gender, and Citizenship in the German Colonial Empire', in F. Cooper and L.A. Stoler (eds), *Tensions of the Empire: Colonial Cultures in a Bourgeois World* (Berkeley, CA: University of California Press, 1997), 263–83.

Wingfield, N.M. (ed.). *Creating the Other: Ethnic Conflict and Nationalism in Habsburg Central Europe*. New York: Berghahn Books, 2003.

———. *Flag Wars and Stone Saints: How the Bohemian Lands Became Czech*. Cambridge, MA: Harvard University Press, 2007.

Winkler, E. *Wahlrechtsreformen und Wahlen in Triest 1905–1909: Eine Analyse der politischen Partizipation in einer multinationalen Stadtregion der Habsburgermonarchie*. Munich: Oldenbourg, 2000.

Winter, E. 'Neither "America" nor "Québec": Constructing the Canadian Multicultural Nation'. *Nations and Nationalism* 13(3) (2007), 481–503 (doi: 10.1111/j.1469-8129.2007.00295.x).

Wolff, R.D. *The Economics of Colonialism: Britain and Kenya, 1870–1930*. New Haven, CT: Yale University Press, 1974.

Young, R.J.C. *The Idea of English Ethnicity*. Malden, MA: Blackwell, 2008.

Zahra, T. *Kidnapped Souls: National Indifference and the Battle for Children in the Bohemian Lands, 1900–1948*. Ithaca, NY: Cornell University Press, 2008.

Zettelbauer, H. *'Die Liebe sei Euer Heldentum': Geschlecht und Nation in völkischen Vereinen der Habsburgermonarchie*. Frankfurt am Main: Campus, 2005.

Zimmermann, S. *Divide, Provide, and Rule: An Integrative History of Poverty Policy, Social Policy, and Social Reform in Hungary under the Habsburg Monarchy*, trans. John Harbord. Budapest: CEU Press, 2011.

Index of Names and Places

Index of Subjects